Supporting Users and Troubleshooting Desktop Applications on a Microsoft® Windows® XP Operating System (70-272)

Textbook

Joli Ballew

PUBLISHED BY
John Wiley & Sons Inc.,
111 River Street, Hoboken, NJ 07030, USA

Copyright © 2008 by Microsoft Corporation

Library of Congress Cataloging-in-Publication Data pending.

    ISBN 0-7356-2076-8
    (Microsoft Press)
    ISBN 0-07-225618-4
    (McGraw-Hill)

Printed and bound in Asia.

10 9 8 7 6 5 4 3 2 1

A CIP catalogue record for this book is available from the British Library.

Microsoft Press books are available through booksellers and distributors worldwide. For further information about international
editions, contact your local Microsoft Corporation office or contact Microsoft Press International directly at fax (425) 936-7329.
Visit our Web site at www.microsoft.com/learning/. Send comments to *moac@microsoft.com*.

Microsoft, Microsoft Press, MS-DOS, MSN, Outlook, PowerPoint, and Windows are either registered trademarks or
trademarks of Microsoft Corporation in the United States and/or other countries. Other product and company names mentioned
herein may be the trademarks of their respective owners.

The example companies, organizations, products, domain names, e-mail addresses, logos, people, places, and events depicted
herein are fictitious. No association with any real company, organization, product, domain name, e-mail address, logo, person,
place, or event is intended or should be inferred.

This book expresses the author's views and opinions. The information contained in this book is provided without any express,
statutory, or implied warranties. Neither the authors, Microsoft Corporation, nor its resellers or distributors will be held liable
for any damages caused or alleged to be caused either directly or indirectly by this book.

Acquisitions Editor: Linda Engelman
Project Editor: Barbara Moreland
Technical Editor: Rozanne Whalen

ISBN 978-0-470-17061-8

CONTENTS AT A GLANCE

CONTENTS

ABOUT THIS BOOK

Welcome to *Supporting Users and Troubleshooting Desktop Applications on a Microsoft Windows XP Operating System (70-272)*, a part of the Microsoft Official Academic Course (MOAC) series. Through lectures, discussions, demonstrations, textbook exercises, and classroom labs, this course teaches students the skills and knowledge necessary to support end users who run Windows 2000 Professional Edition, Microsoft Windows XP Professional in a corporate environment, or Microsoft Windows XP Home Edition in a home environment, and the Microsoft suite of productivity applications. The eleven chapters in this book walk you through key concepts of end user and computer management including configuring and troubleshooting Office applications, Internet Explorer, and Outlook Express, and resolving issues with usability and customization of both the operating system and applications.

TARGET AUDIENCE

This textbook was developed for beginning information technology students who want to learn to support computers and end users who run the most recent Microsoft operating systems and the Microsoft suite of productivity applications. The target audience will provide direct, front-line, corporate and home, end user support, either at a Help Desk or call center, or they will use their knowledge to work in their own computer support business.

PREREQUISITES

This textbook requires students meet the following prerequisites:

- Six months experience with the latest Microsoft operating sytems and applications. Applications include Internet Explorer and Outlook Express, as well as Microsoft Office applications.

- A working knowledge of the impact of the desktop PC operating in a workgroup.

- Prerequisite knowledge and course work as defined by the learning institution and the instructor.

THE TEXTBOOK

The textbook content has been crafted to provide a meaningful learning experience to students in an academic classroom setting.

Key features of the Microsoft Official Academic Course textbooks include the following:

- Learning objectives for each chapter that prepare the student for the topic areas covered in that chapter.

- Chapter introductions that explain why the information is important.

- An inviting design with screen shots, diagrams, tables, bulleted lists, and other graphical formats that makes the book easy to comprehend and supports a number of different learning styles.

- Clear explanations of concepts and principles, and frequent exposition of step-by-step procedures.

- A variety of readeraids that highlight a wealth of additional information, including:

  - ❏ Note – Real-world application tips and alternative procedures, and explanations of complex procedures and concepts

  - ❏ Caution – Warnings about mistakes that can result in loss of data or are difficult to resolve

  - ❏ Important – Explanations of essential setup steps before a procedure and other instructions

  - ❏ More Info – Cross-references and additional resources for students

- End-of-chapter review questions that assess knowledge and can serve as homework, quizzes, and review activities before or after lectures. (Answers to the textbook questions are available from your instructor.)

- Chapter summaries that distill the main ideas in a chapter and reinforce learning.

- Case scenarios, approximately two per chapter, provide students with an opportunity to evaluate, analyze, synthesize, and apply information learned during the chapter.

- Comprehensive glossary that defines key terms introduced in the book.

THE SUPPLEMENTAL COURSE MATERIALS CD-ROM

This book comes with a Supplemental Course Materials CD-ROM, which contains a variety of informational aids to complement the book content:

- An electronic version of this textbook (eBook). For information about using the eBook, see the section titled "eBook Setup Instructions" later in this introduction.

- The Microsoft Press Readiness Review Suite built by MeasureUp. This suite of practice tests and objective reviews contains questions of varying complexity and offers multiple testing modes. You can assess your understanding of the concepts presented in this book and use the results to develop a learning plan that meets your needs.

- Microsoft PowerPoint slides based on textbook chapters, for note taking.

- Microsoft PowerPoint Viewer.

Readiness Review Suite Setup Instructions

The Readiness Review Suite includes a practice test of 300 sample exam questions and an objective review with an additional 125 questions. Use these tools to reinforce your learning and to identify areas in which you need to gain more experience before taking your final exam for the course, or the certification exam if you choose to do so.

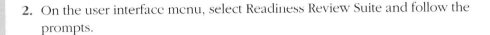

▶ **Installing the Practice Test**

1. Insert the Supplemental Course Materials CD into your CD-ROM drive.

2. On the user interface menu, select Readiness Review Suite and follow the prompts.

eBook Setup Instructions

The eBook is in Portable Document Format (PDF) and must be viewed using Adobe Acrobat Reader.

▶ **Using the eBooks**

1. Insert the Supplemental Course Materials CD into your CD-ROM drive.

2. On the user interface menu, select eBook.

THE LAB MANUAL

The Lab Manual is designed for use in either a combined or separate lecture and lab. The exercises in the Lab Manual correspond to textbook chapters and are for use in a classroom setting supervised by an instructor.

The Lab Manual presents a rich, hands-on learning experience that encourages practical solutions and strengthens critical problem-solving skills:

- Lab Exercises teach procedures by using a step-by-step format. Questions interspersed throughout Lab Exercises encourage reflection and critical thinking about the lab activity.

- Lab Review Questions appear at the end of each lab and ask questions about the lab. They are designed to promote critical reflection.

- Lab Challenges are review activities that ask students to perform a variation on a task they performed in the Lab Exercises, but without detailed instructions.

- A Troubleshooting Lab, which appears after a number of regular labs and consists of mid-length review projects, is based on true-to-life scenarios. This lab challenges students to "think like an expert" to solve complex problems.

- Labs are based on realistic business settings and include an opening scenario and a list of learning objectives.

Students who successfully complete the Lab Exercises, Lab Review Questions, Lab Challenges, and Troubleshooting Labs in the Lab Manual will have a richer learning experience and deeper understanding of the concepts and methods covered in the course. They will be better able to answer and understand the testbank questions, especially the knowledge application and knowledge synthesis questions. They will also be much better prepared to pass the associated certification exams if they choose to take the exam.

NOTATIONAL CONVENTIONS

The following conventions are used throughout this textbook and the Lab Manual:

- Characters or commands that you type appear in **bold** type.

- Terms that appear in the glossary also appear in **bold** type.

- *Italic* in syntax statements indicates placeholders for variable information. *Italic* is also used for book titles and terms defined in the text.

- Names of files and folders appear in Title caps, except when you are to type them directly. Unless otherwise indicated, you can use all lowercase letters when you type a filename in a dialog box or at a command prompt.

- Filename extensions appear in all lowercase.

- Acronyms appear in all uppercase.

- Monospace type represents code samples, examples of screen text, or entries that you might type at a command prompt or in initialization files.

- Square brackets [ ] are used in syntax statements to enclose optional items. For example, [*filename*] in command syntax indicates that you can type a filename with the command. Type only the information within the brackets, not the brackets themselves.

- Braces { } are used in syntax statements to enclose required items. Type only the information within the braces, not the braces themselves.

KEYBOARD CONVENTIONS

- A plus sign (+) between two key names means that you must press those keys at the same time. For example, "Press ALT+TAB" means that you hold down ALT while you press TAB.

- A comma (,) between two or more key names means that you must press the keys consecutively, not at the same time. For example, "Press ALT, F, X" means that you press and release each key in sequence. "Press ALT+W, L" means that you first press ALT and W at the same time, and then you release them and press L.

COVERAGE OF EXAM OBJECTIVES

This book is intended to support a course that is structured around concepts and practical knowledge fundamental to this topic area, as well as the tasks that are covered in the objectives for the MCSE 70-272 exam. The following table correlates the exam objectives with the textbook chapters and Lab Manual lab exercises. You may also find this table useful if you decide to take the certification exam.

NOTE The Microsoft Learning Web site describes the various MCP certification exams and their corresponding courses. It provides up-to-date certification information and explains the certification process and the course options. See http://www.microsoft.com/traincert/ for up-to-date information about MCP exam credentials about other certification programs offered by Microsoft.

Textbook and Lab Manual Coverage of Exam Objectives For MCDST Exam 70-272

Objective	Textbook Chapter	Lab Manual Content
Configuring and Troubleshooting Applications		
Configure and troubleshoot Internet Explorer.	Chapter 5	Lab 5
Configure and troubleshoot Outlook Express.	Chapter 4	Lab 4
■ Answer end-user questions related to configuring Outlook Express.	■ Chapter 4	■ Lab 4
■ Configure and troubleshoot newsreader account settings.	■ Chapter 4	■ Lab 4
■ Configure and troubleshoot e-mail account settings.	■ Chapters 4 and 7	■ Lab 4
Configure the operating system to support applications.	Chapter 6	Lab 6
■ Answer end-user questions related to configuring the operating system to support an application.	■ Chapter 6	■ Lab 6
■ Configure and troubleshoot file system access and file permission problems on multiboot computers.	■ Chapter 11	■ Labs 9 and 11
■ Configure access to applications on multiuser computers.	■ Chapter 11	■ Lab 11
■ Configure and troubleshoot application access on a multiple user client computer.	■ Chapter 11	■ Lab 11
Resolving Issues Related to Usability		
Resolve issues related to Office application support features. Tasks include configuring Office applications and interpreting error messages.	Chapter 7	Lab 7
Resolve issues related to Internet Explorer support features. Tasks include configuring Internet Explorer and interpreting error messages.	Chapter 5	Lab 5
Resolve issues related to Outlook Express features. Tasks include configuring Outlook Express and interpreting error messages.	Chapters 4 and 7	Lab 4

Textbook and Lab Manual Coverage of Exam Objectives For MCDST Exam 70-272

Objective	Textbook Chapter	Lab Manual Content
Resolve issues related to operating system features. Tasks include configuring operating system features and interpreting error messages.	Chapters 2, 3, and 10	Labs 3, 10, and 11
Resolving Issues Related to Application Customization		
Resolve issues related to customizing an Office application.	Chapters 4 and 6	Labs 4 and 6
■ Answer end-user questions related to customizing Office applications.	■ Chapter 6	■ Labs 6 and 7
■ Customize toolbars.	■ Chapter 6	■ Lab 6
■ Configure proofing tools.	■ Chapter 6	■ Lab 6
■ Manage Outlook data, including configuring, importing, and exporting data, and repairing corrupted data.	■ Chapters 4 and 7	■ Lab 4
■ Personalize Office features.	■ Chapter 6	■ Lab 6
Resolve issues related to customizing Internet Explorer.	Chapter 5	Lab 5
Resolve issues related to customizing Outlook Express.	Chapters 4 and 7	Lab 4
Resolve issues related to customizing the operating system to support applications.	Chapters 3 and 6	Lab 6
■ Answer end-user questions related to customizing the operating system to support an application.	■ Chapters 3 and 6	■ Labs 3 and 6
■ Customize the Start menu and taskbar.	■ Chapter 3	■ Lab 3
■ Customize regional settings.	■ Chapter 3	■ Lab 3
■ Customize fonts.	■ Chapter 5	■ Lab 5
■ Customize folder settings.	■ Chapter 3	■ Lab 3
Configuring and Troubleshooting Connectivity for Applications		
Identify and troubleshoot name resolution problems. Indications of such problems include application errors.	Chapter 8	Lab 8
Identify and troubleshoot network adapter configuration problems. Indications of such problems include application errors.	Chapter 8	Lab 8
Identify and troubleshoot LAN and Routing and Remote Access configuration problems. Indications of such problems include application errors.	Chapter 8	Lab 8
Identify and troubleshoot network connectivity problems caused by the firewall configuration. Indications of such problems include application errors.	Chapter 10	Lab 10
Identify and troubleshoot problems with locally attached devices. Indications of such problems include application errors.	Chapters 2, 8, and 12	Lab 8

Textbook and Lab Manual Coverage of Exam Objectives For MCDST Exam 70-272

Objective Configuring Application Security	Textbook Chapter	Lab Manual Content
Identify and troubleshoot problems related to security permissions.	Chapter 9	Lab 9
■ Answer end-user questions related to application security settings.	■ Chapter 9	■ Lab 9
■ Troubleshoot access to local resources.	■ Chapters 8 and 9	■ Lab 8
■ Troubleshoot access to network resources.	■ Chapters 8 and 9	■ Lab 8
■ Troubleshoot insufficient user permissions and rights	■ Chapter 8	■ Lab 9
Identify and respond to security incidents.	Chapter 10	Lab 10
■ Answer end-user questions related to security incidents.	■ Chapter 10	■ Lab 10
■ Identify a virus attack.	■ Chapter 10	■ ---
■ Apply critical updates.	■ Chapter 10	■ Lab 10
Manage application security settings.	Chapter 9	---

THE MICROSOFT CERTIFIED PROFESSIONAL PROGRAM

The MCP program is one way to prove your proficiency with current Microsoft products and technologies. These exams and corresponding certifications are developed to validate your mastery of critical competencies as you design and develop, or implement and support, solutions using Microsoft products and technologies. Computer professionals who become Microsoft certified are recognized as experts and are sought after industry-wide. Certification brings a variety of benefits to the individual and to employers and organizations.

> **MORE INFO**   For a full list of MCP benefits, go to http://www.Microsoft.com/ learning.

Certifications

The MCP program offers multiple certifications, based on specific areas of technical expertise:

- **Microsoft Certified Professional (MCP)**   In-depth knowledge of at least one Windows operating system or architecturally significant platform. An MCP is qualified to implement a Microsoft product or technology as part of a business solution for an organization.

- **Microsoft Certified Systems Engineer (MCSE)**   Qualified to effectively analyze the business requirements for business solutions and design and implement the infrastructure based on the Windows and Windows Server 2003 operating systems.

- **Microsoft Certified Systems Administrator (MCSA)**   Qualified to manage and troubleshoot existing network and system environments based on the Windows and Windows Server 2003 operating systems.

- **Microsoft Certified Database Administrator (MCDBA)**   Qualified to design, implement, and administer Microsoft SQL Server databases.

- **Microsoft Certified Desktop Support Technician (MCDST)**   Qualified to support end users and to troubleshoot desktop environments on the Microsoft Windows operating system.

MCP Requirements

Requirements differ for each certification and are specific to the products and job functions addressed by the certification. To become an MCP, you must pass rigorous certification exams that provide a valid and reliable measure of technical proficiency and expertise. These exams are designed to test your expertise and ability to perform a role or task with a product, and they are developed with the input of industry professionals. Exam questions reflect how Microsoft products are used in actual organizations, giving them "real-world" relevance.

- Microsoft Certified Professional (MCP) candidates are required to pass one current Microsoft certification exam. Candidates can pass additional Microsoft certification exams to validate their skills with other Microsoft products, development tools, or desktop applications.

- Microsoft Certified Systems Engineer (MCSE) candidates are required to pass five core exams and two elective exams.

- Microsoft Certified Systems Administrator (MCSA) candidates are required to pass three core exams and one elective exam.

- Microsoft Certified Database Administrator (MCDBA) candidates are required to pass three core exams and one elective exam.

- Microsoft Certified Desktop Support Technician (MCDST) candidates are required to pass two core exams.

ABOUT THE AUTHORS

The textbook, Lab Manual, pretest, testbank, and PowerPoint slides were written by instructors and developed exclusively for an instructor-led classroom environment.

Joli Ballew is a Microsoft Windows XP expert. Over the last four years, she has written over a dozen books including *Windows XP Professional, the Ultimate User's Guide* (Paraglyph Press), *Windows XP: Do Amazing Things* (Microsoft Press), *Degunking Windows* (Paraglyph Press), and most recently, the text for Microsoft Press' self-paced training course *MCDST Exam 70-272 - Supporting Users and Troubleshooting Desktop Applications on a Microsoft Windows XP Operating System*. Joli is also a regular and popular Microsoft Windows XP Expert Zone columnist, and is currently under consideration for Microsoft's coveted MVP award. Joli is an MCSE and MCDST, has a B.A. in Mathematics, and teaches Windows XP and FrontPage classes at Eastfield Community College. She also participates in various beta programs, newsgroups, and online communities.

Earlier in her career, Joli authored *Windows 2000 Professional Test Yourself* (Syngress Media), had a chapter published in the book *Mission Critical Internet Security* (Syngress Media), published several Windows XP e-books for Expert-Guides.com, and had an article on the Windows boot process published in Microsoft Professional Magazine (July 2001). In addition to these publications, Joli has four books available on Photoshop, digital photography, and creating artwork digitally using various graphics applications.

Owen Fowler worked as a Tier II Support Agent for one of the largest electronic tax filing centers in the United States. He has also run his own computer consulting business, covering networking and operating system issues, in both Colorado and Washington. In 2003, he assisted Verizon Wireless in consolidating their nationwide network into a single domain. He has been an author, technical editor, and development editor on many titles for Microsoft Press.

FOR MICROSOFT OFFICIAL ACADEMIC COURSE SUPPORT

Every effort has been made to ensure the accuracy of the material in this book and the contents of the CD-ROM. Microsoft Learning provides corrections for books through the World Wide Web at the following address:

http://www.microsoft.com/learning/support/

If you have comments, questions, or ideas regarding this book or the companion CD-ROM, please send them to Microsoft Learning using either of the following methods:

Postal Mail:

Microsoft Learning

Attn: *Supporting Users and Troubleshooting Desktop Applications on a Microsoft Windows XP Operating System (70-272)*, Editor

One Microsoft Way

Redmond, WA 98052-6399

E-mail: moac@microsoft.com

Please note that product support is not offered through the above addresses.

CHAPTER 1

INTRODUCTION TO DESKTOP SUPPORT

Upon completion of this chapter, you will be able to:

- Differentiate among workgroups, domains, and multiple domains

- Identify your role in the tier structure

- Identify the key differences among the various types of support environments

- Identify the traits of a successful desktop technician

The purpose of this course is to teach you to support end users who run Microsoft Windows 2000 Professional or Windows XP Professional in a corporate environment, or Windows XP Home Edition in a home or small business environment, and to prepare you for the 70-272 certification examination. This course assumes that you have approximately 6 months of hands-on experience and the following prerequisite knowledge:

- Basic experience using a Microsoft Windows operating system such as Windows XP

- Basic understanding of Microsoft Office applications and Windows accessories, including Microsoft Internet Explorer

- Basic understanding of core operating system technologies, including installation and configuration

- Basic understanding of hardware components and their functions

- Basic understanding of the major desktop components and interfaces and their functions

- Basic understanding of Transmission Control Protocol/Internet Protocol (TCP/IP) settings

- How to use command-line utilities to manage the operating system

- Basic understanding of technologies that are available for establishing Internet connectivity

The goal of this chapter is to introduce you to desktop support and common network configurations, and to teach you how to best support the end user in these varied settings. The chapter begins with an introduction to corporate environments, the help-and-support tier structure, and common job titles and duties. A discussion on workgroups, domains, and reasons for multiple domains is also included. Noncorporate environments are introduced, including Internet service providers (ISPs), call centers, and large and small repair shops, and an introduction to the end user and how you can best provide support is detailed.

OVERVIEW OF CORPORATE ENVIRONMENTS

There are several types of environments in which you might be employed. Understanding these environments and your place in them is crucial to your success. This section provides a brief overview of the corporate environment, including common network setups, tier structure, job titles, and job requirements.

Types of Networks

From a user's perspective, there are three basic types of logical networks: **workgroups**, **domains**, and multiple domains. In each of these environments, users are able to share common resources such as files, folders, and printers, and there are security measures that can be put in place to keep users' personal data, network resources, and company data secure and protected from outside forces.

Workgroups

Workgroups are logical groupings of networked computers that share resources, and are often referred to as peer-to-peer networks. Of the three network types, the workgroup is the easiest to set up and maintain, but the least secure. Each computer maintains its own local security database, which contains the valid user accounts for logging on to and using that computer. The user accounts secure data on the computer and protect the computer from unwanted access. Because there is no single computer that provides centralized security of user accounts for all of the computers on the network, the network is considered decentralized.

Workgroups are usually the best choice for small networks where the computers are in close proximity to one another because this configuration is easy to maintain, allows each individual to decide on what they want to share with others and to what degree, no network administrator or overhead related to domains exist, and the computers can all be linked using a single hub. Having the ability to connect using a single hub makes creating and managing the network quite easy, as well as inexpensive. Figure 1-1 shows an example of a workgroup.

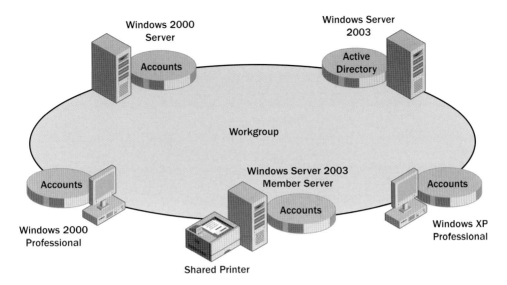

Figure 1-1   A workgroup is often referred to as a peer-to-peer network.

NOTE   When Workgroups Are Used   Workgroups are typically configured for home networks, small home offices, and small businesses where the computers are in close proximity to one another and can be connected using a hub, switch, or router. Because they are not the most secure option for a network, they are not often used in larger corporations.

Domains

Domains are logical groupings of networked computers that share a common database of users and centrally managed security on a single server (or servers) called a domain controller. A single domain must have one or more domain controllers, and these computers provide **Active Directory** directory services such as providing access to resources, security, and a centralized database. Domains are logical groupings, so they can span a building, city, state, or across countries, or they can be configured for a small office. The computers can be connected by dial-up, Ethernet, Integrated Services Digital Network (ISDN) lines, satellite, or even wireless connections. Figure 1-2 shows an example of a domain with two domain controllers.

NOTE   When Domains Are Used   Domains are typically configured for networks in larger companies because they are the most secure option for a network, offer centralized security and management, and are extensible. Smaller companies generally opt against domains, because they have more overhead and require more time to administer than workgroups do.

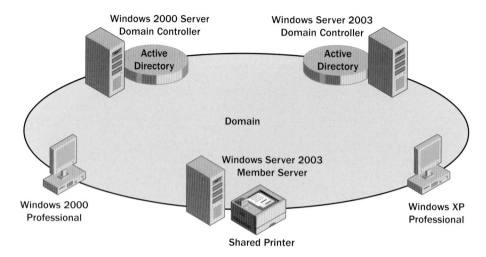

Figure 1-2   Domains share a common database and are centrally managed.

NOTE   Logical Groupings vs. Physical Layouts   Workgroups, domains, and multiple domains describe the logical grouping of computers. Referring to a physical (rather than logical) topology describes the way information moves through the network—for example, in a straight line (bus topology) or in a circle (ring topology). Don't confuse this logical grouping with the physical layout of the network. A small network of three computers connected by a single hub can be logically grouped into a domain, just as a larger network consisting of thousands of computers across multiple subnets can also be grouped into a domain.

Multiple Domains

Multiple domains are logical groupings of computers that combine two or more separate domains as a single, cohesive, yet decentralized unit. Multiple administrators manage the network, and the domains represent specific parts of a larger organization. Multiple domains are generally created when the network (and corporation) spans multiple countries or when two established companies merge. In a multiple-domain configuration, multiple domain controllers exist.

MORE INFO   Learn More About Domains and Active Directory   To learn more about domains and Active Directory, visit http://www.Microsoft.com/technet, select Products & Technologies, and select Windows Server 2003 or Active Directory.

Tier Structure

Corporations define technical support roles in tiers, and generally there are four, as detailed in Table 1-1. Each of these four tiers can also have its own tier structure. The position that we're concerned with is Tier 1, highlighted in the table. The employees in the corporate Tier 1 group are also categorized in three additional, internal, tiers. The internal Tier 1 employees usually provide front-line support, and internal Tiers 2, 3, and 4 employees accept escalations. These roles are defined in more detail in the section "Telephone Call Centers" later in this chapter. Your position in the corporation will be in the Tier 1, Help Desk position. An overview of the general tier structure is presented in Table 1-1.

Table 1-1   An Overview of the Corporate Tier Structure

Tier 4, Architect	Strategic: Analyzes and designs enterprises. Makes budget and purchasing decisions and collaborates with business.
Tier 3, Engineer	Tactical: Analyzes and designs within a single technology and implements the technology. Handles complex troubleshooting including escalations from administrators.
Tier 2, Administrator	Operational: Day-to-day server and software troubleshooting. Performs operating system (OS) management and support.
Tier 1, Help Desk	Support: Day-to-day client OS, application, and hardware troubleshooting. Follows prescriptive guidelines and provides end user phone support.

Corporate tier structures allow for growth by clearly defining technical support roles and requirements for moving up the tier ladder. The Microsoft Certified Desktop Support Technician (MCDST) certification prepares candidates for jobs in the Tier 1 environment and provides a good foundation for moving up in the corporation.

Job Titles and Requirements

As a Tier 1, entry-level technical support employee, your job is to provide direct end user support. At a high level, you should be prepared to perform the following tasks:

- Perform basic troubleshooting of the operating system and installed applications

- Provide customer service, including listening to the customer, defining and solving the problem, and educating the user on how to avoid the problem in the future

- Install, configure, and upgrade software, including applications and operating systems

- Monitor and maintain systems

- Document calls and close them or escalate them as required by company policy and time limits set by **service level agreements** (SLAs)

More specifically, you will be consulted to troubleshoot and provide information on a variety of products, including operating systems and applications such as Microsoft Outlook, Microsoft Access, and Microsoft Excel, and operating system components like Internet Explorer and Microsoft Outlook Express. You will also be called on to resolve connectivity issues, troubleshoot dual-boot or multiuser computers, and install and configure handheld devices. You will be expected to resolve or escalate 80 percent of the incident requests you receive from end users, employ proper procedures to document the incident, and operate within the environment's SLAs. SLAs might require a call to be resolved in a particular amount of time or within a specified budget.

There are various job titles and job roles for desktop support technicians; common Tier 1 entry-level job titles are listed next. When creating a resumé, looking for employment, or interviewing, make sure you are familiar with these titles. Each of these job titles is a Tier 1 entry-level job, and all are quite similar in nature.

- Call Center Support Representative
- Customer Service Representative
- Help Desk Specialist (or Technician)
- Product Support Engineer
- PC Support Specialist

> **NOTE   Join a Newsgroup**   To supplement your desktop technician training, join a relevant newsgroup. With a newsgroup you can exchange ideas, ask for help, and get answers to common questions quickly. Visit http://www.Microsoft.com/ windowsxp/expertzone/newsgroups/default.asp.

OVERVIEW OF NONCORPORATE ENVIRONMENTS

Not all desktop support technicians will acquire or hold jobs in a large, corporate environment; many will obtain employment through telephone call centers, repair shops, and private businesses, or ISPs.

Telephone Call Centers

Telephone call centers accept calls from end users and resolve problems over the telephone. These calls can be hardware or software related, depending on the company and its clients. A desktop technician's place in these environments is defined using a tier system similar to that in a corporate environment. Table 1-2 shows a general tier structure for a telephone call center. An entry-level desktop technician falls in either of the first two tiers, depending on his or her experience.

Table 1-2   An Overview of the Telephone Call Center Tier Structure

Tier 4: Experience 4+ years	Resolves calls escalated from Tier 3 personnel and tries to resolve them. This involves complex troubleshooting, and employees in this tier are hardware and software engineers and architects.
Tier 3: Experience 1–2 years	Receives calls escalated from Tier 2 personnel and tries to resolve them. This involves a combination of experience, directed training in specific hardware and software, and application of previous knowledge. These employees might have other certifications.

Table 1-2 An Overview of the Telephone Call Center Tier Structure

Tier 2: Experience 6 months–1 year	Receives calls escalated from Tier 1 personnel and tries to resolve them. As with Tier 1 employees, the employee works using a set of predetermined questions and solutions. Supports OS, application, and hardware troubleshooting.
Tier 1: Experience Less than 6 months	Answers the phone and works using a script. The employee instructs the user to reboot the computer, disconnect and reconnect, stop and restart an application, and perform other common troubleshooting tasks.

Repair Shops and Private Businesses

Desktop technicians can also find their niche as members of small repair shops, large repair shop chains, computer sales chains, computer manufacturers, or hardware testing labs. They can also start their own computer-repair business.

If you intend to work as a desktop support technician in any of these settings, you should also be either A+ or Network + certified. Unlike a desktop technician, an employee at a repair shop or one that owns his or her own business has much more hands-on computer work than those who answer phones. These technicians replace hardware, add memory, repair printers, and perform similar tasks, in addition to the tasks required of a desktop technician.

Internet Service Providers

ISPs are companies that provide Internet access to subscribers for a monthly fee. Subscribers can be individuals or entire corporations. Some ISPs do more than offer Internet access, though; they design Web pages, consult with businesses, provide feedback concerning Web page traffic, and send out virus warnings. Some also set up, secure, and maintain **e-commerce** Web sites for clients.

If you choose to work for an ISP, you will most likely answer the phones and perform general help desk duties as previously defined. The most common tasks required of an ISP desktop technician include the following:

- Set up new accounts using Outlook or Outlook Express, Netscape Mail, Apple OSX Mail, Eudora, and other e-mail clients
- Configure settings to filter spam by creating rules and blocking senders
- Troubleshoot Internet and e-mail access
- Troubleshoot servers and physical connections
- Resolve problems with various connection types, including dial-up modems, Digital Subscriber Line (DSL), cable, and wireless modems
- Resolve and escalate calls when necessary

ISP desktop technicians will need to be familiar with Internet technologies, **Domain Name System** (DNS) name resolution, connection types, available modems, and other common ISP tools. ISPs, as with other technician's employers, generally work using a tier system, and moving up the tier is dependent on your experience, education, and training.

SUPPORTING AND UNDERSTANDING THE END USER

The job of desktop technician involves much more than answering the phone and resolving a problem. It also involves understanding, communicating with, and pleasing the end user. You must be able to listen to a customer, gather information from that customer, diagnose and resolve or escalate the problem, and properly document the resolution of the problem in the manner dictated by company policy. The end user must also be satisfied with the solution and believe he or she was treated fairly and with respect. The goal of this section is to introduce you to the types of end users you will encounter, detail how previous interactions with desktop support could have gone, discuss traits of a good desktop support technician, and detail what end users expect from you.

An End User's Level of Expertise

There are many types of end users. Each has a different level of expertise, and each one has that expertise in varying degrees. Some end users will have no computer experience at all and will barely understand basic computer terms; some will have targeted experience; still others will have many years of experience. Table 1-3 details the different types of users you might encounter.

Table 1-3   End Users Have Varying Skill Levels

Highly experienced	These users are extremely experienced and most likely know more than you do concerning the problem at hand. Their problems will generally need to be escalated quickly.
Generally experienced	These users can e-mail, use the Internet, download and install programs, follow wizards, install and configure programs, set up simple networks, and do minor troubleshooting. Tier 1 or Tier 2 support personnel can generally assist these users.
Targeted experience	These users have experience in one or two applications that they use daily to do their jobs. Besides this experience, they have almost no computing skills. Depending on the application in question, Tier 1 or Tier 2 support personnel can generally assist these users.
No experience	These users are completely new to computing and have little or no experience with e-mail, the Internet, or installing or using applications. Tier 1 personnel should be able to handle most of these calls.

After you've gained some experience as a desktop technician, you'll be able to determine how experienced users are after speaking with them for only a few minutes. In the interim, you'll learn how to work with and assist the different types of end users by communicating with them through written scripts and by following specific (and proven) troubleshooting guidelines.

> **CAUTION** *Be Careful!* Keep in mind at all times that you will be assisting all levels of users; never assume that the user knows less than you.

Previous Experiences with Technical Support

Chances are that the end user you are speaking with on the phone or visiting at her desk has dealt with a desktop support technician before. If that experience wasn't satisfactory, you might have to deal with an angry, dissatisfied, or frustrated client. You might also be the second or third technician to try to solve the problem, or the problem might be a recurring one. If this is the case, concentrate on verifying the problem, be polite and respectful, and use whatever resources it takes to solve the problem quickly and effectively.

Traits of a Good Desktop Support Technician

Companies and clients want to hire and keep the best desktop technicians they can find, and there are several specific traits and qualities they look for. It doesn't matter whether you work in a corporate environment or offer in-home computer-repair services, the traits and skills are the same. To be the best desktop technician you can be, work to demonstrate as many of these qualities as possible.

- **Excellent customer service skills** Successful desktop technicians have the ability and emotional intelligence to teach highly technical content to users with any level of experience. They can speak to any user about any problem and define that problem in terms the user can understand (without making the user feel inadequate or "dumb"). They have skills that any customer service employee would have; they are polite, concerned for the customer, and have a sincere desire to service the customer's needs. Beyond emotional intelligence, they also have social intelligence. This involves the ability to handle their own or others' anxieties, anger, and sadness; being self-motivated; and having empathy for others.

- **Talent for communicating** Good technicians can communicate with end users of any level of experience, any personality, and on any level of the corporate ladder. They can communicate technical information to nontechnical users and acquire technical information from those who cannot explain the problem clearly. Good technicians also take the time to explain in simple terms why the problem occurred, how it can be avoided in the future, and how and where to get help when no technical support technician is available.

- **Ability to multitask and stay calm under pressure**   Desktop technicians must deal with ongoing problems, multiple open troubleshooting tickets, deadlines for meeting SLAs, accountability to bosses and end users, and ambiguous problems. Throughout, they must be able to work effectively and coolly under pressure. Desktop technicians must also be able to respond calmly when an end user becomes frustrated or angry, and must maintain a professional demeanor at all times.

- **Technical aptitude**   Desktop technicians have a natural aptitude for computers, hardware, and software, and for configuring each. They enjoy working with the technologies, have workstations at home where they troubleshoot problems in their spare time, welcome new technologies, and show a talent for seeing the whole picture in terms of networks, components, shared files and folders, and even problems. Having the ability to see things holistically is the first step to becoming an expert in your field.

- **Capacity to solve problems**   Talented desktop technicians have the capacity to solve problems quickly. They are good at solving logic problems, uncovering hidden clues, chasing leads, and discovering and attempting solutions without exacerbating the problem further. Communication and linear and logical troubleshooting are the top skills employers look for. The technical aspect can be taught much more easily than these skills because these have more to do with overall intelligence, personality, and social abilities than technical skills do. You must strive to develop critical thinking and problem-solving skills, and learn to "read the signs" when dealing with a problem. The better you get at seeing the signs and the overall picture, the better you'll be as a technician. The capacity to solve problems can be improved through training, experience, trial and error, observation, and working with higher level technicians.

SUMMARY

- Desktop support technicians must be prepared to work in various environments including workgroups, domains, and multiple domains.

- A desktop technician's place in the corporate, ISP, or company hierarchy is generally in the Tier 1 position and is considered an entry-level position.

- ISPs, corporations, small and large repair shops, manufacturers' factories, and small computer-repair home businesses require different skills, but in each instance, the technician must be friendly, helpful, capable, and competent.

- Desktop technicians must have technical knowledge in many areas, including the operating system, components such as Outlook Express and Internet Explorer, and applications, including Outlook, Excel, Access, and others.

- The MCDST certification opens a doorway into Tier 1 jobs, identifies the employee as qualified to hold the desired job, and identifies the business owner as qualified to determine and resolve home end user problems.

REVIEW QUESTIONS

1. Briefly, what types of businesses, corporations, or companies would choose to configure a workgroup? A domain? A multiple domain? Why?

2. Which of the following is not a job function of a Tier 1 corporate desktop technician? (Choose all that apply.)

    a. Perform general troubleshooting of the operating system

    b. Perform general troubleshooting of operating system components such as Internet Explorer and Outlook Express

    c. Troubleshoot network problems that do not directly affect the end user

    d. Install, configure, and upgrade software, including applications and operating systems

    e. Set group or local security policies for end users, including what security settings a user should have, and determine what he can or cannot access on the network

3. You have just gotten a job at an ISP and you've been assigned a Tier 1 position. Which of the following can you expect in your first week at work? (Choose all that apply.)

    a. To walk users through re-creating their e-mail account or reconfiguring their Internet security settings

    b. To configure local security policies

    c. To answer phones and instruct users to reboot their computer, close and restart applications, and disconnect and reconnect to the ISP

    d. To read from a script of questions and make decisions based on their answers

    e. To help users reinstall their e-mail clients

4. For each of the following descriptions, decide if each refers to a workgroup, a domain, or multiple-domain network configurations. If the description applies to more than one, list all that apply.

    a. This network configuration is a logical grouping of computers created for the purpose of sharing of resources such as files and printers.

    b. This network configuration does not use Active Directory services.

    c. This network configuration can include multiple domain controllers.

    d. This network configuration provides centralized security.

    e. This network configuration is easy to design and implement and is best configured for users in close proximity to one another.

5. Taking into account what you've learned about workgroups and domains, network topologies, corporate and noncorporate tier structures, call center environments, hands-on repair shops, and ISPs, describe which environment you would most like to work in. Cite five reasons for your decision.

6. Allot yourself five minutes to list as many traits as you can relating to the three categories listed here.

    a. Communication skills

    b. Aptitude skills

    c. Personal skills

CASE SCENARIOS

Scenario 1-1: Choosing the Best Entry Level Job

John has decided to earn his MCDST and is in the process of obtaining an entry-level job in information technology. He enjoys working with people, but he also enjoys the hands-on aspect of the technology. He has several computers at home and he has connected them and configured a small domain just for the fun of it. He likes working inside the computer, too, adding memory, replacing cards, and so on, and he's certain that someday he wants to own his own computer-repair or network consulting business. He wants to make sure he gets the best work experience possible. What type of entry-level job is best for John while he works to meet his goals? Why?

Scenario 1-2: Strengthening Personal Skills

You recently earned your A+ certification and are currently working in a small, family-owned repair shop. You work in the back and do a lot of hands-on computer work but you don't have much interaction with the public. Although you are extremely talented at repairing hardware, adding memory, repairing printers, and performing similar tasks, and you have exceptionally good problem-solving skills, you know you lack some of the delicate personal skills required of a successful desktop technician. Your boss has even mentioned that you could be a little more personable. Which of the following offer the best solutions to this problem? (Select two.)

1. Consider moonlighting two or three nights a week as a telephone-call support technician. There, you'll learn some of the basic personal skills required of a good desktop technician.

2. Quit the repair shop and go to work immediately for an ISP. You can learn to create Web sites, you'll learn about e-commerce and, if you're lucky, you'll only have to deal with people face to face occasionally.

3. Take a course on interpersonal skills at your local community college. There, you'll learn basic communication skills such as how to listen and how to converse effectively with all types of people.

4. Consider a different line of work. Communication skills, ability, talent, and personal skills come naturally to good desktop technicians and can't be taught.

CHAPTER 2
RESOLVING A SERVICE CALL

Upon completion of this chapter, you will be able to:

■ Ask relevant questions

■ Identify possible solutions

■ Determine a solution or resolution

■ Document the problem and the solution

■ Inform and teach the end user

The purpose of this chapter is to teach you the logical processes involved in resolving a service call. Resolving a call involves gathering information, determining a solution or course of action, attempting and finding solutions or escalating the call, and informing the end user of your findings.

In the first section you'll learn what questions to ask and what specific things to make note of, such as whether or not the user has made any recent changes to the operating system or applications. Following that, you'll learn what steps are involved in determining a solution, starting with locating information, then listing and trying possible solutions, and finally either solving the problem or escalating it. With the problem solved (or out of your hands), you'll then need to document the call and communicate with the end user about the problem and its solutions.

Understanding these concepts is fundamental to becoming a good desktop technician, and using problem-solving and personal skills such as these is required on a daily basis.

KNOW WHAT TO ASK

The most important part of troubleshooting is to ask pertinent questions and listen to and make note of the answers. You will not be able to resolve a call if you cannot determine what the problem is. The end user has many of the answers you need, but you have to get the end user to share this information with you. You must listen, communicate, and ask the appropriate questions, all while making the end user feel helpful (and not the one to blame for the problem).

When you first start work at a telephone call center, company, home business, or Internet service provider (ISP) as a Tier 1 desktop technician, you should expect to ask your end users specific questions already written out for you in the form of a script. However, as you move up the ladder and work through the natural progression of gaining expertise and experience, you'll move from following a script to building your own repertoire of queries. As you internalize your knowledge, you'll start to learn and understand how to resolve problems on your own. Keeping in mind you'll probably start your first Tier 1 position reading questions already written for you, in this chapter you'll learn what types of questions to ask when you are required to work through the resolution process on your own.

Asking Who, When, What, Why, and How

A reporter or police detective asks these questions to obtain the required information to perform her job, and you will ask the same questions in your role as a desktop technician. The information you acquire will help you find out why the problem occurred, and with that knowledge you can often resolve the problem on your own. The following sections offer some common questions you should ask and what insight they yield.

Who?

- Who was at the computer when the problem first occurred?
- Who else has been using the computer and have they experienced similar problems?
- Who has worked on this problem prior (if it has happened before)?
- Who has the same problem on another computer (that you know of)?

What the Answers Tell You

The answers to these questions tell you who has firsthand knowledge of the problem and if other users who access the same computer (under a different account) also encounter the problem. If multiple users have access but only one user encounters the problem, you've already narrowed down the issue. You'll also learn from these questions who has worked on the problem before (you might find out the user has), and whether other users on the network are having the same problem on their computers. If the latter is true, the problem could be a network-wide problem such as a **security policy** issue, virus, or other glitch in the entire system.

When?

- When did this problem occur the first time and has it occurred since?
- When was the last time you downloaded or installed an application?
- When was the last time you installed new hardware?
- When did you last clean up the computer with Disk Cleanup or Disk Defragmenter, delete **temporary files** or **cookies**, or perform similar deletions of data?
- When was the last time you uninstalled any applications?

What the Answers Tell You

The answers to these questions tell you how long the user has had this problem, if the problem occurred after the user installed a new piece of hardware or new application, and if the user routinely maintains the computer. If the problem occurred after installing or uninstalling hardware or software, you have a good lead. Asking pointed questions about maintenance can also be helpful in finding out if the user has recently cleaned out program or system folders or deleted any necessary files.

What?

- What are your thoughts on what caused the problem?

- What have you tried to do to troubleshoot the problem yourself?

- What do you think can be done to solve the problem?

What the Answers Tell You

The answers to these questions tell you what the user believes happened and give you an opportunity to involve him in the solution. Asking the user what he thinks can be done to solve the problem could also bring up a very simple solution. If the user recently reconfigured settings for a program or uninstalled a necessary file or program, you know where to begin. If the user has tried to troubleshoot the problem already, you'll need to know what changes he has made. Finally, if the user thinks reconfiguring the e-mail account will solve the problem, it's likely because he was doing something to it earlier, but does not want to admit it.

Why and How?

- Why do you think the problem occurred?

- How do you think the problem occurred?

What the Answers Tell You

The answers to these questions can often summon up a solution quickly. If the user says, "The problem occurred because I spilled coffee on the keyboard" or "The problem occurred because I opened an attachment in an e-mail," you know exactly where to start. Keep in mind, though, that these answers won't always be useful and might sometimes even be deceitful. (A user might have opened an attachment but might tell you she didn't, for instance.) Remember, you're the expert.

As you work through these questions with an end user, document the answers carefully, listen to everything he has to say, be polite and professional, and make notes of possible solutions as you think of them. If you need to, leave the situation for a few minutes to digest the information, and check company documentation, online help and support, or other resources for answers.

Reproducing the Problem

If you or the end user can reproduce the problem, you will have quite a bit more to go on. Problems that can't be reproduced (like applications that shut down for no apparent reason) are much more difficult to diagnose than those that can (like the failure to send or receive e-mail). If the end user can reproduce the problem, make a note of what applications were open and what components were being used, and troubleshoot those applications and their configurations.

> **CAUTION** *Be Careful* Don't try to reproduce any problem that has previously caused loss of data or is a known network problem such as a virus or worm. Doing so can cause additional problems and further damage.

DETERMINE A SOLUTION

Once you have asked the proper questions and made notes of the answers, you'll need to formulate a plan of action for resolving the call. If you work for an ISP or telephone call center, your plan of action might involve only reading a set of directions from a script and escalating the call up a tier, but that is still a course of action. If you've already determined a solution and solved the problem, you only need to document your solution.

If you own your own business, though, or are otherwise on your own when fielding a service call, solving the problem might involve more groundwork. When physically assisting a user either in her home or at her desk, it isn't quite so easy to turn the call over to someone else. If you own your own business, conferring with someone else can cost you time and money, as well as clients; if you've walked across the corporate campus to field a call, calling in someone else produces the same results. In either instance, when given more responsibility for servicing calls, you'll need to have a plan of action for uncovering, documenting, and resolving the call without another technician. In this section you'll learn the steps involved in resolving a service call on your own, as opposed to calling in another technician or escalating the call. In general, a specific procedure should be followed, and a common technique is listed here.

To locate answers and to determine a solution after speaking with the end user, perform these general steps in order (each of which will be detailed in later sections):

1. Locate a solution by searching the computer's help and support files. If a solution is found, attempt to solve the problem and document the solution. If the solution does not work, document that as well, and undo any changes made to the computer.

2. Locate a solution by searching the company's help and support files. If a solution is found, attempt to solve the problem and document the solution. If the solution does not work, document that as well, and undo any changes made to the computer.

3. Search manufacturers' Web sites. If a solution is found, attempt to solve the problem and document the solution. If the solution does not work, document that as well, and undo any changes made to the computer.

4. Search technical sites. If a solution is found, attempt to solve the problem and document the solution. If the solution does not work, document that as well, and undo any changes made to the computer.

5. Search newsgroups. If a solution is found, attempt to solve the problem and document the solution. If the solution does not work, document that as well, and undo any changes made to the computer.

6. If no solution is found, document the information and attempted solutions, and undo any changes made to the computer during the troubleshooting process.

7. Escalate the call.

8. When the problem is solved, document the solution.

The troubleshooting process covered in the chapter is further detailed in the flow-chart shown in Figure 2-1.

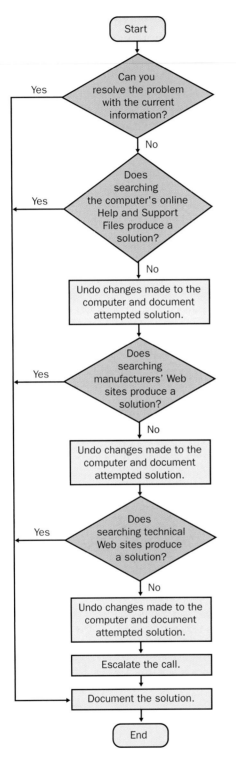

Figure 2-1   Troubleshooting a problem is best done systematically.

In the next few sections, you'll learn more about each of these steps and options.

Locating the Answers

There are several places to look for help in troubleshooting a computer problem, and if you have good research skills you'll most likely be able to locate a solution without escalating the call. Because escalations require more manpower, more downtime, and more expense for both you and the end user, you should do all you can to resolve calls without having to call in someone else to help. As for finding a solution, chances are quite good that this isn't the first time an end user has encountered this problem, and the answer will probably be easy to find either in company documents or on the Internet.

> **NOTE   It's All in the Training**   The ability to research and find answers isn't an innate ability; a good researcher simply has to know where to look for answers.

Online Help and Support

Online help and support should be the first place you look for information about common operating system problems. Windows Help and Support Center offers information ranging from performing basic tasks like logging on and off to complex ones like working remotely. It also offers tools to help you access advanced system information, check network diagnostics, and run software and hardware troubleshooting wizards. Figure 2-2 shows the default Help and Support Center for Microsoft Windows XP Professional. It's easy to use; simply browse the categories or type in a few keywords.

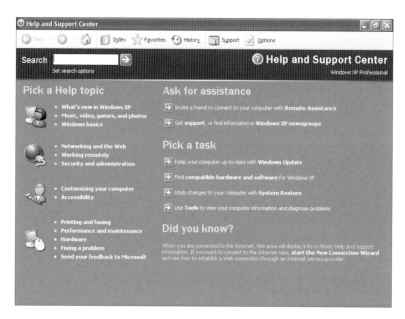

Figure 2-2   The Windows XP Professional default Help and Support Center page offers an abundance of information.

Company Documentation

As time passes, more and more companies and corporations will customize the Help files in the Help and Support Center so that the files offer resources to end users that are specific to their department, job role, company, or domain. This localized help information is not only useful to the end user, but also for desktop technicians who don't work for the company and are instead hired as vendors or contract employees. Computer manufacturers already personalize help files for home users and include help files directly related to the user's specific computer configuration. The Microsoft Office System has online resources available directly from the application, too, and these are updated often so the information is always current.

Targeted help such as this allows users to locate answers to their own problems easily, and it allows you to access information quickly as well. Figure 2-3 shows an example of a customized Help and Support Center interface, created by a computer manufacturer for the home user. Notice that there are additional Help topics including VAIO User Guide, VAIO Multimedia, and VAIO Support Agent Help. These topics are specific to the machine and can be quite helpful when troubleshooting computer problems.

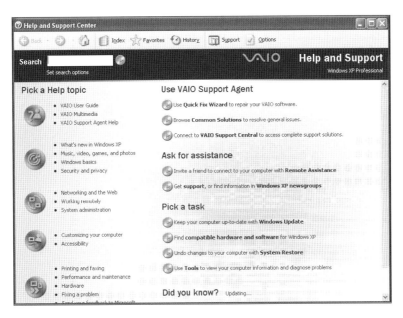

Figure 2-3   Help and Support Center pages can be customized.

Depending on your work environment, this type of customized documentation might be available. At the very least, almost every company will offer some access to a databank that contains answers to commonly asked questions. If you can't find the answer to your troubleshooting query using the default Windows Help and Support files, try these.

Manufacturers' Web Sites

Many times a problem occurs because a piece of hardware has failed, a **device driver** is corrupt, new software is incompatible, or a computer's **basic input/output system (BIOS)** needs updating. These problems and others can be researched through a manufacturer's Web site. This is an especially appropriate tool when troubleshooting a home user's computer or a computer that has recently been upgraded from one operating system to another. If you have yet to find the problem, and a troubleshooting wizard has listed hardware, software, or BIOS problems as the culprit, visit the manufacturer's Web site for help and updates.

> **NOTE   About the Home User**   Home users will be more likely to install new drivers, applications, and third-party utilities than office users will, mainly because of the lack of limitations placed on them as users. Office users are often not allowed to install devices and applications due to network policies. When troubleshooting a home user's computer, make sure you know what has been installed recently; a new hardware device might be causing the problem.

The Microsoft Knowledge Base

The Microsoft Knowledge Base (which can be accessed at *http://support.microsoft.com/ default.aspx*) offers answers to known issues and can be of significant help when you are trying to solve seemingly irresolvable issues. Figure 2-4 shows the Microsoft Help And Support page where the Knowledge Base and other resources can be accessed. Notice that you can also access announcements, link to visitors' top links, acquire downloads and updates, get product support, and locate other support centers (for Microsoft Outlook, Windows 2000, and so on).

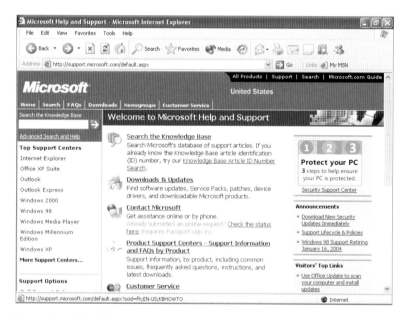

Figure 2-4   The Microsoft Knowledge Base offers solutions to known issues.

The Knowledge Base contains support articles that are identified by an ID number, and you can search for information using that number or using keywords. These articles address known issues with the operating system, third-party software, and hardware, and they provide workarounds and solutions. The Knowledge Base also offers how-to articles, such as KB 291252, "How To: Publish Pictures to the Internet in Windows XP," and KB 813938, "How to Set Up a Small Network with Windows Home Edition," part 1 of a series of articles on the subject.

Search the Knowledge Base after you've tried the previous options, and when you need to know the following:

- Why a specific piece of hardware such as a camera, scanner, printer, or other device does not work as expected, and the problem can be reproduced easily

- Why a specific third-party application won't install, won't start, won't work as expected, or produces error messages

- How to resolve operating system errors including boot errors, problems during installation, **access violation errors** and standby problems, and resolve other known issues

- How to create boot disks, view system requirements, configure file associations, or perform other common tasks

- How to resolve errors that occur when using operating system components such as when accessing System Properties, using Whiteboard, or using System Restore

- What a Stop Error Message means and how to resolve it

- How to resolve errors that occur after installing updates

> **NOTE** Search for a Specific Error Message   Search the Knowledge Base for the specific error message if a text message exists. This is an especially helpful resource when the error is caused by third-party software or hardware. Information on third-party tools is not available in the Windows XP Help files.

TechNet

TechNet (*http://www.Microsoft.com/technet/*) offers comprehensive help on applications, operating systems, and components like Active Directory directory service, Microsoft Internet Explorer, Windows XP Professional, and Office applications, including how to plan, deploy, maintain, and support them. You can also access information on security, get downloads, read how-to articles, read columns, and access troubleshooting and support pages. Because your job will revolve around troubleshooting and resolving end-user requests, you'll likely spend most of your time accessing the troubleshooting pages. A sample TechNet page is shown in Figure 2-5.

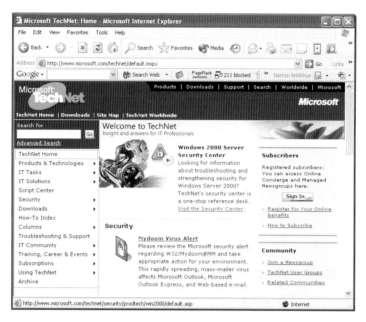

Figure 2-5   A sample Microsoft TechNet Troubleshooting page.

Although you'll find some overlap between TechNet and the Knowledge Base, TechNet generally offers quite a bit more depth on subjects than the Knowledge Base does. Search the TechNet support pages after you've tried the Knowledge Base and when you need to do any of the following:

- Locate product documentation

- View the latest security bulletins

- Get information about service packs, Windows updates, and drivers

- Visit the "Bug Center"

- Get help with **dynamic-link library (DLL)** errors

- Subscribe to TechNet

- Locate highly technical information about technologies

> **NOTE TechNet Subscriptions**   TechNet offers two types of annual subscriptions for a single user or a single server, TechNet Standard and TechNet Plus. Prices for subscriptions range from around $350 to $1,000 (U.S.). A one-year subscription delivers up-to-date technical information every month including the complete Knowledge Base and the latest Resource Kits, service packs, drivers and patches, deployment guides, white papers, evaluation guides, and much more, all on a CD that can be accessed anywhere, at any time, even when you can't get online. Installing service packs from a CD is much faster than downloading them, too, offering yet another reason for considering the subscription. Finally, TechNet Plus offers beta and evaluation software, allowing you to gain experience with software before it's released to the public.

Newsgroups

Newsgroups can be accessed from the Knowledge Base home page, from TechNet, from the Windows XP Expert Zone (*http://www.microsoft.com.windowsxp/expertzone/ default.asp*), and from various other areas of the Microsoft Web site. These can be a valuable resource for locating answers you are unable to resolve using any other method. Members of newsgroups are your peers in IT, computer enthusiasts, beginners, and advanced business or home users, and they have various abilities: some are looking for answers, and some frequent the newsgroup to provide answers to issues they've resolved and to share their expertise. You can join a newsgroup that addresses the application or operating system you need help with, immediately post your question, and almost as quickly receive an answer. Sometimes answers even come from Microsoft experts such as Microsoft Most Valuable Professionals (MVPs). Microsoft chooses Microsoft MVPs based on their practical expertise in Microsoft technologies and these MVPs are deemed experts in their fields.

> **NOTE**   **Try the Knowledge Base Newsgroups First**   Start with the Knowledge Base newsgroups; they'll offer good troubleshooting information. TechNet newsgroups are for IT professionals, MSDN newsgroups are for developers, and Windows XP Expert Zone newsgroups are for Windows XP enthusiasts. If you do not find what you need using the Knowledge Base newsgroups, try one of these others. Third-party newsgroups are also available. Some popular third-party sites include *www.whatis.com*, *www.windrivers.com*, *www.kellys-korner-xp.com*, *www.dougknox.com*, and *www.theeldergeek.com*.

To access a list of newsgroups, visit the Knowledge Base Web site, the Windows XP Expert Zone, or the TechNet Web site and click Newsgroups. You'll find newsgroups for a variety of applications, operating systems, components, and levels of end user. Table 2-1 lists some of the available Knowledge Base newsgroups, but you can find different groups in different areas.

Table 2-1   Selecting the Right Newsgroup

For help with	Join these Knowledge Base newsgroups
Operating systems	Windows XP, Windows 2000, Windows XP Media Center.
Internet Explorer	Internet Explorer 6.0, Internet Explorer 5.5.
Office applications	Access, Excel, FrontPage, Office, Outlook, PowerPoint, Publisher, Word.
Connectivity and networking	For a domain environment, join Active Directory. In a domain, small office, or home environment, join the XP Expert Zone newsgroups Networking and the Web and Wireless Networking.
Security	Virus Discussion, Windows XP Security Administration, Windows 2000 Security, General Security Discussion.
Handheld devices	Tablet PC, Windows CE, Pocket PC.

Working with Possible Solutions

Working through a solution once you've found one requires a little more savvy than simply performing a few mouse clicks and keystrokes and walking away or hanging up the phone. You'll have to perform some pre-repair and post-repair tasks like ordering the solutions (if there are more than one), backing up the user's data, and attempting the solutions and documenting the results. If a solution doesn't work, you'll have to undo it, try another, and possibly escalate the problem as required by the company.

Attempting Solutions

Most of the time after researching the problem, you will find a single solution to it, and working through that solution will resolve the problem. Solutions you'll uncover in a Tier 1 position generally involve running a command at the Run line, reconfiguring an e-mail account, installing a patch, re-creating a network connection, reseating a card on the motherboard, or even simply rebooting the computer or removing a floppy disk from the A drive. However, no matter how simple the solution seems, you should always prepare for the worst. Before attempting any solution (besides removing a floppy disk or rebooting), perform as many of the following tasks as you can within your time frame, job scope, and corporate limitations.

- Locate and make a note of previous settings so that you can revert back to those if your solution fails or causes additional problems.

- Order the solutions by listing solutions obtained from reputable sources first. (List Help and Support Center, Knowledge Base, TechNet, the manufacturer's Web site, and so on first and save solutions found through newsgroups or third-party sites for last.)

- Back up the end user's data to a network resource, CD-R, or external hard disk.

- Create a system restore point.

- Perform any additional tasks required by your company.

- Completely document all attempted solutions and their results.

The higher you move up the tier ladder, the more of these you'll need to be able to perform. If you provide phone support and work from a script, you might not be able to do any of these, but if you own your own business and visit the user on site, or if you go to a user's desk to solve the problem, you'll likely have more leeway (and responsibility) and can do more.

> **CAUTION** *Protect the User's Data!*   *Protect the end user's data at all costs. If that means postponing an attempt at a risky or undocumented solution until another technician can back up the data or until you can bring in a CD-R drive to back up a home user's data, you must wait.*

While working to repair the problem, if you attempt a solution and it doesn't work, any changed settings, configurations, uninstalled programs, or other specific alterations to a computer must be undone before you attempt another solution. This is especially critical if you need to escalate the call; the next technician needs to see the computer in its previous state. In addition, fully test the solution you think resolves the problem. For instance, verify e-mail can be sent and received after changing Post Office Protocol 3 (POP3) mail settings, or make sure the user can access a Web site after changing Internet Explorer privacy settings. Attempt solutions that are within your realm of responsibility, too; don't do a repair installation if that's not on your list of repair options.

Documenting the Problem and Attempted Solutions

Documenting the problem, attempted solutions, and solutions that work are a major part of a desktop technician's job. Although companies, call centers, ISPs, repair shops, and small business owners each have their own way of documenting, documentation tasks usually involve creating (or accessing) a file for a specific client, subscriber, end user, or company computer, and updating that file each time there is a service call regarding it. The documentation might be handwritten on a documentation worksheet and then transferred to a computer file later (as in home or desktop tech support), or it might be immediately input into a computer (as in a call center or ISP tech support).

Depending on the job you hold and your position in the tier structure, you might only be required to fill in a few fields of a documentation worksheet. However, if you own your own company and keep your own records, you'll want to keep much more. Listed next are a few items you should almost always document, no matter what type of job or position you hold:

- The date and time the service call was initiated
- The name, address, phone number, logon information, and any other pertinent data that identifies the end user
- The computer ID, the operating system version, connection type, and installed applications as appropriate
- The problem in definite terms, with as much detail as time allows
- The attempted solutions and the results
- The solution or escalation information
- How long it took to resolve the issue
- Whether the issue has yet to be resolved

Keeping customer and service call documentation (with even minimal information) is crucial to being a good desktop technician, running a successful business, acquiring experience, or advancing in your field. Keeping a separate log of problems and solutions that you've dealt with can also become quite a reference tool; you can refer to your own personal documentation when the problem arises again with another client. In the next section, you'll learn to create a personal knowledge base.

Creating a Personal Knowledge Base

There are several options for collecting and maintaining the data you'll compile while performing your job as a desktop technician. Microsoft Excel and Microsoft Access make good databases and organizational tools, and third-party software such as ACT! or Crystal Reports might also be appropriate, depending on how much data you want to keep. Keeping your own personal knowledge base of problems you've encountered and their solutions will make it easier for you to access the answers to those problems the next time they arise.

When creating a personal knowledge base of problems and their solutions, document the following:

- The problem in detail, using keywords so a search for the problem or one similar to it will produce results
- The cause of the problem, using keywords so a search for the problem or one similar to it will produce results
- The resource that offered a solution to the problem, including a Uniform Resource Locator (URL)
- The solution
- Problems that resulted from the solution (if any)
- How many times the problem has been encountered and solved

INFORM AND TEACH THE END USER

The final part of the service call resolution process is to inform the end user what the problem was and how it was resolved. You can then teach end users how to avoid the problem in the future and how to locate help on their own from the Help and Support Center, company documentation, or other available resources. Finally, you can spend a few minutes teaching the user some basic maintenance tasks like using Disk Defragmenter or Disk Cleanup, as well as some other easy-to-use tools.

> **NOTE** **Understand Your End User** If you get the impression that the end user has absolutely no interest in the information you want to provide, make it brief. Although your main objective is to repair the problem without loss of data, a secondary objective is to avoid annoying the end user. Likewise, if the end user is interested and you own your own business, spending a little extra time educating the user will help to improve your relationship and increase the likelihood that she will call on you again.

Explaining the Problem and Solution to the End User

If a user understands what the problem was and how it was solved, that user can likely solve the problem himself the next time it occurs, if it does. This not only reduces overall costs for the company, but it also frees you to spend more time working on other tasks. In addition to saving both you and the company time and money by reducing service calls, informing users of the problem and solution is empowering to them, too. Consider this:

- Although it might require some downtime on the users' end, having end users solve the problem themselves is probably less aggravating to them than reporting the problem and waiting for a technician to call or show up.

- Many users, particularly home or home office users, will appreciate knowing how to prevent or solve problems in the future. Most want to know how to prevent and solve problems on their own.

- When users can solve their own problems, it's generally cheaper and minimizes downtime for small business owners and freelance vendors.

Consider the problems, solutions, and end results of interacting positively and proactively with end users about problems and their solutions, as detailed in Table 2-2.

Table 2-2   Teach and Inform the End User

Problem and Solution	Solution as Detailed to the End User	Result of Informing and Teaching the End User
User reports that computer will not boot. The user has a floppy disk in the drive and needs to remove it.	You inform the end user that when the computer boots, it looks to the floppy disk first for system files. Because there are no system files on the disk, the computer cannot boot.	The next time the user encounters this problem, the user removes the disk and boots the computer without help from technical support.
User reports she cannot access network resources. You find the user is not logged on to the domain.	You inform the user that logging on to the domain is what allows her to access shared resources and that it is a security feature of a domain.	The user understands the idea of being authenticated on the domain and remembers to log on to access network resources.
User reports he cannot use System Restore. You determine it has been disabled.	You inform the user that System Restore must have at least 200 MB of hard disk space to function, and it must be enabled.	User keeps System Restore enabled.
User complains that every time she clicks the Outlook Express icon, Outlook opens instead. You determine that Outlook is configured as the default e-mail client, and make the appropriate changes.	You inform the end user that she can set defaults for the e-mail client, Web browser, newsgroup reader, calendar, and more on the Programs tab of the Internet Options dialog box.	The end user no longer needs help setting default Internet programs, and also learns about available Internet options.

Each time you teach end users a new task, they become more confident in their abilities and are more apt to solve their own problems rather than calling for technical support. Although this is good in reducing overall costs and use of resources, this can work against you as well. The old saying "a little knowledge is a dangerous thing" certainly holds true in this case. While teaching end users new skills, also make sure to let them know (gently) that they can cause problems, too.

> **NOTE** **Understand the End User**   If you can clearly see that the end user you are working with does not have enough experience to deal with the technical information you want to offer, you might be better off not telling the user of the solution. As a desktop technician, you need to have a sense of the end user's prior knowledge to know how much to explain or share. If there is a danger that the new information will result in a misunderstanding or a naive understanding—both of which could get the user into serious trouble in the future—then you're probably better off keeping the explanation to a minimum with a caveat that the end user probably should not "try this at home."

If a user understands what the problem was and it was solved, that user can likely avoid the problem in the future. When an end user can avoid a problem completely, productivity increases and the overall cost to support that user decreases. It is a waste of resources to simply correct a problem and go back in a week to correct it again. It's much more productive to explain to the user how to keep the problem from happening in the first place. As shown earlier in Table 2-2, end users can often avoid problems if they understand a problem's cause.

Helping the User Solve Problems with Online Help and Support

You can teach end users (in small steps) how to find information and solve problems on their own. There is much information available in the Help and Support Center on a user's own computer, and the information is easy to locate, access, and use. There are also how-to files as well as lengthy articles on how to perform tasks that range from setting up a home network to working remotely. The troubleshooting wizards are especially helpful, and they provide a great way to get to know the troubleshooting process.

When possible, encourage end users to access the help files and browse through them when they encounter a problem. Most users want to know how to solve problems on their own without waiting for a technician. Small-home-office users, especially, appreciate being able to solve their own problems, particularly when a problem occurs late at night or on the weekend, when technicians and technical support aren't available.

> **NOTE** **Troubleshooters Are Good Training Tools**   You can use the troubleshooting wizards to practice and enhance your troubleshooting skills and to look for answers to common problems. The troubleshooters work through the problem-solving process as you should, suggesting obvious solutions first, and then moving on to more complex ones.

Using a Troubleshooting Wizard

Consider the following scenario. A home user is having a problem with Internet Connection Sharing. Although the user can surf the Internet on his computer, a computer recently connected as a client computer is unable to connect to the Internet through this shared connection. The client computer is the only other computer on the network and connects to the host through a hub. The user states he only recently acquired the hub and connected the computers to it. The user wants you to resolve this problem.

Although this sounds like a potentially difficult situation, this problem can easily be solved using the Internet Connection Sharing Troubleshooter in the Help and Support Center.

▶ **Locating a troubleshooter**

To locate the Internet Connection Sharing Troubleshooter (or any other troubleshooter) and resolve this particular problem, follow these steps:

1. From the Start menu, select Help And Support.

2. Select Fixing A Problem.

3. In the left pane under Fixing A Problem, select Troubleshooting Problems.

4. In the right pane, click List Of Troubleshooters.

5. Select the Internet Connection Sharing troubleshooter.

6. On the What Problem Are You Having? page, select I Cannot Browse The Internet From An Internet Connection Sharing Client Computer, and click Next.

7. On the Can You Browse The Internet From The Host Computer? page, select Yes, I Can Browse The Internet From the Host Computer, and click Next.

8. On the Can You Browse the Internet From Another Client Computer? page, select No, I Can't Browse From Any Client Computers On The Home Or Small Office Network, and click Next.

9. As prompted by the wizard, ask the user if he has run the Network Setup Wizard. If the user has not, run the Network Setup Wizard as defined in the troubleshooting guide. This is the likely cause of the problem because the user stated that the client computer was recently connected to the host through a hub, but made no mention that a network was officially configured. This should solve the problem. (If this does not solve the problem, continue working through the wizard until the problem has been determined and solved.)

The home user could have accessed this troubleshooter and the problem could have been solved without your assistance if the user had the proper knowledge of the available tools. However, with the problem solved and the information now at hand, the user can solve the same problem on his own the next time it occurs.

NOTE   **About Informing the End User**   *Although you want to inform end users of places to obtain information, you don't want them finding a solution on TechNet that requires they access the registry, change BIOS settings, or perform other potentially dangerous actions. Make sure end users understand the potential risk of working outside their area of expertise or comfort, and verify that they are only working with the Help and Support Center and company-approved documents.*

Teaching Common Maintenance Tasks

The end user can be taught how to maintain the computer if company policy allows it. If it is in your job description, if you are visiting an employee's desktop, or if you support home users, take a few minutes to make sure the client understands basic maintenance options. Routine maintenance can be quite useful in keeping a computer running properly, it can actually prevent problems, and it can even enhance performance.

Using Disk Cleanup

Disk Cleanup is a safe and simple maintenance tool that users can employ to keep their computers running smoothly. Disk Cleanup searches the drives on the computer and then shows the user temporary files, **Internet cache files**, and unnecessary program files that the user can safely delete. Deleting these files frees up space on the hard disk, which helps the computer run faster and more efficiently. Removing temporary files also helps performance because these files can build up on the computer, take up lots of space, and hinder performance.

▶ **Running Disk Cleanup**

To use Disk Cleanup or instruct a user to do so, follow these steps:

1. From the Start menu, select All Programs, Accessories, System Tools, and Disk Cleanup. Disk Cleanup will take a few minutes to open, because it first calculates how much space you'll be able to free up on the computer's hard disk.

2. If the computer has multiple partitions, in the Select Drive dialog box, select the drive to clean up from the drop-down list. If this is the first time the drive is being cleaned and more than one drive or partition exists, choose the **system partition** first. Click OK.

3. In the Disk Cleanup dialog box, review the files to be deleted. Select the check boxes for the file types you want to delete, and select the Recycle Bin check box to empty it also. Figure 2-6 shows an example. Click OK when finished.

4. Click Yes to verify you want to perform these actions.

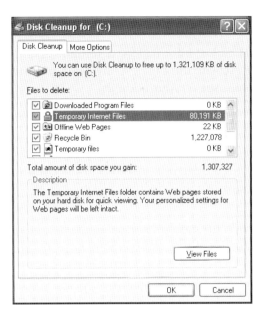

Figure 2-6   Teach end users to use Disk Cleanup weekly.

Using Disk Defragmenter

Disk Defragmenter is another tool that can be used to keep the user's computer running smoothly. The hard disk becomes fragmented as users delete files, move files, delete and install programs and applications, and empty the Recycle Bin. The files on the hard disk aren't stored contiguously as they once were, and this causes the computer to work harder than necessary to locate the file fragments, put them together, and bring up the data.

Convince the end users you service to run Disk Defragmenter once a month. They'll see better computer performance, have fewer problems in the long term, and learn that maintaining the computer benefits them greatly.

▶ **Running Disk Defragmenter**

To use Disk Defragmenter, follow these steps:

1. Close all open programs.

2. Turn off screen savers and antivirus software and disconnect from the Internet.

3. From the Start menu, select All Programs, Accessories, System Tools, and Disk Defragmenter.

4. Select a drive to defragment and either click Analyze to see whether the disk needs defragmenting or click Defragment to begin the process immediately.

Although you might already be familiar with these maintenance tasks, your end users might not be. Share this knowledge with them, and you'll likely see them a little less often.

SUMMARY

- To resolve a service call, you must gather information, determine a solution, find and attempt solutions or escalate the call, test any solutions that you implement, and inform the end user of your findings.

- To solve a problem, first get answers to the questions who, what, when, why, and how. The answers often point up a solution quickly.

- To find a solution, search these resources in the following order: online Help and Support files, company documentation, manufacturers' Web sites, technical sites, and newsgroups. Apply possible answers in the same order.

- Before attempting any solution, back up the user's data, create a system restore point, and document previous settings and configurations if it is within your job role.

- Always document the service call fully, including the user's name, computer ID, problem, attempted solution, result, and how long it took to resolve the call.

- To lower costs, create informed end users, and reduce how often you have to speak with the same end users, inform them briefly of the problem, the solution, and how to avoid the problem in the future.

- To reduce the likelihood a computer will develop future problems, inform the user about how to perform routine maintenance tasks like using Disk Defragmenter and Disk Cleanup.

REVIEW QUESTIONS

1. Questions asked of clients often trigger quick solutions to basic problems. Match the question on the left to the solution it triggered on the right.

1. Who is affected by this problem?	a) The user states that he recently deleted all temporary files and cookies from his computer, explaining why he is no longer able to automatically sign in to Web sites he visits.
2. When was the first time you noticed the problem? Was it after a new installation of software or hardware?	b) John cannot send or receive messages using Outlook. It is determined that the problem is only related to his configuration of Outlook, because other users who log on to the same computer under a different account can use Outlook to send and receive e-mail without any problem.
3. Has the user recently deleted any files or performed any maintenance?	c) The keyboard keys are sticky because coffee was spilled on the keyboard.
4. How did this problem occur?	d) The user states that the first time the computer acted strangely was after she installed a new screen saver.

2. You work for an ISP and receive a call from a client stating that she has not been able to retrieve her e-mail all morning. You check the network servers and everything is working on your end. Which of the following questions could you ask the user that would most likely yield results in this situation? Pick three.

    a. When was the last time you installed new hardware?

    b. How long have you been a subscriber with us?

    c. Have you recently installed or switched over to a new e-mail client?

    d. Have you opened any suspicious attachments?

    e. When did you last clean up the computer with Disk Cleanup?

3. Decide where to look first for answers to the scenarios listed here. Match each question on the left to the appropriate choice on the right.

1. After a recent upgrade to Windows XP Professional, a user's scanner no longer functions as it should. You remember that it was listed as incompatible during the upgrade and believe it might be a driver issue. Where will you likely find the new driver?	a) Newsgroup
2. A user cannot access a network application. The application was designed specifically for the company and is not a Microsoft product or any other common third-party application. Where will you likely find information about this application?	b) TechNet
3. You've searched the Knowledge Base and TechNet for the solution to a problem, but haven't had any luck. Where should you look now?	c) Knowledge Base
4. You need to search through the latest security bulletins to find out if the problem you are having is related to a known security problem. Which online resource offers access to these bulletins?	d) Manufacturer Web site
5. You need to find out why a home user's camera doesn't work with the Windows Picture and Fax Viewer. Specifically, the Rotate tool causes the computer to freeze up each time it's used. Where should you look first?	e) Company documentation
6. You want to access the Hardware Troubleshooter to resolve a problem with a user's sound card. Where can this troubleshooter be found?	f) Help and Support Center

4. Create three simple questions you could ask an end user who is having a problem accessing data on the network server, which would in turn provide answers to common connectivity problems. Explain what each solution might uncover. For instance, an answer of "yes" to the question "Has the computer been moved or bumped recently?" could indicate that a network card is loose inside the computer.

5. Which of the following are tasks you would encourage an average home-based end user to do on his own to maintain and support his own computer? Choose all that apply.

    a. Use Disk Defragmenter monthly.

    b. Access TechNet when in need of technical support and follow the directions to solve problems on his own.

    c. Use Disk Cleanup weekly.

    d. Use Scheduled Tasks to schedule Disk Cleanup to run regularly.

    e. Access the Help and Support Center for how-to articles and to perform specific tasks.

    f. Enable System Restore and keep it enabled.

CASE SCENARIOS

Scenario 2-1: Resolving Problems with Attachments

An end user who runs Windows XP Professional has called technical support regarding his e-mail account. He is certain he was able to open attachments last week, but one just came in today and he can't open it. The user says the paper clip in Outlook Express is grayed out. The technician asks the user if he's made any changes to Outlook Express and he says no. He is firm in his answer. The following five steps describe how the technician solved the problem. Put them in the correct order.

1. Inform the user to open Outlook Express, click Tools, click Options and, on the Security tab, make the appropriate changes.

2. Ask the user what operating system he uses, if any new software or hardware has been installed, if he has switched e-mail clients recently, and other pertinent questions. The user informs you he recently installed a new printer, he uninstalled a screen saver, and he installed Service Pack 1 last weekend.

3. Take a few minutes to inform the user about the maintenance features of Outlook Express including using Clean Up Now.

4. Look for help in various places and locate the answer in the Knowledge Base. The technician discovers that installing Service Pack 1 resets the security setting associated with opening attachments in Outlook Express.

5. Verify the user can now open attachments and document the results.

Scenario 2-2: Helping a User Solve a Printer Problem

An end user calls to report a problem with a locally attached printer. The user is in an office on the other side of the corporate complex, you're busy, and no other technician is available. You find out after asking a few questions that the printer actually works fine, but it just prints slowly. You won't be able to visit the user's desk in person until tomorrow, and you've gleaned from the user that she has quite a bit of experience with computers. Which of the following solutions (they are all valid) is best under these circumstances?

1. Tell the user to join a printer newsgroup and ask other users for advice.

2. Tell the user to open Help and Support, locate the printer trouble-shooter, and work through the options. There is an option to allow Windows to investigate the problem, and this might produce a solution.

3. Tell the user to visit *www.windrivers.com* and download a new driver for the printer.

4. Tell the user to uninstall and reinstall the printer.

CHAPTER 3
TROUBLESHOOT THE OPERATING SYSTEM

Upon completion of this chapter, you will be able to:

- Identify and repair problems involving the taskbar and Start menu

- Configure and troubleshoot regional settings

- Add or remove input languages and troubleshoot language-related problems

- Configure and troubleshoot folder settings

- Add, change, and troubleshoot file associations

- Use the troubleshooting tools included with Windows XP (Msconfig, Msinfo32, Chkdsk, Disk Defragmenter, and SFC /Scannow) to resolve operating system errors and problems

The purpose of this chapter is to teach you how to resolve many of the most common end user requests involving basic operating system components. The components covered in this chapter include the taskbar, Start menu, regional settings, folder settings, and file association settings.

The chapter begins with the taskbar and Start menu and introduces the most common issues you'll see as a Tier 1 desktop technician. Issues involving the taskbar usually revolve around missing icons, a locked or missing taskbar, or the automatic grouping of items. Common issues with the Start menu involve personalizing it by adding or removing items, reordering items, or performing similar customizations.

You'll also learn how to configure and troubleshoot various regional settings such as currency, date, and time; to configure input languages; and to resolve language-related keyboard problems. Additionally, you'll learn about folder settings and file associations, and the most common end user requests associated with these components. Common requests include changing how a folder opens and what is shown, viewing hidden or system files, and changing the way a particular program or file opens. Finally, you'll learn how to use the troubleshooting tools included with Microsoft Windows XP to resolve common problems with the operating system, such as errors on startup, replacing missing system files, and more.

THE TASKBAR AND START MENU

The taskbar and the Start menu are the two main liaisons between the end user and his computer. The taskbar defines for the user the files and programs currently open and running, as well as the programs that are running in the background. The taskbar also allows the user to switch between open files and applications easily, group items, and open the most often used programs quickly. The Start menu provides access to the other available programs, network places, connections, help and support files, recent documents, and more.

Because of the amount of time the end user spends using these two components, she might have several configuration (or troubleshooting) requests, including the following:

- The taskbar is always disappearing and I'd like that to stop. I also want to be able to move the taskbar to another area of the screen.

- John, my colleague down the hall, has an icon next to his Start menu that he uses to open our accounting program. I don't have any icons there. How do I create one of those so I don't always have to locate the program in the Start menu or place a shortcut on the desktop?

- I don't have enough room on my taskbar to show all of my open programs, and I have to scroll to see the additional programs. Is there some way of grouping the programs together?

- Can I remove or hide the icons for my antivirus software, my pop-up stopper program, and other programs that run in the background? If I remove them, do they stop running?

- There are a lot of icons in the notification area I don't think I need. How can I get rid of those for good? I don't think they should be running in the background and I don't even know what some of them are.

- There are lots of programs in my Start menu I don't need, and some I need that aren't there. Can you fix that for me?

- I want to be able to open My Network Places, open the Control Panel, and access System Administrative Tools from the Start menu, but I don't want my recent documents to be listed. I also don't want to see the My Music or My Pictures folders, or any other folders that are not work related.

To answer these questions, you have to understand the options available and how to access and configure them. By the time you reach the end of this section, you'll be able to resolve all of these issues and more.

NOTE   **The Answers**   *These questions and their answers constitute Review Question 1.*

The Notification Area

The notification area shows the time, volume control, and icons for programs that start and run automatically. These program icons can be for antivirus programs, music programs, CD-burning programs, or third-party programs that have been downloaded or purchased. If an item is in the notification area, its program is running in the background, making it quickly available when needed. The notification area also shows icons for network connections, and can show if the connections are enabled or disabled.

In this section, you'll learn to configure and troubleshoot the notification area. Troubleshooting can also include cleaning up the area by removing unnecessary programs. After completing this section you'll be able to do the following:

- Add items to the notification area if the program supports it
- Hide inactive icons so the notification area doesn't take up too much room on the taskbar
- Remove icons and close running programs temporarily
- Remove icons and close running programs permanently

Adding Items to the Notification Area

An icon can be added to the notification area only if the program supports that feature in its preferences or configuration options, and many times icons are added by default when a new program is installed. (There is no support for dragging and dropping a program in the notification area.) Icons can be added for network connections too, including **Ethernet** connections to **local area networks (LANs)**, wireless connections through wireless **access points**, and dial-up connections to the Internet.

If a user requests that you add an icon to the notification area for an application such as an antivirus program, open the program and browse through the available options and preferences.

> **NOTE** **Remove Items from the Notification Area** You can also clear the relevant option to remove the item from the notification area. Removing an item in this manner does not disable the program; it only removes it from the tray.

▶ **Adding an icon for a network or Internet connection**

If a user requests that you add an icon to the notification area for any network or Internet connection on a computer running Windows XP, follow these steps:

1. From the Start menu, select Connect To, and then select Show All Connections. If this is not available, in Control Panel, open Network Connections.

2. Right-click the connection you want to show in the notification area, and select Properties.

3. On the General tab of the connection's Properties dialog box, select the Show Icon In Notification Area When Connected check box, and click OK.

Figure 3-1 shows a notification area that has three active network connections. One is a wireless connection, one is a dial-up Internet connection, and one is to a LAN. It also shows the new mail icon, antivirus software, and a third-party pop-up stopper application.

Figure 3-1   The notification area shows active programs and connections.

Hiding Inactive Icons

If the computer has several programs that start automatically when Microsoft Windows does and there are multiple icons in the notification area as shown in Figure 3-1, the end user might complain that the notification area is taking up too much space on the taskbar. If this happens, enable Hide Inactive Icons, and the icons for programs that are not active (but are still running in the background), will be hidden. To do so, follow these steps:

1. Right-click an empty area of the taskbar and select Properties.

2. On the taskbar tab, select the Hide Inactive Icons check box. Click OK.

The inactive icons will now be hidden behind the arrow. Figure 3-2 shows a notification area configured with hidden icons. Compare this to Figure 3-1; both show the same notification area.

Figure 3-2   Access hidden icons in the notification area by clicking the arrow.

> **NOTE   Hidden Icons**   Keep in mind a user might call you and ask where specific items in the notification area are. The items could be hidden behind the arrow. Check there before you access the program's preferences or restart the program.

Removing Icons and Closing Running Programs Temporarily

To close a program and remove an item from the notification area temporarily so that you can free up resources, disable the program, or briefly unclutter the tray, right-click the icon and look at the choices. Figure 3-3 shows the choices for MSN Messenger 6.1, a program a home user might have installed.

Figure 3-3   Click Exit to close this program and remove the icon from the notification area.

The choices for removing the icon and editing the program will differ depending on the application or connection. Common options include the following:

- Exit
- Disable
- Close
- End
- Preferences (locate the Exit command in the dialog box)

Removing icons from the notification area in this manner is not permanent; it only removes an icon until the program is started again or the computer is rebooted. Removing items permanently requires a little more work.

Removing Icons and Closing Running Programs Permanently
A cluttered notification area is a good indicator that too many programs are starting when Windows boots. This can be the cause of many common performance problems, including a slower than necessary boot-up process, a bogged down system that performs poorly, or a computer that generally displays slow response times when accessing applications or performing calculations. When a user complains that the system exhibits these symptoms, check the notification area first.

Even if the computer seems to be running smoothly, you should remove items from a computer's notification area if the applications are never used. There is no reason to continue to allow unused programs to start each time Windows does; this only drains necessary system resources.

▶ Removing icons permanently

If you decide to remove programs from the notification area permanently, follow these steps:

1. From the Start menu, select Run.
2. In the Run dialog box, type **msconfig.exe** and click OK.
3. In the System Configuration Utility dialog box, select the Startup tab.
4. Scroll down to the bottom of the list, as shown in Figure 3-4, and clear the check box for any third-party item you do not want to start automatically when Windows does. In this example, the Wallpaper Changer PowerToy, the TrayMinimizer program, and WMPImporter can all be cleared. Click OK.

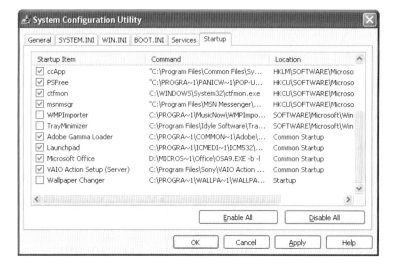

Figure 3-4   The System Configuration Utility dialog box offers lots of information.

5. Restart the computer and verify that you understand that changes have been made when prompted by the System Configuration Utility.

Locking and Unlocking the Taskbar

By default, the taskbar's position on the desktop is locked, which means it cannot be moved to any other location on the desktop, it cannot be resized, and toolbars displayed on the taskbar cannot be changed. If a user wishes to unlock the taskbar, the procedure is easy: right-click an empty area of the taskbar and, from the resulting menu, clear Lock The Taskbar.

Grouping Similar Items and Enabling Quick Launch

Two additional ways to enhance the taskbar are enabling Group Similar Taskbar Buttons and enabling and configuring Quick Launch, both available options in the Taskbar And Start Menu Properties dialog box. Grouping similar open items saves room on the taskbar by grouping similar entries together; enabling Quick Launch lets you permanently add icons to the Quick Launch area of the taskbar for any program a user accesses often.

> **NOTE**   **Quick Launch and the Taskbar**   If Quick Launch is enabled and the taskbar is locked, there will be no dotted lines in front of or behind the Quick Launch area. If Quick Launch is enabled and the taskbar is unlocked, the dotted lines will be apparent, as shown in the figures in this chapter.

Enabling Group Similar Taskbar Buttons

As a desktop technician, you'll work with users of all levels. Some users will just be learning how to e-mail, some will work with a single program and one or two files most of the day, and others will work with multiple programs and have multiple open files. Users who multitask between multiple programs and have several open files will likely have a crowded taskbar and might ask you about their options for organizing the files and programs shown on the taskbar.

Figure 3-5 shows a crowded taskbar, and Figure 3-6 shows the same taskbar with the grouping option enabled. Both taskbars include three open Windows Explorer folders, three open Microsoft Excel worksheets, two open graphics in Microsoft Paint, and three open Microsoft Word documents. In Figure 3-5, some of these open files can't be seen without using the arrow on the taskbar.

Figure 3-5   An unlocked and crowded taskbar might make the taskbar seem disorganized.

Figure 3-6   A locked and crowded taskbar might seem better organized with grouping enabled.

If the user wants you to configure his computer to use these grouping options, open the Taskbar And Start Menu Properties dialog box as detailed earlier. On the Taskbar tab, select the Group Similar Taskbar Buttons check box and click OK.

Enabling Quick Launch

Quick Launch is the area of the taskbar directly to the right of the Start menu that contains icons for your most used programs. When you first enable Quick Launch, you'll have three icons: E-Mail, Launch Internet Explorer Browser, and Show Desktop, as shown in Figure 3-7. Clicking their respective icons opens these programs. However, you can customize the Quick Launch area to include whatever programs you access most often, and even resize it if the taskbar is unlocked. (Figures 3-7 and 3-8 show a customized Quick Launch area.)

Figure 3-7   Quick Launch is shown here with the taskbar unlocked.

▶ **Using Quick Launch**

If a user contacts you and wants to use Quick Launch or asks you to add or remove program icons from it, follow these steps:

1. Right-click an empty area of the taskbar and select Properties.

2. In the Taskbar And Start Menu dialog box, select the Taskbar tab.

3. Select the Show Quick Launch check box, then click OK.

4. To remove any item from the Quick Launch area, right-click it and select Delete. Click Yes in the Confirm File Delete dialog box. (You won't be deleting the program, only removing the icon from the Quick Launch area.)

5. To add any item to the Quick Launch area, locate the program in Windows Explorer, the Start menu, or the All Programs list, right-click it, and drag the program to the Quick Launch area, then select Create Shortcuts Here. If this option is not available, select Copy Here. A new icon will be added.

Figure 3-8 shows a personalized Quick Launch area with icons (from left to right) for Microsoft Outlook Express, Microsoft Internet Explorer, Adobe Photoshop 7.0, Microsoft Photo Editor, MSN Messenger 6.1, Help and Support, Backup, and Control Panel. Depending on the user's needs and preferences, you might be called on to create a Quick Launch area like this one.

Figure 3-8   A personalized and resized Quick Launch area is shown here with the taskbar unlocked.

Troubleshooting a Locked, Hidden, or Missing Taskbar

If an end user contacts you about a locked, hidden, or missing taskbar, it is most likely a simple procedure to repair. Most of the time, the Start Menu And Taskbar Properties dialog box simply has the Lock The Taskbar, Auto-Hide The Taskbar, or Keep The Taskbar On Top Of Other Windows check boxes selected. Clearing these check boxes solves the problems immediately.

- **Lock The Taskbar**   When this check box is selected, the user will not be able to move or resize the taskbar by dragging. The user might complain that the taskbar is "locked."

- **Auto-Hide The Taskbar**   When this check box is selected, the taskbar will be hidden automatically until the user moves her mouse over the area where the taskbar should be. The user might complain that the taskbar is "missing" or "malfunctioning."

- **Keep The Taskbar On Top Of Other Windows**   When this check box is selected, the taskbar stays on top of all other running applications. The user might complain that the taskbar is "always in the way."

In other instances, the user might complain that the taskbar is too large or in the wrong area of the desktop. When this happens, inform the user that he can drag the top of the taskbar (when the mouse pointer becomes a two-headed arrow) to resize it. Moving the taskbar to another area of the screen is achieved by dragging it there.

Advanced Troubleshooting

If the problem with the taskbar cannot be solved using the previous techniques, the problem is more advanced. Table 3-1 lists some known issues with the taskbar on the left, and the Knowledge Base article number and brief solution on the right.

Table 3-1   Advanced Taskbar Problems and Solutions

Problem	Knowledge Base Article Number and Brief Solution
The taskbar is missing when you log on to Windows.	KB 318027; This behavior can occur if the Windows settings for a particular user account are corrupted. The solution involves checking for bad drivers, followed by creating a new user account, followed by performing an in-place repair of the operating system.
The taskbar stops responding intermittently.	KB 314228; This is caused if the Language Bar is minimized and a Windows-based program is busy. Installing the latest service pack solves this problem.

Table 3-1 Advanced Taskbar Problems and Solutions

Problem	Knowledge Base Article Number and Brief Solution
After moving the taskbar from the bottom of the screen to the right side, the background picture is not displayed correctly.	KB 303137; Microsoft has confirmed this is a problem. To solve this problem, click once on an empty area of the desktop and then press F5 to refresh the background.
A part of the ToolTips or a message from the status area remains behind or partially displayed on the status area of the taskbar after it should be gone.	KB 307499; To resolve this behavior, right-click another location that does not contain the leftover message, click the displayed message, move the mouse pointer over the icon, or resize the taskbar.

If the end user's problem is among these, search the Knowledge Base for additional articles and solutions.

> **MORE INFO** **More Information**   Refer to Chapter 2, "Resolving a Service Call," for more troubleshooting techniques, including in what order available information should be sought and techniques should be attempted.

Taskbar Toolbars

Adding any taskbar toolbar adds a link on the taskbar that can be used to quickly access the component chosen. For instance, adding the Desktop toolbar allows you to easily access items on the desktop by clicking the link to them on the taskbar. Adding the Links toolbar allows users to access Internet sites stored in their Links folder (in Internet Explorer Favorites) from the taskbar.

Toolbars can be added to the taskbar by right-clicking the taskbar, pointing to Toolbars, and making the appropriate selection from the choices available. Some choices you can add include the following:

- Address
- Windows Media Player
- Links
- Language Bar
- Desktop
- Quick Launch
- New Toolbar

If users need access to any of these items often, inform them of the ability to add them.

Troubleshooting the Start Menu

The majority of the time, service calls regarding the Start menu involve what is or is not on it. A CEO might want My Network Connections, My Recent Documents, Internet, E-Mail, and the company's accounting program. The lead artist in the graphics department might want My Pictures, Printers and Faxes, My Music, and her favorite art program. When you are queried to personalize the Start menu, the combinations of ways in which the service call comes in are numerous. Figure 3-9 shows an example of a personalized Start menu.

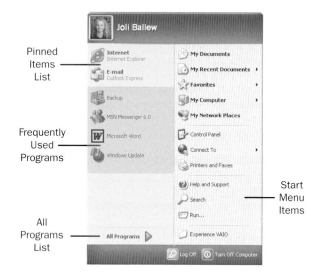

Figure 3-9   A customized Start menu offers personalized access to programs.

There are two types of Start menus available in Windows XP, the Start menu and the Classic Start menu. In this section, you learn about the Start menu and how to resolve the most basic troubleshooting calls. The tasks include adding or removing programs or Start menu items, permanently pinning items to the Start menu, and reordering the All Programs list. The Classic Start menu is discussed briefly in the next section.

Items Need to Be Added or Removed in the All Programs List

Adding and removing items from the All Programs list in the Start menu are common requests from end users. Adding a program can be achieved in a number of ways, but you'll learn the easiest way here. Removing a program is the simpler of the two tasks.

▶ **Adding an item to the All Programs list**

To add an item to the All Programs list, follow these steps:

1. Right-click the Start menu and select Open All Users.

2. From the File menu, point to New, and select Shortcut.

3. In the Create Shortcut dialog box, click Browse.

4. Locate the local or network program, file, folder, computer, or Internet address to create a shortcut for and click OK.

5. Click Next. On the Select A Title For The Program page, type a name for the shortcut and click Finish.

6. Close the Documents And Settings\All Users\Start Menu window.

To see the new addition, from the Start menu, point to All Programs, and look toward the top of the All Programs list. You can now move that item by dragging it to any other area of the All Programs list, the Frequently Used Programs area of the Start menu, or the pinned items list.

To remove an item from the All Programs list, simply right-click it and choose Delete. Click Yes when prompted to verify this action.

> **NOTE** **Reorder the All Programs List**   *You can reorder items on the All Programs list by dragging and dropping, or you can order them alphabetically by right-clicking any entry and selecting Sort By Name.*

Start Menu Items Need to Be Added or Removed

End users will often initiate a service call because a colleague one cubicle over has something on the Start menu that they don't, or there are items on the Start menu they simply don't need. They might call to say that sometimes the program they want is in the frequently used area of the Start menu and sometimes it isn't, and they would like it to always be available. Start menu items can include just about anything, such as frequently accessed programs, pinned items, and operating system components such as Control Panel, My Network Places, Help and Support, Search, Run, and similar items.

Items are added to the frequently used programs area as they are opened, and they are moved up or down the list automatically depending on how often they are used. When a computer is new and there are no items in this list, a program is added to it by opening it once. As programs continue to be opened and used, the list automatically lists the programs by how frequently they are used. If specific items on the list aren't needed, they can be removed by right-clicking and selecting Remove From This List. In addition, all items can be removed and the frequently used programs can be disabled, cleared, or reconfigured from the Customize Start Menu dialog box by following these steps:

1. Right-click Start and select Properties.

2. In the Taskbar And Start Menu Properties dialog box, verify that Start Menu is selected, and click Customize.

3. In the Customize Start Menu dialog box, in the Programs section, click Clear List to clear all items from the frequently used programs area of the Start menu.

4. To increase or decrease the number of programs shown, change the value for Number Of Programs On Start Menu using the arrows. Zero disables it. Figure 3-10 shows an example. Click OK and click OK again to apply the changes.

Figure 3-10   The Customize Start Menu dialog box offers many ways to personalize the Start menu.

You can pin or unpin an item to or from the Start menu by right-clicking the item in the Start menu or All Programs list and selecting Pin To Start Menu. Pinning an item to the Start menu places it in the top left corner of the Start menu with other pinned items like Internet and E-Mail, allowing for easier access. This option is also available for items in the frequently used items area.

Finally, if a user asks you to add or remove an operating system component, such as Favorites, Control Panel, Run, My Documents, or My Pictures to or from the Start menu or to configure how it is displayed, follow these steps:

1. Right-click Start and select Properties.

2. In the Taskbar And Start Menu Properties dialog box, verify that Start Menu is selected and click Customize.

3. In the Customize Start Menu dialog box, select the Advanced tab.

4. In the Start Menu Items window, scroll through the options. Selecting an item will show it on the Start menu. Other choices for an item include the following:

   ❑ **Display As A Link–**   The item will be displayed on the Start menu.

   ❑ **Display As A Menu–**   The item will be displayed and a menu will be available that contains the objects in that folder.

   ❑ **Don't Display This Item–**   The item will not be displayed.

5. In the Recent Documents area, click Clear List to clear the list of recently opened documents, or clear the List My Most Recently Opened Documents check box to prevent items from being shown. Click OK twice to apply the changes and exit.

NOTE   Advanced Troubleshooting   Remember, if the troubleshooting call goes beyond these basic configuration issues, visit the Knowledge Base for help.

Troubleshooting the Classic Start Menu

The Classic Start menu is another option for end users. If, after an upgrade, end users complain that the Start menu is too complicated or that they want it to look more like their old Microsoft Windows 98 or Windows 2000 computer did, this is the menu you pick. Troubleshooting the Classic Start menu is similar to troubleshooting the Start menu as detailed earlier, except for the minor differences in the Customize dialog box. Figure 3-11 shows the Customize Classic Start Menu dialog box.

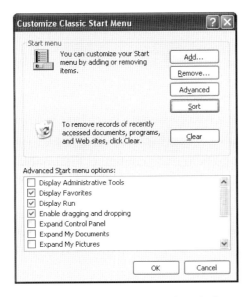

Figure 3-11   Customizing the Classic Start menu is also achieved through a dialog box.

In this dialog box you can do the following:

- Click Add to add any item to the Start menu.

- Click Remove to remove any item from the Start menu.

- Click Advanced to start Windows Explorer to add or remove items from the Start menu.

- Click Clear to remove records of recently accessed documents, programs, and Web sites.

- Click any item in the Advanced Start Menu Options list to show that item.

REGIONAL AND LANGUAGE OPTIONS

Regional and language options, available from Control Panel, define the standards and formats the computer uses to perform calculations; provide information such as date and time; and display the correct format for currency, numbers, dates, and other units. These settings also define a user's location, which enables help services to provide local information such as news and weather. Language options define the input languages (one computer can accept input in many different languages); therefore, the computer must be configured with the proper settings. Almost all regional and language configuration and troubleshooting tasks are performed using the Regional And Language option in Control Panel. Figure 3-12 shows the Regional And Language Options dialog box.

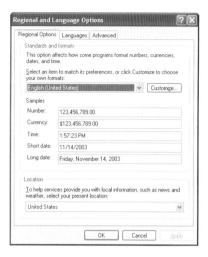

Figure 3-12   The Regional And Language Options dialog box offers a place to configure regional and language options.

As a desktop technician, you'll often be asked to help users configure and trouble-shoot these settings. In many instances, users need to add an additional region or input language because they travel, work, or live in two different countries or regions; an input language needs to be added because users who share a computer speak different languages; or a currency, time, and date need to be changed tem-porarily on a user's laptop while he is on a business trip. You learn how to perform these tasks in this section.

Configuring Correct Currency, Time, and Date

When a user requests a change to the currency, time, or date standards and formats on a computer, you make those changes in the Regional And Language Options dialog box, on the Regional Options tab, shown earlier in Figure 3-12. Changing the standard and format is as simple as clicking the drop-down list in the Standards And Formats area and selecting a new option. In Figure 3-13, English (United States) is no longer selected, French (France) is. Notice that the date is written in French, that the currency has changed, and that the date, January 12, 2004 is writ-ten 12/01/2004, which is different from the English version, which is 1/12/2004.

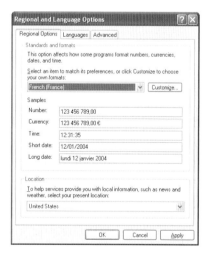

Figure 3-13   Changing standard and format options changes the currency, date, language, and more.

▶ **Using the Regional And Language Options dialog box**

To make this change and to access the other options for the Regional And Language Options dialog box, follow these steps:

1. Open Control Panel. In Category view, select the Date, Time, Language, & Regional Options link and then the Regional And Language Options link. (In Classic view, double-click Regional And Language Options).

2. Select the Regional Options tab.

3. In the Standards And Formats section, click the drop-down list to view the additional choices. Select one of these choices.

4. In the Location section, choose a country from the list to change the default location.

5. To further customize the settings, click Customize.

6. When finished, click OK in each open dialog box to exit.

Customizing Regional Options

If a user requests a specific change to the default settings, such as changing the currency symbol, the time or date format, or the system of measurement, but wants to keep other default settings intact, click Customize, as shown in Figure 3-12, and make the appropriate changes. Each option has a drop-down list, and selecting a different option only requires selecting it.

Troubleshooting Input Languages

The input language configured for the computer tells Windows how to react when text is entered using the keyboard. A user might want you to add a language if she works or travels between two or more countries that use different languages, and she needs to work in those languages or perform calculations with the currencies in those countries. With multiple languages configured, the user can toggle between them as needed. In addition, users might want to change language settings even if they do not travel, but do work with an international group or conduct business with other countries.

▶ **Adding an input language**

To add (or remove) an input language, follow these steps:

1. From Control Panel, open Regional And Language Options.

2. Select the Languages tab, and in the Text Services And Input Languages section, click Details.

3. In the Text Services And Input Languages dialog box, click Add to add an additional language.

4. In the Add Input Language dialog box, select the language you want to add. To choose a specific keyboard layout, select the Keyboard Layout/ IME check box and choose the appropriate layout. To add a keyboard layout or **input method editor (IME)**, you must have installed it on your computer first. Click OK.

5. Back in the Text Services And Input Languages dialog box, select which language should be the default language from the Default Input Language drop-down list, and click OK.

Figure 3-14 shows two available languages, English (United States) - US and Italian (Italy) - Italian. The user can now switch between these languages easily using the Language Bar (located on the taskbar).

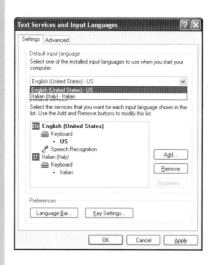

Figure 3-14   Two languages are now available for the user.

Troubleshooting Language-Related Problems

When users have multiple languages configured, language-related problems are bound to occur. One of the more common issues occurs when a user with multiple languages configured accidentally changes the default language in use by unintentionally hitting the key combination that switches between them. By default, pressing LEFT ALT + SHIFT switches between languages. Users who accidentally hit that combination might suddenly find themselves with a keyboard that doesn't act as it's supposed to, and they won't have any explanation for why it happened. You'll have to use the Language Bar to switch back to the default language, and you might want to disable this feature while you're at the computer.

Here are some other common things to look for:

- If a user complains that while using the On-Screen Keyboard accessibility tool, most keys on the screen do not blink when he presses a key on the physical keyboard, inform the user that this behavior is intended and correct (see KB 294519).

- If after installing a new IME as the default keyboard layout, the user complains that the previous keyboard layout is still being used, install the latest service pack to resolve the problem (see KB 318388).

- If a user complains that after choosing a new language she is unable to view the menus and dialog boxes in that language, inform the user that the Windows Multilingual User Interface Pack must be purchased and installed for these items to be changed (see Microsoft Help and Support Center).

Less common and more complex problems are addressed in the Knowledge Base. Remember to search there for answers if the problem cannot be resolved through general reconfiguration and common troubleshooting techniques.

FOLDER SETTINGS

Folder settings can be accessed from Control Panel or from the Tools menu in Windows Explorer. These settings are used to specify how folders function and what content is displayed. Folder Options can be used to resolve many types of service calls and requests from end users. Listed next are brief descriptions of the four available tabs in the Folder Options dialog box and some common tasks that can be achieved using them:

- **General Tab**   Use the options on this tab to change how folders look and how they open. Windows can be configured to use Windows Classic folders for a pre–Windows XP look and feel, and opening a folder inside another folder can be configured to appear in different ways. Folders can be configured so that the new folder either opens in the same window or in a different one. Folders can also be configured to open with a single or double click.

- **View Tab**   Use the options on this tab to apply folder views system-wide (Details, Tiles, Icons, and so on) or to reset the folder views to their default. Configure advanced settings to remember (or not remember) each folder's view settings, to show (or not show) pop-up descriptions of folder and desktop items, to use (or not use) Simple File Sharing, to automatically search for network folders and printers, and more.

- **File Types Tab**   Use the options on this tab to view, add, or reconfigure what types of files open with what particular program. When an end user requests that a specific file open with a specific program, make that change here.

- **Offline Files Tab**   If **Fast User Switching** is not enabled, offline files can be enabled here. When offline files are enabled, a user can work on network files even if he isn't connected to the network. (Offline Files are a tested objective on the 70-271 exam.)

   NOTE   Folder Options Are Available in Control Panel   Open the Folder Options dialog box by opening Control Panel, clicking Appearance And Themes, and opening Folder Options.

Troubleshooting Folder View Settings

When a user requests help involving how folders are viewed, how windows open, and what can and cannot be seen inside a folder, check the configured Folder Options first. There you can discover the cause of many common problems and resolve them easily.

Before starting any troubleshooting in the Folder Options dialog box, ask the user if she has made any changes there already. If a user tells you she has made changes to the Folder Options but can't remember what the changes were, use the Restore Defaults button on the General tab and the View tab to restore the defaults. Many times, this solves the problem. Table 3-2 shows some other common problems and their resolutions, all of which are available in the Folder Options dialog box.

Table 3-2   **Common Folder View Issues and Their Solutions**

Common Problem	Solution
A user reports that each time he opens a folder or clicks an icon in Control Panel, it opens a separate window. Sometimes he has 15 open windows on his desktop, and he finds it quite annoying. He wants you to change this behavior.	In the Folder Options dialog box, on the General tab, in the Browse Folders area, select Open Each Folder In The Same Window.
A user reports that she needs to view encrypted and compressed folders in a different color when using Windows Explorer to locate them. She wants to know how to do this.	In the Folder Options dialog box, on the View tab, select the Show Encrypted Or Compressed Files In Color check box.
A user reports that his coworkers often see new folders and printers in My Network Places, but he never does. He has to search for and add them manually. He wants you to resolve this problem.	In the Folder Options dialog box, on the View tab, select the Automatically Search For Network Folders And Printers check box.
Your CEO fancies herself a power user, and wants to be able to view and access protected system files and hidden files and folders. How do you allow this?	In the Folder Options dialog box, on the View tab, select the Show Hidden Files And Folders check box and clear the Hide Protected Operating System Files (Recommended) check box.
A user who has recently upgraded from Windows 98 to Windows XP does not like the "Web" look associated with the folders and the interface. What can you do in the Folder Options dialog box to make the user more comfortable?	In the Folder Options dialog box, on the General tab, click Use Windows Classic Folders.

NOTE   Missing Category View?   If you change the Tasks setting in the Folder Options dialog box (on the General tab) to Use Windows Classic Folders instead of Show Common Tasks In Folders, you won't have the option in Control Panel to switch to Category view. Users might miss this feature and have a difficult time connecting the missing options with selecting this setting.

Adopting Best Practices

Because changing default folder behavior is so simple (just select or clear any check box in the Folder Options dialog box), you might think that changes performed here are harmless. This is not true. Here are some reasons to leave the default options configured:

■ Although you can easily allow users to view hidden files and folders or access system files, you should avoid it at all costs. Changes made to these files, especially system files, can make the computer inoperable. If the changes are severe enough, you might have to perform a repair installation.

■ Although you might be tempted to disable Simple File Sharing to give a user more options for configuring security on his small workgroup or home network, it isn't always necessary and might confuse the end user.

In addition, the user might try to configure complicated options and create unnecessary file-sharing problems.

■ Although you might think that switching a user to use Windows Classic folders just because she is initially uncomfortable with the interface is helpful, in the long run it might be better for that user to learn to work with the new technology. Technologies will change, and it is generally beneficial to keep up.

FILE ASSOCIATIONS

File extensions define the file type. A file with a .doc extension is a document; a file with an .mp3 extension is an MP3 music file. The file extension tells Windows what type of file it is opening and what program should be used to open it. A document file will most likely be configured to open in Word; a music file will most likely be configured to open in Windows Media Player.

As a desktop technician, you'll be called on to troubleshoot file associations. Specifically, you'll be asked to add and troubleshoot file types that aren't recognized by the operating system and to configure a specific file type to always open with a specific program. You might also want to inform the end user how he can change the default behavior temporarily. In this section, you learn to do all of these things.

Common File Types

Table 3-3 shows some common file types and the programs they will most likely be configured to open with automatically. In the far right column, additional programs are listed that can be used to open the same file. Users might ask you to change which program is used to open a specific file type because they prefer one program to another or because company policy requires them to use a specific program.

Table 3-3   Common File Types and the Programs Used to Open Them

File Extension	Common Default Programs	Alternate Programs
.avi	Windows Media Player	RealPlayer, Quick Time
.bmp	Paint	Microsoft Photo Editor, third-party graphics programs, Internet Explorer
.doc	Word	WordPad, Notepad, or third-party word processing programs
.gif, .jpg, .jpeg, .tiff	Paint, Windows, Picture and Fax Viewer	Third-party graphics programs, Internet Explorer
.htm, .html	Internet Explorer, Notepad	WordPad, Microsoft FrontPage
.mp3, .wav	Windows Media Player	RealPlayer, Quick Time
.txt	Notepad	WordPad, Internet Explorer, Word
.xls	Excel	Third-party database applications

This is by no means a complete list; these are only a few of the hundreds of available file types. However, it does make clear that different files can be opened using various programs. Although the CEO's secretary might be happy with .jpeg files opening in Windows Picture and Fax Viewer, chances are good that a member of the graphics department will need that file to open in a more advanced graphics program.

Changing the Way a File Type Opens by Default

If a user requests that a specific type of file open with a specific program every time that file type is encountered, you'll want to change the details for that particular file extension to create a permanent default for that file type. For instance, if a user requests that all .gif files always open with Windows Picture and Fax Viewer, you can set this by following these steps:

1. Open Control Panel and open Folder Options.

2. Select the File Types tab, scroll down, and select GIF.

3. In the Details for GIF Extension area, next to Opens With: *<program name>*, click Change.

4. In the Open With dialog box, shown in Figure 3-15, select Windows Picture And Fax Viewer and click OK. Click Close in the Folder Options dialog box.

Figure 3-15   The Open With dialog box offers personalization options for the user.

From here on, or until this new default behavior is changed manually, all .gif files will open using Windows Picture and Fax Viewer. You can use this same procedure to change any file type and the program it opens with.

Changing the Way a File Type Opens Once

If a user only wants the file to open with a different program once, it's as simple as right-clicking. Perhaps a user who has never edited a picture has one she wants to brighten using the tools in Photo Editor, but all of her graphics files open in the Windows Picture and Fax Viewer by default. You can instruct the user to open the picture in another program easily, following these steps:

1. Browse to the file by using Windows Explorer or My Computer, or by opening My Documents, My Pictures, or another folder that contains the file.

2. Right-click the file to open, point to Open With, and select the program from the list. The file will open in the designated program.

NOTE *Select a Default Program* The Open With dialog box includes the Always Use The Selected Program To Open This Kind Of File check box. If this check box is selected, the program will always open with this type of file. Do not select this check box if you do not want to make this the default program.

Problems occur when there are no choices in the Open With list. This happens because Windows does not recognize the file and does not know what program to use to open it. This problem is covered in the next section.

Troubleshooting File Associations

There are two common file association problems that end users encounter. Either they right-click the file, point to Open With, and see no available choices, or they attempt to open the file and fail because the file type is not recognized. (These unknown files and their file types are almost exclusively created using third-party applications or a company's specially designed applications.)

If, after right-clicking a file, the Open With dialog box provides no choices, you need to inform the user to select Choose Program (available from the Open With list choices) to tell Windows what program to use to open the file. If there are no recommended programs, the user needs to browse to the program that opens it. After selecting the appropriate program, the user can open the file. If the program is unavailable, you'll need to install a program that can be used and is compatible with that particular file type.

When Open With is unavailable and the user selects Open, or if a user attempts to open a file with an unknown file extension, the user receives the message shown in Figure 3-16. This message appears when a user tries to open a file and the associated program is not installed or available, or when the file type isn't registered and recognized by the operating system. In this dialog box you can either use a Web service to locate the program the file opens with, or you can manually select the program from the list. To manually select a program, select Select The Program From A List, locate the program, and click OK.

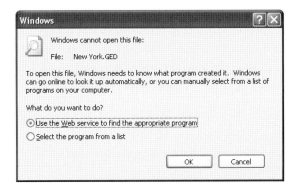

Figure 3-16 The result when a file type is not recognized by Windows is shown here.

Adding a New File Extension

If you've encountered a file type that Windows isn't familiar with, you'll need to add that file extension on the File Types tab of the Folder Options dialog box. This way, Windows knows that the file type is valid and what program to associate it with.

▶ **Adding a file type**

To add a file type, follow these steps:

1. Open Control Panel and open Folder Options.

2. On the File Types tab, click New.

3. In the Create New Extension dialog box, type the file extension in the File Extension field. Click OK.

4. Locate the new file type at the top of the Registered File Types list as shown in Figure 3-17. Notice the new file type does not have a program associated with it. In the Opens With area, click Change to choose the program to open it with.

Figure 3-17   Adding a file type is achieved through the Folder Options dialog box.

5. In the Windows dialog box, select Select The Program From A List and click OK.

6. In the Open With dialog box, select the program. (An installed program must be able to open the file.) Click OK. In the Folder Options dialog box, click Close.

   NOTE **Modify File Types**   You can also modify file types by clicking Advanced on the File Types tab. Actions such as Open, Play, and Print can be set as the default action when a file is selected and opened.

COMMONLY USED TROUBLESHOOTING TOOLS

There are several troubleshooting tools that ship with Windows XP that can be extremely helpful in resolving many of the problems you'll encounter while performing your job as a desktop technician. These tools are generally employed when the user receives error messages (or prompts by applications) as the computer boots, when the user receives errors while opening or saving files, or when the user accesses applications or hardware. In this section you'll learn about five of these tools:

- **Msconfig**   A run-line command that opens the System Configuration Utility, which can be used to troubleshoot and resolve boot errors and get rid of unwanted prompts by third-party applications.

- **Msinfo32**   A run-line command that opens the System Information window, which provides detailed information about the computer system configuration.

- **Chkdsk**   A command-line tool that creates a status report of the integrity of the hard disk and corrects errors on the disk.

- **Disk Defragmenter**   A program included with Windows XP that analyzes hard disks and locates and consolidates fragmented files and folders.

- **SFC /Scannow**   A command-line tool that scans and verifies all protected system files on the computer and replaces any missing files.

Next, you are briefly introduced to these tools; for more information, see the related Windows XP Help files.

▶ **Using Msconfig**

Use Msconfig when troubleshooting errors that occur during the boot process, to rid the computer of third-party software prompts after booting, to discover and resolve problems with running services, or to resolve errors regarding the boot paths configured on multiboot computers. To use Msconfig to open and use the System Configuration Utility, follow these steps:

1. From the Start menu, select Run.

2. In the Run dialog box, type **msconfig** and click OK.

3. In the System Configuration Utility dialog box, browse through the available tabs and make changes as appropriate:

    ❏ **General**   Use the options on this tab to tell Windows XP how to boot the machine. There are three choices: Normal Startup, which loads all device drivers and services; Diagnostic Startup, which loads only basic devices and services; and Selective Startup, which loads only the items manually configured from the other tabs. System Restore can also be launched from this tab. Experiment with these choices to resolve boot problems.

    ❏ **System.ini**   Use the options on this tab to tell Windows XP what items configured in the System.ini file to load when booting. You'll need to have quite a bit of experience with the boot files, drivers, and other items to use these tools effectively.

    ❏ **Win.ini–**   Use the options on this tab to tell Windows XP what items configured in the Win.ini file to load when booting. You'll need to have quite a bit of experience with the boot files, drivers, and other items to use these tools effectively.

❑ **Boot.ini** Use the options on this tab to configure dual-boot computers, check boot paths, set a boot path as a default, configure how long to wait before booting to the default, and more.

❑ **Services** Use the options on this tab to select or deselect what services on the Windows XP computer will load during the boot process. Deselecting services can help you pinpoint the exact service that is causing problems on the machine.

❑ **Startup** Use the options on this tab to select or deselect what startup items are loaded during the boot process. Deselecting third-party startup items will rid the computer of that software's prompts to register, upgrade, update, or purchase, and will stop the item from loading on startup. Use this option to rid the notification area of unnecessary running programs.

4. Click OK and reboot. You'll be prompted on reboot that the startup configuration has changed.

CAUTION Be Careful Be careful when modifying the boot files, or you might render the computer unbootable. Many of these options should be reserved for experienced, advanced technicians. When in doubt, consult a more experienced technician or the Windows XP or Knowledge Base help files.

▶ **Using Msinfo32**

Use Msinfo32 when you need to obtain information about the local or remote computer's hardware configuration, computer components, installed software, drivers (signed or unsigned), or need to get information about the BIOS version, verify that memory is installed and available, check product activation status, determine hardware conflicts, and more. To use Msinfo32 to open the System Information window and to browse through the available data, follow these steps:

1. From the Start menu, select Run.

2. In the Run dialog box, type **msinfo32** and click OK.

3. From the left pane, expand each of the trees to view the available data (this is shown in Figure 3-18):

❑ **Hardware Resources** View and determine conflicts between hardware devices, see hardware's interrupt requests (IRQs), memory, and more.

❑ **Components** View information about multimedia hardware, sound and display devices, modems, storage, printing devices, and more.

❑ **Software Environment** View information about system drivers, print jobs, network connections, running tasks, services, and more.

❑ **Internet Settings** View information about Internet settings, including the browser version and type, content and cache settings, and more.

❑ **Applications** View installed applications and information logged while using the applications. Figure 3-18 shows an example of the Microsoft Office 2003 Environment tree, and a description of the last Web connection error encountered by the application.

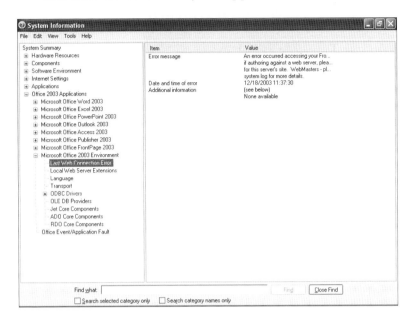

Figure 3-18 The System Information Utility offers an incredible wealth of information.

4. Close the System Information window when finished.

▶ **Using Chkdsk**

Use Chkdsk (Check Disk) to view the file system type (NTFS or FAT), and to verify the integrity of the disks installed on the computer. Adding the appropriate parameter (/F), you can also fix errors on the disk. To use chkdsk to check the integrity of the hard disk and automatically fix any errors it finds, follow these steps:

1. From the Start menu, point to All Programs, point to Accessories, and select Command Prompt.

2. To see all of the Chkdsk parameters, at the command prompt type **chkdsk /?**. The Help report is shown in Figure 3-19. (If you don't have any experience at the command line, review these options carefully. Do some independent study to become familiar with command-line tools.)

Figure 3-19 Chkdsk offers several parameters.

3. At the command prompt, type **chkdsk /F** to run Check Disk and automatically correct disk errors.

▶ **Using Disk Defragmenter**

Disk Defragmenter looks for and consolidates fragmented files, those that are saved in various areas of the hard disk rather than in one place. Opening defragmented files takes less time than opening fragmented ones, because the information is stored together on the disk rather than haphazardly. Use Disk Defragmenter when the user complains that the computer seems slower than usual, when the user has not used Disk Defragmenter in the past or does not use it on a regular basis, and when no distinct problems can be found for the slowdown. To use Disk Defragmenter, follow these steps:

1. From the Start menu, point to All Programs, point to Accessories, point to System Tools, and select Disk Defragmenter.

2. To analyze the disk to see if it needs defragging, select the disk from the top pane, and select Analyze from the bottom.

3. If the computer's hard disk needs to be defragmented, you'll be prompted, as shown in Figure 3-20. Click Close.

4. Back up the user's files.

5. Disconnect from the Internet, turn off all antivirus software, turn off all screen savers, and close all running programs (except Disk Defragmenter).

6. To defragment the volume, click Defragment. Close all dialog boxes and windows when the process is complete.

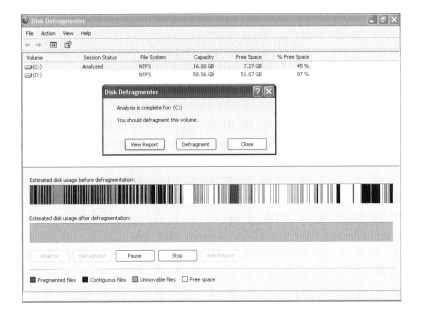

Figure 3-20   After analyzing the disk, Disk Defragmenter prompts to defragment the disk.

NOTE   Defragmenting is a Long Procedure   Disk Defragmenter might take quite some time to complete, depending on the disk size and the level of fragmentation. Consider running this application at the end of the day or at night, and do not disturb the computer while it is running.

▶ Using SFC /Scannow

System File Checker (SFC) is a command-line utility that allows a technician or user to determine if any protected system files are missing. Missing system files can cause problems with the boot process, or problems when operating system components are opened. To use the SFC /Scannow utility to determine if there are any missing files and to replace them, follow these steps:

1. From the Start menu, point to All Programs, point to Accessories, and select Command Prompt.

2. Type **SFC /scannow** and press ENTER.

3. If prompted, insert the Windows XP CD-ROM.

4. Wait while Windows verifies that all protected files are intact and in their original versions.

There are many other command-line tools to choose from; to locate information about these tools, open the Windows Help and Support Center and search for "command line tools."

SUMMARY

- To resolve problems involving the taskbar, use the Taskbar And Start Menu Properties dialog box. On the Taskbar tab, you can lock or hide the taskbar, group similar items, show Quick Launch, hide inactive icons, and keep the taskbar on top of other windows.

- To resolve problems involving the Start menu, use the Taskbar And Start Menu Properties dialog box. On the Start menu tab, click Customize to define what should and should not appear on the taskbar, clear the taskbar of recently used programs or documents, and more.

- To enable a user to work in different languages on one computer, make changes in the Regional And Language Options dialog box. There, you can select and configure options for currency, time and dates, and select input languages.

- To configure how folders open, how they look, and what they contain, use the Folder Options dialog box. There, you can choose to show hidden files and folders, open folders with a single click, configure how encrypted and compressed files look, and more.

- To troubleshoot file associations, to define what program should be used to open a specific file type, to add new file types, and to edit what happens when a particular program opens a file, use either the Open With dialog box by right-clicking on a file and selecting Open With, or the Folder Options dialog box by clicking the File Types tab.

- To troubleshoot common operating system errors, use the troubleshooting tools included with Windows XP: Msconfig, Msinfo32, Chkdsk, Disk Defragmenter, and SFC /Scannow.

REVIEW QUESTIONS

1. Match the end user request on the left with the solution on the right.

1. The taskbar is always disappearing and I'd like that to stop. I also want to be able to move the taskbar to another area of the screen.	a) Open the Taskbar And Start Menu Properties dialog box. On the Taskbar tab, select the Show Quick Launch check box. Then, from the Start menu, locate the program to show in the Quick Launch area, right-click it, and drag and drop it there. Select Copy Here.
2. John, my colleague down the hall, has an icon next to his Start menu that he uses to open our accounting program. I don't have any icons there. How do I create one of those so I don't always have to locate the program in the Start menu or place a shortcut on the desktop?	b) Open the Taskbar And Start Menu Properties dialog box. On the Taskbar tab, select the Group Similar Taskbar Buttons check box.

3. I don't have enough room on my taskbar to show all of my open programs, and I have to scroll to see the additional programs. Is there some way of grouping the programs together?

c) Open the Taskbar And Start Menu Properties dialog box. On the Taskbar tab, clear the Auto-Hide The Taskbar check box. Then, verify that the Lock The Taskbar check box is cleared. Instruct the user to move the taskbar by dragging.

4. Can I remove or hide the icons for my antivirus software, my pop-up stopper program, and other programs that run in the background? If I remove them, do they stop running?

d) Notification area icons can be removed by setting preferences in the program's configuration choices. If you right-click an item in the notification area and its shortcut menu enables you to choose Exit or Close, the program will stop running when you choose the appropriate option.

5. There are a lot of icons in my notification area I don't think I need. How can I get rid of those for good? I don't think they should be running in the background and I don't even know what some of them are.

e) Open the Taskbar And Start Menu Properties dialog box. On the Start Menu tab, click Customize. In the Customize Start Menu (or Customize Classic Start Menu) dialog box, make the appropriate changes.

6. There are lots of programs in my Start menu I don't need, and some I need but aren't there. Can you fix that for me?

f) From the Start menu, select Run. At the Run line, type **msconfig.exe** and click OK. On the Startup tab, clear the check boxes for the items that you do not want to start when the computer boots.

7. I want to be able to open My Network Places and the Control Panel, and access System Administrative Tools from the Start menu, but I don't want my recent documents to be listed. I also don't want to see My Music, My Pictures, or anything else that is not work-related.

g) Open the Taskbar And Start Menu Properties dialog box. On the Start Menu tab, select Classic Start Menu and click Customize. Use the Add and Remove buttons to customize the menu. Apply the changes. If desired, select Start Menu to return to the default Start menu look.

2. You are an architect who creates blueprints for clients all over the world, so you use the metric system instead of the U.S. system of measurement. Your company handles all other communications, including billing. Your regional settings are configured to use the English (United States) standard. Which of the following is the best option for changing the default system of measurement on your computer from U.S. to metric?

   a. Change the default regional options for standards and formats to English (Canada). Canada is the nearest country that uses the metric system.

    b. Change the default regional options for standards and formats to English (United Kingdom). The United Kingdom uses the metric system and many of your clients live there.

    c. Keep the English (United States) setting, but customize the measurement system to use the metric system. Don't make any other changes.

    d. Install a metric keyboard.

3. In the following table, match the user request on the left with the part of the operating system that is used to resolve that request on the right.

1. A user wants to open folders using a single-click, not a double-click.	a) Taskbar And Start Menu Properties dialog box, Taskbar tab.
2. A user wants open programs to be grouped on the taskbar.	b) Configure the folder options from the View menu of any open folder. Open the Folder Options dialog box and, on the View tab, click Apply To All Folders.
3. A user wants all of her folders to open and display folder items as icons, not the current setting of tiles.	c) Folder Options dialog box, File Types tab, Registered File Types window, Change.
4. A user wants his JPEG files to always open in Paint.	d) Folder Options dialog box, General tab.
5. A user complains that there is no Security tab when she shares a file.	e) Folder Options dialog box, View tab, Advanced Settings.
6. A user complains that the pop-up descriptions for folder and desktop items no longer appear when he hovers over the item with the mouse.	f) Folder Options dialog box, View tab, disable Simple File Sharing.

4. After configuring Folder Options, you notice you can no longer switch to Category view in Control Panel. What must you do to resolve this problem?

    a. Clear the Use Windows Classic Folders check box in the Folder Options dialog box.

    b. Select the Use Windows Classic Folders in the Folder Options dialog box.

    c. In Control Panel, click View, select Choose Details, and select the Show Tasks check box.

    d. In Control Panel, select the View tab, select Choose Details, and clear the Hide Task Options check box.

5. You want to have as few items as possible on the taskbar. Which of the following items can easily be removed from the taskbar? (Choose all that apply.)

   a. The Start button

   b. The system clock

   c. The notification area

   d. Quick Launch items

   e. Inactive icons in the notification area

6. There are many ways to access the Folder Options dialog box. Which of the following are valid examples?

   a. In Windows Explorer, from the Tools menu, select Folder Options.

   b. In the My Documents folder, from the Tools menu, select Folder Options.

   c. In Control Panel, open Folder Options.

   d. In My Computer, from the Tools menu, select Folder Options.

   e. From the All Programs list, under Accessories, select Folder Options.

7. A user has multiple languages configured on her laptop and needs access to the Language Bar quite often. However, she does not want the Language Bar to continually be open, taking up space on the taskbar. What can you tell the user to do? Select the best answer.

   a. In Regional And Language Options, remove and reinstall the languages each time she needs them.

   b. In the Text Services And Input Languages dialog box, select the Turn Off Advanced Text Services check box.

   c. Add the Language Bar to the taskbar only when it's needed by right-clicking the taskbar, pointing to Toolbars, and choosing Language Bar.

   d. None of the above. When multiple languages are configured, the Language Bar is always on the taskbar.

8. Which of the following allows you to open a file with an unknown file type? (Each choice offers a complete solution. Choose two.)

   a. Install the application used to create the file, and then open the file in that program.

   b. Register the file type in the Folder Options dialog box and associate it with a program already installed on the computer that has the capability to open the file.

   c. Use the Web to determine which programs can be used to open the file.

   d. Register the file type and let Windows choose a program to open the file with.

9. Which of the following troubleshooting tools included with Windows XP should be used to repair problems related to missing protected system files?

   a. Msconfig

   b. Msinfo32

   c. Chkdsk

   d. Disk Defragmenter

   e. SFC /Scannow

CASE SCENARIOS

Case Scenario 3-1: Finding the Missing Icon

Jessica calls the technical support line to report that she can no longer locate her messaging program. When you ask her to explain the problem in more detail, you discover that she believed the icon was taking up too much space "in the area of the taskbar where the clock is," so she removed it by right-clicking and selecting Exit. Now, she can't find it and is afraid she's deleted it from her system. What is the problem and how can it be resolved?

1. Jessica completely removed the program from her system when she removed it from the notification area. Reinstall the component from the operating system's CD-ROM.

2. Jessica has exited the program but not uninstalled it. Because it is an application configured to start when Windows boots, you inform her that the only way to start the program again is to reboot the computer.

3. Jessica must log on to the network domain so that the missing program files can be downloaded.

4. Jessica removed the program icon and closed the program only temporarily. The icon can be added back to the notification area by rebooting the computer or by starting the program from the All Programs menu.

Case Scenario 3-2: Making a User More Comfortable with an Upgrade

After an upgrade from Microsoft Windows 2000 Professional to Windows XP Professional, a user reports that "the Start menu is too confusing and everything looks weird" and he wants you to remove Windows XP and put Windows 2000 back on his computer. Knowing that you can't do that because the company is upgrading all of its machines, which of the following can you do to make this user more comfortable with the new operating system?

1. Change the Start menu type to the Classic Start menu.

2. Disable Hide Inactive Icons.

3. Use the Windows Classic theme.

4. Do not show the Favorites, My Music, or My Pictures folders on the Start menu.

5. In the Folder Options dialog box, select Use Windows Classic Folders.

6. Use Classic view in Control Panel.

CHAPTER 4

MICROSOFT OFFICE OUTLOOK 2003 AND OUTLOOK EXPRESS

Upon completion of this chapter, you will be able to:

■ Create, configure, and troubleshoot POP3, SMTP, and IMAP e-mail accounts

■ Import address books and messages from other accounts

■ Join a newsgroup and configure Outlook to be the default newsreader

■ Maintain Outlook by using the available utilities

■ Leave e-mail messages on a server when users access e-mail from multiple computers

■ Troubleshoot and resolve common end user requests

The purpose of this chapter is to teach you to support end users who run Microsoft Windows 2000 Professional, Windows XP Home Edition, or Windows XP Professional and who use Microsoft Outlook or Outlook Express as their e-mail client. In this chapter you'll learn to create, configure, and troubleshoot e-mail accounts and newsgroups, keep Outlook and Outlook Express running smoothly by maintaining the stored data, and resolve common end user requests such as these:

■ Importing address books and messages from other computers or exporting address books and messages to laptops and other portable devices

■ Setting up a newsgroup

■ Configuring a home account so e-mail can be retrieved from the network server

■ Leaving a copy of e-mails on the network server

■ Resolving problems related to user name, display name, or e-mail account settings

The MSCDT Exam 071-272 covers both Outlook and Outlook Express, but most of the focus in this chapter is on Outlook. Because Outlook Express is a limited version of Outlook, the procedures involved in using it are similar to the procedures for using Outlook, with only minor changes. Of course, the full version of Outlook is much more comprehensive, and offers many more features. Make sure you are familiar with both versions and that you can perform the tasks outlined in this chapter in either application.

POP3, SMTP, AND IMAP E-MAIL ACCOUNTS

Post Office Protocol 3 (POP3) and Simple Mail Transfer Protocol (SMTP) are two **protocols** for moving e-mail across the Internet. Basically, SMTP is used to send e-mail from one server to another or from a client computer to a mail server, and POP3 or Internet Message Access Protocol (IMAP) is used to retrieve e-mail from those servers. With a POP3 account, e-mail is received and held on a network or Internet service provider (ISP) server, and the end user then accesses and downloads those messages at his convenience. IMAP, an extension of POP3, is similar, except the e-mail remains on the server even if the end user deletes it on her local computer. As a desktop technician you'll need to be able to configure POP3, SMTP, and IMAP accounts using Outlook and Outlook Express. Creating accounts also includes testing, troubleshooting, and importing (or exporting) existing address books and messages.

> **NOTE**   *Outlook 2003*   In this section, you'll learn to create new e-mail accounts in Microsoft Office Outlook 2003; Outlook Express is briefly discussed at the end of this section.

Creating Accounts

Creating accounts using either Outlook 2003 or Outlook Express is achieved using a wizard. There are several types of e-mail accounts that can be set up using Outlook 2003, including an e-mail account for Microsoft Exchange Server, POP3 and SMTP, IMAP, **Hypertext Transfer Protocol (HTTP)**, and additional e-mail account types including those that access third-party mail servers. As a desktop technician in a Tier 1 or Tier 2 position, you'll be called on to set up only POP3, SMTP, IMAP, and HTTP accounts. Domain administrators will set up accounts to Exchange servers and third-party servers.

▶ **Adding a POP3 account**

In this example, you'll learn to add a POP3 account, but similar procedures can be followed for adding an IMAP or HTTP account. To add a POP3 (and SMTP) e-mail account for an Outlook 2003 client, follow these steps:

1. Open Outlook 2003.

2. From the Tools menu, select E-Mail Accounts to start the E-Mail Accounts Wizard.

3. On the E-Mail Accounts page, choose Add A New E-Mail Account, and click Next.

4. On the Server Type page, click POP3, and click Next.

5. On the Internet E-Mail Settings (POP3) page, shown in Figure 4-1, type the required information.

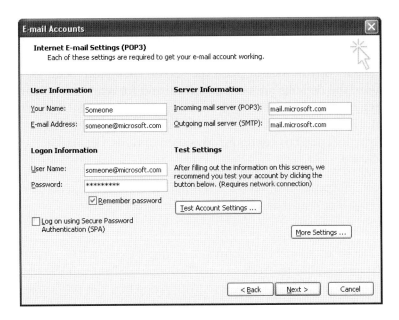

Figure 4-1   Configure Internet e-mail settings using the wizard.

- ❑ **Your Name**   The user's name as it should appear in the From: line of an e-mail message.

- ❑ **E-Mail Address**   The user's full e-mail address, including the suffix.

- ❑ **User Name**   The user name required to authenticate to the mail server. This can be a name or the e-mail address.

- ❑ **Password**   The password required to authenticate to the mail server.

- ❑ **Incoming Mail Server (POP3)**   The name of the incoming mail server.

- ❑ **Outgoing Mail Server (SMTP)**   The name of the outgoing mail server.

- ❑ **Log On Using Secure Password Authentication (SPA)**   Select this check box if the server requires it.

6. Click Test Account Settings. If an error occurs as shown in Figure 4-2, double-check the information input in step 5. If problems persist, contact your network administrator for the correct settings, and if an administrator is not available, refer to the section "Troubleshooting Outlook" at the end of this chapter.

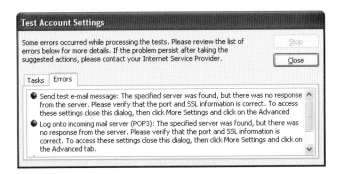

Figure 4-2   Test account settings before committing the changes.

7. If you know you need to configure advanced options such as additional user information, additional SMTP settings (such as a user name and password for the SMTP server), connection options, or to configure the account to leave a copy of messages on the server, click More Settings. For a home user, the defaults are generally fine, and for many corporate users, the same is true. Click Next, and then click Finish to close the wizard. (If advanced options are necessary or the e-mail account doesn't work properly, you'll need to configure advanced options, detailed in the following section.)

With the e-mail account configured, send a test e-mail from the new account to the new account to verify that e-mail can be both sent and received.

More Settings

If you need to configure additional (or advanced) settings, either while you are creating an e-mail account or after it's been created, you can do so from the Internet E-Mail Settings dialog box shown in Figure 4-3. This dialog box can be accessed by clicking More Settings while creating the account on the Internet E-Mail Settings wizard page (shown earlier in Figure 4-1), or by editing an existing account.

Figure 4-3   The Internet e-mail settings dialog box offers additional configuration options.

There are several additional settings, detailed in Table 4-1.

Table 4-1   **Internet E-Mail Settings**

Tab	Setting and Description
General	■ **Mail Account** The name of the account as the user would like to refer to it. This can be any name. Creating the account name can be an important decision if the user has multiple e-mail addresses and might wish to follow one account name with (at work) and another with (at home). ■ **Organization** The name of the user's organization. This is not required. ■ **Reply E-Mail** The e-mail address that should be used to accept replies to messages sent to this address. If no address is configured, all replies will be sent to the configured e-mail address. A reply e-mail address can be used when a secondary e-mail is configured for a Web site or public computer, so that all e-mail received at that location is handled by a primary address that is more convenient.
Outgoing Server	■ **My Outgoing Server (SMTP) Requires Authentication** Select this check box to specify that the SMTP server requires a user name and password. When this is selected, other options become available: Use The Same Settings As My Incoming Mail Server, Log On Using (User Name, Password), Log On Using Secure Password Authentication (SPA). ■ **Log On To Incoming Mail Server Before Sending E-Mail** Select this option if applicable.
Connection	■ **Connect Using My Local Area Network (LAN)** Select this option to connect to the mail server using the LAN. ■ **Connect Via Modem When Outlook Is Offline** Select this option when a user connects over a LAN, but needs to connect with a modem if working offline. ■ **Connect Using My Phone Line** Select this option when a user always connects to the mail server using his own phone line. ■ **Connect Using Internet Explorer's Or A 3rd Party Dialer** Select this option when a third-party connection is used. ■ **Modem** Select a dial-up connection from the drop-down list. ■ **Properties** Click the Properties button to access advanced modem properties. ■ **Add** Click the Add button to add another networking connection.

Table 4-1   Internet E-Mail Settings

Tab	Setting and Description
Advanced	■ **Incoming Server (POP3)** Type the port number of the POP3 server. Generally, it is 110.
	■ **This Server Requires An Encrypted Connection (SSL)** Select this check box if the server requires an encrypted connection.
	■ **Outgoing Server (SMTP)** Type the port number of the SMTP server. Generally, it is 25.
	■ **This Server Requires An Encrypted Connection (SSL)** Select this check box if the server requires an encrypted connection. Encrypted connections are more secure than those that are not encrypted, and might be required by corporate policies.
	■ **Server Timeouts** Specifies how long to wait for a response from the mail server before giving up. Slower connections require more time to respond; faster connections require less. (If a user has a slow connection and receives timeout errors, increase this number.)
	■ **Leave A Copy Of Messages On The Server** Select this check box if messages are to be left on the server even after users have deleted them from their inboxes. Be careful when configuring this, though; if a user's quota is met at the server, incoming e-mail will be rejected until additional space becomes available.
	■ **Remove From Server After ___ Days** If the e-mail account is configured to leave messages on the server, this tells Outlook how long to leave them there before deleting them.
	■ **Remove From Server When Deleted From Deleted Items** If the e-mail account is configured to leave messages on the server, this deletes those e-mails when they are deleted from the user's Deleted Items folder.

If you need to set any of these additional options and did not do so during the creation of the account, you can do so by modifying an existing account. To configure the additional settings for an existing account, follow these steps:

1. Open Outlook 2003 and, from the Tools menu, select E-Mail Accounts.

2. On the E-Mail Accounts page, click View Or Change Existing E-Mail Accounts, and click Next.

3. On the E-Mail Accounts page, select the account to change, and click Change.

4. On the Internet E-Mail Settings (POP3) page, click More Settings.

5. In the Internet E-Mail Settings dialog box, click any tab and input or configure the required information. Click OK when finished to close the Internet E-Mail Settings dialog box.

6. On the Internet E-Mail Settings (POP3) page, click Next.

7. Click Finish on the E-Mail Accounts page.

With the e-mail account configured, send a test e-mail from the new account to the new account to verify that e-mail can be both sent and received. If there are problems, refer to the section "Troubleshooting Outlook" at the end of this chapter.

Working with Address Books and Messages

When Outlook 2003 is installed on a user's computer, Outlook offers to import mail, addresses, and mail account settings from an existing e-mail application already installed on the computer. For many users, this is generally Outlook Express, but it can also be Eudora Light or Eudora Pro. In addition, data from previously saved files, such as Microsoft Excel or Microsoft Access files, can be imported.

Users might also need to export address books and messages for the purpose of backing them up or moving them to another location. Importing and exporting tasks are performed using the Import and Export Wizard, available on the Outlook File menu.

Importing Address Books and Messages

Address books and mail messages can be imported in a number of ways, and in this section we cover two of them. You'll learn to import mail messages and address books from Outlook Express and Eudora (Pro and Light), and you'll learn to import mail and messages from an Excel file. Although there are other options, including importing the data from a previously exported text or comma-separated values (CSV) file, an Access file, a personal folder file, or an application like Lotus Organizer or ACT!, the procedures are basically the same as the two you'll see here.

▶ Importing mail and addresses

To import Internet mail and addresses from Outlook Express, Eudora Light, or Eudora Pro, follow these steps:

1. Open Outlook. From the File menu, select Import And Export.

2. On the first page of the Import and Export Wizard, click Import Internet Mail And Addresses, and click Next.

3. On the Outlook Import Tool page, select the Internet Mail application to import from. Figure 4-4 shows this page with Outlook Express selected.

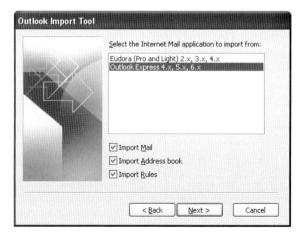

Figure 4-4   The Outlook Import Tool can be used to import many items.

4. Select the items to import. Choose any combination of Import Mail, Import Address Book, or Import Rules. Click Next.

5. If you are only importing e-mail messages or rules, click Finish. If you are also importing an address book, click Next.

6. If importing addresses, on the Import Addresses page, choose one of the following options and then click Finish:

   ❏ **Replace Duplicates With Items Imported** Existing data will be over-written with the data imported. This is an appropriate option if the imported data is newer than the stored data.

   ❏ **Allow Duplicates To Be Created** Existing data will not be overwritten, and duplicates will be added. This is an appropriate option if the user wants to keep all existing data and import additional data.

   ❏ **Do Not Import Duplicate Items** Existing data will be kept, and duplicate information will not be copied. This is an appropriate option if the imported data is older than the stored data.

7. To save a report of the Import Summary, click Save In Inbox on the Import Summary page.

▶ **Importing data**

To import data from another program or file, follow these steps:

1. Open Outlook. From the File menu, select Import And Export.

2. In the Import and Export Wizard, select Import From Another Program Or File, and click Next.

3. On the Import A File page, select Microsoft Excel. (To import from another program, select another option.) Click Next.

4. Click Browse to locate the file. Select the appropriate option for dealing with duplicate entries. Click Next.

5. On the Import A File page, choose the appropriate folder from the Select Destination Folder list. Figure 4-5 shows an example. Click Next.

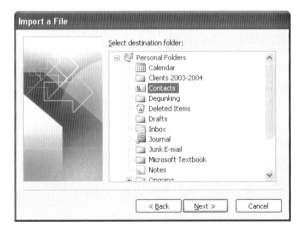

Figure 4-5   Import an address book to the Contacts folder with the Import and Export Wizard.

6. To map custom fields or to change the folder selected, click Map Custom Fields or Change Destination. When mapping custom fields, drag and drop the field on the left (configured fields) to the field on the right (address book fields). When finished, click Next. Click Finish.

Exporting Address Books and Messages

For the purpose of backing up an address book or a message, or to store the information on a hard drive for the purpose of exporting to another computer later, use the Import and Export Wizard as detailed in the previous sections. When prompted, select Export To A File (instead of selecting any importing choice). You'll be prompted to save the file as one of the following:

- **Comma Separated Values (DOS)**   Choose this if you need to export the data so it can later be imported to a third-party e-mail client.

- **Comma Separated Values (Windows)**   Choose this if you need to export a file for use in Microsoft Word, PowerPoint, or third-party applications.

- **Microsoft Access**   Choose this to save the data in a Microsoft Access file.

- **Microsoft Excel**   Choose this to save the data in a Microsoft Excel file.

- **Personal Folder File (.pst)**   Choose this if you need to organize and back up your Outlook data. These data files can only be read by Outlook. Only the content is preserved; permissions, rules, forms, views, and descriptions are not preserved.

- **Tab Separated Values (DOS)**   Choose this if you need to export the data so it can later be imported to a third-party e-mail client.

- **Tab Separated Values (Windows)**   Choose this if you need to export a file for use in Word, PowerPoint, or third-party applications.

After making the appropriate choice, click Next and continue through the wizard as detailed in earlier sections.

Using Outlook Express

The goal of this section is to introduce you to Outlook Express and to detail the most common tasks you'll be asked to perform. Although using Outlook Express is similar to using Outlook, the processes aren't exactly the same for both. As a desktop technician, you need to be able to support both Outlook (commonly used in corporations, companies, and small businesses) and Outlook Express (commonly used by home users and small home-based businesses). In this section you'll learn the most basic Outlook Express tasks; you'll learn to create a POP3 or IMAP account for a home user, test and troubleshoot that account, and import an existing address book and messages.

> **NOTE**   **Exporting Is an Excellent Backup Tool**   Teach your end users to export their address book to a floppy disk. The floppy disk makes an excellent backup.

▶ Creating a POP3 or IMAP account

To create a POP3 account using Outlook Express for a small business owner or home user, follow these steps:

1. Open Outlook Express.

2. From the Tools menu, select Accounts.

3. Select the Mail tab. Click Add, and then click Mail.

4. Using the Internet Connection Wizard, on the Your Name page, type in the name of the user as she wants it to appear to others. Because this is a display name only, any name is fine. Click Next.

5. On the Internet E-Mail Address page, type the e-mail address. Click Next.

6. On the E-Mail Server Names page, in the My Incoming Mail Server Is A ___ Server drop-down list, choose POP3 or IMAP. In the Incoming Mail (POP3, IMAP, Or HTTP) Server box, type the name of the incoming mail server. In the Outgoing Mail (SMTP) Server box, type the name of the outgoing mail server. Figure 4-6 shows an example. Click Next.

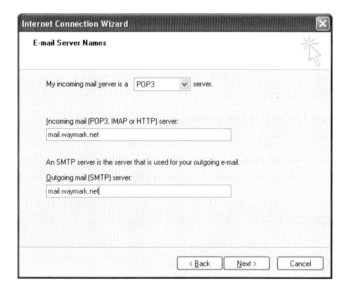

Figure 4-6   Configure e-mail server names using the Internet Connection Wizard.

7. On the Internet Mail Logon page, type in the account name and password. If the home user requests it, select the Remember Password check box. Click Next.

8. Click Finish when prompted, and click Close in the Internet Accounts dialog box.

Importing and Exporting

With the account working properly, you can now import a user's address book and existing messages. There are multiple ways to import an address book, as you learned earlier. However, when configuring a new account for a home user, the easiest way to import an address book is to have previously exported it as a CSV text file. Working with an address book using this technique works in almost any situation, including moving address books between computers (such as from a home PC to a laptop or from an old computer to a new one), and moving an exist-ing address book from an old e-mail account configuration to a new one on the same or on different computers. It also provides an excellent way to back up the address book, and teaching the end user to do this is a good idea.

In this example, you'll learn how to first export an existing address book as a CSV text file and then to import it to the new account.

▶ **Exporting an address book**

To export the address book, follow these steps:

1. Open Outlook Express on the old computer, laptop, or existing com-puter, click File, point to Export, and click Address Book.

2. In the Address Book Export Tool, select Text File (Comma Separated Val-ues) and click Export.

3. In the CSV Export dialog box, click Browse and choose a location in which to save the file.

4. In the Save As dialog box, type a name for the file and then click Save. Click Next.

5. In the second CSV Export dialog box, select the fields to export. Make sure to select First Name, Last Name, and E-Mail Address. Click Finish.

6. Click OK when prompted that the export process is complete and then click Close to close the Address Book Export Tool.

▶ **Importing an address book**

To import the address book, follow these steps:

1. From the File menu, point to Import, and select Other Address Book.

2. In the Address Book Import Tool dialog box, shown in Figure 4-7, select Text File (Comma Separated Values). Click Import.

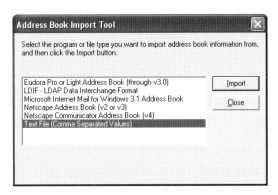

Figure 4-7   Import an address book using the Address Book Import Tool.

3. In the CSV Import dialog box, click Browse. Locate the exported address book and click Open. Click Next in the CSV Import dialog box.

4. In the second CSV Import dialog box, select the fields to import and click Finish. Make sure to select First Name, Last Name, and E-Mail Address.

5. Click OK when prompted that the import process is complete and then click Close to close the Address Book Import Tool.

▶ **Importing existing messages**

Finally, importing existing messages is achieved as follows:

1. Open Outlook Express and, from the File menu, point to Import, and select Messages.

2. In the Select Program dialog box, select the program from which to import messages. Click Next.

3. In the Import dialog box, if prompted, select the appropriate identity and click Next. You'll be prompted for an identity only if multiple identities exist. (For more information on identities, see "Creating Multiple Identities in Outlook Express" later in this chapter.)

4. In the Location Of Messages dialog box, accept the defaults (unless the mail folder has been moved) and click Next. If the mail folder has been moved, you'll need to use the Browse button to locate it before clicking Next.

5. In the Select Folders dialog box, select All Folders or Selected Folders. Many of the folders you'll see here are automatically created in both Outlook and Outlook Express (as well as in other e-mail clients) to hold the data saved or created by the user. Folders automatically created include Drafts, Inbox, Outbox, Deleted Items, Sent Items, and more. Folders can also be created manually. If Selected Folders is chosen, select the folders to import. To select more than one folder, hold down the CTRL key. Click Next.

6. Click Finish after the messages are imported successfully.

> **NOTE   Importing and Exporting**   As with Outlook, there are various ways to import and export data. Make sure you are familiar with the additional techniques.

JOINING A NEWSGROUP

Newsgroups are collections of messages stored on news servers that are posted by members of the groups. These news servers are maintained by third-party entities such as Microsoft for the purpose of assisting others in finding information and answers to questions quickly. Messages posted to the newsgroups can generally be read by anyone, and anyone can post to them. In this section, you'll learn how to add the News entry to the Go menu, how to start the Outlook newsreader, how to use Outlook News as the default news client, how to join a newsgroup, and how to troubleshoot newsgroup accounts.

▶ **Setting up Outlook News as the default news client**

The first time you or an end user sets up Outlook to join a newsgroup, you must add the News command to the Go menu by following these steps:

1. Open Outlook, right-click an empty area of the Standard toolbar, and select Customize.

2. On the Commands tab, in the Categories list, select Go.

3. In the Commands list, select News, and drag it to the Go menu. When the menu list appears, point to where you want News to appear in the list

and release the mouse button. Figure 4-8 shows the new Go menu choices. Click Close in the Customize dialog box.

Figure 4-8   The new Go menu contains a choice for accessing newsgroups.

4. To set up a newsgroup, click Go, and then click News.

> **NOTE   If News Isn't Available**   If the News option is not available in the Customize dialog box, from Control Panel, Internet Options, and the Programs tab, choose Outlook Express to be the default newsreader.

▶ Adding a Newsgroup

If an end user has Outlook Express installed, Outlook Express is most likely already configured as the default newsreader. To configure Outlook News to be the new default newsreader, follow these steps:

1. Open Outlook, click Go, and choose News.

2. Wait while the Outlook Newsreader opens, and click Yes to verify that Outlook should now be the default program used. If the user has currently joined newsgroups using Outlook Express, those newsgroups will be available once this is done.

▶ Joining a newsgroup

If the user has not joined any newsgroups previously, you'll be asked to help the user set up a newsgroup account. The procedure to join a newsgroup is the same in either Outlook or Outlook Express:

1. From the Tools menu, select Accounts, and in the Internet Accounts dialog box, select the News tab.

2. Click Add, and click News.

3. On the Internet Connection Wizard page, type the display name and click Next.

4. On the Internet News E-Mail Address page, type the e-mail address to be associated with this account, and click Next. To avoid spam, consider masking the e-mail account name to protect the user from unsolicited junk e-mail. For instance, type johndoe@nospam.myisp.com instead of the real address, johndoe@myisp.com. Additionally, consider creating a disposable e-mail address for this purpose, such as a Hotmail address, and use the address solely for newsgroups.

5. On the Internet News Server Name page, type the name of the News (NNTP) Server. This name must be obtained from the newsgroup host. The Microsoft news server name is msnews.Microsoft.com. If the news server requires the user to log on, select the My News Server Requires Me To Log On check box. If this check box is selected, click Next and type in the user name and password.

6. Click Finish to close the wizard, and click Close in the Internet Accounts dialog box.

7. When prompted by Outlook to download newsgroups from the accounts just added, click Yes.

8. In the Newsgroup Subscriptions dialog box, locate the newsgroups to add and click Subscribe. Click OK to close the dialog box.

9. In the left pane, select an added newsgroup to connect.

Common Newsgroup Service Calls

Common service calls associated with newsgroups include blocking messages from a particular sender, blocking unwanted messages, and resolving problems with sending or receiving **posts**. Users might also need to cancel a subscription to a newsgroup or view newsgroups without subscribing at all.

Blocking (and Unblocking) Senders and Unwanted Messages

Users might decide that some posts or newsgroup participants are not desirable or useful, and might ask you to block those senders or messages. Blocked messages go directly to the Deleted Items folder and are not displayed.

▶ Blocking messages

To block messages from a sender or a domain, follow these steps:

1. Open the newsreader and, from the list of messages in a newsgroup, select a message from the sender to block.

2. From the Message menu, select Block Sender. Click Yes to remove all messages from that sender.

▶ Unblocking senders

To unblock a sender or a domain, follow these steps:

1. Open the newsreader and, from the Tools menu, select Message Rules, Blocked Senders List.

2. On the Blocked Senders tab, select the e-mail address or domain name to unblock. Click Remove.

3. Click OK to close the Message Rules dialog box.

Resolving Send and Receive Errors

Send and receive errors can be caused in a number of ways, including misspelled news server names, server **timeouts**, problems with passwords, and problems with ISP settings. Listed here are some common problems and solutions:

- **Timeout errors**   Newsgroup servers will time out and give an error message if it takes longer than allotted to download newsgroup messages. To solve this problem, from the Tools menu, select Accounts, select the news server to change, and click Properties. On the Advanced tab, in the Server Timeouts area, move the slider to the right to increase the amount of time allotted. Click OK and click Close.

- **Can connect to ISP, but cannot access newsgroups**   Failure to access a newsgroup when Internet connectivity is working is generally caused by incorrect advanced options settings. From the Tools menu, select Accounts, select the news server, and click Properties. On the Server, Connection, and Advanced tabs, check the settings and verify they are correct. Keep an eye out for typographical errors. Make the appropriate changes, click OK, and click Close.

- **Cannot connect to news server**   The inability to connect to a news server is often related to the settings configured for the news server, including the user name, password, or news server name. From the Tools menu, select Accounts, select the news server name, and click Properties. Check the following:

  - ❑ On the Server tab, verify the New Account name and user information.

  - ❑ On the Advanced tab, verify the server name is spelled correctly. If the server requires the end user to log on, verify the account name and password.

  - ❑ On the Advanced tab, verify the News (NNTP) port number (this is generally 119), clear the This Server Requires A Secure Connection (SSL) check box if a secure connection isn't necessary, and select or clear the Ignore News Sending Format And Post Using check box as desired.

Other common problems with newsgroups can be resolved using newsgroups, the Knowledge Base, and similar resources.

Viewing Newsgroups Without Subscribing

There are several ways a user can view newsgroup content without subscribing, including visiting the newsgroup's Web site, but the easiest way is through the Help options in Outlook. In the following example, you use the Help options available in Outlook to access the Outlook New Users newsgroup:

1. Open Microsoft Outlook and in the top right corner where it shows Type A Question For Help, type **newsgroups** and press ENTER. (You must be online.)

2. Scroll down the Search Results pane and choose Get Answers From Other Users, as shown in Figure 4-9.

Figure 4-9   Visit a newsgroup without joining to access information quickly.

3. The Discussions In Outlook New Users newsgroup Web page opens. There you can browse messages, search for topics, read posts, post replies, and locate other newsgroups.

NOTE   Newsgroups   *Newsgroups can be an effective way to help end users become more autonomous and find solutions to their own problems. If you have time during a service call, point users to this feature.*

Unsubscribing to a Newsgroup

To unsubscribe to a newsgroup, open the newsreader, open the Inbox, and locate the newsgroup to unsubscribe from. Right-click the newsgroup and choose Unsubscribe.

MAINTAINING OUTLOOK

Maintaining Outlook is similar to maintaining Outlook Express; a user can empty the Deleted Items folder when he exits the program, use AutoArchive to manage the mailbox size by deleting old items or moving them to an archive file, and use Mailbox Cleanup to manage the size of the mailbox or delete files that are a certain age or size. Users might also want to configure junk e-mail settings. You'll be called on to perform these tasks, but to reduce service calls to clients, make sure you teach your end users to use these tools regularly.

NOTE   Outlook Express   *The rest of this chapter focuses mainly on Outlook, but tasks done in Outlook Express are performed similarly, as demonstrated in earlier sections.*

Emptying Deleted Items Folder on Exit

One way to keep Outlook maintained is to empty the items in the Deleted Items folder each time Outlook is closed. Emptying the Deleted Items folder when exiting keeps that folder clean and this step might be necessary to keep a user's mailbox within specific file size limits, especially if the user's mailbox is stored on a network server. Deleting files on exit is an option in the Options dialog box, set as follows:

1. In Outlook, from the Tools menu, select Options.

2. In the Options dialog box, select the Other tab.

3. Select the Empty The Deleted Items Folder Upon Exiting check box.

4. Click OK to close the Options dialog box.

> **NOTE Deleted Items**   Don't select this check box unless you absolutely have to. Users will find they access this folder often to review deleted messages.

AutoArchive

AutoArchive can be used to keep a mailbox manageable by archiving old items that users need but access infrequently and by deleting content that meets specific criteria for age. AutoArchive is on by default and runs in the background, clearing items that meet set expiration conditions. These expiration options apply to both e-mail and meeting items with content that is no longer valid after a certain date.

AutoArchive can be configured in a number of ways and can be set to perform (or not perform) the following tasks:

- Run automatically after a specific number of days.

- Prompt the user before it runs.

- Archive or delete old items after a specific number of months, weeks, or days.

- Delete expired items in e-mail folders.

- Show archive folders in the folder list.

- Move items to a specific place.

- Permanently delete old items.

- Set a **retention policy** if it is applied by a network administrator.

Because users often forget to manage and maintain their e-mails, AutoArchive should be configured to run using its defaults unless the user or corporate policy prevents it.

▶ **Setting up AutoArchive**

AutoArchive can be accessed from the Options dialog box as follows:

1. From the Tools menu, select Options, and select the Other tab.

2. Click AutoArchive.

3. Make changes by selecting or clearing check boxes and using the arrows to set numerical configurations.

4. Click OK twice to save your changes.

Mailbox Cleanup

When possible, inform users of Mailbox Cleanup. This application allows users to easily manage the size of their mailboxes to improve the overall performance of Outlook. From the Mailbox Cleanup dialog box, users can do the following:

- View the total size of the mailbox and the individual folders in it, including the Deleted Items folder.

- Sort, delete, and archive items by date or size.

- Find and delete unread e-mail (junk e-mail or spam), e-mail from a particular sender, e-mail that has an attachment, items in the Deleted Items folder, items sent to a particular person, and more.

- View and delete items in the **Conflicts folder**.

▶ **Using Mailbox Cleanup**

To open and use the Mailbox Cleanup utility (shown in Figure 4-10), follow these steps:

1. From the Tools menu, select Mailbox Cleanup.

   ❑ To view the mailbox size, click View Mailbox Size. Click Close to return to the Mailbox Cleanup dialog box.

   ❑ To use AutoArchive, configure the settings for date and size using the arrows next to the Find Items Older Than and Find Items Larger Than areas, and click AutoArchive.

   ❑ To view the size of the Deleted Items folder, click View Deleted Items Size. Click Close to return to the Mailbox Cleanup dialog box.

   ❑ To empty the Deleted Items folder, click Empty. Click Yes to verify your choice.

2. To perform an advanced search for messages in the Mailbox Cleanup dialog box, set the criteria using the arrows next to the Find Items Older Than and Find Items Larger Than areas, and then click Find. The Advanced Find dialog box opens with three tabs: Messages, More Choices, and Advanced. You use these tabs to configure advanced search options, and you use the Edit menu to select and delete the items if desired. See the following section for more information on these options.

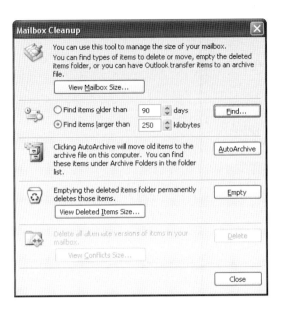

Figure 4-10   Mailbox Cleanup can be used to delete specific messages.

Advanced Find Options

Each tab in the Advanced Find dialog box offers multiple options for sorting the files that matched the original criteria in step 3 in the previous example. For instance, to locate all unread e-mail and delete it (this is almost always junk e-mail), select the More Choices tab, select the Only Items That Are check box, and choose Unread from the drop-down list. Every item stored that has not been read that matches the criteria for age and size set earlier will appear. To delete these files, from the Edit menu, select Select All, and press DEL on the keyboard.

E-mail can also be sorted by who sent it, who it was sent to, whether or not it contains an attachment or is flagged, and if it meets specific size requirements. E-mail can also be sorted based on what words appear in the subject line or body. This is an excellent tool for getting rid of unwanted e-mail stored on the computer, e-mail regarding a specific project that has been completed, or e-mail from a group or specific person.

Junk E-Mail Options

Outlook has a Junk E-Mail option in the Actions menu. The Junk E-Mail Options dialog box is shown in Figure 4-11. Junk e-mail options can be set to move messages that appear to be unwanted to a special junk e-mail folder. As you can see in Figure 4-11, the Junk E-Mail Options dialog box has the following four tabs:

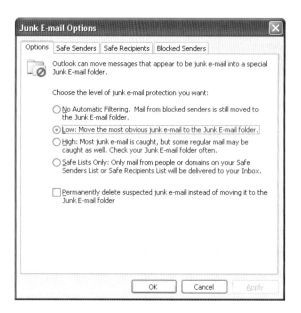

Figure 4-11   Junk E-Mail options can be configured to catch and reroute unwanted e-mail.

- **Options**   Use the options on this tab to configure the level of junk e-mail protection. The level can be configured for no protection, for low or high protection, or so that the recipient receives e-mail only from specified contacts. These settings can also be configured so that suspected junk e-mail is automatically deleted and bypasses the Junk E-Mail folder.

- **Safe Senders**   Use the options on this tab to configure a safe senders list. E-mail from addresses or domain names on this list will never be treated as junk e-mail. Also available is the Always Trust E-Mail From My Contacts check box.

- **Safe Recipients**   Use the options on this tab to configure a safe recipients list. E-mail sent to addresses or domain names on this list will never be treated as junk e-mail.

- **Blocked Senders**   Use the options on this tab to configure a blocked senders list. E-mail from addresses or domain names on this list will always be treated as junk e-mail.

As a desktop technician you'll be asked to address issues involving junk e-mail. For clients who use Outlook, your first suggestion should be to configure junk e-mail options. (For Outlook Express users, configure rules and block senders.) Make sure to inform users to check their Junk E-Mail folder occasionally, though, because sometimes valid e-mail gets sent there.

▶ **Using Junk E-Mail options**

To use and configure Outlook's default Junk E-Mail options, follow these steps:

1. From the Actions menu, point to Junk E-Mail, and select Junk E-Mail Options.

2. On the General tab, shown in Figure 4-11, choose the desired level of junk e-mail protection.

CAUTION **Junk E-Mail Settings** *If junk e-mail levels are set to High, most junk e-mail will be caught, but some valid mail might be caught as well. Be careful when choosing this setting, and make sure that safe senders are configured for important contacts.*

3. On the Safe Senders, Safe Recipients, and Blocked Senders tabs, click Add to add a particular sender or domain. Click OK.

Users can also easily add senders to the safe senders or blocked lists as e-mail arrives. With the e-mail selected in Outlook, click Actions, point to Junk E-Mail, and click any of the following:

- Add Sender To Blocked Senders List

- Add Sender To Safe Senders List

- Add Sender's Domain (@example.com) To Safe Senders List

- Add Recipient To Safe Recipients List

- Mark As Not Junk (only available when the user is accessing e-mail from the Junk E-Mail folder)

These settings allow users to add blocked senders, safe senders, and save recipients easily. Teach end users how to do this when possible.

TROUBLESHOOTING OUTLOOK

Most problems that occur with Outlook have to do with incorrect user names, passwords, and e-mail addresses, and these issues result in problems sending and receiving e-mail. Other problems occur when end users make their own changes to the application, which can cause problems with the interface or the ability to connect to the ISP or e-mail server. In this section, you learn how to resolve common problems such as these.

Resolving an Incorrect Name or E-Mail Address

If any typographical errors were made during the creation of the user's e-mail account, if the user changed departments and needs her e-mail name or address altered, if the user wants replies to go to a different e-mail address than the one configured, or if the user has independently made changes to her e-mail settings, she might encounter problems in sending or receiving e-mail, or she might report that the name or organization is not correct on e-mails sent to others. Users who change positions, get promoted, earn degrees or certifications, or get married might want a new title (or name) in their e-mail as well.

▶ **Changing names and e-mail addresses**

If a user reports errors or needs changes along these lines, make the changes from the E-Mail Accounts Wizard as follows:

1. Open Outlook, and from the Tools menu, select E-Mail Accounts.

2. In the E-Mail Accounts Wizard under E-Mail, click View Or Change Existing E-Mail Accounts. Click Next.

3. On the E-Mail Accounts page, select the e-mail account to configure. Click Change.

4. Verify the values for User Information, Server Information, and Logon Information, and make changes as needed. Click Test Settings to verify the information is correct.

5. Click More Settings, and in the Internet E-Mail Settings dialog box, view the tabs and make changes as needed. Click OK when finished. Click Next and Finish to close the E-Mail Accounts Wizard.

Almost all problems relating to typographical errors or changing a user's name or e-mail address can be solved using this utility.

Common Interface Problems

The Outlook interface can be changed to reflect the needs and preferences of any user. For the most part, changes made to the interface are achieved using the View menu options, using the Go menu options, and by customizing the toolbars using the Customize dialog box. Although interface changes are generally easy to configure, when new users make changes on their own they sometimes encounter problems later in locating items they need. Table 4-2 details some items a user might report as missing and the procedure for getting those particular components back. Figure 4-12 shows Outlook 2003 and the available panes and toolbars.

Table 4-2   **Missing Interface Components**

Report	Procedure for Resolution
Navigation pane is missing	From the View menu, select Navigation Pane.
Reading Pane is missing or in the wrong area of the interface	From the View menu, select Reading Pane, and then select Right or Bottom.
E-mails are arranged in the wrong order	From the View menu, select Arrange By, and then select Date, Conversation, From, To, Folder, Size, Subject, Type, Flag, Attachments, E-Mail Account, Importance, Categories, or Custom.
Can't preview e-mail messages in Inbox	From the View menu, select AutoPreview.
Missing Task pane, Standard toolbar, Advanced toolbar, Web toolbar	Right click the Menu bar, and select the missing item.
Missing Status Bar	From the View menu, select Status Bar.
Can't view items in the Navigation pane or the Navigation pane has changed	From the Go menu, select the item to show in the Navigation pane.
Needed commands are missing from the toolbars and menus	Right-click an empty area of the Menu bar, click Customize and, on the Commands tab, choose the items to add. Drag the item to the correct area of the toolbar or menu. Select the Options tab to reset menus and toolbars and perform other customizations.

Table 4-2   **Missing Interface Components**

Report	Procedure for Resolution
Items in the Navigation pane aren't needed	From the Tools menu, select Options, and then select the Other tab. Click Navigation Pane Options, and in the Navigation Pane Options dialog box, clear unwanted items.

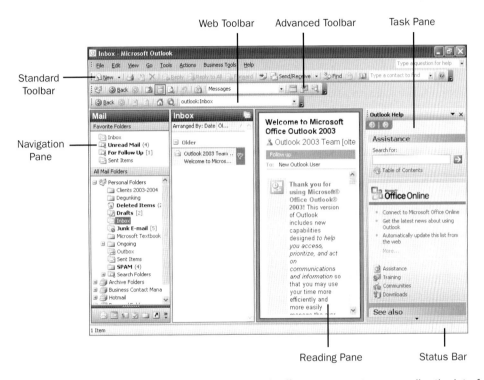

Figure 4-12   Default panes and toolbars in Outlook offer many ways to personalize the interface.

There are many other settings available for end users, all of which can be configured through the available menus and dialog boxes. Familiarize yourself with all aspects of both Outlook and Outlook Express.

TROUBLESHOOTING OUTLOOK EXPRESS

Although most of the emphasis in this chapter has been on Outlook, some attention needs be given to troubleshooting and maintaining Outlook Express. This section covers three areas:

- Resolving problems involving sending and receiving e-mail after a new account has been created

- Resolving and preventing problems by configuring maintenance and security options

- Creating and using the Outlook Express Log file

Resolving Problems with New Accounts

Each time you create a new account, you need to verify the account works as it should before leaving the client or ending the call. Testing the account verifies the account was created properly and is in working order. In addition to testing the account on creation, though, when troubleshooting a call, sending a test e-mail can also give insight into what might be causing the user's current problem.

▶ **Testing a new account**

To test and troubleshoot a new account, follow these steps:

1. Open Outlook Express and click Create Mail.

2. In the To box, type the address of the e-mail account you just created or the e-mail address of the user that is problematic. This is the user's account. In the Subject box, type **Test**, and then click Send.

3. After the e-mail has been sent, click Send/Recv. Verify the e-mail was sent and received. If an error occurs or if the display name is incorrect, troubleshoot the account using the steps listed next.

▶ **Troubleshooting an account**

If an error was received while testing the account, specifically a failure notice was issued by the ISP that the e-mail could not be sent, an error occurred when trying to receive the e-mail, or the display name is incorrect, follow these steps:

1. From the Tools menu, select Accounts.

2. On the Mail tab, select the account that was just configured or is not working.

3. Click Properties.

4. On the General tab, verify the user information, including name and e-mail address. Make the appropriate corrections.

5. On the Servers tab, verify the server information, including incoming server name, incoming and outgoing mail servers, account name, password, and authentication settings. If in doubt, contact the ISP to double-check the settings. Make the appropriate corrections. Click OK, and then click Close. Send another test e-mail.

6. If the e-mail still fails, verify the user is connected to the Internet, verify with the ISP that the e-mail address used is the correct one, and verify the names of the mail servers.

Maintenance Tasks

You can also avoid and resolve problems by configuring the maintenance and security options in Outlook Express. These options are available from the Tools menu, by selecting Options. Figure 4-13 shows the options on the Maintenance tab.

Figure 4-13   Users can configure maintenance options to avoid problems.

Using the Maintenance tab, users or technicians can resolve problems that have to do with the configuration of the available items including the following:

- Emptying messages from the Deleted Items folder on exiting the program to avoid saving unnecessary e-mail

- Purging deleted messages when leaving IMAP folders to avoid meeting server quota limits

- Compacting messages in the background to save space on the local hard disk

- Deleting newsgroup messages after a specific period of time to keep folders organized and under quota limits

- Using the Clean Up Now utility to compact, remove, or delete messages, or reset newsgroup headers and message bodies

- Using the Store Folder option to change where e-mail messages are stored by default

In addition to these options on the Maintenance tab, there are also a few important options on the Security tab:

- Selecting the Internet zone to protect the computer from viruses and other unwanted Internet content

- Warning the user when other applications try to send e-mail on the user's behalf

- Allowing or disallowing attachments

- Encrypting all outgoing e-mail messages

- Providing a **digital signature** for all outgoing messages

Creating and Using a Log File

If a user has problems with his e-mail or newsgroup account that cannot be resolved by techniques listed thus far, you can configure Outlook Express to save commands to and from the mail server in a log file for troubleshooting purposes.

The log file must be enabled on the Maintenance tab of the Options dialog box before it can be used:

1. Open Outlook Express and, from the Tools menu, select Options.

2. On the Maintenance tab, in the Troubleshooting section, select the items to log. You can log Mail, News, IMAP, or HTTP folders.

3. Click OK.

> **NOTE   Deleting the Log File**   Log files can be quite large. When you are finished troubleshooting, make sure you clear the log file option in the Options dialog box and delete the log file as detailed next.

To locate, read, and then delete the log file:

1. From the Start menu, select Search.

2. In the Search Results window, in the Search box, type *.**log**. Verify the search will contain the root drive. Click Search.

3. Sort the files by date, if there are multiple files, by clicking Date Modified on the heading bar. Look for pop3.log, smtp.log, or a similar name that represents the server type toward the top of that list.

4. Leave the Search Results window open, and open the appropriate log file.

5. Use the information in the log to determine what operation failed or passed, what time errors occurred, and the user name encountering the problems. The ISP or network administrator can help you determine the cause of the problem.

6. Close the log file.

7. Open Outlook Express and, from the Tools menu, select Options.

8. On the Maintenance tab, clear all log files and click OK. Close Outlook Express.

9. In the Search Results window, still open, right-click the log file and select Delete. Click Yes to verify. Close the Search Results window.

COMMON END USER REQUESTS

End users will eventually need help configuring other Outlook features in addition to setting up e-mail accounts, adding newsgroups, or troubleshooting connectivity. Common end user requests include the following:

- Configuring Outlook so that the user can work from home, from a hotel, or while on vacation, at the same time leaving e-mails on the network server so they are there when the user gets back to the office

- Configuring advanced composition settings such as message formats, editing, spelling, and other issues relating to e-mail composition

■ Creating signatures for outgoing messages

■ Importing and exporting Internet accounts files (.iaf) for users who use Outlook Express

Leaving a Copy of E-Mail on the Server

When users travel, they have an account on their laptop so that they can access e-mail while on the road. Creating this account is similar to creating any e-mail account, except the users need to be able to dial into (or otherwise connect to) the e-mail server at their workplace. Sometimes a user dials directly into a company server; at other times a user accesses the server through their ISP. (You'll learn to create accounts such as these in Chapter 8, "Common Connectivity Problems.")

Once the account is set up, you'll need to configure Outlook or Outlook Express to leave e-mail on the network server until the user returns to work to retrieve it and delete it permanently. If this is not set up properly, the user will have some e-mail messages on the laptop, some on the home computer, and some on the office computer. Keeping track of e-mail using this type of system is inefficient.

▶ **Configuring Outlook e-mail to stay on the server**

To configure a user's laptop so that Outlook will leave messages on the network server or ISP server until the user deletes them manually from her office computer, follow these steps:

1. From the Tools menu, select Options, and select the Mail Setup tab.

2. Click E-Mail Accounts and, on the E-Mail Accounts page, click View Or Change Existing E-Mail Accounts, and click Next.

3. On the E-Mail Accounts page, select the e-mail account to configure, and click Change.

4. On the Internet E-Mail Settings page, click More Settings.

5. In the Internet E-Mail Settings dialog box, select the Advanced tab, shown in Figure 4-14.

6. Select the Leave A Copy Of Messages On The Server check box and, if applicable, select the Remove From Server After ___ Days or the Remove From Server When Deleted From Deleted Items check boxes.

7. Click OK, click Next, and click Finish.

8. Click OK to close the Options dialog box.

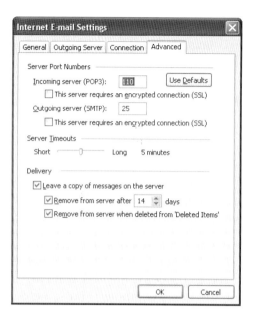

Figure 4-14   Leave a copy of messages on the server.

▶ **Configuring Outlook Express e-mail to stay on the server**

To configure a user's laptop so that Outlook Express will leave messages on the network server or ISP server until the user deletes them manually from his office computer, follow these steps:

1. Open Outlook Express and, from the Tools menu, select Accounts.

2. On the Mail tab, select the account to configure, and then click Properties.

3. In the Properties dialog box for the account, select the Advanced tab.

4. Under Delivery, select Leave A Copy Of Messages On Server.

5. To remove the messages after a specified number of days, select the Remove From Server After ___ Day(s) and/or Remove From Server When Deleted From Deleted Items check boxes.

6. Click OK in the Properties dialog box, and click Close in the Internet Accounts dialog box.

Depending on the choices made here, messages will remain on the server for a specified number of days or until they are manually deleted. This gives the user a method for keeping the e-mail account synchronized when multiple computers are used.

Configuring Composition Options

Because most users will use Outlook to send and receive e-mail on a daily basis, composition options will certainly be important to them. There are several options available, including formatting, spelling and grammatical editing, and creating signatures. End users might ask you to assist them in configuring these options.

All of the composition options a user needs are located in the Options dialog box (from the Tools menu, select Options). On the Mail Format tab, a user can configure the following settings:

- Compose messages in Hypertext Markup Language (HTML), rich text, or plaintext.

- Choose an editor (for example, Microsoft Office Word 2003).

- Choose stationery and fonts for new messages, when replying and forwarding, and when sending e-mail using plaintext.

- Create signatures.

On the Spelling tab, the user can configure the following settings:

- Suggest replacements for misspelled words.

- Check spelling before sending an e-mail.

- Ignore words in uppercase, words with numbers, or original text in a reply or forward.

- Configure AutoCorrect options and edit the custom dictionary.

- Choose an international dictionary.

Making these configuration changes is achieved by configuring the available drop-down lists, selecting or clearing options, or accessing other dialog boxes by clicking buttons.

> **NOTE   Outlook Express**   You can make similar changes for Outlook Express users using the Tools menu and selecting Options. In the Options dialog box, you can access tabs for Spelling, Read, Send, Compose, and Signatures and you can configure preferences.

Creating Multiple Identities in Outlook Express

You can configure multiple identities for Outlook Express users who share a computer or who share Outlook Express. Each user can have his or her own identity with personalized settings, contacts, e-mail addresses, preferences, and more. When logging on to Outlook Express, either a default identity can be used or a list of identities can be offered. In this section you'll learn to do the following:

- Add an identity
- Switch users
- Delete an identity

▶ **Adding a new identity**

To add a new identity in Outlook Express, follow these steps:

1. Open Outlook Express.
2. From the File menu, select Identities, and then select Add New Identity.

3. In the New Identity dialog box, type the name of the new user and select Require A Password if desired. Click OK.

4. When prompted to switch to the new identity, click Yes or No. Click Close in the Manage Identities dialog box.

▶ **Switching users**

To switch identities, follow these steps:

1. From the File menu, select Switch Identity.

2. In the Switch Identities dialog box, select the user to switch to and click OK.

3. When and if prompted, click Yes or No to keep the current connection to the Internet.

▶ **Deleting an identity**

Deleting identities is necessary when an identity is no longer needed. Deleting identities is also achieved from the Manage Identities dialog box as follows:

1. Open Outlook Express.

2. From the File menu, select Identities, and then select Manage Identities.

3. In the Manage Identities dialog box, select the user to delete. Click Remove, and then click Delete to verify.

4. Click Close in the Manage Identities dialog box.

The .iaf File

Outlook Express can be used to create an .iaf, or Internet Accounts file, to back up and store information about the mail folders and mail and news account settings for a single Outlook Express identity. Backing up this information makes it easy to restore if necessary, because of a computer crash or in the event a new computer is obtained or purchased. These .iaf files won't store subscribed newsgroup information, message rules, or blocked senders, and won't retain information about custom toolbars either, but they offer a quick and easy way to back up and restore settings.

▶ **Exporting settings to an .iaf file**

To export the settings to an .iaf file using Outlook Express, follow these steps:

1. In Outlook Express, from the Tools menu, select Accounts.

2. In the Internet Accounts dialog box, select an account and click Export.

3. In the Export Internet Account dialog box, browse to a location to save the file or accept the defaults. Name the file and click Save.

4. In the Internet Accounts dialog box, click Close.

As necessary, use the same procedure (clicking Import instead of Export) to restore the file to the e-mail account.

SUMMARY

- To create, test, and troubleshoot e-mail accounts in Outlook and Outlook Express, use the Internet Accounts dialog box. From there you can add accounts, view properties, and make changes to existing accounts.

- To join a newsgroup and set Outlook as the default newsgroup reader, drag the News command to the Go menu, and use the News option to add or remove newsgroup accounts.

- To maintain Outlook and Outlook Express, configure maintenance settings such as emptying the Deleted Items folder on exiting and compacting messages, AutoArchive, and Mailbox Cleanup.

- To resolve common end user requests, learn techniques such as leaving a copy of the e-mail on a network server, exporting .iaf files, and setting composition options for spelling, grammar, and signatures.

REVIEW QUESTIONS

1. A user has a POP3 e-mail account from an ISP and he reports he cannot send e-mail. He can receive e-mail. Which of the following is most likely the problem?

   a. The Mail Account name in the Internet E-Mail Settings dialog box (accessed by clicking More Settings in the E-Mail Accounts dialog box) has a typographical error.

   b. The SMTP server name is incorrectly configured in the user's e-mail settings.

   c. The ISP's POP3 mail server is down.

   d. The user has not typed in the correct password.

2. A client who has been using Outlook Express has recently installed the Microsoft Office System. He reports that when he opened Outlook for the first time, he tried to create an e-mail account, but as the procedure progressed, he got confused and clicked Cancel in the remaining dialog boxes instead of working through them. He now reports that he can send and receive e-mail, but he can't access his address book and he can't locate his old mail messages. What should you tell the user to do?

   a. Uninstall and reinstall Outlook 2003. After the application has been reinstalled, tell him to call back and you'll walk him through the procedure.

   b. Delete the existing account using the E-Mail Accounts Wizard. Re-create the account using the same wizard, and follow the prompts for importing the address book and mail messages.

   c. From the Tools menu, select Address Book. In the Address Book window, click File, and click Import And Export. Import the address book used for Outlook Express.

   d. Open Outlook and, from the File menu, select Import And Export. Work through the Import and Export Wizard to import both mail messages and the address book.

3. A user reports she received an error message from the company's e-mail server. The message stated that she has met her quota for space on the server and needs to delete some of the e-mail she has stored there. She informs you she has deleted some unnecessary folders from Outlook, reduced the items in her Sent Items folder, and emptied the Deleted Items folder. She wants help configuring the computer so she does not receive these messages in the future. Which of the following applications or utilities is the best choice for configuring her computer?

   a. AutoArchive

   b. Mailbox Cleanup

   c. Junk E-Mail

   d. Macros

4. There are several ways to export address books and e-mail messages. Match the user's requirements on the left to the best export option on the right.

   1. The address book will be stored in a Word document.   a) Personal folder files

   2. The address book will be stored as a database file.   b) Microsoft Excel

   3. Messages will be stored as a backup of Outlook data and will not be used by any other program.   c) CSV (Windows)

   4. The address book will be stored as an .xls file.   d) Microsoft Access

5. Configuring a newsgroup in Outlook 2003 involves several steps, each of which is listed next. Place the steps in the correct order.

   a. Open the newsreader from the Go menu.

   b. Type the name of the news (NNTP) server.

   c. Subscribe to the downloaded newsgroups.

   d. Use the Customize dialog box to drag the News command to the Go menu on the Menu bar.

   e. Create a news account from the Tools menu by selecting Accounts and, on the News tab, clicking Add.

6. A user reports he set up AutoArchive in Outlook 2003 to permanently delete items that are two weeks old, no matter what folder they are in. However, the items are not being deleted after 14 days but instead are being deleted every 21 days. What is the likely cause of this?

   a. A retention policy has been set by network administrators.

   b. The deleted items have been moved to the junk e-mail folder.

   c. The settings configured in Mailbox Cleanup conflict with the settings configured in AutoArchive. Mailbox Cleanup has priority when conflicts arise.

d. AutoArchive has been disabled because there is less than 200 MB of free space on the computer hard disk.

7. A user reports she configured specific fonts to use when composing a new message, when replying and forwarding messages, and when using stationery. However, each time she composes a message or replies or forwards one, the same font is always used. It's the 12-point Courier New font that she configured for composing and reading plain text. When she closes the Fonts dialog box, she selects the Always Use My Fonts check box, but she still can only compose e-mail using 12-point Courier New. What is the cause of the problem?

   a. The fonts chosen for new mail, for replying, and for forwarding are not installed on the computer or are corrupt. Reinstall the fonts.

   b. The display settings on the computer are set to 800 by 600 pixels. Reconfigure the display settings to 1024 by 768.

   c. The mail format settings are configured to compose messages in plaintext. Configure this to use HTML or rich text.

   d. The advanced settings for Internet Format (on the Mail Format tab of the Options dialog box) are set to encode attachments in UUEN-CODE format when sending a plaintext message.

CASE SCENARIOS

Scenario 4-1: Transferring an Address Book

A home user has purchased a new computer and plans to get rid of the old one. She has backed up her My Documents, My Pictures, and My Videos folders to three CD-R disks. The only other thing the user wants to transfer to the new computer is her address book. She does not want to transfer her messages, e-mail account settings, or news account settings. What is the fastest way to move this data to the new computer? She uses Outlook Express.

   1. From the old computer, use Outlook Express to export the address book to a floppy disk, and then use that disk to import the address book at the new computer. Use the CDs already burned to transfer the folder data.

   2. Connect the two computers using a null-modem cable and use the Files and Settings Transfer Wizard to transfer the data.

   3. Connect the two computers using a hub and Ethernet cables, and then drag and drop the folders between computers. At the new computer, import the address book using the Import command.

   4. At the new computer, use Outlook Express to import the address book from the old computer. Use a null-modem cable to connect. Use the CDs already burned to transfer the folder data.

Scenario 4-2: Getting the Most Out of the Junk E-Mail Options

A small business user in a graphics company reports that he recently set his junk e-mail option to High because he's been getting an incredible amount of spam lately. After asking a few questions, you discover he joined three newsgroups last month and created his own company Web site where he posted his e-mail address. He reports that although most junk e-mail is caught, he's getting complaints from his clients that he isn't responding to their e-mails in a timely fashion. He wants to block the junk e-mail but he also wants to receive the large attachments and pictures Outlook thinks are junk e-mail. What should you advise this user to do? Although some of the answers are viable, choose the single best answer.

1. Unsubscribe from the newsgroups. As long as he's subscribed to them he'll continue to get junk e-mail. Remove his e-mail address from his Web site, and replace it with his phone number.

2. Add each client to the safe senders list in the Junk E-Mail Options dialog box.

3. Open the junk e-mail folder and, for each item, click Actions, point to Junk E-Mail, and select Add Sender To Blocked Senders List.

4. Open the junk e-mail folder and, for each item that is a valid e-mail, click Actions, point to Junk E-Mail, and select Add Sender To Safe Senders List.

CHAPTER 5
CONFIGURE INTERNET EXPLORER

Upon completion of this chapter, you will be able to:

- Configure Accessibility and Language settings

- Resolve common end-user requests

- Use Profile Assistant, Content Advisor, and digital certificates to personalize and secure Internet Explorer

- Maintain Internet Explorer by deleting temporary files, using Disk Cleanup, and performing similar maintenance tasks

- Resolve problems associated with viewing Web pages by configuring Internet Options and setting screen resolution, screen colors, and fonts

- Troubleshoot Security Zones

- Configure disk caching to enhance performance

The purpose of this chapter is to introduce Microsoft Internet Explorer and to explore common end-user requests. As a desktop technician, you'll be asked to resolve a wide range of service calls regarding Internet Explorer, including personalizing the interface, changing how Web pages look on the monitor, and showing users how to access History files or search for related Web sites. You'll also be called on to perform troubleshooting tasks. These calls generally have to do with the inability to view Web pages or problems with the speed at which Web pages are loaded, but the requests can also be about performing maintenance tasks like deleting temporary files or asking for advice on dealing with cookies.

PERSONALIZING INTERNET EXPLORER

As a desktop technician, many of the requests you receive will have more to do with making something "look right" than actually performing an advanced troubleshooting task. In addition to making the interface pleasing to the eye, though, you'll also be asked to make it more functional. In this section, you learn how to resolve many requests including the following:

- Format colors, font styles, and font sizes on Web pages so they can be read more easily.

- Add language preferences so that Web sites, if content is available, can be viewed in another language.

- Import Internet Favorites from another computer or account.

- View data including Web browsing history, related sites, search results, and folders.

- Set a home page.

- Personalize Internet Explorer's Title bar.

Configuring Accessibility

Users who have trouble viewing Web pages because of the colors, font size, or font type might ask you to configure Internet Explorer so that Web pages are easier to read and view. These changes can be made using Internet Explorer menus and the Internet Options dialog box as detailed in the next two sections. However, these changes are not always applied when a user visits a Web site. To use these settings at all Web sites visited, you'll need to apply the changes using the accessibility options, and tell Internet Explorer to use these settings to override existing Web page defaults.

In the following three sections, you'll learn to change the text size and default colors and fonts, and how to configure the new settings to override any existing and specific Web settings.

▶ Changing text size

If an end user asks you to change the default text size on a Web page, follow these steps:

1. Open Internet Explorer, choose View, and then choose Text Size.

2. Select from the following choices: Largest, Larger, Medium, Smaller, and Smallest.

▶ Changing colors and fonts

If an end user asks you to change the default colors and fonts used when she visits Web pages, follow these steps:

1. Open Internet Explorer and, on the Tools menu, choose Internet Options.

2. In the Internet Options dialog box, select the General tab, and click Colors.

3. In the Colors dialog box, shown in Figure 5-1:

   a. Under Colors, clear the Use Windows Colors check box, and select the color box next to Text. Select a new color for the text, and click OK.

   b. Under Colors, select the color box next to Background. Select a new color for the background, and click OK.

   c. Under Links, select the color box next to Visited. Select a new color, and click OK.

   d. Under Links, select the color box next to Unvisited. Select a new color, and click OK.

   e. Under Links, select the Use Hover Color check box. Select the color box next to Hover. Select a color, and click OK.

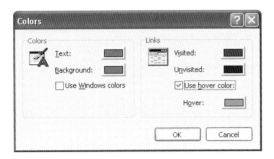

Figure 5-1 The Colors dialog box lets users customize the colors they see when visiting Web pages.

4. Click OK to close the Colors dialog box.

5. In the Internet Options dialog box, click Fonts.

6. In the Fonts dialog box, select a language script (if a change is needed), select a Web page font, and select a plaintext font. Internet Explorer uses Web page fonts to display formatted text on a Web page; it uses plaintext fonts to display unformatted text. Click OK.

7. Click OK to close the Internet Options dialog box.

Overriding Settings Specified by Web Sites

The settings configured in Internet Explorer for text size, colors, and fonts might or might not be applied, depending on the Web site visited. Web pages that have no colors specified will use the colors the user configured, and the same is true of fonts. However, if a Web page does have a specific color or font, these choices will be overridden.

▶ Overriding color and font preferences

To ensure that the end user's preferences for colors and fonts are always applied, follow these steps:

1. Open Internet Explorer and, on the Tools menu, choose Internet Options.

2. In the Internet Options dialog box, select the General tab, and click Accessibility.

3. In the Accessibility dialog box, under Formatting, select the appropriate check boxes:

   ❑ Ignore Colors Specified On Web Pages

   ❑ Ignore Font Styles Specified On Web Pages

   ❑ Ignore Font Sizes Specified On Web Pages

4. Click OK in the Accessibility dialog box and click OK again in the Internet Options dialog box.

Toolbar Button Icon Size

While on the phone or at an end-user's desk resolving an accessibility option call, ask the user if he would like to customize the size of the Toolbar button icons while you're there. If a user has asked you to make the Web text larger, he might also appreciate making larger Toolbar icons, too. If the user has asked you to make Web page text smaller, he might also appreciate smaller Toolbar icons.

▶ **Customizing toolbar buttons**

If the user wants to customize the Toolbar button icons, walk him through the following procedure:

1. Open Internet Explorer and right-click any Toolbar button or icon. On the shortcut menu, select Customize.

2. In the Customize Toolbar dialog box, in the Icon Options drop-down list, choose Large Icons or Small Icons based on the user's preference.

3. In the Text Options drop-down list, choose Show Text Labels, Selective Text On Right, or No Text Labels to finish the customization. Because the changes are applied immediately, the user can decide what he wants before committing by closing the dialog box. Once an appropriate choice has been made, click Close.

Using the Profile Assistant

The Profile Assistant is another option available to Internet Explorer users. The Profile Assistant allows a user to enter personal information that can then be automatically sent to a Web site when that information is requested. The information entered in the Profile Assistant is saved in a secure location on the client's computer and the user is prompted to send information if the Web site supports this technology. Users can accept or deny this service each time they encounter it. This saves time for users because they do not have to enter the same information each time they visit a new Web site, and it allows users to determine when and for which sites the Profile Assistant is used.

▶ **Configuring Profile Assistant**

To configure the Profile Assistant, open Internet Explorer and follow these steps:

1. On the Tools menu, choose Internet Options.

2. On the Content tab, under Personal Information, click MyProfile. In the Address Book – Choose Profile dialog box, verify that Create A New Entry In The Address Book To Represent Your Profile is selected and click OK.

3. In the Properties dialog box for the user, configure as much information as desired by accessing the following tabs: Name, Home, Business, Personal, Other, **NetMeeting**, and Digital IDs. (Digital IDs is detailed later in this chapter.)

4. Click OK to close the Properties dialog box when complete; click OK in the Internet Options dialog box to close.

NOTE   When the Profile Assistant Isn't Available   If the Profile Assistant is not available in Internet Explorer, read Microsoft Knowledge Base article 178342.

Configuring Languages

Internet Explorer can display Web pages in many different languages, and if users' Web surfing takes them to sites that are written in another language, Internet Explorer can update the computer with the character sets needed to view those sites. If you have bilingual or multilingual end users and clients, you might be asked to configure Internet Explorer to work with these languages.

▶ **Changing language settings**

To specify another language for Web page content, follow these steps:

1. Open Internet Explorer and, on the Tools menu, choose Internet Options.

2. On the General tab, click Languages.

3. In the Language Preference dialog box, click Add.

4. In the Add Language dialog box, select the language to add as shown in Figure 5-2, and click OK.

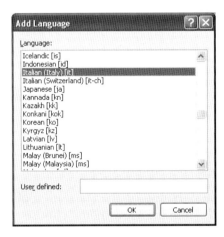

Figure 5-2   Users can add almost any language to Internet Explorer.

5. Arrange the languages in order of priority by selecting them and using the Move Up or Move Down buttons. If a Web site offers multiple languages, content will appear in the language that has the highest priority. Click OK in the Language Preference dialog box.

6. Click OK to close the Internet Options dialog box.

> **NOTE   Web Page Encoding**   Most Web pages contain information that tells Internet Explorer what language and character set to use. However, not all pages contain that information. When this is the case, Internet Explorer can usually determine what character set to use if Auto-Select is turned on. In Internet Explorer, from the View menu, point to Encoding, and make sure Auto-Select is selected. If it isn't, select it. Notice that you can also select a specific encoding from the list.

Resolving Common Interface Requests

End users often have requests that deal with locating information while using Internet Explorer and customizing Internet Explorer's interface. Users might need to locate a Web site they visited last week; they might be searching for information that is related to information they've previously found; they might need to be able to view search options, their Favorites, the Media bar, History, or their hard disk folders while they browse the Internet; or they might ask you to configure a home page, or troubleshoot why they can't set one themselves. You'll learn how to resolve all of these requests in this section.

Viewing History

Users sometimes call to ask how they can access a site they've previously visited. Users might add that they've forgotten the site name and **Uniform Resource Locator (URL)**, but require the information they found earlier on the site. You will be required to help them locate the site again.

The History files can help you locate previously viewed Web sites that have been visited over the last three weeks, and the sites can be viewed in various ways:

- By date
- By site
- By most visited
- By order visited today

▶ **Locating a previously seen site**

To assist a user in locating a previously viewed site, follow these steps:

1. Open History by either clicking the History button on the Standard toolbar or accessing it from the View menu. From the View menu, choose Explorer Bar, and then choose History.

2. On the Explorer bar, select View to see the History categories. Sort the files by choosing By Date, By Site, By Most Visited, or By Order Visited Today. Figure 5-3 shows the categories in the Explorer bar viewed by date.

Figure 5-3   The Explorer bar with History sorted by date offers customized searching.

3. Select any category to expand it, and choose any site in the list to return to the site.

   NOTE   Viewing by Site   *Viewing the History sites by name organizes the site alphabetically. This can be useful if the user remembers a company name. Often, a company's name is the same as its Web site name.*

Viewing Related Sites

The Related button is an available Standard toolbar button that can be an extremely helpful tool for users who need to access related information quickly. Clicking the Related icon opens the Explorer bar and offers a list of other Internet sites that contain similar information to what the user is currently viewing. Figure 5-4 shows an example. In this figure, the user is viewing the Windows XP Expert Zone, and the related information in the Explorer bar shows Web sites that offer similar information.

Figure 5-4   Locate related information using the Related button.

By default, Internet Explorer does not include the Related button on the toolbar, so the first step is to put it there. This procedure also works for adding or removing other icons:

▶ **Using the Related button**

1. Open Internet Explorer and right-click any Standard toolbar button. Choose Customize.

2. In the Customize Toolbar dialog box, in the left pane under Available Toolbar Buttons, locate Related.

3. Select Related, click Add, and the Related button appears in the left pane under Current Toolbar Buttons.

4. Use the Move Up or Move Down buttons to place the new button anywhere on the toolbar. Click Close when finished.

Now, any time users need to locate information that is similar to what they are viewing, they only need to click the Related button. The Explorer bar will open automatically.

Viewing and Customizing the Explorer Bar

The Explorer bar was introduced briefly in the previous section, but there are other Explorer bar options. To access these options, on the View menu, choose Explorer Bar, and select from the following:

- **Search** The Search Explorer bar can help an end user find a Web page, a person's address, a business, or a map; or look up a word, find a picture, or look through previous searches. You can also use the Search Explorer bar to search Web sites by keywords, as with any other **search engine**. MSN Search performs these searches.

- **Favorites** The Favorites Explorer bar shows all of the end user's Favorites in the Explorer bar. This allows the user easy access to all of her favorite Web sites.

- **Media** The Media Explorer bar opens WindowsMedia.com, where music videos, movie previews, radio stations, and news can be accessed quickly.

- **History** The History Explorer bar leaves the History folders open and available at all times. Using the History bar, a user can access previously viewed Web sites easily.

- **Folders** The Folders Explorer bar shows the folders on the user's hard disk. This makes accessing those folders as easy as clicking them. When a user opens a folder, the folder's contents appear in the right pane of Internet Explorer. Using the Back button returns the user to the previously viewed folder or Web page.

    NOTE **Closing the Explorer Bar** Users can close the Explorer bar by clicking the X in the top right corner of it or by clearing it on the View, Explorer Bar menu.

Finally, although not technically an Explorer bar, selecting Tip Of The Day from the Explorer Bar menu opens a third pane at the bottom of the Web page; Internet Explorer displays tips in this pane. This might be a good choice for a new user, and you could suggest it when troubleshooting his Internet Explorer configuration either on the phone or at his desk.

Setting a Corporate Home Page

Another common request of end users is to configure a home page that will open each time Internet Explorer is used. This home page can be the company's Web site home page, a search engine, or a small business owner's own Web site, among others.

▶ Configuring a home page

To configure a home page, follow these steps:

1. Use Internet Explorer to browse to the Web site to set as the home page.

2. On the Tools menu, choose Internet Options.

3. In the Internet Options dialog box, select the General Tab.

4. In the Home Page area, click Use Current.

> **NOTE** **Group Policy Restrictions** If a user complains that he cannot change his home page, chances are that it is against company policy. The home page is probably set and rules are in place for changing it in the company's **Group Policy**.

Personalizing the Title Bar

If a home user or a computer administrator wants to customize the Title bar of Internet Explorer with a browser title or custom logo, or if she wants to make customizations to the Standard toolbar, such as changing the toolbar background or adding buttons, you'll need to know how to create and modify Group Policy settings. Administrators of a single computer or administrators in a workgroup can configure Group Policy. Group Policy settings configured on a single Microsoft Windows XP Professional computer affect everyone who logs on to that computer. (In a domain, network administrators configure Group Policy, and these changes affect everyone who logs on to the domain.)

▶ **Creating a customized toolbar**

To use Group Policy to change how the Internet Explorer interface looks by creating a customized title bar, or to further customize it for a small business owner or home user, follow these steps:

1. On the Start menu, choose Run.

2. In the Run dialog box, type **gpedit.msc**. Gpedit.msc opens the Group Policy console. Click OK.

3. In the Group Policy console, expand User Configuration (if necessary), expand Windows Settings, and expand Internet Explorer Maintenance. The left pane of the Group Policy console is shown in Figure 5-5.

Figure 5-5 The Group Policy console's left pane offers various customizable options.

4. Select Browser User Interface in the left pane and, in the right pane, double-click Browser Title.

5. In the Browser Title dialog box, select the Customize Title Bars check box, and then type in the user's name, company name, or other customization. The new Internet Explorer Title bar will read "Microsoft Internet Explorer Provided By" followed by what you type. Click OK.

6. In the right pane of the Group Policy console, double-click Custom Logo.

7. In the Custom Logo dialog box, select the Customize The Static Logo Bitmaps or Customize The Animated Bitmaps check box (you can configure either or both). Click Browse to locate the image. In the Browse dialog box, locate the image and click Open. Click OK in the Custom Logo box to apply it.

8. Open Internet Explorer and view the changes. If satisfied, close the Group Policy console.

There are many other changes you can make to Internet Explorer using the Group Policy console. You might have noticed that under Browser User Interface there is also an option for Browser Toolbar Customizations, which enables the user to customize and even add toolbar buttons. In addition, you can make the following customizations under Internet Explorer Maintenance to customize URLs (refer to Figure 5-5):

■ Select URLs in the left pane and, in the right pane, choose Important URLs. Here, you can customize the home page URL, the Search bar URL, and the online support page URL. The online support page is created by the company and then made available to users.

■ Click URLs in the left pane and, in the right pane, choose Favorites And Links. Here, you can customize the Favorites folder and the Links bar by adding links to sites related to the company or service the company offers. For instance, you can add Favorites folders for Help And Support or Corporate Online Help Pages.

NOTE **Group Policy and Automatic Updates**   For information on how to configure Automatic Updates by using Group Policy, refer to Knowledge Base article 328010. This article also contains a white paper on software update services.

Configuring Content Advisor

Another customizable option a user might ask about is Content Advisor. Content Advisor allows a user to control the Internet content that can be viewed on a single computer. The Content Advisor dialog box, shown in Figure 5-6, allows an administrator to configure what Web sites and content can and cannot be viewed based on the Internet Content Rating Association (ICRA) guidelines and the user's preferences. ICRA's goal is to protect children from potentially harmful content, while still preserving free speech on the Internet. Rating categories include Language, Nudity, Sex, and Violence. The Content Advisor also allows the user to specify customized and approved or disallowed sites.

Figure 5-6   The Content Advisor can be used to limit what Web content can or cannot be viewed.

▶ **Configuring and using Content Advisor**

You access and configure the Content Advisor using Internet Explorer's Internet Options dialog box, following these steps:

1. Open Internet Explorer, choose Internet Options and, in the Internet Options dialog box, select the Content tab.

2. In the Content Advisor section, click Enable. (If Content Advisor is already enabled, Disable and Settings will be available instead. If that's the case, skip to step 4.)

3. In the Content Advisor dialog box, click OK to enable it. In the Create Supervisor Password dialog box, enter the supervisor password you want to use in the Password and Confirm Password text boxes. In the Hint text box, type a hint that you can use to help you remember this password if you forget it. Click OK when you're done. In the message box stating that Content Advisor has been enabled, click OK.

4. With Content Advisor enabled, click Settings. Enter the supervisor's password and click OK.

5. On the Ratings tab, select a category. Move the slider to the left for more restrictive settings; move the slider to the right for less restrictive settings. As you move the tab, read the description of the ratings level in the Descriptions area. Repeat this step for all four categories: Language, Nudity, Sex, and Violence.

6. To add a site to the Approved Sites list or to disallow access to any Web site, select the Approved Sites tab and enter the name of the Web site in the Allow This Web Site text box. Choose Always to make the page always viewable, or choose Never to make sure it cannot be viewed. Click OK.

7. On the General tab under User Options, if desired, select the Users Can See Sites That Have No Rating or Supervisor Can Type A Password To

Allow Users To View Restricted Content check box. If desired, click Create Password and configure an administrator password. Click OK to close this dialog box.

8. To configure advanced settings such as using a specific ratings bureau or importing or installing rules, select the Advanced tab and make the appropriate changes. Click OK to close Content Advisor.

9. Click OK to close the Internet Options dialog box.

Understanding Digital Certificates

Finally, you can customize Internet Explorer to use digital certificates. Digital certificates identify people and organizations on the Internet, much like a driver's license or passport identifies a person to the appropriate authorities. For instance, when accessing a Web site that is secure (starts with https://), the Web site must send the computer a certificate verifying they are who they say they are and that it is safe for the user to send information such as a credit card number or bank account number. After the Web site's identity has been verified by a third party, the customer and the company can then set up a secure channel for exchanging information. When there is a problem with a certificate, Internet Explorer displays a warning dialog box. Certificates help keep the Internet safe for both buyers and sellers. Certificates can be obtained from third-party certificate authorities such as VeriSign (*http://www.verisign.com*) and Thawte (*http://www.thawte.com*).

You view the digital certificates on a user's computer from the Internet Options dialog box, available from the Tools menu in Internet Explorer. Certificate information can be found on the Content tab, under Certificates. For more information on digital certificates, read the informative article entitled "Obtaining and Installing a Digital Certificate," by Gary King, available from *http://www.win2000mag.com/Articles/Index.cfm?ArticleID=4773*.

> **MORE INFO**   **For More Information about Certificates**   To learn more about digital certificates, specifically the Clear SSL State Option in Windows XP, read Microsoft Knowledge Base article 290345.

MAINTAINING INTERNET EXPLORER

Maintaining Internet Explorer is an important task, but many end users either do not take the time to maintain it or do not know what should be done or how often. As a desktop technician, you'll be called on to help end users resolve problems that stem from this lack of maintenance.

In this section you learn some basic maintenance tasks including using Disk Cleanup, managing and maintaining the temporary files saved to the computer, manually deleting temporary files, and deleting temporary files on exiting Internet Explorer. Cookies are also discussed, and the process for deleting those is detailed.

Temporary Files

Temporary Internet files are files that are automatically saved to the hard disk for the purpose of speeding up the display of frequently visited Web pages. Internet Explorer saves the files in the Temporary Internet Files folder, which can contain **cookies**, graphics, Web pages, and **JavaScript** files, among other things. Because Internet Explorer can open files saved to the computer faster than it can obtain and open files from the Internet, maintaining the files in this folder is quite important to successful, fast Web browsing.

Problems occur when the Temporary Internet pages **cache** is full, and resolving these problems is as simple as deleting the files in the Temporary Internet Files folder. Unfortunately, recognizing problems caused by a full Temporary Internet Files folder can be difficult. Here are some common warning signs of a full Temporary Internet Files folder:

- An end user reports he cannot use the Save Picture As command to save a graphics file to his hard disk as a JPEG or GIF, but the file can be saved as a BMP file. The file name might also appear as Untitled.

- An end user reports problems viewing History files by date, or no data appears.

- An end user reports that when she selects Source from the View menu to view the source for a Web page, the source code does not appear as expected.

- An end user reports that when he visits the Windows Update Product Catalog Web site, he receives the message Cannot Display Page. (This happens because the user has an earlier version of the site control in his browser cache and the cache is full.)

- An end user reports she gets unrecoverable errors (faults) when using Internet Explorer.

Although these problems can occur for other reasons, often, deleting the files in the Temporary Internet Files folder solves the problem. In the next few sections, you learn several ways to manage and delete temporary Internet files.

Using Disk Cleanup

Disk Cleanup is a maintenance tool that you can use to resolve problems, but it is also one you can teach your end users to use to maintain their computers on their own. Disk Cleanup enables you or the end user to delete files in the **Downloaded Program Files** folder, Temporary Internet Files folder, the **Temporary Files** folder, the Recycle Bin, and more. Deleting these files regularly will help keep the computer running smoothly.

▶ Deleting files with Disk Cleanup

To use Disk Cleanup, follow these steps:

1. From the Start menu, point to All Programs, point to Accessories, point to System Tools, and select Disk Cleanup.

2. In the Select Drive dialog box, select the drive to clean up from the Drives drop-down list, and click OK.

3. In the Disk Cleanup dialog box, shown in Figure 5-7, select the folders and the items to clean up. You can read a description of what is in each folder by clicking it once.

Figure 5-7   Disk Cleanup can be used to delete unnecessary files.

4. To view any of the files, click View Files.

5. Click OK to start the cleaning process. Click Yes to verify you want to perform these actions.

   NOTE   Disk Cleanup   Urge your end users to use Disk Cleanup at least once a month.

Manually Deleting Files

There is another way to delete temporary Internet files besides using Disk Cleanup; you can manually delete the files yourself from the Temporary Internet Files folder. This folder is located in the *<root drive>*\Documents And Settings*<user name>*\ Local Settings\Temporary Internet Files folder. You'll have to have Show Hidden Files And Folders selected on the View tab of the Folder Options dialog box if you want to browse to this folder. If you don't want to enable the option to view hidden files on an end user's computer, though, there is another way to access the folder.

▶ Deleting files manually

To access the Temporary Internet Files folder and manually delete the files in it, follow these steps:

1. Open Internet Explorer and, on the Tools menu, choose Internet Options.

2. In the Internet Options dialog box, on the General tab in the Temporary Internet Files area, click Settings.

3. In the Settings dialog box, shown in Figure 5-8, click View Files.

4. To delete the files, on the Edit menu, choose Select All and, in the Folder Tasks pane, click Delete The Selected Items. You can also press the DEL key on the keyboard.

5. Click Yes to verify you want to delete these files. Close the Temporary Internet Files window.

6. Click OK to close the Settings dialog box, and click OK again to close the Internet Options dialog box.

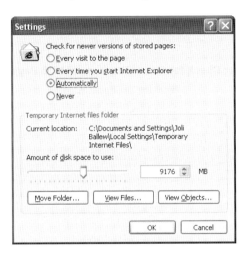

Figure 5-8 The Settings dialog box allows a user to work with temporary Internet files manually.

NOTE **ActiveX and Java Controls** *You can also view ActiveX and Java controls that have been downloaded and installed on the computer by clicking View Objects in the Settings dialog box. These files can also be deleted if desired.*

Deleting Files on Exit

If you have a user who has recurring problems with a full Temporary Internet Files folder, if a user does not want to have temporary Internet files saved to her computer, or if company policy requires that no temporary files be saved to any users' hard disks, you can configure temporary Internet files to be deleted each time the user closes Internet Explorer.

▶ **Deleting files when exiting**

To configure Internet Explorer to delete the files in the Temporary Internet Files folder each time the user closes Internet Explorer, follow these steps:

1. Open Internet Explorer and, on the Tools menu, choose Internet Options.

2. On the Advanced tab, scroll down to the Security section.

3. Select the Empty Temporary Internet Files Folder When Browser Is Closed check box. Click OK.

Each time the user closes Internet Explorer, the temporary files will be automatically deleted.

Configuring Temporary Internet File Settings

As shown in Figure 5-6, there are several settings that you can configure for temporary Internet files, including how often Internet Explorer checks a Web page for newer versions, how much disk space should be set aside to hold temporary files, and where the Temporary Internet Files folder is stored. It is important to understand what each of these settings offers, because end users will often have specific needs that will require you to make changes to these default settings.

There are four settings for how often Internet Explorer should look for newer versions of stored pages, and these options are detailed in Table 5-1. Reasons for changing the settings are also outlined.

Table 5-1   **How Often Should Internet Explorer Check for Newer Versions of Web Pages?**

Setting	When It Should Be Selected	What the End Result Will Be
Every Visit To The Page	Choose this option when you always need a newer version of the page, such as a stock page, weather alert page, or news page.	Selecting this option slows down browsing for pages already viewed because a new page must be retrieved from the Internet each time the page is visited. Retrieving pages from the Internet takes much longer than retrieving them from the Temporary Internet Files folder on the hard disk.
Every Time You Start Internet Explorer	Choose this option when you need to see the latest version of the file when you first open Internet Explorer each day (or each session). This might be necessary for corporate users who have to check for daily changes to the company's Web site.	Selecting this option increases browsing speed throughout a session, but is slower than the following two options.
Automatically	Choose this default option when you want Internet Explorer to look for newer versions of pages automatically. This is generally the best option for home users and most company personnel.	Selecting this option configures Internet Explorer to check for new versions of pages for pages viewed in a previous session. Internet Explorer determines over time how often you view the page and makes allowances for how often the site should be checked for new content.
Never	Choose this option if you don't want Internet Explorer to ever check for newer versions of previously viewed pages. This setting is appropriate for users who access sites that rarely change. Instruct users to click the Refresh button to check for changes at any time.	Selecting this option speeds up browsing because all previously viewed pages are cached, and the information for those pages is retrieved from the hard disk each time the site is accessed.

In the Settings dialog box, you can also configure how much hard disk space is allotted to the Temporary Internet Files folder. Because temporary Internet files make surfing previously viewed pages faster, you should configure an ample amount of space. If a user complains that browsing is slower than he thinks it should be, slower than it used to be, or if you've already seen the warning signs or dealt with a full Temporary Internet Files folder, consider allotting more space for the folder. If the end user is low on disk space, you should reduce the amount of space that is reserved for temporary Internet files.

Finally, if it's necessary for backup, or if you want to store the Temporary Files folder on another drive or partition, you can move the folder by selecting Move Folder. In the Browser For Folder dialog box, browse to the new folder and click OK.

About Cookies

Cookies are small text files placed on a computer by the Web sites that are visited. These text files are read by the Web site the next time a user visits the site, and this enables the Web site to keep track of a user's preferences. This way, the Web browsing experience is personalized because sites can remember details such as a logon name, what operating system is used, what version of Media Player is running, and what a user prefers to view while visiting. A Web site might also know what has been previously purchased, and it can guess what a user will want to see the next time she visits the site.

> **NOTE** **Personally Identifiable Information**   Cookies can also store personally identifiable information such as a name, e-mail address, telephone number, or even a person's marital status. However, Web sites only gain this information by asking for it outright. Make sure your end users know that cookies cannot obtain any personally identifiable information from them unless they specifically provide it.

Although most cookies are legitimate, some are not. Unsatisfactory cookies are those that are used to provide personally identifiable information for a secondary purpose, such as selling your e-mail address to third-party vendors, or sharing your name and address with other companies. Because there are unsatisfactory cookies, it is important to understand the different types of cookies, how to delete cookies, and how to change privacy settings to prevent different types of cookies from being saved to the computer. Your company might require that changes be made to the default settings for cookies, too, so you need to know how to make changes if asked.

Types of Cookies

There are several types of cookies:

- **Persistent**   These cookies remain on a computer even when Internet Explorer is closed, the user has disconnected from the Internet, or the computer has been turned off. Persistent cookies store information such as logon name, password, e-mail address, color schemes, purchasing history, and other preferences, so that when you revisit a site, this information is available and can be applied.

- **Temporary**   These cookies are stored on a computer only during a single browsing session and are deleted when Internet Explorer is closed. Web sites use temporary cookies to determine what client browser, language, and screen resolution the user is using. This allows a user to move back and forth among the Web pages at the site without losing previously input information. If you disable temporary cookies, a user will not be able to access a site that requires them.

- **First-party**   These cookies are sent to a computer from the Web site being viewed. They might be persistent or temporary and are generally harmless.

- **Third-party**   These cookies are sent to a computer from a Web site not currently being viewed. They generally come from advertisers on the Web site being viewed for tracking Web page use for advertising and marketing purposes. They might be persistent or temporary, and most third-party cookies are blocked by default using the Medium privacy setting.

- **Session**   A session cookie is a temporary cookie that is deleted from a computer when Internet Explorer is closed.

Internet Explorer offers companies and end users several options for working with cookies, and the cookies stored on a computer can be deleted easily. Users have complete control over what types of cookies are stored, and users can even be prompted before a cookie is placed on the computer.

▶ Deleting Cookies

Because cookies can store user names, passwords, and other personally identifiable information, deleting cookies is necessary when a computer is transferred to another user at a company or sold when a new computer is purchased. For security reasons, you might also be asked to delete cookies occasionally.

To delete the cookies on any Windows XP computer, follow these steps:

1. Open Internet Explorer and, on the Tools menu, choose Internet Options.

2. On the General tab, click Delete Cookies.

3. In the Delete Cookies dialog box, click OK to verify you want to delete the cookies in the Temporary Internet Files folder. Click OK to close the Internet Options dialog box.

   NOTE   Make a Note of User Names and Passwords!   When you delete cookies from a computer, no user names, member names, passwords, ID numbers, or similar information is retained. When a user revisits a site that requires this information, he will have to reenter this information.

Configuring Privacy Settings

The privacy settings of Internet Explorer allow users and companies to personalize what types of cookies can be saved to the computer and under what circumstances. You can configure Internet Explorer to prompt a user every time a cookie is to be placed on the computer; it can be configured to handle cookies differently for different Web sites, some cookies can be allowed and some blocked, or all cookies can be blocked. These settings apply to Web sites in the Internet zone only; Local Intranet, Trusted Sites, and Restricted Sites zones all have their own configurations.

▶ Changing default privacy settings

When asked by an end user, asked by a boss, or required by company policy to change the default privacy settings for cookie handling, follow these steps:

1. Open Internet Explorer and, on the Tools menu, choose Internet Options.

2. Select the Privacy tab. If the Default button is unavailable, no advanced cookie-handling settings have been configured. If the Default button is available, advanced settings have already been configured. To view the default settings, click Default if it is available. Figure 5-9 shows the default settings.

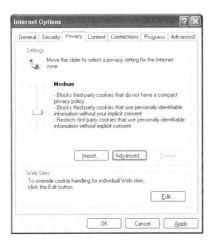

Figure 5-9   Default privacy settings can be changed on the Privacy tab of the Internet Options dialog box.

3. Move the slider to select one of the following (from least secure to most secure):

- ❑ **Accept All Cookies**   All cookies will be saved and Web sites can read the cookies they created.

- ❑ **Low**   Only third-party cookies that do not have a **compact privacy policy** or that use personally identifiable information without a user's implicit consent will be restricted.

- ❑ **Medium**   The same as the low setting, but also restricts first-party cookies that use personally identifiable information without a user's implicit consent.

- ❑ **Medium High**   The same as the medium settings, but also restricts third-party cookies that collect personally identifiable information with a user's explicit consent.

- ❑ **High**   Blocks all cookies that do not have a compact privacy policy and all cookies that use personally identifiable information without a user's explicit consent.

- ❑ **Block All Cookies**   All cookies are blocked and existing cookies on the computer cannot be read by the Web sites that created them.

4. Click OK to close the Internet Options dialog box and apply the changes, or click Advanced on the Privacy tab to override any particular privacy setting's defaults. If Advanced is selected, continue to step 5.

5. In the Advanced Privacy Settings dialog box, select the Override Automatic Cookie Handling check box. From the First-Party Cookies choices, select Accept, Block, or Prompt as desired, and in the Third-Party Cookies area, select Accept, Block, or Prompt as desired. To always allow session cookies, select the Always Allow Session Cookies check box (see Figure 5-10). Click OK, and click OK again in the Internet Options dialog box to apply the changes.

Figure 5-10   The Advanced Privacy Settings dialog box can be used to tweak privacy settings.

Some Web sites require cookies, so blocking all cookies can cause a user to have problems viewing a site; the site might fail to function properly. In addition, changing cookie settings can also affect how cookies already stored on the computer act when they are needed. Be alert when making changes to the default; you can create more problems than you are solving if not careful.

TROUBLESHOOTING INTERNET EXPLORER

Desktop technicians are often called on to troubleshoot problems with Internet Explorer, and these service calls are generally one of three types. They are end user requests to make Internet Explorer work faster and smarter, look better, have more functionality, or resolve simple interface issues; corporate requests to configure security zones (which usually results in additional security zone service calls); and end user requests to resolve problems that have to do with the inability to view Web pages properly. This section covers all of these topics.

NOTE   Connectivity Issues   This section assumes that Internet Explorer is connected to the Internet properly. Chapter 8, "Common Connectivity Problems," focuses on connectivity problems.

Common End User Requests

End users will have various requests that involve how Internet Explorer looks and acts, and they will ask you to resolve problems with the interface. You can resolve many of these problems by customizing the Standard toolbar, changing what is selected from the View menu, or personalizing the Advanced settings in the Internet Options dialog box.

Missing Toolbar, Links Bar, or Status Bar

A common complaint from end users is that a toolbar is missing or the toolbar they used to have isn't available anymore. The toolbars that can be configured include the Standard toolbar, the Address bar, and the Links bar. Users might also complain that they can't see the information at the bottom of the screen that shows what security zone they're in, denoting a missing Status bar. You can add and remove these toolbars using the View menu, and you can customize the placement of the Standard toolbar, Address bar, and Links bar by dragging and dropping. To show or hide any of the toolbars, follow these steps:

1. Open Internet Explorer and, on the View menu, choose Toolbars.

2. The Toolbars list contains Standard Buttons, Address Bar, Links, Lock The Toolbars, and Customize selection. Toolbars marked with a check are showing; toolbars without a check are not. To select or clear a toolbar, select it from the list. Figure 5-11 shows an example of all three toolbars. In this example, the Links bar is incorporated into the Address bar.

Figure 5-11   The toolbars can be customized to suit any user's needs.

To customize the placement of the Standard toolbar, Address bar, or Links bar, follow these steps:

1. In Internet Explorer, position the cursor at the far left of the toolbar you want to move.

2. Click and hold the mouse button; the cursor will change to a four-headed arrow.

3. Drag the toolbar to a new position to combine it with an existing toolbar or to move its position on the screen.

4. Position the cursor on the light dotted lines that separate combined toolbars until the cursor becomes a two-headed arrow. Drag to resize the toolbar.

NOTE Toolbar Positions   The Standard toolbar, Address bar, and Link bar must remain at the top of the Internet Explorer window. They cannot be moved to the left, right, or bottom of the screen (like the Taskbar can).

Locked Toolbar

If a user complains the toolbar is locked and cannot be moved, click View, point to Toolbars, and clear Lock The Toolbars by selecting it.

Personalizing the Favorites Menu

When users call to report that they cannot access all of their favorites, or that they have saved favorites but they aren't listed in the Favorites list, it's most likely because the Personalized Favorites Menu option is enabled in the Advanced options of Internet Explorer. Personalized menus keep the Favorites list clean by hiding links that aren't used very often. The list only shows the links that are accessed frequently. Tell the users they can access the less frequently accessed links by clicking the down arrow at the end of the Favorites list.

▶ **Enabling personalized Favorites menus**

If the user requests you change this behavior, or if the user wants you to enable personalized favorites, follow these steps:

1. Open Internet Explorer and, on the Tools menu, choose Internet Options.

2. On the Advanced tab, scroll down to the Browsing section, and select or clear the Enable Personalized Favorites Menu check box. Click OK.

   NOTE Restart Internet Explorer   Applying the change to personalized favorites might require you to close and restart Internet Explorer.

Using AutoComplete

AutoComplete is a feature that helps end users work, browse, and purchase items on the Internet faster than they could normally by automatically listing possible matches for Web addresses, forms, and user names and passwords on forms. Although this can be a good feature for a computer administrator who does not share a computer, for the average home user or the owner of a small, home-based business, it is not a good idea under all circumstances.

You should not use AutoComplete when the computer is located in a nonsecure environment, such as a break room, lunchroom, or kiosk, or when two or more people share a computer and computer account. In addition, when a computer is transferred to a new user or sold to another person, the AutoComplete form and password information should be cleared.

▶ **Enabling or disabling AutoComplete**

As a desktop technician, you'll be asked to enable or disable AutoComplete (depending on the circumstance), enable or disable Internet Explorer's ability to save passwords, and clear the AutoComplete history, by following these steps:

1. Open Internet Explorer and, on the Tools menu, choose Internet Options.

2. On the Content tab, in the Personal Information area, click AutoComplete.

3. To enable or disable AutoComplete, in the AutoComplete Settings dialog box, select or clear the Use AutoComplete for Web Addresses, Forms, and User Names And Passwords On Forms check boxes.

4. To clear the AutoComplete history for forms, click Clear Forms.

5. To clear the AutoComplete history for passwords, click Clear Passwords.

6. To remove the ability of Internet Explorer to save any passwords in the future, clear the Prompt Me To Save Passwords check box.

7. Click OK to close the AutoComplete Settings dialog box, and click OK to close the Internet Options dialog box.

NOTE Don't Confuse AutoComplete with Inline AutoComplete Inline Auto-Complete completes entries in the Address bar as you type based on entries you've used before and offers a list of choices under the Address bar or other links that start the same way. AutoComplete offers choices under the Address window as well, but doesn't complete the entry in the Address bar as you type.

Using Inline AutoComplete

Inline AutoComplete completes entries in the Address bar as you type based on entries you've used before and offers a list of choices under the Address bar for other links that start the same way.

▶ Enabling Inline AutoComplete

You can enable Inline AutoComplete, using the Advanced options of Internet Explorer, by following these steps:

1. Open Internet Explorer and, on the Tools menu, choose Internet Options.

2. On the Advanced tab, scroll down to the end of the Browsing section.

3. Select the Use Inline AutoComplete check box. Click OK.

Using Default Search Actions

Users can perform searches in a number of ways including using the Search Explorer bar, using a Web browser or search engine, or typing their requests in the Address bar. If a user's choice is to search for information using the Address bar, there are several ways the results for that search can be shown. In addition, searching from the Address bar can be disabled. Here are the advanced choices for searching from the Address bar:

- Display results, and go to the most likely site.
- Do not search from the Address bar.
- Just display the results in the main window.
- Just go to the most likely site.

▶ Changing default actions

The default is to go to the most likely site, but you can change that default as follows:

1. Open Internet Explorer and, on the Tools menu, choose Internet Options.

2. Select the Advanced tab and scroll down to Search From The Address Bar.

3. In the When Searching list, select the appropriate choice. Click OK.

Changing the HTML Editor

Some end users' jobs require them to view the source code on a Web page, and they need a Hypertext Markup Language (HTML) editor program to use with Internet Explorer to view and edit that source code. By default, Internet Explorer uses Notepad. However, if a user wants to use Microsoft FrontPage or another HTML editor, you need to change this default.

▶ **Changing the default editor**

To change the default HTML editor in Internet Explorer, follow these steps:

1. Open Internet Explorer and, on the Tools menu, choose Internet Options.

2. Select the Programs tab.

3. In the HTML Editor drop-down list, choose the appropriate program. Click OK.

Script Errors

Users might report that script error notifications appear on their monitors while surfing Web sites, and they might also complain they are continually asked if they want to debug those errors. You might also have users with the opposite problem; a developer or technician might need to see these errors when testing a new Web site. Whatever the case, script options exist in the Advanced options of Internet Explorer, and they can be easily enabled or disabled.

▶ **Enabling and disabling script debugging**

To enable or disable script debugging or if a user should be notified of all script errors, follow these steps:

1. Open Internet Explorer and, on the Tools menu, choose Internet Options.

2. On the Advanced tab, in the Browsing section, select or clear the Disable Script Debugging and Display A Notification About Every Script Error check boxes and click OK.

3. Click OK to close the Internet Options dialog box.

▶ **Enabling download complete notification**

Finally, if a user reports that she is not notified when a download completes and would like to receive a message to indicate such, follow these steps:

1. Open Internet Explorer and, from the Tools menu, select Internet Options.

2. On the Advanced tab, in the Browsing section, select the Notify When Downloads Complete check box.

3. Click OK to close the Internet Options dialog box.

As you learned in this section, you can resolve many problems by using the View menu or the Internet Options dialog box. The Content tab, Programs tab, and Advanced tab of the Internet Options dialog box allow you to change the program defaults and personalize Internet Explorer. The View menu enables personalization of the toolbars. Many user requests can be handled by making changes here.

Troubleshooting Zones

There are four security zones: Internet, Local Intranet, Trusted Sites, and Restricted Sites. The Internet zone contains all Web sites. Intranet, Trusted Sites, and Restricted Sites zones don't include any sites by default, and thus must have Web sites manually placed in them. Each of the four zones has default security settings (Low, Medium-Low, Medium, and High) that determine what type of content can be downloaded and run (such as **ActiveX controls**) and what users have the ability to do (such as install desktop items). For any zone, you can change the security level and modify the security defaults.

You'll be asked to resolve problems that have to do with zone configurations; these will mainly be issues regarding the inability to view or access something or to comply with company security directives. To resolve these types of calls, you'll need an understanding of the default settings for each zone. Table 5-2 details the four zones and their default settings for ActiveX controls and installation of desktop items. There are other settings for each zone, but these are the items you'll commonly need to modify. (Default settings can be changed.)

> **NOTE** **Know Security Zone Settings**   Make sure you understand and are familiar with all of the security zone settings.

Table 5-2 **Security Zones and Default Settings**

Security Zone	Default Security Levels
High (default for the Restricted Sites zone)	■ **Disable** Download unsigned ActiveX controls, initialize and script ActiveX controls not marked as safe. ■ **Enable** Run ActiveX controls and plug-ins, script ActiveX controls marked safe for scripting. ■ **Prompt** Download signed ActiveX controls, installation of desktop items.
Medium (default for the Internet zone)	■ **Disable** Download unsigned ActiveX controls, initialize and script ActiveX controls not marked as safe. ■ **Enable** Run ActiveX controls and plug-ins, script ActiveX controls marked safe for scripting. ■ **Prompt** Download signed ActiveX controls, installation of desktop items.
Medium-Low (default for the Local Intranet zone)	■ **Disable** Download unsigned ActiveX controls, initialize and script ActiveX controls not marked as safe. ■ **Enable** Run ActiveX controls and plug-ins, script ActiveX controls marked safe for scripting. ■ **Prompt** Download signed ActiveX controls, installation of desktop items.

Table 5-2   **Security Zones and Default Settings**

Security Zone	Default Security Levels
Low (default for the Trusted Sites zone)	■ **Disable** Download unsigned ActiveX controls, initialize and script ActiveX controls not marked as safe. ■ **Enable** Run ActiveX controls and plug-ins, script ActiveX controls marked safe for scripting. ■ **Prompt** Download signed ActiveX controls, installation of desktop items.

NOTE   Downloads   File and font downloads are enabled by default on all Internet security zones.

Service calls involving security zones can have to do with an end user's need to have more (or less) access to Web content than he currently has or to place a Web site in a specific zone and use that zone's default security settings. You might also receive calls to configure users' computers to comply with a company security policy requirement to enable or disable a specific security setting. In this section, you'll learn to do all of these things.

▶ **Changing Internet zone defaults**

To make changes to the Internet zone's default settings (this same technique works to change any zone's default settings), follow these steps:

1. Open Internet Explorer and, on the Tools menu, choose Internet Options.

2. On the Security tab, select the Internet zone if it is not selected already.

3. Move the security slider up or down to change the default security setting for the zone. If the slider is not available, click Default Level. It is best to leave the Internet zone at either Medium (the default) or Medium-High. Lower settings will reduce security; higher settings will reduce functionality.

4. Click Custom Level.

5. In the Security Settings dialog box, scroll down the list to select the item to change. Make the appropriate change by selecting the desired option. Click OK to close the Security Settings dialog box, and click OK to close the Internet Options dialog box.

▶ **Adding to the Trusted Sites zone**

To add a Web site to the Trusted Sites zone (this same technique works to add a site to the Restricted Sites zone), follow these steps:

1. Open Internet Explorer and, on the Tools menu, choose Internet Options.

2. Select the Security tab.

3. Select Trusted Sites, and click Sites.

4. In the Add This Web Site To The Zone text box, type the address to add. If adding a trusted site, you must begin the Web site URL with https://, which denotes a secure site. Click Add.

5. Click OK to close the Trusted Sites dialog box and click OK again to close the Internet Options dialog box.

▶ **Adding to the Local Intranet zone**

To add a Web site to the Local Intranet zone, follow these steps:

1. Open Internet Explorer and, on the Tools menu, choose Internet Options.

2. Select the Security tab.

3. Select Local Intranet, and then click Sites.

4. In the Local Intranet dialog box, select the Web sites that should be included in the Local Intranet zone. Figure 5-12 shows the choices.

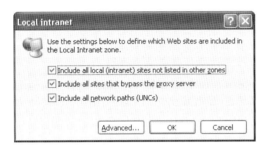

Figure 5-12   Local Intranet zone settings can be set to configure local sites.

5. In the Local Intranet dialog box, click Advanced.

6. In the Add This Web Site To The Zone box, type any additional Web sites to add. Click Add to add each.

7. Click OK in the Local Intranet dialog box, click OK again in the first Local Intranet dialog box, and click OK to close the Internet Options dialog box.

Common Service Calls

As a desktop technician you'll need to know when to change which security setting, and you'll often be asked to make the change without giving the user a security setting that is too lenient or one that is against company policy. This takes familiarity with the process (shown earlier) and an understanding of the security setting options. To help you become more familiar with common requests, Table 5-3 shows some examples of service calls and their resolutions.

Table 5-3   **Common Security Service Calls and Resolutions**

Service Call Scenario	Resolution
A Web designer calls to report that he needs to be able to download signed ActiveX controls for the purpose of testing a Web site he is creating. However, each time a signed ActiveX control is downloaded, he gets a prompt. He wants this behavior to stop.	Personalize his default security settings and change the setting for Download Signed ActiveX controls from Prompt to Enable.

Table 5-3   **Common Security Service Calls and Resolutions**

Service Call Scenario	Resolution
A user reports that when she connects to a site on her local intranet, she can't download unsigned ActiveX controls. She needs to be able to do this to perform work-related tasks. You need to change this so she can download unsigned ActiveX controls without changing the security zone.	Personalize her default security settings and change the setting for Download Unsigned ActiveX Controls from Disable to Enable or Prompt.
Your boss tells you that he doesn't want his workers to be able to install desktop items for anything they've downloaded from the Internet. He asks you not to change any other behavior on their machines.	Personalize the default security settings on each machine and change the setting for Install Desktop Items from Prompt to Disable.

As you become more familiar with the terms and security settings options, you'll be able to quickly identify problems and their solutions. In many instances, you can resolve problems by making simple changes to the default security settings.

Resolving Problems Viewing Web Pages

There are several reasons why users won't be able to view Web pages properly, and many times it is because they have made changes to the defaults on their own. Problems can also occur because of default security settings: a site is in the Restricted Sites zone or the site requires cookies be placed on the machine and cookies are not allowed. Users might report specific errors as well; they get internal page faults, or they can't hear sounds, see videos, or view pictures. These are common problems and solutions to them are detailed in this section.

Screen Resolution

If a user reports problems viewing a single Web page, but other pages look fine, check to see if there is a note at the bottom of the page that says, "This page is best viewed using 800 by 600 screen resolution" or something similar. If it is a corporate Web site or one the user relies on heavily, he might need to reconfigure his display settings permanently. Display settings can be changed from Control Panel.

Cookie Handling

Many Web sites require that cookies be enabled on a user's machine if the user wants to visit and browse the site. A user will be unable to view Web pages that have this requirement if the user's privacy settings are configured to block all cookies, if the privacy settings are set to High, or if the company has a strict cookie policy that blocks first-party cookies or does not allow session cookies.

Allowing a user access to sites requires that the default privacy settings be changed. Changing privacy settings was detailed in the section "Configuring Privacy Settings" earlier in this chapter.

Sounds, Videos, and Pictures

Some of the Advanced options of Internet Explorer restrict what can and cannot be seen on a Web page. These settings are often configured to speed up access to a page by not playing videos or showing pictures when the site is loaded, and sound can be disabled as well. If a user reports problems associated with sound, video, or pictures, check the advanced options first, following these steps:

1. Open Internet Explorer and, on the Tools menu, choose Internet Options.

2. Select the Advanced tab and scroll down to the Multimedia section shown in Figure 5-13.

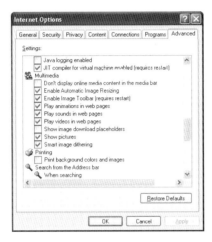

Figure 5-13   Use the Advanced tab for configuring multimedia and similar options.

3. Verify that the appropriate items are selected:

   ❑ Play Animations In Web Pages

   ❑ Play Sounds In Web Pages

   ❑ Play Videos In Web Pages

   ❑ Show Pictures

4. On the Advanced tab, verify that the Show Image Download Placeholders check box is cleared. Click OK.

Internal Page Faults

Internal **page faults** are often difficult to diagnose. Connectivity settings; a full Temporary Internet Files folder; and third-party Internet software including fire-walls, file-sharing software, Internet optimizers, and on-screen animation programs can cause page faults. Network protocols, cookies, corrupted Favorites, services, and Internet software installations can also cause page faults. In addition to the number of things that can cause them, these errors come in many forms. Here are a few of them:

■ Invalid page fault

■ Iexplore.exe has generated errors and must be shut down

- Page could not be displayed

- Could not open the search page

- An access violation occurred in MSHTML.DLL

If specifics are given, as in the last item, visit the Microsoft Knowledge Base (*http://support.Microsoft.com/default.aspx*) and type in the exact error. Downloading and installing a hotfix can solve this particular error. These are the easiest of all page faults to find solutions for. If no specifics are given, you'll have to resolve the errors using trial-and-error troubleshooting techniques.

> **NOTE   Service Packs**   Before you do too much troubleshooting, verify that the user has the most recent version of Internet Explorer and the latest service packs for both the operating system and Internet Explorer. To check the version number and what service packs are installed, open Internet Explorer and, from the Help menu, select About Internet Explorer.

If you are at the user's desk when the error occurs, use the Internet Explorer Reporting tool to report the error, then view the error details. If the error report gives any indication of the cause of the error, disable the program or service associated with it. If that doesn't work and the user has the most up-to-date service packs installed, continue troubleshooting in this order:

1. Verify that the proxy settings for the local area network (LAN), if they exist, are correctly configured. You can locate these settings by clicking LAN Settings on the Connections tab of the Internet Options dialog box.

2. Disable third-party browser extensions such as Bonzai Buddy, Comet Cursor, or other third-party downloaded components. Applications like these can often be disabled from the notification area or from the application itself, and uninstalling the component from Control Panel is the best option if one of these programs caused the page fault.

3. Delete all temporary Internet files and ActiveX controls. You can do this on the General tab of the Internet Options dialog box.

4. Delete cookies. You can do so on the General tab of the Internet Options dialog box.

5. Delete Favorites. Exploring to the Favorites folder and deleting the files contained there is one way to do this.

6. Verify the system has enough RAM and the RAM is performing properly.

If these techniques don't solve the problem, consult the Microsoft Knowledge Base, TechNet, and newsgroups as detailed in Chapter 2, "Resolving a Service Call."

SUMMARY

- To personalize Internet Explorer, users can change the text size, colors, fonts, and font styles shown on Web pages, and customize the toolbars.

- To configure languages so Web sites can be viewed in a user's native language, change the language option in the Internet Options dialog box of Internet Explorer.

- To secure and personalize a Web user's experience, you can configure Content Advisor, digital certificates, and the Profile Assistant.

- To resolve common end-user requests, you will have to import favorites, configure settings for cookies, set a home page, personalize the Title bar, and configure the Explorer bar.

- To maintain Internet Explorer, use Disk Cleanup regularly and configure temporary Internet File folder settings.

- To troubleshoot Internet Explorer, check security zones, privacy settings, and the Advanced configuration options of Internet Explorer.

REVIEW QUESTIONS

1. A company has placed a computer in a break room so users can access it on their lunch and coffee breaks. How should the computer be configured? Choose all that apply.

    a. Disable AutoComplete.

    b. Clear forms and clear passwords from the AutoComplete Settings dialog box.

    c. Disable Personalized Favorites.

    d. Set Privacy settings to block all cookies.

    e. Configure a custom level for the Internet zone to disable the installation of desktop icons.

2. A user reports that he has changed his text size to Largest, but when he visits sites, sometimes the text on the sites is large and sometimes it isn't. He reports this happens occasionally with colors and font styles, too. What does the user need to do to make sure these settings are always used, no matter what Web site he visits?

    a. Use the Internet Options dialog box of Internet Explorer and, on the General tab, click Accessibility, and make the appropriate changes in the Accessibility dialog box.

    b. Open Control Panel, open Accessibility Options, and on the Display tab, select the Override Web Settings check box.

    c. Use the Internet Options dialog box in Internet Explorer, select the General tab, click Advanced and, in the Accessibility choices, select the Override Web Settings check box.

d. Use the Internet Options dialog box in Internet Explorer, select the General tab, click Accessibility and, in the Accessibility dialog box, select the Format Documents Using My Style Sheet check box.

3. A small business owner wants to personalize the Internet Explorer Title bar on the computer that visitors access when they come into her store. She also wants to configure a default home page that users cannot change. Which of the following commands is used on the Run line to open the appropriate application for configuring these computer-wide settings?

    a. msconfig.exe

    b. sigverif.exe

    c. cmd.exe

    d. gpedit.msc

4. Which of the following are indications of a full Temporary Internet Files folder? Choose all that apply.

    a. When using the Save As command, pictures can only be saved as bitmaps, and cannot be saved as JPEG or GIF files.

    b. No History files appear in the History folder.

    c. Page faults appear.

    d. Access to frequently accessed Web pages is slow.

5. Match the type of cookie on the left with its description on the right.

1. Persistent	a) These cookies are sent to a computer from the Web site being viewed. They can be persistent or temporary, and are generally harmless.
2. Temporary	b) These cookies are sent to a computer from a Web site not currently being viewed. They generally come from advertisers on the Web site being viewed for the purpose of tracking Web page use for advertising and marketing purposes. They can be persistent or temporary, and most third-party cookies are blocked by default using the Medium privacy setting.
3. First-party	c) These cookies are only stored on a computer during a single browsing session and are deleted when Internet Explorer is closed. They are used by Web sites to determine what client browser, what language, and what screen resolution is used, and they allow a user to move back and forth among the Web pages at the site without losing previously input information. If these cookies are disabled, a user will not be able to access a site that requires them.

4. Third-party   d) A temporary cookie that is deleted from a computer when Internet Explorer is closed.

5. Session   e) These cookies remain on a computer even when Internet Explorer is closed, the user has disconnected from the Internet, or the computer has been turned off. These cookies store information such as logon name, password, e-mail address, color schemes, purchasing history, and other preferences, so that when a site is revisited, this information is available and can be applied.

6. Company policy requires that all cookies saved to a user's computer must have a compact privacy policy that conforms to P3P standards. No cookies shall be saved if they do not conform. Which of the following default privacy settings can be used? Select all that apply.

  a. Accept All Cookies

  b. Low

  c. Medium

  d. Medium-High

  e. High

  f. Block All Cookies

7. You need to configure a security setting for the Internet zone for users who access Web sites from a computer located in the company's lunchroom. Network administrators have configured a group policy, physically secured the computer, and performed similar tasks, and have asked you to configure a security level for the Internet zone that will apply the following rules by default:

  ❏ **Disable**   Download unsigned ActiveX controls, initialize and script ActiveX controls not marked as safe.

  ❏ **Enable**   Run ActiveX controls and plug-ins, script ActiveX controls marked safe for scripting.

  ❏ **Prompt**   Download signed ActiveX controls, installation of desktop items.

Which security level offers these default settings for the Internet zone?

8. A home user wants you to configure his Windows XP computer so that his 12-year-old son cannot access Web sites that contain offensive language, nudity, sexual references, or violence that involves fighting or killing. He'd like to be able to override those settings, if ever necessary, by using an administrator password. The user wants to spend the least amount of money possible. What should you tell the user to do?

  a. Tell the user to purchase and install inexpensive third-party parental control software. Teach the user how to configure it.

    b. Configure Content Advisor, included with Windows XP.

    c. Create a separate account for the son, and purchase and install parental control software. Apply the software only to the son's account.

    d. Configure digital certificates, included with Windows XP, and only accept digital certificates from reputable sites.

    e. Configure the Profile Assistant to limit what sites the son has access to.

CASE SCENARIOS

Scenario 5-1: Configuring Internet Explorer Settings

All computers in your office have recently been upgraded from Microsoft Windows 98 to Windows XP. A clean installation was performed on each computer and all service packs were installed. The installation went smoothly. However, the stockbrokers in your office are complaining that they aren't getting up-to-date quotes when they visit their favorite, frequently viewed Web sites. They've been accessing these sites for two years without incident. What is most likely wrong and how can this problem be resolved?

1. The application the stockbrokers use to get stock quotes is not compatible with Windows XP and needs to be replaced with a newer version.

2. The Temporary Internet Files folder is full and needs to be emptied.

3. The settings for the temporary files need to be changed to check for newer versions of stored pages every time the page is visited.

4. The Temporary Internet Files folder was moved during the upgrade; Internet Explorer does not know where to store temporary files and, therefore, isn't saving any.

Scenario 5-2: Understanding and Configuring Zones

A user reports that each time she accesses a particular Web site, she is inundated with content she doesn't want to see and she thinks this might have to do with ActiveX, Java applets, or scripts running on the site. The user reports that the site takes a long time to load, too. She wants to visit this site and only read the data; she has no interest in the other items on the site. You need to make this site available without making any changes to the default settings for the Internet zone. What should you do?

1. Add this site to the Local Intranet zone.

2. Add this site to the Trusted Sites zone.

3. Add this site to the Restricted Sites zone.

CHAPTER 6
INSTALL AND CONFIGURE OFFICE APPLICATIONS

Upon completion of this chapter, you will be able to:

■ Perform preinstallation tasks including verifying compatibility, licenses, and minimum hardware requirements

■ Install the Microsoft Office System applications and their updates

■ Personalize Office features including customizing toolbars, commands, formatting, layout, default file locations, and more

■ Configure proofing tools including spelling, grammar, AutoCorrect lists, and Auto-Summarize rules for Office applications

The goal of this chapter is to teach you to install and configure Office applications for end users in either a corporate or home environment. Installation includes verifying that the software to be installed is compatible with the computer's operating system and hardware, understanding and verifying license and minimum hardware requirements, testing the applications in a lab, and using program compatibility mode when software isn't compatible. After installation, you'll learn how to configure the applications to meet the user's specific needs.

There are several configuration tasks you'll become familiar with, including the following:

■ Proofing in English, Spanish, and French

■ Using fonts and localized templates

■ Personalizing dictionaries, editing modes, and AutoCorrect options

■ Adding, removing, and customizing toolbars, menus, commands, and file locations

■ Configuring print options, layout options, backgrounds, and formatting options

141

PREINSTALLATION TASKS

Although many people (mostly end users) simply put a program's installation CD into the CD-ROM drive and follow the prompts to install it, this is not a prudent way for a professional desktop technician to install applications for end users. Part of a technician's job is to verify that the program to be installed is compatible with the user's operating system and hardware, that the computer meets the application's specified minimum requirements, that the company or user has a valid license, and that the program will function as it should in the environment in which it will be used. You should perform all of these tasks *before* you install the application. These preinstallation tasks are detailed in this section.

Verifying Compatibility

When a user asks you to install an application, your first job is to check the software box, the CD, online support (such as the manufacturer's Web site), or other documentation to verify that the software is compatible with Microsoft Windows XP. In most instances, the information is readily available. Figure 6-1 shows an example of some basic online documentation that states that the application is compatible with Windows XP.

Click Here to Learn More...

Works with Windows 95/98/ME/NT/2000 & XP

Figure 6-1   Verify compatibility from the software's box or other documentation.

Some applications offer much more information, usually from a page that lists system requirements. These requirements might state that specific hardware must be installed on the computer for components in the application to work (and thus be compatible). For example, although Microsoft Office System can be installed on almost any computer that runs Microsoft Windows 2000 with Service Pack 3 or Windows XP or later, to use certain features, other hardware must be installed for the features to function correctly. For instance, the following components need specific hardware to work.

- **Speech recognition** For speech recognition to work properly with Windows 2000 (with Service Pack 3 or later) or Windows XP, the computer must have a close-talk microphone and an audio output device.

- **Advanced Outlook functionality** For advanced Microsoft Office Outlook 2003 options to work properly, a Microsoft Exchange server is required.

- **Collaboration functionality** For advanced collaboration functionality, Microsoft Windows Server 2003 must be available, and Windows SharePoint must be installed.

- **Internet functionality** For Internet tools and options, such as online support features, updating the Office system, and Outlook 2003 to work properly, Internet connectivity must be available.

Verifying an application's compatibility is an important part of the installation procedure. If you determine that a program is incompatible, consider your options, including purchasing new hardware, searching for an upgrade to the application, or choosing not to install the program at all.

Meeting Minimum Requirements

Documented minimum requirements list the basic hardware and operating system components necessary for the program to function minimally (usually without additional features such as speech recognition or advanced functionality). Minimum requirements detail what type of processor is needed, how much random access memory (RAM) is required, how much hard disk space must be available, what type of operating system can be used, and what kind of display is needed for the program to open and run.

Recommended requirements are also generally included in the same documentation. Recommended requirements state what hardware is necessary for the application to function effectively and efficiently. These standards are often required to prevent the computer from bogging down while performing tasks.

Table 6-1 shows an example of the documented minimum and recommended requirements for Microsoft Office Professional Edition 2003. You can also find this information online at *http://www.microsoft.com/office/editions/prodinfo/sysreq.mspx*.

Table 6-1 Office Professional Edition 2003 Minimum Requirements

Component	Minimum Requirement	Recommended Requirement
Computer and processor	Personal computer with a 233-MHz processor	Personal computer with an Intel Pentium III or equivalent processor; Pentium 4 provides optimal performance
Memory (RAM)	128 MB	More than 128 MB
Hard disk space	400 MB	An additional 290 MB of space for options and installation files cache
Operating system	Windows 2000 (with Service Pack 3 or later) or Windows XP	Windows 2000 (with Service Pack 3 or later) or Windows XP
Display	Super VGA (800 by 600)	Super VGA (800 by 600) or higher

Installing additional options requires more hardware. Using the optional installation of Outlook 2003 with Business Contact Manager requires a PC with a Pentium 450-MHz or faster processor, 260 MB or more of RAM, and 190 MB of additional disk space.

> **TIP Recommended Requirements** Most of the time, you'll want the user's computer to exceed the minimum requirements. Simply meeting minimum requirements will allow the program to run, but exceeding the requirements will help the program run faster and more efficiently. In almost all cases, meeting or exceeding recommended requirements is best.

Having the Proper Licenses

Installing and running a software program almost always requires a license, an activation code, a validation code, or a product identification number. Generally, you find these numbers on the CD itself, on the CD case, on the box or, if the application was downloaded from the Internet, in an e-mail.

In some instances, you must input the code prior to installation, as with the Office System. Other times you must input a product ID during installation, and activation occurs after you complete the installation, as with Windows XP. Sometimes, you enter an unlock code the first time you use the application, which then activates the program. Whatever the case, you need to verify that the end user or the company has a valid license, product ID, or activation code prior to beginning the installation. Figure 6-2 shows an example of a product ID requirement prior to installation.

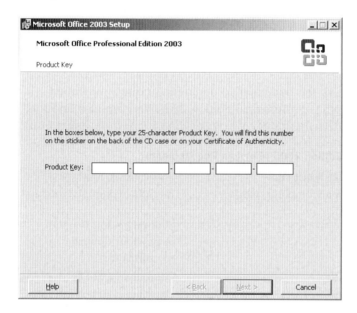

Figure 6-2   A Product Key must be available to install most software.

Testing in a Lab

If you need to install a program that you have never installed before, especially one that does not list compatibility with Windows XP in its documentation or one that will be deployed company-wide, install the program in a lab setting first, using the same environmental variables under which you or your users will normally use the program. The same is true for home users who use older operating systems like Microsoft Windows 98, and who want to install a newly released application. Not all newer programs list Windows 98 as a compatible operating system, and if you aren't sure, testing the software first before attempting to install it on a user's computer is a wise move.

When testing the program in a lab, verify that:

■ The program opens normally and does not cause system instability including blue screens, internal page faults, or memory errors.

■ The computer shuts down properly after the program is closed, and can be booted without errors.

■ The program's cut, copy, and paste commands, spell check, import and export commands, acquire, and other components work properly (if available).

■ The program can be used to open and save data in the required file types, and can save files to the network server (if necessary).

■ The program can be used to send and receive data from hardware attached locally and on a network, including scanners, cameras, printers, and disk drives.

■ The program closes normally from the File menu and with the Close button in the top right corner.

Even if all of these tasks work fine in a lab, there is still a slim chance that problems will arise if the program is not listed as compatible. When in doubt, install the program under its native operating system using the Program Compatibility Wizard in Windows XP, or run the program in a specific program compatibility mode. Both of these options are detailed next.

Using Program Compatibility Options

Although most programs will run properly on Windows XP, some older games and third-party applications that were written for a specific operating system like Microsoft Windows 95 or Windows 98 won't work as expected (or won't install at all). When this happens, install or run the program using one of the available program compatibility options. Choosing a program compatibility mode for a program allows that program to run in its native environment, which should cause the program to run properly and perform as expected.

When Not to Use Compatibility Modes
Program compatibility modes aren't for all programs, especially programs that are system tools such as CD-burning software or firewalls. System tools such as these run at a very low **kernel mode** and can cause serious problems if installed and run incorrectly. System tools include, but are not limited to, the following:

■ Antivirus software

■ Firewalls

■ CD-burning software

■ Backup utilities

■ Disk management software

When in doubt, purchase a newer version or an upgrade to the software or do not install it.

Program Compatibility Modes

If a program is already installed and is not performing properly, you can change the compatibility mode for it by right-clicking the program's icon and selecting the Compatibility tab. You can choose to run the program in one of four compatibility modes—Windows 95, Windows 98/Me, Windows NT 4.0 (Service Pack 5), or Windows 2000—by following these steps:

1. Locate the problem application in the All Programs list or by browsing to it using Windows Explorer.

2. Right-click the program name or icon and select Properties. In the Properties dialog box, select the Compatibility tab, shown in Figure 6-3.

Figure 6-3   Program compatibility settings are located on the Compatibility tab.

3. In the Compatibility Mode area, select the Run This Program In Compatibility Mode For check box and choose an operating system from the drop-down list.

4. In the Display Settings area, select any of these check boxes: Run In 256 Colors, Run In 640 × 480 Screen Resolution, or Disable Visual Themes. If the program has problems handling the higher quality video of Windows XP, you should try one of these settings. (If, after configuring these settings you still find that the program doesn't run properly, try tweaking these settings.)

5. If available in the Input Settings area, select the Turn Off Advanced Text Services For This Program check box. Advanced Text Services can interfere with earlier software, especially games.

6. Click OK, then start the program and verify it runs properly.

Program Compatibility Wizard

The Program Compatibility Wizard lets you install and test the program in different environments and with various settings to see which mode can best run the application. For instance, if the program was originally designed to work on a Windows 95 machine, installing it using the Windows 95 program compatibility mode will allow the program to run in its native environment, and it will likely run properly.

▶ Installing a legacy program

To use the Program Compatibility Wizard to install a legacy program, follow these steps:

1. On the Start menu, select Help and Support.

2. In the Search box, type **Program Compatibility Wizard**.

3. In the Search Results box, click Getting Older Programs To Run On Windows XP, and in the right pane, locate the step to Start The Program Compatibility Wizard. Click the link.

    NOTE **Help and Support**   *You can also access the Program Compatibility Wizard by selecting Start, Run, typing* **hcp://system/compatctr/compatmode.htm** *in the Open text box, and clicking OK.*

4. Click Next to start the wizard.

5. On the How Do You Want To Locate The Program That You Would Like To Run With Compatibility Settings? page, select how you want to locate the program:

    a. Want To Choose From A List Of Programs

    b. Want To Use The Program In The CD-ROM Drive

    c. Want To Locate The Program Manually

6. If you choose to select the program from a list, do so and click Next. If you choose to browse to the program, do so, and click Next. If you choose to use the program in the CD-ROM drive, place the CD in the drive and click Next.

7. On the Select A Compatibility Mode For The Program page, make the appropriate selection (Microsoft Windows 95, Microsoft Windows NT 4.0 [Service Pack 5], Microsoft Windows 98/Windows Me, or Microsoft Windows 2000) or choose not to apply a compatibility mode. Click Next.

8. On the Select Display Settings For The Program page, select a display setting. Read the program's documentation to verify you are making the correct selection. (You don't have to make a selection.) Click Next.

9. Install the program.

10. On the Did The Program Work Correctly page, make a selection based on the results in step 9, and then click Next:

    a. Yes, Set This Program To Always Use These Compatibility Settings

    b. No, Try Different Compatibility Settings

    c. No, I Am Finished Trying Compatibility Settings.

11. On the Program Compatibility Data page, choose Yes or No to send a compatibility data report to Microsoft. Click Next and/or Finish.

If later the program does not run as expected, right-click the program icon, select the Compatibility tab, and select another compatibility option.

Letting Users Install Their Own Programs

Many companies have local or group policies in place that prevent users from installing their own programs. In these environments you can expect service calls from end users who are upset about this policy, because they want to install the latest holiday screen saver, greeting card software, or music file-sharing download application. Let the users know that these policies are in place for many reasons, but stress that letting them install any program they'd like can be quite dangerous for the company, the computer, and for the users' data. (Many programs such as these are also detrimental to a user's productivity.)

If a user does have the appropriate permissions to install a program, make sure he is aware of the preinstallation tasks detailed in this section, that he creates a system restore point prior to installation, and that his data is backed up.

INSTALLATION

Once you have verified that the application is compatible with the operating system and the computer's hardware setup, that the user has the proper licenses, and that the computer meets the minimum or recommended requirements, installing the program can occur in a number of ways. Installing the application can be achieved using an installation CD or accessing the files from a network location or network server. Some companies automate application installations by using Group Policy or a Systems Management Server (SMS) server, further simplifying the process for users. There are a few concepts to be aware of before beginning any installation, though:

- Understanding the terms of the license agreement
- Deciding which components you should install
- Selecting a location in which to save the application's files
- Deleting temporary, backup, or installation files after installation is complete

Each of these concepts is detailed fully in the following sections.

General Installation Concepts

During the installation of many applications, you'll be prompted throughout to answer questions about or agree to the license agreement, and to state what should be installed and where and what to do with temporary files after the installation is complete.

License Agreements

Generally, license agreements document for the user or the company how the software can be used including, but not limited to, the following:

- Guidelines for how often and where you can install the software. You can install some applications on only a single personal computer, others on a personal computer and a laptop, and others on multiple computers. Some software can be installed on network servers and requires a license for each user or computer that accesses the software on the network.

- Guidelines for Remote Desktop and Remote Assistance usage.

- Guidelines for mandatory product activation (covered in the next section).

- Restrictions on using the application to create or promote inappropriate content, or any item that can damage or disable Internet-based services.

- Guidelines for selling, renting, or transferring the application.

- Warranties, applicable laws, severability clauses, and other legal issues.

You should read the license agreement carefully, and then agree to it. Understand that agreeing to the license agreement is equivalent to signing a legal contract and it is legally binding. Make sure you read the agreement and truly agree with and are aware of the rules and regulations stated in it. (You won't be able to install the program without accepting the license agreement.)

More About Product Activation

As mentioned in the previous section, many software manufacturers, including Microsoft, require the user to activate the product online or by phone or fax within a specified number of days from the time the software was installed or first used. If the product isn't activated in that specified period, the software will cease to work, and will only prompt the user to activate it each time it is opened. As an example, a user must activate Microsoft Windows XP within 30 days of its first use. If the user does not or cannot activate the product (perhaps because it is a pirated copy), the operating system fails to function after the 30-day grace period. Product activation is part of Microsoft's effort to combat piracy and unauthorized use of its products.

> **NOTE To Activate Windows XP by Phone or Get More Information** To activate Windows XP by phone in the United States, call (888) 652–2342. For more information about product activation, read Microsoft Knowledge Base articles 302806 ("Description of Microsoft Product Activation") and 302878 ("Frequently Asked Questions About Microsoft Product Activation).

Product activation prevents users from installing the software on multiple computers, sharing the software with users who do not want to purchase the software, and casually copying the software.

Choosing Components

When you install an Office system (or other multifaceted application) such as Microsoft Office Professional Edition 2003, you'll be prompted to select an installation type and to decide what components to install. The components you choose can be installed in various ways, depending on the amount of resources on the computer.

Installation types for Office Professional Edition 2003 include Upgrade, Complete Install, Minimal Install, Typical Install, and Custom Install (all of which are common options). Figure 6-4 shows these options, as well as the option to browse to a new location to save the installation files.

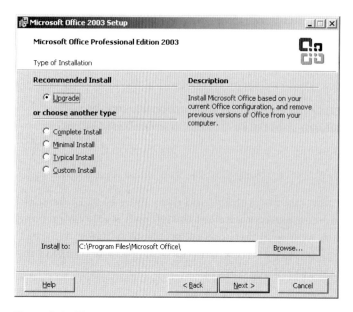

Figure 6-4   There are several installation types to choose from.

Components included in Office Professional Edition 2003 include Microsoft Office Word 2003, Excel 2003, PowerPoint 2003, Outlook 2003, Publisher 2003, and Access 2003. When installing Office Professional Edition 2003, choosing Custom Install is almost always the best choice, because you control what programs are installed, where they are installed, and what additional components are included with the installation.

When installing using the Custom Install, you can choose how to install each component:

■ **Run From My Computer**   Copies files and writes registry entries and shortcuts for the selected components. This allows the user to run the components locally, without having to insert the CD or access the files from a network drive.

■ **Run All From My Computer**   Copies files and writes registry entries and shortcuts for the selected components and all of their subfolders. This allows the user to run the components locally, without having to insert the CD or access the files from a network drive.

■ **Installed On First Use**   Does not copy the files to the user's hard disk until the first time the component is used. At that time the component is automatically copied either from the CD or a network location.

■ **Not Available**   Does not copy and will never copy the selected component.

Figure 6-5 shows a custom installation with all of the components selected to run from the computer. When performing an installation, you'll be prompted to make the appropriate choices.

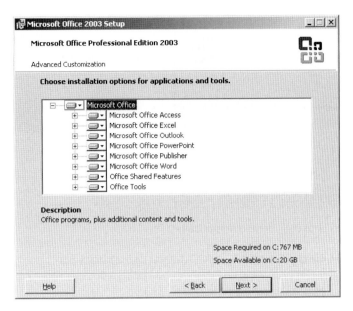

Figure 6-5   In this example, all components are selected to run from the computer.

Install to File Folder

You might be asked to configure the computer to store the installation files in a location other than the user's hard disk. The files might be stored on a different partition or a network drive. If company policy requires it or if a user's computer has multiple partitions, click Browse in the installation type stage (shown in Figure 6-4) and select the desired location.

Deleting Temporary, Backup, or Installation Files

Depending on the program you install, you might be prompted to delete backup files, temporary files, or installation files. Most of the time, temporary files are deleted automatically, but running Disk Cleanup after an installation isn't a bad idea if you didn't see any temporary files being deleted toward the end of the installation and feel they have been left on the computer.

Backup files are usually deleted automatically, too, but if you have enough disk space and are prompted to save or delete them, it won't hurt to leave them on the computer. Installation files can be deleted if you are prompted, but for the most part, accepting the defaults offered during the installation process is fine. When installing the Office System, it is recommended you keep the installation files. Figure 6-6 shows an example of the backup files being automatically deleted.

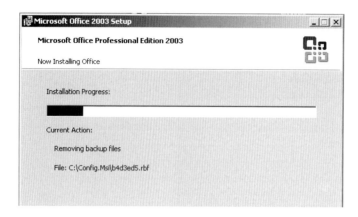

Figure 6-6   Deleting backup files is usually done automatically.

NOTE   Using the Program for the First Time   *When an end user opens a program or a component of it for the first time, she might be asked to input specific user information including e-mail address, name, business, and so on. Make sure you start the program and input this information before leaving the user's desk or ending the service call.*

Getting Required Updates After Installation

After installing Office Professional Edition 2003, you'll most likely be prompted to obtain the newest updates from the Microsoft Office Online Web site. If prompted, simply follow the directions for obtaining the updates; the updates will be downloaded and installed automatically.

▶ **Checking for updates manually**

An experienced technician will remember to manually check for updates often. Checking for updates on a schedule, for instance once a week or once a month, will help keep the computer safe and running properly. To check for Office updates manually, follow these steps:

1. Open any Office application (Excel, Word, PowerPoint, Access, and so on). From the Help menu, select Check For Updates. Figure 6-7 shows the option from Excel.

Figure 6-7   Manually check for updates using the Help menu in any Office application.

2. Internet Explorer automatically opens to *http://office.microsoft.com/ officeupdate/default.aspx*. Select Check For Updates.

3. If new updates are available, select the checkboxes for the ones you want to install and click Start Installation. Figure 6-8 shows the Office Update Web site with two updates available.

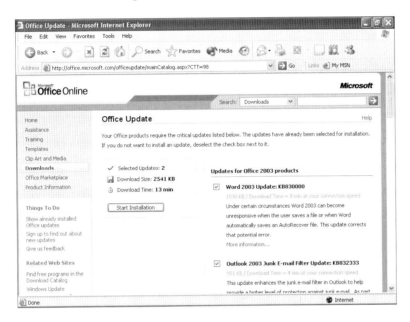

Figure 6-8   Here, two updates are available.

4. When prompted, click Next to confirm installation. Continue following the Office Update Installation Wizard prompts until the updates are installed. Depending on the updates selected, this might require you to insert the Microsoft Office CD, close running applications, and restart your computer on completion.

> **NOTE   Sign Up to Find out About New Updates**   *To receive notices about new updates for Office applications, visit http://office.microsoft.com/officeupdate/ default.aspx, and select Check for Updates. On the Office Update page, in the Things To Do area, select Sign Up To Find Out About New Updates.*

Common Installation Problems

Problems that occur during installations vary, but most are caused by a lack of hardware resources on the computer, compatibility problems, a bad CD, corrupt or inaccurate downloaded files, a user's failure to follow installation instructions, or an incorrect product ID or validation code. Table 6-2 lists some of the most common problems, possible causes, and their solutions.

Table 6-2   **Common Installation Problems**

Installation Problem	Possible Cause	Possible Solution
Disk space or RAM errors	The computer does not meet the minimum requirements documented for the software.	Install an additional drive or free up enough drive space, or add more physical memory (RAM).
Missing or corrupt files	The CD might be bad or downloaded files might be corrupt or missing.	Request a new CD from the manufacturer or download the files again.
Permission denied errors	An administrator might need to install the software or network policies prevent software installations.	Contact an administrator or log on as one.
Errors including Can't Copy File To Disk, Permission Denied, and Can't Access Hard Disk	Antivirus software might be preventing the application from installing.	Disable the antivirus software temporarily.
Product ID, validation code, or unlock code doesn't work	You might have made typographical errors when inputting the code; for example, you might have entered a zero instead of the letter O. In addition, validation codes might be case sensitive. The code might be invalid because the program has already been installed on another computer.	Try inputting the code again, substituting zeros for the letter O, and vice versa. Make sure you input the code using the correct case. If the code continues to fail, call the company's tech support line, ask an administrator for assistance, or read the license agreement to see if there are limitations on installations.
Activation failure	The activation might fail because the program has already been installed on another computer or because the computer is not connected to the Internet.	Read the license agreement to see if there are limitations on installations, connect to the Internet if necessary, or activate the product over the phone.
Installation hangs, gives illegal-operation errors, or installation fails	These problems can be caused any number of ways including the failure to close open programs before installing, failure to follow installation instructions, having incompatible hardware, or not having enough memory.	Try reinstalling and carefully follow the instructions shown. Access the company's Web site and search for installation help and support files if necessary. Many programs have known issues with specific hardware and operating systems.

Chances are that someone else has already seen any error message you see and a solution has been found and documented. Most manufacturers have Web pages that address these specific problems. If an installation problem persists, visit the Web site and see if a solution is available.

Using the Log Files

If the installation problems can't be solved by the techniques listed in the previous section or by researching the Microsoft Knowledge Base, consider taking a look at the log files that Office creates during installation; you can use these files to troubleshoot installation problems. There are four file types (depending on the installation), and these log files are automatically created in the \Temp folder on the user's hard disk:

- **Office Professional Edition 2003 Setup(000x).txt**   The Setup.exe log file

- **Office Professional Edition 2003 Setup(000x)_Task(000x).txt**   The Windows Installer log files

- **MSI*.log**   The Windows Installer log files

- **Offcln11.log**   A log file created if you've uninstalled the Office System previously

You can get more information about these files and how to read them from the Microsoft Knowledge Base article 826511, "HOW TO: Use an Office 2003 Setup Log File to Troubleshoot Setup Problems."

PERSONALIZING OFFICE FEATURES

Once you have installed a program, it needs to be personalized to suit the user who will be working with the program. Personalization comes in many forms, but for the most part users will want you to help them (or teach them) to do the following:

- Add, remove, and customize toolbars

- Customize menus and the commands shown on them

- Customize formatting options, print options, and editing options

- Change the default location of saved files or backup files

Adding, Removing, and Customizing Toolbars

Every application has a toolbar, others have two or three, and still others offer multiple toolbar choices. Both Microsoft Office Excel Professional Edition 2003 and Microsoft Office Word Professional Edition 2003 offer 20 toolbars. Users will not want all of the available toolbars on their screen at the same time, but they might want to add the ones they use often or remove the ones they don't use. In addition, users might want to customize their toolbars by using the available toolbar options (such as showing items on a single row or on two rows, or using large icons).

Common Toolbars

Some toolbars are fairly common and appear in multiple Office applications. To customize an application for a specific user in a specific department, you'll need to be aware of the most common options:

- **Standard**   This toolbar contains standard features, including options for opening a new or existing document, saving and printing, and using features such as spell check and cut, copy, and paste. This toolbar should be made available to most users.

- **Formatting**   This toolbar contains features including font selection and size; formatting options such as bold, italic, and underline; and justification and numbering options. This toolbar should be made available to most users, especially those who create presentations, graphics, or publications.

- **Web**   This toolbar contains options for accessing Favorites, a home page, and previously viewed network documents and Web sites. This toolbar should be made available to those whose work requires they access the Internet or network places frequently.

- **Task pane**   This toolbar offers a fast and easy way to obtain information about the Office program or component. This toolbar should be made available to new users and those who need to locate information from the Knowledge Base, newsgroups, or other technical help sites quickly.

- **Drawing**   This toolbar offers options to quickly draw shapes, and to insert WordArt, clip art, pictures, diagrams, or charts. This toolbar should be made available to users who create publications, company memos, or other documents with images, or otherwise need access to the drawing tools.

Figure 6-9 shows these toolbars (and the Menu bar) in Word 2003.

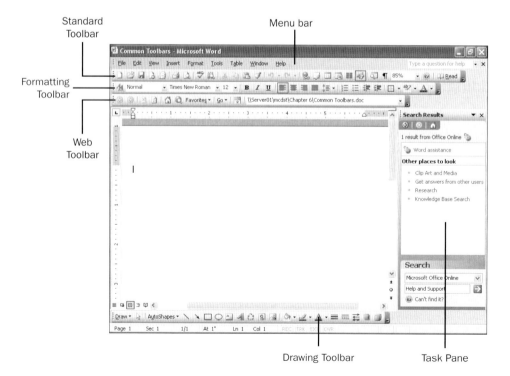

Figure 6-9   Common toolbars are shown here.

Toolbar Customizations

Toolbars can be added or removed, and toolbars can be customized. To add or remove toolbars in any Microsoft Office application, from the View menu, point to Toolbars, and select or clear any toolbar to show or hide it. Figure 6-10 shows an example. (You can also add or delete toolbars by right-clicking on the Menu bar.)

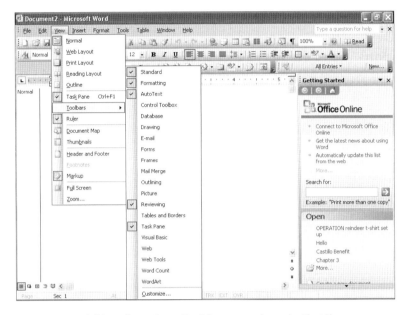

Figure 6-10   Add toolbars from the View menu by selecting them.

You can also customize toolbars, and there are several ways to access the customization options:

- Right-click the Menu bar, select Customize, and select the Options tab.

- On the View menu, select Toolbars, Customize, and then select the Options tab.

- On the Tools menu, select Customize, and select the Options tab.

In the Customize dialog box shown in Figure 6-11, several options are available:

- **Show Standard And Formatting Toolbars On Two Rows**   Selecting this check box places both toolbars on the same row to save space on the user's screen.

- **Always Show Full Menus**   Selecting this check box causes menus to always show all of their options, and does not show **personalized menus**.

- **Show Full Menus After A Short Delay**   Selecting this check box causes menus to show personalized menus, and then shows the full menu after a short delay.

- **Reset Menu And Toolbar Usage Data**   Clicking this button restores the default set of commands on the menus and toolbars, and undoes any explicit customization.

- **Large Icons**   Selecting this check box causes the icons on the toolbars to become larger.

- **List Font Names In Their Font**   Selecting this check box causes lists of font names to be displayed in their fonts. This makes selecting a font easier; the font list contains a preview of each font available.

- **Show ScreenTips On Toolbars**   Selecting this check box shows ScreenTips on toolbars.

- **Show Shortcut Keys In ScreenTips**   Selecting this check box shows shortcut keys in ScreenTips.

- **Menu Animations**   Selecting an option from this drop-down list enables menus to be shown using a specified animation: System Default, Random, Unfold, Slide, or Fade.

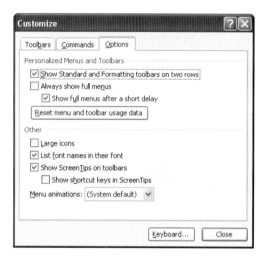

Figure 6-11   The Customize dialog box allows a user to personalize Office applications.

NOTE *Combining Toolbars   You can combine toolbars by dragging from their ends. The mouse pointer becomes a four-headed arrow when placed over the correct area for moving the toolbar.*

Further Customizing Menus, Toolbars, and Their Commands

Some end users will have very specific requests concerning the customization of their toolbars; they might ask you to make several adjustments including these:

- Adding commands to the Menu bar

- Adding commands to menu lists

- Rearranging the categories in the Menu bar

- Rearranging the commands in the menu lists

- Resetting the menus and toolbars to their defaults

The Customize dialog box offers these options.

Sample Service Call

A user in the graphics department of your company uses Microsoft Office PowerPoint 2003 to create company documentation and slides for presentations. He needs to have as much workspace as possible, and wants you to make several changes:

- Remove all of the toolbars and the Task pane.
- Add the commands Insert Table and Publish As Web Page to the Menu bar.
- Add the Draw Table command to the Tools menu list.
- Move the Can't Repeat or Repeat command to the top of the Edit menu.
- Move the Slide Show category on the Menu bar to the end of the Menu bar.

▶ **Maximizing workspace**

Here's how you'd make these changes:

1. On the Start menu, select All Programs, Microsoft Office, and select Microsoft Office PowerPoint 2003.

2. To remove the toolbars and Task pane, right-click the Menu bar and clear every item's check box.

3. Right-click the Menu bar and select Customize.

4. On the Commands tab, in the Categories pane, select Table.

5. In the Commands pane, select Table, and drag and drop it on the Menu bar.

6. In the Categories pane, select Web.

7. In the Commands pane, select Publish As Web Page, and drag and drop it on the Menu bar. The Menu bar now has the available commands added.

8. In the Categories pane, select Table.

9. In the Commands pane, drag the Draw Table command to the Tools menu list. Figure 6-12 shows how this will look. Drop the Draw Table command underneath the Spelling command.

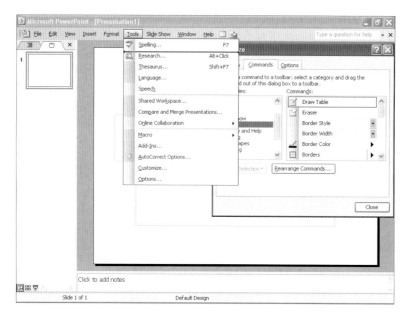

Figure 6-12   Add a command to a menu list by dragging.

► **Rearranging commands**

You can rearrange commands in the Menu bar and in the menu lists by using the Rearrange Commands dialog box. To make these changes, follow these steps:

1. In the Customize dialog box, click Rearrange Commands.

2. In the Rearrange Commands dialog box under Choose A Menu Or Toolbar To Rearrange, verify that Menu Bar is selected and, from the Menu Bar drop-down list, select Edit.

3. In the Controls area, select Can't Repeat. Click Move Up to move this item to the top of the list.

4. Under Choose A Menu Or Toolbar To Rearrange, click Toolbar. Menu Bar will be selected.

5. In the Controls area, select Slide Show. Click Move Down four times to move this to the end of the Menu Bar list.

6. Note that Reset is available in the Rearrange Command dialog box. Click Close. Click Close to exit the Customize dialog box. Figure 6-13 shows the result.

Figure 6-13   A customized Menu bar is shown here.

Customizing Using the Options Dialog Box

There are literally thousands of ways to customize the various Office applications in the Office System. Many of these options are available through the Tools menu and the Options choice. The Options dialog box configuration choices and tabs differ depending on the program selected. You should familiarize yourself with the available options in all of the Office applications as well as any third-party applications you see regularly.

Figures 6-14, 6-15, and 6-16 show various Options dialog boxes. Although there isn't enough room to cover all of the options for each Office application in this chapter, we cover some of the more common options through the Word 2003 Options dialog box.

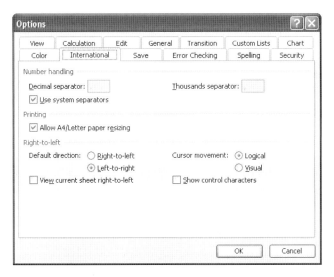

Figure 6-14   The Excel Options dialog box offers some familiar and customizable options.

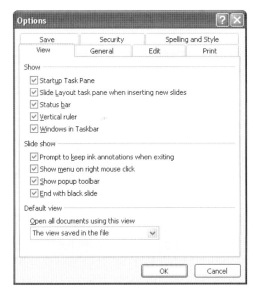

Figure 6-15   The PowerPoint Options dialog box offers some familiar and customizable options.

Figure 6-16   The Word Options dialog box offers some familiar and customizable options.

> **NOTE**   *Options Dialog Boxes*   In the remaining sections of this chapter, Word 2003 is used as the default application for detailing the options for configuring Office applications. Other components and programs offer comparable options and are used similarly.

View Options

The options on the View tab of the Word 2003 Options dialog box are shown in Figure 6-16. You can make many customizations with the options on this tab. Common options users might want you to modify include these:

- **Startup Task Pane**   The Startup Task Pane is the pane on the right side that offers links to Microsoft Office Online, search options, and a list of recently viewed documents.

- **Tab Characters, Spaces, Paragraph Marks, Hidden Text, Optional Hyphens**   Formatting marks can be shown for tab characters, spaces, paragraph marks, and more.

- **Drawings**   Clearing the Drawings check box hides objects created with the Word drawing tools to speed up the display of documents that contain drawings.

- **Wrap To Window**   Wraps text to the document window, making it easier to read on the screen.

> **NOTE**   *Familiarize Yourself with Other Options*   As with the remaining sections, familiarize yourself with all of the available options. To see what each option does, click the question mark in the top right corner of the Options dialog box., and then click any option with the mouse.

General Options

You can make many customizations with the options on the General tab. Common options users might want you to modify include these:

- **Provide Feedback With Animation and Provide Feedback With Sound**   Users might want to use sound (by selecting the Provide Feedback With Sound check box) or not view animations (by clearing the Provide Feedback With Animation check box) when using Word 2003.

- **Help For WordPerfect Users**   Selecting this check box allows WordPerfect users to view Help files.

- **Allow Background Open Of Web Pages**   Users might want to open Hypertext Markup Language (HTML) files and still use Word to complete other tasks.

- **Allow Starting In Reading Layout**   Users might not want documents to automatically open in Reading layout.

Edit Options

You can also make many customizations with the options on the Edit tab. Common options users might want you to modify include these:

- **Typing Replaces Selection**   Deletes the selected text when you begin to type. Clear this checkbox to insert new text in front of the selected text instead.

- **Picture Editor**   Microsoft Office Word is the default picture editor, but you can change this option if you have another picture editor installed.

- **Enable Click And Type**   Click and Type allows a user to insert text, graphics, tables, and other items in a blank area of a document by double-clicking. This might not be desirable.

Print Options

You can make many customizations with the options on the Print tab. Common options users might want you to modify include these:

- **Draft Output**   This setting prints the document with minimal formatting, which speeds up the print process. Not all printers support this function.

- **Reverse Print Order**   This setting prints pages in reverse order.

- **Include With Document; Field Codes**   This setting prints codes, Extensible Markup Language (**XML) tags**, background colors and images, and more.

- **Default Tray**   Configure a default print tray for printers that support this feature.

Save Options

You can make many customizations with the options on the Save tab. Common options users might want you to modify include these:

- **Always Create Backup Copy**   Select this check box to create a backup copy of each document.

- **Allow Background Saves**   Documents are automatically saved in the background every 10 minutes. A user might want to disable this to avoid saving changes to a file before she is ready.

- **Save Word Files As**   You can save Word files as Word documents, XML documents, single-file Web pages, Web pages, or document templates.

File Locations

You can make many customizations with the options on the File Locations tab. Common options users might want you to modify include these:

- Changing the location where documents are stored

- Changing the location where clip art is stored

- Changing the location of **AutoRecover files**

Making changes on this tab requires more than selecting or clearing a check box, or making a selection from a drop-down list. To modify the location of saved files, click Modify. In the Modify Location dialog box, browse to the new location and click OK. Note that you can create a new folder in the desired location by selecting the Create New Folder icon in the Modify Location dialog box. A user might want to change the default location of saved files to make backing up documents easier, or to make locating AutoRecover files more intuitive.

> **NOTE**   **Lost Files**   When a user reports that his computer or application shuts down unexpectedly and a working file was lost, browse to the location of the AutoRecover files. You will almost always find the last saved version there.

Security Options

You can make many customizations with the options on the Security tab. Common options users might want you to modify include these:

- Creating a password to open a file and setting advanced **encryption** options

- Creating a password to modify the file

- Configuring the file for read-only

- Removing personal information from the file's properties when the file is saved

These options and others can be used to keep a user's files and information safe even when others have access to the files.

CONFIGURING PROOFING TOOLS

Proofing tools are components of Microsoft Word and other applications that allow users to check their spelling and grammar in their own language or another; create and use AutoCorrect, AutoSummarize, AutoFormat, and AutoText; use configured dictionaries; and work with fonts and localized templates. In this final section, you'll learn how to configure these tools for end users.

Proofing in Other Languages

The Office System offers users the ability to edit documents in multiple languages. Word 2003 can automatically detect many languages including (but not limited to) Chinese, French, German, Italian, Japanese, Russian, and Spanish. Editing documents in various languages requires that you install the spelling and language tools for the language from the Office System Language Settings, turn on Automatic Language Detection, and set spelling and grammar options.

▶ **Installing spelling and grammar tools for a language**

To install the spelling and grammar tools for a specific language, follow these steps:

1. Click Start, point to All Programs, point to Microsoft Office, point to Microsoft Office Tools, and select Microsoft Office 2003 Language Settings.

2. Select the Enabled Languages tab.

3. In the Available Languages dialog box, select the language to enable. Click Add.

4. If any Office programs are running, you must quit and restart all open Office applications to apply the changes. Click Yes if prompted.

   NOTE   Limited Functionality   *Depending on the operating system and languages selected, you might only have limited functionality of the editing tools. If this is the case, you'll be prompted on how to gain full functionality in these languages.*

▶ **Turning on Automatic Language Detection**

Once you've installed the spelling and grammar tools, you need to turn on Automatic Language Detection by following these steps:

1. Open Word 2003 and, from the Tools menu, point to Language, and then select Set Language.

2. Select the Detect Language Automatically check box, as shown in Figure 6-17, and click OK.

Figure 6-17   You can configure Word to detect language automatically by configuring preferences in the Language dialog box.

▶ **Setting spelling and grammar options**

To set the spelling and grammar options for the new language, follow these steps:

1. In Word 2003, from the Tools menu, select Options.

2. On the Spelling & Grammar tab, configure the language options as desired. Click OK.

To edit a document in the new language, open the document in Word 2003. Word automatically scans the document for spelling errors, and denotes them as necessary. If additional proofing tools are required, you'll be prompted with a dialog box.

> **NOTE** **Microsoft Proofing Tools** Microsoft Office System Proofing Tools is an add-in package that contains the proofing tools that Microsoft makes for more than 30 languages. It includes fonts, spelling and grammar checkers, AutoCorrect lists, AutoSummarize rules, translation dictionaries and, for Asian Languages, **input method editors** (IMEs). These proofing tools are available at http://www.shop.microsoft.com.

Troubleshooting Automatic Language Detection

Several things can go wrong when using Automatic Language Detection, including common problems that occur when Microsoft doesn't support the language or when Word doesn't correctly detect the language (which are addressed in the Microsoft Office Word Help files), and other less common problems (as detailed in various Microsoft Knowledge Base articles). For most issues, a technician's best resources are the Microsoft Word Help files and the Microsoft Knowledge Base. Almost any problem you will encounter while using Automatic Language Detection is addressed in these two areas.

Some of the Microsoft Office Word Help files you might be interested in reading include the following:

■ Troubleshoot Automatic Language Detection

■ Languages Word Can Detect Automatically

■ Automatically Switch Keyboard Languages

■ Automatically Correct Text As You Type In Another Language

■ Install System Support For Multiple Languages

■ Enable Editing Of Multiple Languages

Some Knowledge Base articles you might be interested in reading include the following:

■ 292106: Changes to the Default Language Settings Are Not Retained

■ 831030: Cannot Install German Language MUI Files

■ 831591: "The Dictionary For This Language Was Not Found" Error Message When You Try to Use Handwriting on the Language Bar

Familiarize yourself with these articles and other common problems so you can resolve service calls that revolve around these problems quickly and effectively.

AutoSummarize

Word 2003 can be used to automatically summarize a document. Users can choose to have Word 2003 highlight the important aspects and main points of the document in the document itself, insert a summary at the beginning of the document, create a new document and put the summary there, or create a summary in the document and hide everything else.

▶ **Automatically summarizing a document**

To automatically summarize a document, follow these steps:

1. Open the document in Word 2003.

2. On the Tools menu, select AutoSummarize.

3. Select the type of summary you want. There are four options:

    ❑ Highlight Key Points

    ❑ Insert An Executive Summary Or Abstract At The Top Of The Document

    ❑ Create A New Document And Put The Summary There

    ❑ Hide Everything But The Summary Without Leaving The Original Document

4. In the Percent Of Original box, type or select the level of detail to include in the summary. Using higher numbers includes more detail; lower numbers include less. There are several preconfigured options: 10 Sentences, 20 Sentences, 100 Words Or Less, 500 Words or Less, 10%, 25%, 50%, and 75%. Once you make a selection, the Summary and Original Document figures change to reflect your selection.

5. If you don't want AutoSummarize to replace your existing keywords and comments, in the AutoSummarize dialog box, clear the Update Document Statistics check box.

6. Click OK.

AutoSummarize is an extremely powerful tool that allows users to create summaries of their work quickly. In addition, users who receive long documents can use AutoSummarize to view the key points before reading it, review key points before a meeting, or create notes for study. When visiting a new user's desk, ask if she is familiar with this feature.

Understanding Templates

When you create documents, they contain specific fonts, font styles, and font sizes so that headings, paragraphs, notes, tips, numbered and bulleted lists, summaries, and other components of the document are easily recognizable. Templates can also contain AutoText entries, page layout information, and **macros**. All documents created in Word 2003 use the Word Normal template by default. Templates define what a document, publication, Web site, e-mail message, or fax looks like when published, printed, or viewed. Templates also define what options are available to the creator of the document (macros, font sizes and styles, and so on).

You can access and configure templates in the Templates And Add-Ins dialog box (from the Tools menu, select Templates And Add-Ins). Templates created specifically for a type of publication can be attached to any working document. You can also modify templates by opening the template, making changes, and resaving the template.

▶ **Attaching a template**

To attach a localized or global template, follow these steps:

1. In Word 2003, on the Tools menu, select Templates And Add-Ins.

2. On the Templates tab, click Attach to attach a document template. The template listed is the template currently attached to the active document.

3. In the Attach Template dialog box, select the template to add. You might have to browse for the template. Click Open.

4. To automatically update the document styles, select the Automatically Update Document Styles check box. Click OK.

When you modify a template, the template is changed permanently (or until it is changed again). These changes affect any new documents created using the template.

▶ **Modifying an existing template**

With that in mind, to modify an existing template, follow these steps:

1. On the File menu, select Open, and locate the template to modify.

2. Make any changes desired to the template's text and graphics, styles, formatting, and so on.

3. On the File menu, select Save.

Spelling and Grammar

End users create documents and end users edit documents. Any end user can tell you that creating documents involves much more than typing words on a page, just as editing documents involves much more than checking spelling and grammar. As a desktop technician, you'll be called on to help end users work smarter and faster by teaching them to use the available editing tools. These tools can make both creating and editing documents easier, and there are many tools available.

AutoCorrect is one such tool. It can be used to automatically correct spelling errors as a user types, capitalize days of the week, capitalize the first letter in sentences, and more. You can use AutoFormat to automatically apply styles such as bulleted lists, fractions, and hyperlinks. AutoText enables you to automatically complete text entries such as Dear Madam or Sir, Special Delivery, To Whom It May Concern, and even personal entries created by the user.

In addition to these tools, users can add words to the dictionaries and configure spelling and grammar options. Users can even add words to the AutoCorrect list so the dictionary recognizes them (these can include symbols, too).

AutoCorrect

You can configure AutoCorrect options from the AutoCorrect dialog box or by right-clicking on the misspelled word. Adding an entry to the AutoCorrect list using either procedure places the misspelled word in the AutoCorrect list in case the word is ever misspelled again. When a misspelling occurs, the word is automatically corrected while the user types. Figure 6-18 shows an example of adding a misspelled word to the AutoCorrect list by right-clicking it.

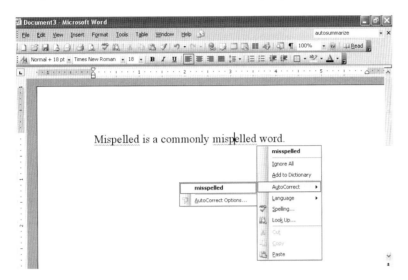

Figure 6-18   You can add AutoCorrect entries by right-clicking.

You can also add AutoCorrect entries using the AutoCorrect dialog box. To add words in this manner, follow these steps:

1. From the Tools menu, select AutoCorrect Options.

2. In the Replace area, type the word that is commonly misspelled.

3. In the With text box, type the desired replacement.

4. Click OK.

> **NOTE Work Faster and Smarter**   Most people have words they commonly misspell. Take a few minutes to teach your users how to add their troublesome words to the AutoCorrect list. They'll work faster and smarter, which has several benefits, one being a happier end user.

AutoFormat

AutoFormat options allow text to be formatted while the user types and creates documents. For instance, when you use bullets or numbered lists, Word 2003 automatically adds the next bullet or the proper number in the list. Straight quotes can be replaced with smart quotes (the quotes point in the right direction), and Internet or network paths can automatically be configured as hyperlinks in the documents. All of these formatting options and more can be selected or cleared in the Auto-Correct dialog box on the AutoFormat and AutoFormat As You Type tabs.

AutoText

AutoText is a feature of Microsoft Office that allows a user to type in the first few letters of a common word or entry such as Best Regards, Attention, or Dear Mom and Dad, and have the rest of the word or phrase offered so the user does not have to type the entire entry. Figure 6-19 shows an example. To add the word or complete the entry, the user simply presses ENTER.

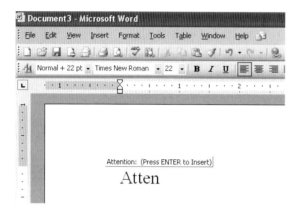

Figure 6-19 AutoText offers the entire word or phrase when applicable.

▶ **Adding AutoText entries**

Users can add their own entries to the AutoText entry list by following these steps:

1. On the Tools menu, select AutoCorrect Options, and select the AutoText tab.

2. In the Enter AutoText Entries Here text box, type the entry to add. This might be a company name, a user name, a Web site, or a word or words the user types often.

3. Click Add to add the entry to the AutoText database, and then click OK to close the AutoCorrect dialog box.

AutoText entries are perfect for long words, phrases, or titles that a user types often. Consider adding a user's job title, department name, Web address, company name, or address.

Adding Words to the Dictionary

You access the dictionary from the Options dialog box on the Spelling & Grammar tab. You can add entries to the glossary for words that Microsoft Office applications think are misspelled. For instance, user names; zip codes; company names; acronyms such as DVDs, CDs, ISBN, or ASAP; and Web addresses are often underlined as misspelled words. Adding these entries to the dictionary not only causes them not to be underlined in a document the next time they are used, but it also keeps them from being marked as misspellings in Outlook, Excel, PowerPoint, or other Office applications.

▶ **Adding an entry to the dictionary**

To add an entry to the default dictionary, follow these steps:

1. In Word 2003, on the Tools menu, select Options, and select the Spelling & Grammar tab.

2. Click Custom Dictionaries.

3. In the Custom Dictionaries dialog box, select the dictionary to which you want to add the entry, and select Modify.

4. In the dictionary's dialog box, in the Word area, type the word to add. Click Add to add the word to the dictionary. Click OK to close the dictionary's dialog box, click OK to close the Custom Dictionaries dialog box, and click OK to close the Options dialog box.

It's easier to inform users to add words to the dictionary by right-clicking them in their documents. If the user knows that a word in a document is a real word and wants to add it to the dictionary, he can right-click the word and select Add To Dictionary. The word is then added.

Spelling and Grammar Options

There are several spelling and grammar options, and these are set in the Options dialog box on the Spelling & Grammar tab, shown in Figure 6-20. End users might want you to change the default options to suit their personal needs.

Figure 6-20 Configure spelling and grammar options from the Spelling & Grammar tab.

Table 6-3 lists some common end user requests and the best way to resolve them. Each solution is achieved using the spelling and grammar options in the Options dialog box. Make sure you are familiar with all of the options.

Table 6-3   **Common Spelling and Grammar Requests and Resolutions**

Request	Resolution
I don't want to see my spelling errors as I type. It's distracting; I'll check the document when I'm finished with it.	Select the Hide Spelling Errors In This Document check box.
I type using a lot of uppercase letters, but the spell check never checks them.	Clear the Ignore Words In Uppercase check box.
I don't want to see grammatical errors as I type. It's distracting; I'll check the document when I'm finished with it.	Clear the Check Grammar As You Type check box.
I need to see the readability statistics for my documents once a grammar check is complete, including the average number of sentences per paragraph, number of passive sentences, and what grade level the document is written for.	Select the Show Readability Statistics check box.

SUMMARY

■ To install an application successfully, verify that the application is compatible with the operating system and the computer hardware and that the computer meets minimum or recommended requirements. Verify that the proper licenses are readily available.

■ To personalize Office applications, add, remove, or customize toolbars, the Menu bar, and the menu lists.

■ To further personalize Office applications, configure options in the Options dialog box including print, view, save, edit, and security options.

■ To create an Office application that works for the user, configure proofing tools including spelling and grammar, templates, and AutoSummarize options.

REVIEW QUESTIONS

1. A user wants you to install Office Professional Edition 2003 on his computer. He uses Windows XP Home Edition, has a Pentium III processor, 512 MB of RAM, 40 GB of free hard disk space, and a generic plug-and-play Super VGA monitor capable of 800-by-600 resolution. Which of the following will need to be upgraded (if any) so that the program will run well (thus meeting recommended requirements)? Choose all that apply.

   a. Upgrade from Windows XP Home to Windows XP Professional.

   b. Upgrade to a Pentium 4 or equivalent.

   c. Add more RAM.

   d. Partition the hard disk into two 20 GB sections. Office cannot work with large disk drives.

   e. Install Service Packs 1 and 2.

   f. Upgrade to a flat-screen monitor or a monitor with resolution that can be configured at 1024 by 768.

   g. Nothing needs to be upgraded.

2. The following table lists some common installation problems and their causes. To answer this question, match the installation problem on the left with the likely cause on the right.

1. The program installed correctly but fails online activation.	a) The program was probably downloaded from the Internet and the download was not successful.
2. The error Can't Copy File To Disk prevents installation from starting or completing.	b) The computer doesn't meet minimum hardware requirements.

3. The installation of the program stops and an error message appears that states some of the downloaded files are missing or corrupt.

c) An antivirus program is running.

4. Installation stops, hangs, or quits.

d) There might be a typographical error created by the user.

5. The validation code won't validate the software.

e) The program has already been installed on another computer and licensing restrictions and requirements are preventing the successful installation of the program.

3. An employee in the marketing department of your company works in Excel most of the day, but she spends an equal amount of time on the Internet. There, she obtains information from Web sites to create quotes, obtain product information, and get competitors' prices. She's also pretty new to Excel, and often has to access the Help and Support files. You want to help her work faster and smarter. What can you suggest? Choose all that apply.

   a. Add the Web toolbar to Excel.

   b. Customize the toolbars and reset the menu and toolbar usage data.

   c. Add the Task pane to the Excel interface.

   d. Add the Formula Auditing toolbar to Excel.

4. An employee in the graphics department of your company uses Microsoft Office PowerPoint Professional Edition 2003 to create documentation for company meetings with prospective clients. He reports that when he accesses a font from the font drop-down list in the Formatting toolbar, all of the fonts are listed but he can't tell what the font looks like by looking at it in the list. He'd like the list of fonts to appear using the font each represents. For instance, Arial uses Arial font, Century uses Century font, Lucida Sans uses Lucida Sans font, and so on. Is this possible and, if so, what needs to be done?

   a. It is not possible.

   b. It is possible only if the Microsoft Advanced Font Add-In is downloaded and installed.

   c. It is an option in the Customize dialog box on the Options tab.

   d. It is an option in the Fonts toolbar.

5. A user reports that each time she opens Word 2003 the Startup Pane appears, and each time she clicks the X in the top right corner of the pane to close it. She wants to avoid this extra step each time she opens Word and configure the pane so that it does not open every time she opens the program. What do you tell her to do? Select all correct procedures.

   a. With Word open, from the View menu, clear Task Pane.

   b. With Word open, from the View menu, point to Toolbars, and clear Task Pane.

   c. In the Task pane, click the X in the top right corner. From the View menu, point to Toolbars, and verify Task Pane is cleared.

   d. From the Tools menu, select Options. On the View tab, clear the Startup Task Pane check box.

6. A user has created a confidential document in Excel 2003 and needs to configure security settings for the file. He reports that the document must be protected at all costs. How should you instruct the user to configure security settings for the file? Select all that apply.

   a. Create a password to open the file.

   b. Create a second password to modify the file.

   c. Configure advanced encryption.

   d. Remove personal information from the file's properties when saving.

7. You support end users who create documents in Word 2003 on Windows XP Professional machines. They often call with problems relating to proofing, editing, and summarizing documents. Common service calls are listed on the left; match them with the appropriate solution on the right.

1. A user is late for a meeting and needs to create a cheat sheet containing the main points in the document he received last week. What should he do?	a) Configure AutoCorrect.
2. A user confides in you that she is not a good speller, and that she always misspells the same words over and over. Instead of right-clicking and choosing the correct spelling of these words time after time, she'd like to know if she can set Word 2003 to automatically correct these words each time she misspells them. What should she do?	b) Configure AutoFormat.

3. A user creates documents that contain hyperlinks to network resources. These documents are posted on the company's internal Web site and users access them when they need help and support. The user complains that he has to manually create the hyperlinks and wants Word to create them automatically. What should he do?

c) Use AutoSummarize and create a summary that highlights the key points.

4. A user is writing a children's book and several of the words she is using aren't real words. She wants to add these words to the dictionary, but the underlining throughout the document makes it hard to concentrate. What should she do?

d) Configure spelling options on the Spelling & Grammar tab.

CASE SCENARIOS

Scenario 6-1: Personalizing Microsoft Word

The company you work for is named Contoso Pharmaceuticals. Users complain that every time they create a document in Word, PowerPoint, Excel, or another Office application, the company name is underlined because it is believed to be misspelled. Users want this behavior to stop. In addition, users want the entire company name typed automatically each time they type in the first few letters of it. They are tired of typing the words *Contoso Pharmaceuticals* every time they want to type the company name. What should you tell each user in the company to do?

1. Add the word *Contoso* to the dictionary. Add *Contoso Pharmaceuticals* to the AutoText list.

2. Add the word *Contoso* to the AutoText list. Add *Contoso Pharmaceuticals* to the AutoCorrect list.

3. Add both *Contoso* and *Pharmaceuticals* to the AutoCorrect list.

4. Add both *Contoso* and *Pharmaceuticals* to the AutoText list.

Scenario 6-2: Understanding Microsoft Office Licensing Requirements and Minimum Requirements

A small business owner wants you to install Microsoft Office Professional Edition 2003 on the computers in his office. He reports he has 10 computers, three of which use Windows 98, two of which use Windows Me, and five that use Windows XP Professional. They are configured as a workgroup. Each of these computers runs Microsoft Office 2000. He purchased five Microsoft Office CDs because a friend told him that he installed his Microsoft Office CD on his desktop PC and his laptop, and they both run like a charm. He figures he'll just use the five CDs to install Office System Professional Edition 2003 on the 10 computers. Where is the flaw in his logic? Pick two.

1. There is a problem with the licensing requirements. Although a user can install Office Professional Edition 2003 on a desktop PC and a laptop, it cannot be installed on two different computers for two different users.

2. Office Professional Edition 2003 can only be installed on Windows XP computers.

3. Office Professional Edition 2003 cannot be installed on the Windows 98 or Windows Me computers.

4. Office Professional Edition 2003 cannot be installed on workgroup computers, only on computers in a domain. He'll need to purchase Microsoft Office Standard Edition 2003.

CHAPTER 7
TROUBLESHOOT OFFICE APPLICATIONS

Upon completion of this chapter, you will be able to:

■ Add missing toolbars, features, and components

■ Use Microsoft Office Online to learn to format text data

■ Link and embed sounds and images

■ Create and troubleshoot macros

■ Configure macro security and enable macro virus protection

■ Resolve issues with attachments, options, and encoding in Outlook Express

■ Troubleshoot Outlook 2003 components

■ Recover lost files

■ Obtain Office Updates

The goal of this chapter is to teach you to resolve end-user requests regarding Microsoft Office applications including Word 2003, Excel 2003, PowerPoint 2003, and Outlook 2003. You'll learn how to resolve problems with these applications, including using Microsoft Office Online. You'll also learn how to perform ordinary tasks in each application, and resolve common end-user requests. In addition to these Office applications, Microsoft Outlook Express is covered.

Although it would be impossible to detail all aspects of each of the Office applications effectively in the space provided in this chapter, be aware that you should be familiar with each application's toolbars, features, and components; know how to recover lost files; and be able to use and troubleshoot the main components of each application. You should also know how to use the available online tools to resolve issues that you are not familiar with, and to learn new skills.

> **NOTE** **Learn as Much as You Can** *The more you know about these applications, the better technician you will be. After finishing this course, spend some time concentrating on the applications. Make sure you have at least intermediate functionality when using each of them.*

WORD 2003

In Chapter 6, "Install and Configure Office Applications," you learned to install and configure Word 2003. Some of the configuration tasks included customizing the toolbars, menus, and their commands; setting personalization options; and configuring proofing tools for spelling and grammar. In this section, you learn how to troubleshoot this application.

Once end users begin using Word 2003 and start performing configuration tasks on their own, creating documents with sounds and images, using macros, and accessing some of the more advanced features available in the application, they'll surely run across problems using them. Although troubleshooting tasks will vary, in this section you'll learn how to resolve some of the more common ones, including these:

- Locate and add missing toolbars, features, and components.
- Format bullets and numbered lists, use AutoFormat, change the language format of text, and more using Microsoft Office Online.
- Embed and link images and sounds.
- Recover lost files.

Missing Toolbars, Features, and Components

As end users start tweaking the Word 2003 interface, you'll start receiving calls about missing toolbars, features, and components. Users might accidentally hide or customize a toolbar so that the default options are absent, move or resize toolbars, or remove components and features, thus making them unavailable. You'll need to be able to field these types of calls and locate missing interface items.

Restoring the Defaults

When a computer is transferred to another user or when users simply request that the changes they've made be removed, you'll need to restore the defaults to the menus, buttons, menu choices, and default toolbars. These changes can affect both menus and toolbars. Table 7-1 details how to make three basic changes and reset defaults.

Table 7-1   **Restore Defaults**

To Restore Original Settings for	Perform These Steps
A menu	1. From the Tools menu, select Customize, and select the Commands tab. 2. Click Rearrange Commands. 3. In the Rearrange Commands dialog box select Menu Bar, and from the Menu Bar drop-down list, select the menu to reset. 4. Click Reset. 5. In the Reset Changes Made To 'File' Menu For drop-down list, select Normal and click OK. Click Close, and click Close to exit.

Table 7-1 **Restore Defaults**

To Restore Original Settings for	Perform These Steps
A built-in toolbar	1. From the Tools menu, select Customize, and select the Toolbars tab. 2. In the Toolbars list box, select the toolbar to restore. Click Reset. 3. In the Reset Changes Made To 'Control Toolbox' Toolbar For drop-down list, select Normal and click OK. Click Close to exit.
All default toolbars and menu commands	1. From the Tools menu, select Customize, and select the Options tab. 2. Click Reset Menu And Toolbar Usage Data. 3. Click Yes to configure the menu and toolbar reset, and then click Close to close the Customize dialog box.

You can also restore original settings for a built-in toolbar button or menu command using similar techniques. Remember, you can show or hide any toolbar by right-clicking an empty area of the Menu bar and selecting or deselecting it, or resize or move a toolbar by dragging it.

Creating a Custom Toolbar

When users report that the default toolbars they use and access just don't suit their purposes, you can guide the users through creating a custom toolbar. Custom toolbars allow users to add their own buttons, add various built-in menus, and even create a custom name for the new toolbar. This is the perfect solution for users who are constantly tweaking the default toolbars and menus.

▶ **Creating a custom toolbar**

To create a custom toolbar for an end user, follow these steps:

1. From the Tools menu, select Customize, and select the Toolbars tab.

2. Click New.

3. In the New Toolbar dialog box, in the Toolbar Name text box, type a name for the new toolbar.

4. From the Make Toolbar Available To drop-down list, select the template or document in which you want to make the toolbar available. Click OK.

5. Select the Commands tab.

6. To add a button, select a category in the Categories list box, and drag the command you want to the new toolbar.

7. To add a built-in menu, select Built-In Menus in the Categories list box, and drag the menu you want to the new toolbar. Figure 7-1 shows an example of a customized toolbar.

Figure 7-1   This customized toolbar has several formatting options.

8. Click Close when finished, and drag the new toolbar to an area of the interface to dock it.

Adding or Removing Components

When you originally install Office, certain components are installed with it. If components are missing or are no longer needed, you'll have to locate the original source files (they might be on a network server, CD-ROM, or mapped drive), and use the Windows Add or Remove Programs feature in Control Panel to add or remove them.

Components for Word 2003 include the following:

- **.NET Programmability Support**   Allows for programmability with **Microsoft .NET Framework** version 1.1.

- **Help**   Help for Microsoft Word.

- **Repair Broken Text**   Repairs documents that display text incorrectly (Eastern European and complex script languages only).

- **Wizards And Templates**   Includes various wizards and templates for Word.

- **Address Book**   Provides tools for integrating the Microsoft Exchange Personal Address Book and Microsoft Office Outlook Address Book.

- **Page Border Art**   Includes page borders to enhance documents.

▶ Adding or removing components

When components are missing or not needed, you'll need to add or remove them from Control Panel by following these steps:

1. Open Control Panel, and open Add Or Remove Programs.

2. Select Microsoft Office Professional Edition 2003 (or whatever Office version you have), and click Change.

3. On the Microsoft Office 2003 Setup page, select Add Or Remove Features. Click Next.

4. On the Custom Setup page, clear the check boxes for any applications you'd like to remove (if applicable), select the check boxes for any applications you'd like to install, leave the others selected, select the Choose Advanced Customization Of Applications check box, and click Next.

5. Expand the tree for Microsoft Office Word. (You can use this same technique for components of other Office applications.) Components not installed will have a red X beside them. Figure 7-2 shows an example.

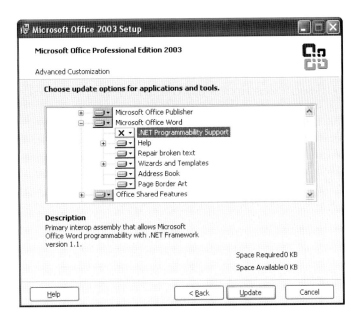

Figure 7-2   Add missing components using Add or Remove Programs in Control Panel.

6. To add a component, click the down arrow beside it, and select Run All From My Computer. That option will be added. To remove a component, click the down arrow beside it and select Not Available. Figure 7-3 shows an example.

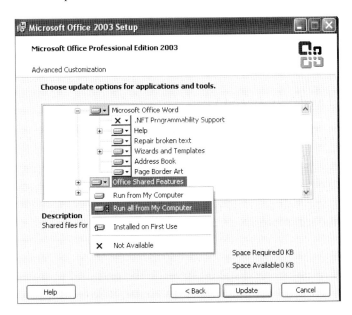

Figure 7-3   Select which components to add or remove from the component's drop-down list.

7. Click Update, and click OK when finished. Click Close to close Add Or Remove Programs.

You might also need to add Office Tools components such as Microsoft Office Picture Manager, Equation Editor, Office Binder Support, Research Explorer Bar, or others. You can view these components and information about them by expanding the Office Tools tree on the Advanced Customization page. When you select a component, you'll see a description listed in the Description area.

MORE INFO **For More Information**   There is a wealth of free information on Office 2003 in the Help files. Just type any query in the Task pane and look through the search results for items that start with Training>. Selecting a Training link takes you to Microsoft Office Online, where a free course automatically starts. There's even a friendly voice to guide you through it. Work through these free training courses in your spare time, and urge your end users to do the same.

Text Formatting

Formatting queries are fairly common in an office environment. Although most users are able to format their own text, you'll be called on to resolve advanced text formatting issues when they arise. These calls might be for you to teach an end user to perform a task, which might require you to search for the procedure using the Task pane and Microsoft Office Online. The queries might also be for you to resolve known issues, which will require you to visit the Knowledge Base or TechNet. As a desktop technician, you should be prepared for anything.

Because queries relating to formatting will be varied, it is far easier to detail where to find answers than how to resolve specific issues. In the following section, you'll learn a little about both.

NOTE **Internet Connectivity**   The Microsoft Office Online Help and Support files work only if the user is connected to the Internet. The rest of this section makes this assumption.

Customizing Bulleted and Numbered Lists

Most users know how to create bulleted and numbered lists, but they might need help customizing the number format, number style, or even the number's position in the list to meet a company's style requirements for Web pages, publications, or documents. Although *you* might have an idea how to do this, walking the user through finding the answer and following a written procedure will be the best solution in the long run. You will not only resolve the call, but most likely prevent some future calls from the same user.

▶ Customizing a list

To customize a bulleted or numbered list, and to teach the end user to use Microsoft Office Online Help and Support at the same time, follow this procedure:

1. Open Word 2003 and the working document.

2. From the View menu, verify that the Task Pane is selected.

3. In the Task pane, click the down arrow and select Help. The Task pane with Help selected is shown in Figure 7-4.

Figure 7-4   The Word Help Task pane offers a wealth of information.

4. Under Assistance, in the Search For text box, type **Customize Bullets And Numbering** and press ENTER on the keyboard or click the green arrow beside the text box.

5. From the Search Results offered, select Modify Bulleted Or Numbered List Formats.

   NOTE   Other Help   Notice you can also choose Troubleshoot Bulleted And Numbered Lists, Restore A Customized List Format To Its Original Setting, Create A Multiple-Level Picture Bullet List, and Convert Bullets To Numbers And Vice Versa.

6. From the Microsoft Office Word Help window, follow the directions offered for modifying any bulleted or numbered list. These procedures cover using a unique symbol or picture bullet, customizing numbered list formats, and formatting bullets and numbers differently.

Changing the Language Format

As with customizing bulleted and numbered lists, you can get help for changing the language format of a document from Microsoft Office Online. Again, walking the user through this procedure reduces further service calls for that user, helps you learn new tasks and skills, and resolves the problem quickly for the end user.

▶ **Resolving language format problems**

To resolve problems with the language format of a document, follow these steps:

1. Open Word 2003 and the working document.

2. From the View menu, verify that Task Pane is selected.

3. In the Task pane, click the down arrow and select Help.

4. Under Assistance, in the Search For text box, type **Language Format**. Press ENTER on the keyboard or click the green arrow next to the text box.

5. From the Search Results offered, select Change The Language Format Of Text.

> **NOTE**   *Other Help*   *Notice you can also choose Install System Support For Multiple Languages, Troubleshoot Automatic Language Detection, Enable Editing Of Multiple Languages, and Change The Language Of the User Interface Or Help In Office Programs.*

6. From the Microsoft Office Word Help window, follow the directions offered for changing the language format of the text.

AutoFormat

AutoFormat quickly applies formatting including headings, bullets, numbered lists, borders, numbers, fractions, and similar items with little effort from the end user either while the document is being created or afterward. Users typically have problems with AutoFormat when it is configured to format text as they create a document, usually because they dislike the formatting Word applies. End users typically have problems when applying formatting to a document after it is created for the same reasons.

AutoFormat has several listings in the Microsoft Office Online Help and Support files, including the following:

- Review AutoFormat Changes
- Turn On Or Off Automatic Formatting
- Troubleshoot Automatic Formatting
- About Automatic Formatting

These Help files, as with others associated with Word, guide you through resolving various AutoFormat issues. For instance, to learn how to review and accept or decline AutoFormat changes, follow these steps:

1. Open Word 2003 and the working document.
2. From the View menu, verify that Task Pane is selected.
3. In the Task pane, click the down arrow and select Help.
4. Under Assistance, in the Search For text box, type **AutoFormat**. Click the green arrow.
5. From the Search Results offered, select Review AutoFormat Changes.
6. From the Microsoft Office Word Help window, follow the directions offered for reviewing, accepting, and rejecting changes.

Embedded and Linked Objects

You can insert objects, which can include files, tables, charts, spreadsheets, images, and sounds, into a working document (a destination file) when you want to include additional information from other sources (source files). For instance, you might insert into a Word document an Excel file that contains sales data that is updated daily, a Publisher file that contains a table that is updated weekly, a Microsoft Access file that contains an employee phone list that is updated monthly, or a simple sound or image that is stored on a network server that is never updated. These inserted objects come from various sources, and are thus referred to as *source files*. Items that you insert into a Word document can be either embedded or linked.

When you embed an object, the information in the destination file doesn't change if you modify the source file. An embedded object is like a snapshot of the object. These objects become part of the destination file, making this type of insertion useful for distributing multiple files in a single document. When embedded objects are edited, they are double-clicked in the destination file, and edited in the source file's native program. Files with embedded data can be quite large.

When you link an object, the information in the destination file is updated when you modify the source file. Linked data is stored in the source file, not the destination file. The destination file stores only information about where the source file is located. With linked files, you can maintain data in a separate program, and when you open the destination file, Word automatically accesses the most up-to-date information. When you edit linked objects, you use the Links command from the Edit menu, and you edit the data in the source file's native application. Files with linked data are generally smaller than those with embedded data.

How to Embed and Link Objects

You embed and link objects by using the Insert and Edit menus, and sometimes by using the Copy and Paste Special commands. The easiest type of object you can add to a document is a new embedded Excel file; all you have to do is click the Insert Microsoft Excel Worksheet icon on the Standard toolbar, and select the size of the worksheet to embed. Figure 7-5 shows an example. Once embedded, you edit the spreadsheet as you would in Excel, using Excel's toolbars. Once you have completed the Excel worksheet, click outside the worksheet area, and Word's toolbars reappear.

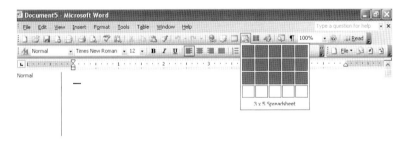

Figure 7-5   Embed a new Excel worksheet.

▶ Embedding existing objects

You can also embed preexisting objects or files that have already been created using the Insert menu and the Object command, as follows:

1. Open Word 2003 and click where the embedded object should be inserted.

2. From the Insert menu, select Object, and then select the Create New tab.

3. In the Object Type list box, select the type of object you want to create.

4. Select the Display As Icon check box.

5. Click OK.

6. In the application that opens, open or create and save the file you want to embed. Minimize or close the file's application. The file will be embedded.

> **NOTE** **When Display As Icon Isn't Selected**   *You can also choose not to select the Display As Icon check box, but doing so changes the default process of embedding a file. For instance, if you embed an Excel file but do not select the Display As Icon check box, an actual Excel document is added to the existing document, not an existing Excel file. If you choose to embed a .wav sound file using this same technique, you'll have to create the sound before it can be embedded. You are not given the option of opening an existing .wav file.*

▶ **Embedding or linking cells from an Excel file**

Here's an example of how to embed or link cells from an Excel file:

1. Open both Word and Excel.

2. In Excel, copy the cells you want to embed or link.

3. In Word, position the mouse pointer on the page where you want the data. From the Edit menu, select Paste Special.

4. Select Paste from the Paste Special dialog box to embed the file; select Paste Link to link the file.

5. If you want to link the object, select the Display As Icon check box to display the linked file as an icon.

6. In the As list, select the format you want to use to embed or link the file. Click OK to save your changes.

Once you've embedded or linked an object, you can edit it by right-clicking and selecting from the options. Links can be updated, edited, opened, and more. Embedded objects can be opened, edited, formatted, converted, hyperlinks can be added, and more. Experiment with the different options for both as time allows.

Troubleshooting Linked and Embedded Files

Users will have problems with embedded and linked files, but problems with linked files can be a little more difficult to diagnose. Table 7-2 lists some common issues with linked files and their solutions. You can find these and other tips and tricks in the Microsoft Office Online Help and Support files.

Table 7-2   **Troubleshooting Linked Files**

Problem	Solution
Cannot Edit error message appears when double-clicking a linked or embedded object.	Verify the program used to create or open the file is installed on the computer and is running. If the object is linked, verify the file has not been moved.
The linked or embedded object cannot be opened because the program used to create it is not installed on the computer.	Convert the object to the file format of a program that is installed by selecting Edit, Linked Worksheet Object, Video Clip Object, Slide Object, or similar option, and then clicking Convert.

Table 7-2   **Troubleshooting Linked Files**

Problem	Solution
The linked or embedded object is cropped around the edges.	In the source program, reduce the size of the data. You can do this by choosing a smaller font, resizing an image, or reducing the column size in a worksheet.
Excel objects don't open in Word.	Open Excel. From the Tools menu, select Options and, on the General tab, clear the Ignore Other Applications check box.

These and other troubleshooting problems and solutions are available from Microsoft Office Online Help and Support, from the Knowledge Base, and from TechNet. You can also get help from newsgroups and third-party Internet sites. A good desktop technician accesses these sites and resources not only to solve problems, but also to learn about common issues before they happen.

Recovering Lost Files

The most disastrous problem from an end user's point of view has to be dealing with lost files. A user can lose a file for many reasons, including a power outage, computer glitch, or user error. Other times, files are lost because the document is damaged or the data is corrupt. When the file is lost due to a power outage, power surge, or computer glitch, as long as the computer can be rebooted, chances are good you can find the file on the hard disk.

NOTE **Preparing for the Worst**   Configure Word to always keep a backup copy of open files. From the Tools menu, select Options, and select the Save tab. Select the Always Create Backup Copy check box. In addition, select the Allow Background Saves and Save AutoRecover Info Every: __ Minutes check boxes.

Using Microsoft Office Application Recovery

If an end user reports that Word 2003 is not responding, you can recover the program. This causes Word to attempt to recover the files the end user was working on and restart the application.

▶ **Recovering Word files**

To access this recovery feature, follow these steps:

1. From the Start menu, select All Programs, Microsoft Office, Microsoft Office Tools, and Microsoft Office Application Recovery.

2. In the Microsoft Application Recovery dialog box, select the program that is not responding, and click Recover Application or Restart Application (only one will be available), or choose End Application if you want to close the application. The latter option causes you to lose recent changes.

3. If you want to report the problem to Microsoft, click Report Problem; otherwise, click Don't Report Problem.

4. Reopen the application if necessary. In the Document Recover Task pane, click the arrow next to the file name and either select Open or Save As. Click Yes if prompted to replace the existing file.

Using AutoRecover

AutoRecover files are the files Word automatically creates in the background every few minutes as specified by the end user. By default, AutoRecover saves files every 10 minutes. If a user encounters a problem with an application, the application offers the last saved version of the file to the user the next time he starts the application. Word stores the AutoRecover files in the folder specified in the Options dialog box (accessed from the File Locations tab).

▶ **Changing AutoRecover settings**

You can change both the file location and AutoRecover default behavior quite easily by following this procedure:

1. Open Word 2003. From the Tools menu, select Options.

2. On the Save tab, verify that the Save AutoRecover Info Every __ Minutes check box is selected and a number between 1 and 120 is configured in the box. You can disable AutoRecover by clearing the check box.

3. On the File Locations tab, select AutoRecover Files, and click Modify to change the location of the recovered files. Browse to a new location, and click OK.

4. Click OK to close the Options dialog box.

> **NOTE**   **Recovery Options**   *You can also manually recover files by browsing to the AutoRecover file location.*

Using Open and Repair

Additionally, you can help end users recover text from a damaged or corrupt document using the Open And Repair option by following these steps:

1. Open Word. From the File menu, select Open.

2. In the Look In drop-down list, browse to the location of the file you want to open. Select the file, but do not click Open.

3. Click the arrow next to the Open button, and then select Open And Repair.

There are other options for recovering lost data, so if none of these options work you might have to restore the data from backup, contact a network administrator, or, if the user created the lost file since the last backup, accept that the file is lost. Encourage users to create backup copies, schedule regular backups, and allow background saves.

> **NOTE**   **Recover Options Work with Other Microsoft Applications**   *These recover options are also available in other Microsoft applications.*

Dealing with User Errors

If a user forgets where she saved the file, you can search for it using the Search Results window available from the Start menu by the date it was created or modified, by its name, or using other options. In addition, all Microsoft applications offer a list of most recently opened documents from the File menu. Finally, clicking Start, pointing to Recent Documents, and accessing a document shown there is also helpful in finding missing files.

EXCEL 2003

In Chapter 6, you learned to install Excel 2003. Although configuration tasks were not included, customizing the toolbars, menus, and their commands; setting personalization options; and configuring the available tools are quite similar to configuring other Office applications. In this section, you'll learn how to troubleshoot this application.

Once end users begin using Excel 2003 and start performing configuration tasks on their own, creating spreadsheets, performing calculations, using macros, and accessing some of the more advanced features available in the application, they'll surely run across problems using them. Although troubleshooting tasks will vary, in this section you'll learn how to resolve some of the more common ones:

- Perform and troubleshoot calculations
- Enable macro security
- Create and troubleshoot macros
- Recover lost files

NOTE **Missing Components and Features** The procedures for resolving issues with missing toolbars, features, and components of Excel 2003 are extremely similar to the procedures detailed for Word 2003 in the previous section.

Calculations

Word 2003 end users do a lot of text formatting; Excel 2003 end users perform a lot of calculations. After calculations are complete, users also sort, filter, validate, consolidate, and group data. You need to have functional familiarity with each of these tasks and be able to troubleshoot various problems with Excel as they arise. In addition to performing calculations and working with their results, Excel users also create tables and charts; format text, cells, rows, and columns; and use AutoFormat in ways similar to Word users. You need to make sure you are well versed in these tasks as well.

As in the last section, in this section you'll learn how to resolve end-user problems using Microsoft Office Online Help and Support. It's the best way to resolve problems, get to know the applications, and learn new skills all at the same time.

Using the Formula Bar

The Formula bar is where you enter formulas, and these formulas determine how calculations are created for cells. You must start a formula with an equal sign (=), followed by the formula itself. For instance:

- =100+200 adds 100 and 200.

- = 15+2*4 adds 15 to 8 (2 times 4).

- =AVERAGE(A1:B6) averages the numbers between the cells A1 and B6.

The plus sign (+), multiplication sign (*), and similar elements of formulas are called *operators*. Users often require help inputting or troubleshooting formulas using these operators. To be able to help them resolve calculation queries, you need to know in what order Excel performs operations, what operators perform what calculations, and how to input the most commonly used formulas.

▶ **Creating a formula**

You can create a formula from scratch or use one of Excel's functions (like Sum or Average) to input a simple formula into the Formula bar. To use a function to create a simple formula and create a calculation, follow these steps:

1. Open Excel 2003 and open a new workbook.

2. Type random numbers in cells A1 through A10.

3. Select cell A11.

4. On the Formula bar, click fx. The Insert Function dialog box opens. Both the spreadsheet and the dialog box are shown in Figure 7-6.

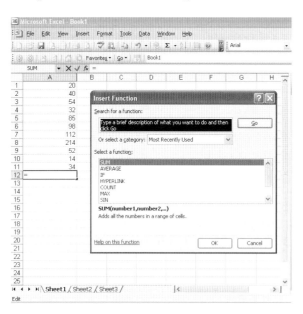

Figure 7-6   Create a simple formula using one of Excel's functions.

5. Double-click Sum in the Insert Function dialog box. In the Function Arguments dialog box shown in Figure 7-7, notice the numbers to be added include cells A1 to A10. In this example, the value is 755. Click OK to insert the formula.

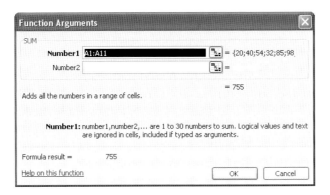

Figure 7-7   The Function Arguments dialog box shows the calculation of a function.

The cell now contains the sum of the cells and a related formula. To view the formula, click the cell and you can view the formula in the Formula bar. You can add various types of formulas in the same manner, or you can type them in manually. As you become more adept with the program, you can decide what you are most comfortable with.

Common Formulas

As you can probably surmise, formulas can be quite complex and can be used to do much more than just add a list of numbers. You can create Excel formulas to perform calculations on dates and times, keep a running balance, calculate the median of a group of numbers, average a set of numbers, round numbers, convert measurements (Celsius to Fahrenheit, for example), and more. Table 7-3 lists several common types of formulas you'll be called on to troubleshoot; the procedure following this table guides you through learning how to create and input any or all of them.

Table 7-3   **Common Formulas**

Formula Type	Common Formulas
Dates and Times	Add dates, add times, calculate the difference between two dates or two times, convert times, count down days until a date, insert the date and time in any cell.
Basic Math	Add, subtract, multiply, divide, round, and average lists of numbers.
Advanced Math	Calculate a percentage of the difference between two numbers, raise a number to a power, calculate the median of a group of numbers, and convert measurements.
Conditional	Calculate based on a previous calculation. For instance, if a number is larger than x, perform some other calculation.

Table 7-3   **Common Formulas**

Formula Type	Common Formulas
Financial	Calculate various interest rates, annuity payments, annual yields, depreciation rates, and accrued interest.
Statistical	Calculate probabilities, deviations, frequency distributions, trends, slope, and variance.

These and many additional formulas are already created and ready to use from Microsoft Office Online Help and Support files. To learn how to create and input any of the formulas listed in Table 7-3 (and many others), follow these steps:

1. Open Excel 2003 and a working document.

2. From the View menu, verify that Task Pane is selected.

3. In the Task pane, click the down arrow and select Help.

4. Under Assistance, in the Search For box, type **List Of Worksheet Functions**, and from the list choose About The Syntax Of Functions. Press ENTER on the keyboard or click the green arrow.

5. Read About The Syntax Of Functions, and then click See Also. In the See Also list, select List Of Worksheet Functions (By Category).

6. Browse through the worksheet functions. To see an example of how you use any worksheet function, select it. A new page appears with information on inputting the formula.

7. Return to the About The Syntax Of Functions page using the Back button, and from the See Also options select Examples Of Commonly Used Formulas. Browse through those options. Figure 7-8 shows instructions for creating a formula to raise a number to a power. These and similar tutorials are available from these Help files.

Figure 7-8   Learn about functions and formulas from the Microsoft Office Help files.

Understanding the Operators

To use a formula, create a formula, or troubleshoot a formula created by an end user, you must understand the operators used in the formula. These can include signs such as plus (+), minus (-), multiply (*), divide (/), less than (<), greater than (>), and raise to a power (^), as well as text operators such as SUM, IF, AVERAGE, POWER, CONVERT, and similar arguments. Although there is no simple way to learn these skills, there is plenty of help available from Microsoft Office Online.

In addition to becoming familiar with operators, you must also understand in which order operators are calculated. For instance, when parentheses are involved, Excel performs the calculations within them first. Multiplication is always performed before addition, and division is always performed before subtraction. Successful troubleshooting of calculations includes knowing the basic order of operations. From left to right, calculations are performed in the following order:

1. Parentheses

2. Exponents

3. Multiply and divide

4. Add and subtract

5. Equal to, less than, greater than, or comparisons

> **NOTE   Learn, Learn, Learn**   To troubleshoot Excel for end users, you need to have a good understanding of basic math, algebra, and formulas. To be the best technician you can be might mean taking an additional math class to brush up on your skills.

Troubleshooting Calculations

When a calculation has a logical error or an error with its syntax, the end user is alerted to it with an error message of #VALUE! in the cell box instead of a numerical value. If it is your job to troubleshoot this error, you have to understand what calculation the user is trying to make, look up the correct formula in the Help files or create your own, or rewrite the formula the user has already written. Excel offers some help as well, and sometimes that help is sufficient.

Figure 7-9 shows an example of an error message. Notice there is a box next to the error, and clicking the arrow in this box opens the drop-down list shown. It is an error in value, and there are options to get help for the error, show calculation steps, edit the formula in the formula bar, and more. Generally, selecting Help On This Error is the best choice for beginners.

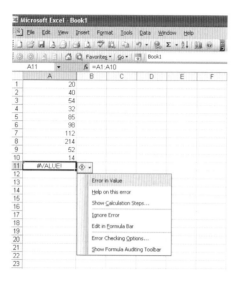

Figure 7-9   Automatic help with errors is available from the drop-down menu.

You'll have to practice creating formulas and performing calculations to get a feel for how Excel works and to troubleshoot problems for end users. If your end users use Excel to perform their daily tasks, you might consider taking a short course in the subject or working through the Microsoft Office Online Excel tutorials.

Working with Macros

Another component of Excel (and other Office applications) that many users employ is the macro. A *macro* is a short program that a user can create to automate tasks. When creating the macro, keystrokes and mouse movements are recorded, and the user can play those movements back at any time with only a few quick clicks of the mouse. For instance, if calculating the company's payroll each month requires the user to repeat the same steps—perhaps selecting a range of cells, selecting various menus and menu options, and creating the same print configurations—the user can automate those steps by recording a macro for it. The next time the user needs to perform that task, he simply plays the macro.

Your role as a desktop technician might require you to create and troubleshoot macros. In the next two sections, you learn to do both.

▶ **Creating macros**

To create a simple macro for an end user in Excel 2003 (the procedure is similar in other applications), follow these steps:

1. From the Tools menu, select Macro and then Record New Macro.

2. In the Macro Name text box, enter a name for the macro. The name of the macro must start with a letter and must not contain any spaces. It cannot be a name used as a cell reference.

3. To create a **shortcut key** for running the macro, type a letter in the Short-cut Key box.

4. In the Store Macro In drop-down list box, select the location in which to store the macro. If you want the macro to be available each time you use Excel, select Personal Macro Workbook. If you want the macro to be available only to this workbook, select This Workbook. If you want the macro to be available for a new workbook, select New Workbook. See Figure 7-10.

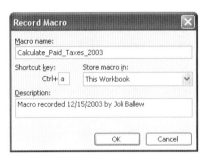

Figure 7-10   Configure the macro using the Record Macro dialog box.

5. In the Description text box, type a description if desired. Click OK.

6. If the macro is to run relative to the position of the active cell (the selected cell), click Relative Reference on the Stop Recording toolbar. Relative reference means the macro will run based on which cell is chosen when the macro is run. When this is not selected, the macro runs using the cells chosen in the initial creation of the macro each time, no matter which cell is chosen and active.

7. Perform the steps involved in the procedure to record the macro. Click Stop Recording when finished.

To run the macro, from the Tools menu, select Macro, Macros, select the macro you want to run, and then click Run. If the macro doesn't work properly, you'll either have to rerecord the macro or troubleshoot it.

Macros and Security

Because macros are **Visual Basic** programs, they can contain viruses or pose security risks. Excel offers several choices for dealing with this risk. There are four security levels that you can set for macros:

- **Very High**   When this level is selected, only macros installed from trusted locations can be run. All other macros are disabled.

- **High**   Unsigned macros are disabled, and signed macros are dealt with depending on their source.

- **Medium**   Unsigned macros are disabled, and signed macros are dealt with depending on their source. This setting is similar to but more lenient than the High security setting.

- **Low**   Almost all macros can be run. This is not a recommended setting.

▶ Setting the security level

To use macros in Excel or any other Office program effectively, you must set the macro security level to Medium or Low. To do so, follow these steps:

1. From the Tools menu, select Options, then select the Security tab.

2. Click Macro Security.

3. On the Security Level tab, select Medium or Low as shown in Figure 7-11.

Figure 7-11   Select the desired security level on the Security Level tab.

4. Click OK to save your changes, and then click OK again to close the Options dialog box.

> **NOTE   Disable All Macros**   To disable macros installed from all sources, even trusted sources, on the Tools menu, select Macro, and select Security. On the Trusted Publisher tab, clear the Trust All Installed Add-Ins And Templates option.

Troubleshooting Macros

There are several reasons why a macro might not run properly or be available, including a user selecting the wrong macro from the list or typing the wrong short-cut key, having the macro security level set too high, or having the macro assigned to a specific workbook that the user doesn't currently have open. Changing the security setting to Low or Medium solves the security issue. The other issues can be resolved using the Macro dialog box, as follows:

1. From the Tools menu, select Macro and then Macros.

2. In the Macros dialog box there are several options:

   ❏ **Run**   Runs the macro.

   ❏ **Cancel**   Closes the dialog box.

   ❏ **Step Into**   Opens the Visual Basic Editor, which you can use to manu-ally debug the macro using its Visual Basic code.

- ❑ **Edit** Opens the Visual Basic Editor, which you can use to manually edit the macro using its Visual Basic code.

- ❑ **Delete** Deletes the macro.

- ❑ **Options** Opens the Macro Options dialog box, where you can view or change the macro's description and shortcut key.

- ❑ **Macros In** Use this list to sort the macros by All Open Workbooks, This Workbook, or by a file name.

Excel might also encounter problems if the macro was recorded incorrectly, if the macro looks for a specific cell that is no longer there, if a cell is formatted incorrectly, or if the macro needs to access data that is no longer available.

If the macro is a fairly simple one, sometimes it's better just to re-create it. If the macro produces an error message, which it often does under these circumstances, that message offers some insight into the problem. If you see an error message when you run a recorded macro, follow this procedure:

1. Copy the macro error and error number.

2. From the Tools menu, select Macro, and then select Visual Basic Editor.

3. In the new Visual Basic Editor window, select Help, and select Microsoft Visual Basic Help. Verify you are connected to the Internet.

4. In the Task pane, type the error number and press ENTER.

5. In the Microsoft Visual Basic Help results, locate the error and the solution.

Some errors are due to known issues with Excel and their solutions can be found in the Microsoft Knowledge Base. If your search using the Visual Basic Editor Help files doesn't produce a solution, try the Knowledge Base articles.

Recovering Lost Files

The first section of this chapter, on Word 2003, detailed options for recovering lost files. The same options available for that application are also available for Excel 2003. When a user reports a file has been lost due to a computer glitch, power outage, or user error, work through those options, which include the following:

- **Using Microsoft Office Application Recovery** From the Start menu, select All Programs, Microsoft Office, Microsoft Office Tools, and Microsoft Office Application Recovery. In the Microsoft Office Application Recovery dialog box, select Microsoft Office Excel. Select either Recover Application or End Application.

- **Using AutoRecover** Restart or recover the application using Microsoft Office Application Recovery or by restarting the computer. In the Document Recovery Task pane shown in Figure 7-12, select the document to recover. You can configure AutoRecover on the Tools menu by selecting Options and selecting the Save tab.

Figure 7-12   The Document Recovery Task pane offers several options.

- **Using Open and Repair**   From the File menu, select Open, and select the file to recover. Click the arrow next to the Open button, and select Open And Repair.

- **Dealing with User Errors**   From the File menu, locate the lost file or from the Start menu, select My Recent Documents and select the file to reopen.

POWERPOINT 2003

In Chapter 6 you learned to install PowerPoint 2003. Although configuration tasks were not included, customizing the toolbars, menus, and their commands; setting personalization options; and configuring the available tools are quite similar to configuring other Office applications. In this section, you learn how to trouble-shoot this application.

Once end users begin using PowerPoint 2003 and start performing configuration tasks on their own, creating presentations, using macros, and accessing some of the more advanced features available in the application, they'll surely run across problems using them. Although troubleshooting tasks will vary, in this section you'll learn how to resolve some of the more common ones:

- Share and package presentations

- Show presentations on any computer

- Recover lost files

> **NOTE   Embedded and Linked Images and Sounds**   Embedding and linking sounds and images is an important part of creating PowerPoint presentations. Embedding and linking were detailed in the Word 2003 portion of this chapter, and procedures for embedding and linking objects are similar in PowerPoint.

Sharing Presentations

Word 2003 users do a lot of text formatting, Excel 2003 users perform a lot of calculations and, in the same vein, PowerPoint 2003 users create a lot of presentations. PowerPoint users' common tasks include creating, moving, and deleting slides; adding and editing text; embedding and linking music and sounds; viewing slide shows; and inserting charts and tables. You should have functional knowledge of these things, too.

PowerPoint users do much more than create presentations, though. They share these presentations. Sharing a presentation, whether it is sent over a network, shown using a laptop and a projector, or burned onto a CD, is often a source of difficulty for the user. This is especially true when there are additional files involved such as a music file that plays in the background, a linked graph or chart, or an image. Users often call for help on these issues.

> **NOTE Tasks** Formatting text, creating macros, and troubleshooting missing toolbars and components can also be a part of resolving PowerPoint calls. These tasks were detailed in the Word 2003 and Excel 2003 sections of this chapter, and procedures for them are similar in PowerPoint.

Packaging and Sharing

When a user is ready to send a completed presentation to a CD, a network file server, or a colleague, that presentation must be packaged so that all of the files included in the presentation (music, graphics, fonts, charts, and so on) are incorporated. The Package For CD feature in PowerPoint 2003 simplifies this process. The Package For CD feature can be used to burn the presentation and all of its included files to a CD, save them to a folder, copy them to a network file server, or even copy them to a floppy disk. In addition (excluding when the presentation is saved to a floppy disk), a PowerPoint Viewer is also added, so that any person using almost any computer can view it.

▶ **Packaging a presentation**

These steps are required to successfully package a completed presentation:

1. Open the completed and saved PowerPoint presentation.

2. From the File menu, select Package For CD.

3. In the Package For CD dialog box, type a name for the CD (or file).

4. Linked files, embedded TrueType fonts, and the PowerPoint Viewer are included by default. To make any changes to the defaults or to apply a password to any of the files, click Options. Make the appropriate changes and click OK.

5. To add additional files, select Add Files. Browse to the location of the files to add, select them, and click Add.

6. To copy the file to a folder or a network file server, click Copy To Folder. Browse to the location in which to save the files. Click Select and click OK.

7. To burn the entire presentation to a CD, click Copy To CD.

8. Wait while the files are packaged and copied. Click Close when finished.

The saved and packaged presentation is now ready for viewing. The folder contains all of the files needed for the presentation, including copies of music, images, charts, graphs, a PowerPoint Viewer, an AutoRun file, and more. Showing the presentation only involves starting it or putting the CD into the CD-ROM drive.

Recovering Lost Files

The first section of this chapter, on Word 2003, detailed options for recovering lost files. The options available for that application are also available for PowerPoint 2003. When a user reports a file has been lost due to a computer glitch, power outage, or user error, work through those options, which include the following:

- **Using Microsoft Office Application Recovery**   From the Start menu, select All Programs, Microsoft Office, Microsoft Office Tools, and Microsoft Office Application Recovery. In the Microsoft Office Application Recovery dialog box, select Microsoft Office PowerPoint. Select either Recover Application or End Application.

- **Using AutoRecover**   Restart or recover the application using Microsoft Office Application Recovery or by restarting the computer. In the Document Recovery Task pane, select the document to recover. You can configure AutoRecover from the Tools menu by selecting Options and selecting the Save tab.

- **Using Open and Repair**   From the File menu, select Open, and select the file to recover. Click the arrow next to the Open button and select Open And Repair.

- **Dealing with User Errors**   Locate the lost file in the File menu, or from the Start menu, select My Recent Documents and select the file to reopen.

TROUBLESHOOTING OUTLOOK EXPRESS

In Chapter 4, "Microsoft Office Outlook 2003 and Outlook Express," you were introduced to Outlook Express, and you learned how to create and troubleshoot e-mail and newsgroup accounts. Although some configuration tasks were included, customizing the toolbars, menus, and their commands; setting personalization options; and configuring the available tools are quite similar to configuring the full version of the application, Outlook 2003, which was also covered in that chapter. This section focuses on Outlook Express and introduces you to some of the more common issues end users encounter.

Although troubleshooting tasks will vary, in this section you learn how to resolve some of the more common ones:

- Open attachments

- Troubleshoot international settings and encoding options

- Recover lost e-mail

Attachments

Service calls regarding attachments can be varied, but they likely revolve around attachments that cannot be opened or attachments that cannot be sent. Sometimes an attachment is unavailable or doesn't have a program associated with it. Sometimes e-mail with attachments remains in the Outbox or causes error messages on sending. The first problem is the most common; almost all service calls regarding the inability to open attachments can be resolved by clearing a single check box. When a user reports that attachments are unavailable and cannot be opened, follow these steps:

1. From the Tools menu, select Options, and select the Security tab.

2. Clear the Do Not Allow Attachments To Be Saved Or Opened That Could Potentially Be A Virus check box. Click OK.

3. Close and reopen Outlook Express.

If this does not solve the problem, or if the problem is one of the others mentioned, you have to delve a little deeper. If the user is a member of a domain, check domain policies for dealing with attachments. In some instances, network policies won't allow attachments to be opened. This policy isn't common, however, because attachments are a large part of corporate life, but if the preceding procedure doesn't resolve the problem, you need to check on this.

No Associated Program
A user won't be able to open the attachment if there is no program associated with it. For instance, if a user tries to open a proprietary file type such as .psd (Photoshop) or .ged (Arts and Letters), and the file's respective program is not installed on the user's computer, opening the attachment fails and an error similar to the one shown in Figure 7-13 appears.

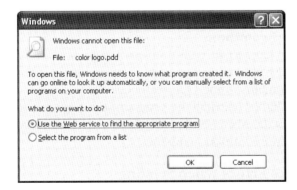

Figure 7-13   A cannot open file error results.

When this happens, instruct the end user to choose Use The Web Service To Find The Appropriate Program. The Microsoft Windows File Associations Web site automatically opens, and information regarding the programs that can be used to open the file is listed. Sometimes, this information includes a link that you can use to download and install a viewer to open the file, or you might need to download and install a trial version of a program. Figure 7-14 shows this Web site; notice you can use Adobe Photoshop, CorelDRAW, and Microsoft Office PhotoDraw to open the .pdd file.

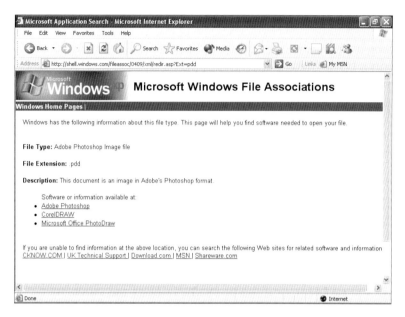

Figure 7-14   Use the Microsoft Windows File Associations Web page to determine programs that can be used to open a file.

If the user does not have Web access, instruct the user to choose Select The Program From A List to see if there are any compatible programs available on the computer. In some instances, the user might have a compatible program installed but Windows doesn't recognize it as a compatible file type. The .pdd file shown in Figure 7-13 was opened easily using Photoshop, even though the error message appeared.

> **MORE INFO**   **File Types**   To learn more about what types of files can be opened with what programs, visit *http://www.oktec.com/help/file_types.htm* and similar sites.

E-Mail with Attachment Remains in Outbox

Problems sending attachments usually have to do with third-party software that is installed on the computer. If an e-mail with an attachment can't be sent even after you click Send/Receive, but instead remains in the Outbox, check for Internet filtering programs (such as Net Nanny). Either uninstall the program or reconfigure it to allow attachments to be sent. Check the Microsoft Knowledge Base for information regarding various third-party software and known issues.

E-Mail with Attachments Produces Errors When Sending

Problems that produce error messages when attachments are sent are usually caused by hardware configuration or compatibility problems. Hardware problems can be caused by incompatible or incorrectly configured modems, firewalls, or similar hardware. These errors might include references including the server unexpectedly terminating the connection, the Simple Mail Transfer Protocol (SMTP) server not responding, or the server timing out. If the only connectivity problems are associated with sending attachments, visit the Knowledge Base or the hardware manufacturers' Web sites for help.

International Settings and Encoding

Users who send and receive e-mail in more than one language might need you to troubleshoot these tasks. A user in the United States who has been successful in sending e-mail to her colleague in France might report that she's been unable to do that lately and ask you to figure out why. A home user who is Italian might want you to teach him to send e-mail to his mother in her own language.

Sending and receiving e-mail in multiple languages using Outlook Express requires a few things. When checking for problems or setting up Outlook Express for the first time, verify that these items are in working order:

- Set Regional Options for the language to be used from Control Panel as detailed in Chapter 5, "Configure Internet Explorer."

- Configure Text Services and Input Languages to include the language to be used, also detailed in Chapter 5.

- Verify the user knows how to switch between languages from the taskbar (next to the Notification Area).

- Verify that any appropriate keyboards are installed, if applicable.

To configure Outlook Express to send and receive e-mail in other languages, you have to configure Internet Explorer to also recognize these different languages when viewing Web pages. Therefore, before continuing, in Internet Explorer, follow these steps:

1. From the Tools menu, select Internet Options, and select the General tab.

2. Select Languages.

3. Click Add to add another language. In the Add Language dialog box, select the language to add and click OK.

4. Verify that the new language is displayed first. If it isn't, select it and use the Move Up button to move it to the top of the list.

5. Click OK to close the Language Preference dialog box, and click OK to close the Internet Options dialog box.

Next, in Outlook Express, follow these steps:

1. From the Tools menu, select Options, and select the Send tab.

2. Under Sending, click International Settings, and make sure that the second language is the default.

3. If prompted, install the necessary language pack.

4. Click OK to close the International Settings dialog box. Click OK to close the Options dialog box.

When creating the message, make sure the user has selected the correct language, select Format, and point to Encoding to verify the correct encoding option is selected.

Other Common Issues

There are some other issues that Outlook Express end users might encounter, and you should try to become familiar with them. You can usually resolve these problems by changing the configuration options in Outlook Express, so you should familiarize yourself with all aspects of the program. Table 7-4 lists some of these problems and their solutions.

Table 7-4   **Other Common Issues**

Problem	Solution
Newsgroup messages automatically download, but the user wants to download messages only after reading the header.	1. From the Tools menu, select Options and select the Read tab. 2. Clear the Automatically Download Messages When Viewing In The Preview Pane check box.
The user wants to automatically hide messages in the Inbox that have already been read.	1. From the View menu, select Current View. 2. Select Hide Read Messages.
The user's e-mail folder is quite large. He wants to reduce the amount of space it takes up without deleting any old messages.	1. Select an e-mail folder. 2. From the File menu, select Folder, and then select Compact.
A user is distracted by the new mail notification sound each time a new e-mail arrives.	1. From the Tools menu, select Options, and select the General tab. 2. Clear the Play Sound When New Messages Arrive check box.

Make sure you can resolve these problems and others related to Outlook Express.

Recovering Lost E-Mail

If a user has accidentally deleted an e-mail she needs, there are a few ways to try to locate and restore it. First, you can see if the message can be located in the Deleted Items folder. If the e-mail is found there, restoring it is as simple as dragging the deleted item to another folder such as the Inbox. If the e-mail is no longer in the Deleted Items folder, you can try to restore it from the Recycle Bin or use a third party's Protected Recycle Bin.

Another option is recovering the missing files from a backup. For a home user, this might be a stretch, because many home users do not know how to back up Outlook Express e-mail messages, so no backup exists. Network users generally have a backup of each day's files on a network server, but obtaining those files might require contacting a network administrator.

> **NOTE** **Exporting as a Backup Tool**   If messages have been recently exported as a means of backup, those messages can be imported as a way to recover lost data. You can import messages by using the File menu and the Import command as detailed in Chapter 4.

Keep in mind that although an end user calls to report that all of the e-mail messages are missing, they might not be. Consider these errors in end-user logic:

- The user might have changed or does not understand the interface. The wrong folder might be selected in the Local Folders list.

- The user might be looking for items in the Deleted Items folder, and those items might be configured to be deleted on exit.

- The folder where the e-mail is stored by default might have been changed. Outlook Express might not be able to find the folder.

- The user might be using two or more e-mail clients and the missing incoming and outgoing e-mail could be in another e-mail-handling program.

- An expected e-mail might have been caught by a spam filter. Check any folders configured to hold messages that are blocked by rules or by filtering programs.

For the most part, you need to teach your Outlook Express users how to back up their messages; there is no automatic recovery tool associated with the program, and no Microsoft Windows or Microsoft Office tool for Outlook Express application recovery.

Teach Users to Back Up Their Data

If you have the time and can teach users (especially home users) how to back up their Outlook Express data, you should do so. Although there are several ways to do this, the method detailed next has been outlined in previous Knowledge Base articles and is generally regarded as the most straightforward.

▶ **Backing up Outlook Express messages**

To back up Outlook Express mail messages, follow these steps:

1. Open Outlook Express and, from the Tools menu, select Options.

2. On the Maintenance tab, select Store Folder.

3. Select the folder location with the mouse, right-click, and select Copy.

4. Click Cancel to close this dialog box, and click Cancel again to close the Options dialog box.

5. From the Start menu, select Run.

6. Place the cursor in the Open text box, right-click, and select Paste. Click OK.

7. In the resulting window, from the Edit menu, select Select All.

8. From the Edit menu, select Copy. Close the window.

9. Right-click the desktop or any other area to store the data, point to New, and select Folder. Name the new folder Mail Folder, followed by the date.

10. Open that folder, right-click in the resulting window, and select Paste. Wait while the data is added. Close the Mail Folder window.

> **NOTE** **Repairing a Damaged E-Mail Folder**   Damaged e-mail folders can be repaired by copying the folder's contents to a temporary folder, deleting the damaged folder, closing and reopening Outlook Express (the folder will be re-created), and then copying the messages back to the newly created folder.

OUTLOOK 2003

In Chapter 4, you learned quite a bit about Outlook 2003. In Chapter 6, you learned how to install and configure it. In this section, you'll learn how to troubleshoot this application.

Once end users begin using Outlook 2003 and start documenting and planning meetings and appointments, configuring contacts, creating Tasks lists, and using the Journal, they'll surely run across problems. Although troubleshooting tasks will vary, in this section you'll learn how to resolve some of the more common ones:

- Set and troubleshoot reminders for meetings
- Add and troubleshoot contacts and contact information
- Add and troubleshoot tasks
- Add journal entries and troubleshoot missing entries
- Recover lost e-mail

The remaining sections cover the Calendar, Contacts, Tasks, and Journal components of Outlook 2003, but only a few troubleshooting tasks are detailed in the usual step-by-step fashion. It is impossible in the space provided here to cover all of the troubleshooting service calls a technician might receive. Instead, a few basic tasks are outlined, with the emphasis on finding the solution rather than learning how to resolve specific troubleshooting calls.

> **NOTE** **Set Up Junk E-Mail Filters** *Chances are good you'll get lots of complaints about junk e-mail while on the job as a desktop technician. Outlook offers several junk e-mail options and filters that you can teach your end users to employ, and they work well. To view and configure these filters, refer to the information in Chapter 4.*

Resolving Problems with the Calendar

The Calendar is an organizational tool for keeping track of meetings, appointments, and reminders. End users are reminded of events before they occur, thus offering them a kind of "virtual secretary." End users who rely on the Calendar to keep track of events often have questions regarding its use. Although service calls will vary, most can be resolved using Microsoft Office Online, the Knowledge Base, or TechNet.

Receiving Reminders for Past Meetings

If a user reports he is receiving reminders for meetings that have already occurred, follow these steps:

1. In Outlook 2003, select Microsoft Office Outlook Help (or press F1) from the Help menu.

2. In the Outlook Help Task pane, type **Troubleshoot Calendar Reminders** and press ENTER.

3. In the Help Task pane, click Troubleshoot Calendar if it is available, or open another appropriate Help file.

NOTE **Additional Help Topics** In the Troubleshoot Calendar Help file there are several Help topics, including I Opened Another Person's Calendar, And I Can't Find A Way To Close It; Other People See My Schedule As Busy When I Don't Have Any Appointments Or Meetings; and I Can't See The Little Calendar.

4. Follow the instructions in the Help file to resolve the problem. This might include dismissing the meeting, removing a duplicate entry, removing a recurrence setting, or modifying the date or time fields, depending on the circumstance.

Appointments and Meetings Are Missing

If a user reports that appointments and meetings are missing from the Calendar, follow this procedure:

1. In Outlook 2003, select Microsoft Office Outlook Help (or press F1) from the Help menu.

2. In the Outlook Help Task pane, type **Troubleshoot Calendar Appointments** and press ENTER.

3. In the Help Task pane, scroll through the available articles and Help files. Select one that has to do with appointments that you feel will most likely offer a solution to missed appointments.

4. Follow the instructions in the Help file to resolve the problem. This might include changing the view of the Calendar or filtering the Calendar entries, depending on the circumstance.

It's up to you to become familiar with all of the components of Outlook 2003, including the Calendar. There are a lot of Help files and books on this subject, and you should try to become well versed in using this component (as well as in using others).

Resolving Problems with Contacts

As with the Outlook Calendar, you can use Microsoft Office Online to resolve problems with the Contacts feature as well. The Contacts folder is used to organize all of the user's e-mail contacts. The options in the Troubleshoot Contacts Help file include detailed instructions on how to resolve many problems, including the following:

- I can't see my contacts.

- Information is missing from my contacts.

- My contacts don't sort in the order I expect.

- The text in the contact card is cut off.

- When I sort, filter, or mail merge my contacts, the address or name fields are not displaying correctly.

- I added a custom field to my contacts but I don't see it.

As with other Outlook components, searching for answers to questions here is generally the best choice.

Resolving Problems with Tasks

You can use Microsoft Office Online to resolve problems with the Tasks feature as well. The Tasks feature allows the user to keep track of tasks that need to be done on a "to do" list. The options in the Troubleshoot Tasks Help file include detailed instructions on how to resolve many problems, including the following:

- I can't see my tasks.
- I assigned a task and it disappeared.
- I received a task update message in my Inbox, but it disappeared.
- I can't skip a recurring task.
- The TaskPad is missing.

Resolving Problems with the Journal

You can also use Microsoft Office Online to resolve problems with the Journal feature. The Journal allows users to keep notes and keep track of long-term and short-term goals, as well as of phone calls, letters, meetings, and more. The options in the Troubleshoot Journal Help file include detailed instructions on how to resolve many problems, including the following:

- When I open a Journal item, I want the item to open to the Journal entry.
- I don't see the Journal button in the Navigation pane.
- The contact I want to automatically record items for does not appear in the For These Contacts list in the Journal Options dialog box.

Recovering Lost E-Mail

Outlook 2003 offers several options for recovering lost e-mail. Users can retrieve e-mail from the Deleted Items folder if it is still there. If the item is gone from the Deleted Items folder, the user might be able to recover the e-mail from the Recycle Bin or from a Microsoft Exchange server (if it's configured to keep deleted items for a period of time after they've originally been deleted). Users might also be able to restore deleted items from Internet Message Access Protocol (IMAP) folders or search for missing e-mail in the Junk E-Mail folder.

Using the Deleted Items Folder

To restore a deleted e-mail that has not been removed from the Deleted Items folder, follow these steps:

1. From the Go menu, select Folder List, and then in the Navigation pane, select Deleted Items.

2. Select the items to retrieve; you can select multiple items by holding down the CTRL key while selecting.

3. Right-click the selected items and select Move To Folder, and in the Move Items dialog box, select Inbox (or any other folder). Click OK to move the items.

You can also drag e-mail items to any folder from the Deleted Items folder.

Restoring from a Microsoft Exchange Server

If the client is looking for e-mail previously deleted, and the Deleted Items folder has been emptied, *and* if the client is using a Microsoft Exchange Server e-mail account on a Microsoft Exchange server (running version 5.5 or newer), you can try to restore the deleted e-mail from the server. An Exchange server can be configured to save deleted items for a period of time after deletion from the user's computer. If this is the case and the previous requirements have been met, follow these steps:

1. From the Go menu, select Folder List, and then in the Navigation pane, click Deleted Items.

2. Select the items to retrieve; you can select multiple items by holding down the CTRL key while selecting.

3. From the Tools menu, select Recover Deleted Items.

Restoring IMAP E-Mail

If the user has an IMAP e-mail account, you can restore messages that have been marked for deletion by selecting the deleted item, clicking Edit, and clicking Undelete. Items marked for deletion can be viewed by clicking View, pointing to Arrange By, pointing to Current View, and clicking Group Message Marked For Deletion.

Inbox Repair Tool

If a user can't open her Personal Folder File (.pst) or Offline Folder File (.ost), or you suspect that either file is corrupt for other reasons, you can use the Inbox Repair tool to check the folders and make sure the file structure is intact. If the file structure is determined to be corrupt, the Inbox Repair tool repairs errors in the file and then rebuilds the file structure.

The Inbox Repair tool is not accessed from inside Outlook. Instead, you must access the application from the following folder: *drive:*\ Program Files\Common Files\System\MSMAPI*LocalID Folder*. The Local ID number is the identifier for the installation of Office. The identifier for English is 1033. The two utilities are named SCANOST and SCANPST. To run either utility, simply double-click its icon.

The Inbox Repair tool then prompts you to browse for the .pst or .ost file to scan, and then it scans and automatically repairs errors in the file. Each of these files is located in the *drive:*\Documents and Settings*user name*\Local Settings\Application Data\Microsoft\Outlook folder. The Inbox Repair tool is often very successful in repairing corrupt files, and it is a good tool to become familiar with.

NOTE   Make Sure Show Hidden Files Is Selected   When browsing for the .pst and .ost files, make sure Show Hidden Files is selected in the Folder Properties dialog box. If it is not, you will not be able to view the Local Settings folder, and will not be able to browse to the data file to scan.

Checking the Junk E-Mail Folder

When the junk e-mail filtering options are set too high, some legitimate e-mail might get deleted and sent to the Junk E-Mail folder. If a user reports that e-mail that should have arrived never did, and the sender verifies the e-mail was sent, check the Junk E-Mail folder. If the missing e-mail is found, lower the Junk E-Mail settings, create a rule for safe recipients, or configure no automatic filtering in the Junk E-Mail options.

REPORTS AND UPDATES

Occasionally when a problem occurs with an Office application, the application will shut down and you or the user will have a chance to report the error to Microsoft and view a Microsoft Online Crash Analysis report. Good technicians will always report the error and read the analysis. Reporting the error helps Microsoft determine what errors are occurring and why, and allows them to create patches and fixes for those problems. Reading the report offers insight into what caused it.

An analysis report can offer different types of information. It might include specific information regarding the cause of the problem, such as an incompatible driver; it might offer only generic advice about drivers and approved hardware and software; or it might include a link to an update that has already been released to fix the problem. Figure 7-15 shows the latter.

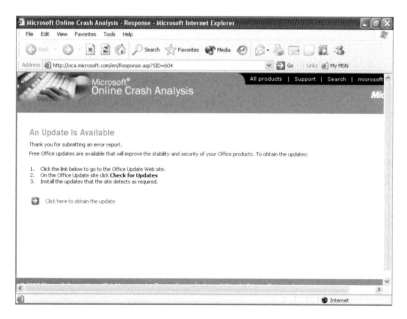

Figure 7-15   A Microsoft Online Crash Analysis report offers information about the problem and offers available updates.

When an update is available, and an Online Crash Analysis offers one, the update should be installed immediately. As a preemptive strike against these types of errors, updates should be manually sought out weekly. This is detailed next.

Obtaining Updates Manually

To obtain an update manually for any Office application, connect to the Internet and, from the Help menu, select Check For Updates. You'll be prompted to either download updates or scan for updates, depending on the situation. Figure 7-16 shows the option to Check For Updates. Notice there are new updates for Word 2003, Outlook 2003, and Office 2003. (When checking for updates, no personally identifiable user information is sent to Microsoft.)

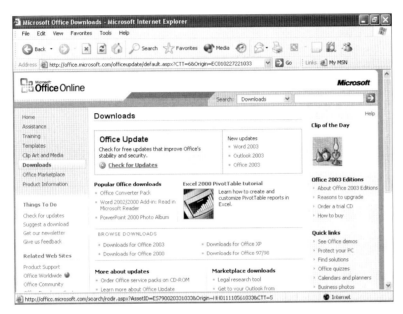

Figure 7-16   Check for updates weekly to make sure your applications are always up to date.

▶ **Installing updates**

To install updates offered after scanning the computer, follow these steps:

1. From the Office Update page, select the updates to install and select Start Installation. As a general rule of thumb, install all offered updates.

2. Confirm your selections on the first page of the Office Update Installation Wizard, and click Next.

3. Verify you have your Office Product CD ready, or know how to access them from your network, and click Next.

4. Wait while the update downloads and installs. This should happen automatically. (Some updates, like service packs must be downloaded, saved to the computer, and installed manually; however, this is not usually the case.)

5. Click Finish when prompted.

6. On the Microsoft Office Online page, click Check For Updates That I Still Need To Install if applicable. Some updates, such as service packs, must be installed separately.

Make sure you repeat this process weekly, or at least monthly. These updates will help your computer run faster and more efficiently, and will prevent further problems.

SUMMARY

- To restore missing toolbars and to customize features in any Office application, use the View menu and select Customize.

- To add or remove Office components, use the Microsoft Office CD and Add or Remove Programs in Control Panel.

- To learn to format bulleted and numbered lists, embed and link objects, create and edit formulas, package and share presentations, and resolve issues with other Office components or tasks, visit Microsoft Office Online.

- To recover lost files, use Microsoft Office Application Recovery, AutoRecover, and the Open and Repair options.

- To manually update Office applications, from the Help menu in the desired application, select Check For Updates.

REVIEW QUESTIONS

1. An Excel 2003 user needs to create a formula for calculating the average of 10 numbers in cells A1 through A11. Which of the following formulas is best?

   a. =AVERAGE(A1:A11)

   b. AVERAGE(A1:A11)

   c. =SUM(A1:A11)\10

   d. =AVERAGE(A1;A11)

2. An Excel 2003 user reports he needs to build his own equations by picking symbols from a toolbar, as well as by typing numbers and variables. You determine he needs the Equation Editor, which is not currently installed on his computer. What should you do?

   a. Download and install the Equation Editor from the Microsoft Office Online Web site.

   b. Install the Equation Editor from the Office System CD, under Office Tools on the Advanced Customization page.

   c. Open Excel 2003. From the Tools menu, select Options and, on the Calculation tab, enable the Equation Editor.

   d. Open Excel 2003. From the View menu, select Equation Editor.

3. A user needs to insert a table, which a colleague has created using Access, into her Word document. The table is updated daily with the latest company statistics and is stored on a network server. The user wants her Word file to always offer the most up-to-date information each time the file is opened. Unfortunately, each time she opens the document, she gets the same information, and the table is never updated. What is the problem?

    a. The user embedded the table instead of linking it.

    b. The user linked the table instead of embedding it.

    c. This user needs to choose Package For CD to package the Word file with the table, so both are available when the file is opened.

    d. The user needs to be made a member of the Domain Power Users group so she can have automatic access to domain resources.

4. Lost files can be recovered in a number of ways, including using Microsoft Office Application Recovery, AutoRecover, Open and Repair, and more. To demonstrate your familiarity with these options and others, match the situation on the left to the best file recovery method on the right.

1. PowerPoint has locked up and is not responding. The user has not saved the presentation he's working on in quite some time and does not want to lose his work. What should you try first?	a) Open and Repair
2. A user deleted an e-mail and needs to retrieve it. She has not emptied her Deleted Items folder, although it is configured to delete items in that folder when she exits Outlook. What should you tell the user to do?	b) The File menu
3. A user reports his Excel file won't open, and he thinks it's corrupt. The computer shut down from a power failure and when he rebooted and started Excel again, nothing happened. He was not offered any recovered files. What should he try now?	c) Microsoft Office Application Recovery
4. A user saved a file yesterday but can't remember where she saved it. She needs to access the file quickly. Where can she look?	d) Open the folder, locate the file, and drag it to a different folder.

5. A user reports he can't open any attachments because the paper clip is unavailable. After questioning the user, you find out that the problem started yesterday after he installed Windows XP Home Edition Service Pack 1 on his computer. What do you tell the user to do?

    a. Choose Use The Web Service To Find The Appropriate Program, locate a program to open the attachment with, and install it.

    b. Uninstall Service Pack 1.

    c. Restart the computer.

    d. From the Tools menu, select Options and select the Security tab. Clear the Do Not Allow Attachments To Be Saved Or Opened That Could Potentially Be A Virus check box. Click OK.

CASE SCENARIOS

Scenario 7-1: Restoring the Default Toolbars in Office Applications

John, the owner of a small company, has begun to travel quite a bit and has purchased a laptop. He wants his wife to use his old computer because she'll take over the duties involved in running the company while he's away. She'll use the same applications, data, and network John used, so there aren't too many changes to make. You've created a new user account; transferred all of John's personal files to his laptop; reset the taskbar, Start menu, background, and screen saver; and made other personal configuration changes. Now, you need to restore the defaults to the menus, buttons, menu choices, and default toolbars in each of the Office applications installed on the computer.

How do you restore all the default toolbars and menu commands in Word 2003, Excel 2003, Access 2003, Outlook 2003, and PowerPoint 2003?

1. In each Office application, select Customize from the Tools menu, and select the Options tab. Then, click Reset Menu And Toolbar Usage Data.

2. In any one of the Office applications, select Customize from the Tools menu, and select the Options tab. Then, click Reset Menu And Toolbar Usage Data.

3. In each Office application, select Customize from the Tools menu and select the Toolbars tab. In the Toolbars box, select the toolbar to restore. Click Reset. In the Reset Toolbar dialog box, select Normal and click OK. Click Close to exit.

4. In any one of the Office applications, select Customize from the Tools menu and select the Toolbars tab. In the Toolbars box, select the toolbar to restore. Click Reset. In the Reset Toolbar dialog box, select Normal and click OK. Click Close to exit.

Scenario 7-2: Creating a PowerPoint Presentation with Music

Theresa, a PowerPoint user, has created a presentation that is almost finalized. All of the slides are created, the transitions have been selected, and a graph and image have been embedded. To finish the presentation, she needs only to add a song that will act as background music for the presentation. She has the song on a CD and has the appropriate licenses to use it. Once the song has been added to the presentation, she wants to burn the final presentation onto a CD that can be played on her instructor's Microsoft Windows Me computer. The steps involved are listed here. Put the steps in order.

1. From the File menu, select Package For CD.

2. Insert the song into the completed PowerPoint presentation.

3. Select Copy To CD.

4. Copy the song to use in the presentation from the CD to the hard disk.

5. Test the presentation to verify it is correct.

6. Open the Custom Animation Task pane and set Effect Options so that the song starts playing at the first slide and stops playing at the last slide.

CHAPTER 8
COMMON CONNECTIVITY PROBLEMS

Upon completion of this chapter, you will be able to:

■ Test, troubleshoot, and repair physical connections

■ Troubleshoot connections configured for Internet, small office, and domain access

■ Diagnose and resolve name resolution problems using Ipconfig, Ping, and other diagnostic tools

■ Troubleshoot DNS and WINS, and HOSTS and LMHOSTS files

■ Resolve problems with Internet Connection Sharing

■ Describe the differences among the various types of handheld and mobile devices

■ Connect mobile devices using IrDA ports, wireless access points, and USB, FireWire, and serial ports

The purpose of this chapter is to teach you to recognize and resolve common connectivity problems that end users encounter in small home-office workgroups, larger local area networks (LANs), and corporate domains. Resolving connectivity problems at the Tier 1 level involves testing the physical connections, testing the hardware, and verifying the servers are online (if applicable), followed by testing and troubleshooting configured connections at the end user's computer. An end user might have several connections configured, including any or all of the following:

■ An Internet connection

■ A shared Internet connection

■ A connection to another computer through a hub, switch, or router

■ A connection to a larger LAN through the Internet

■ A connection to a domain or a domain server

■ A connection to a mobile device

In addition to calls that involve physical and configured connections, you might be asked to resolve more advanced connectivity issues. At the end of this chapter you'll learn about these advanced issues and how to use command-line utilities such as Ping, Ipconfig, and PathPing to determine the problem; how to configure **Domain Name System** (DNS) and Windows Internet Naming Service (WINS) addresses; and how to troubleshoot files such as HOSTS and LMHOSTS. Finally, you'll learn to troubleshoot connections for mobile devices, including handheld PCs, and you'll learn about the available connectivity options for various handheld devices.

PHYSICAL CONNECTIVITY

Many connectivity problems occur because the physical connection between the end user's computer and the hub, router, switch, phone jack, server, or Internet is not working properly. These connectivity problems are virtually the same for both home users and network domain users. Connection problems can be due to malfunctioning cables, network interface cards (NICs), modems, hubs, or **wireless access points**, or they can be caused by the incorrect configuration of these devices.

In this section, you learn some basic troubleshooting techniques that can be used to diagnose physical connectivity problems. This is the hands-on part of troubleshooting. If it is determined that the physical connections are good, you can move on to the second part of troubleshooting connectivity, checking the configurations of the network connections.

Connections

Many of the service calls you'll be asked to handle as a Tier 1 desktop technician are resolved by simply reconnecting the Ethernet cable or phone line to the computer, modem, or hub. This is especially true in an office or corporate environment where the furniture is moved or relocated often, or a cleaning crew comes in each night and works around end users' computers. When a user reports he cannot access the workgroup computers, the LAN, the domain, or the Internet, check these physical connections first.

> **NOTE** *Downed Servers and Computers*   *A workgroup or domain client will not be able to access workgroup or domain resources if its network server is down or the workgroup computer it is trying to reach is not turned on or is otherwise unavailable. Before getting too far into the troubleshooting procedure, verify that network computers are functional.*

In addition to the physical connection of the cable or phone line to the NIC or modem, verify these other items are properly connected (if applicable):

- The Ethernet cable to the hub
- The Ethernet cables from the hub to other computers
- The physical connections to and from servers, routers, and firewalls
- The phone line to the phone jack

- The modem, hub, and other devices that need power to the wall jack

- The universal serial bus (USB) or FireWire cable from and to the personal digital assistant (PDA), handheld PC, or other device

- Any other connection to and from any other device on the user's computer

In addition, if a wireless access point is configured, make sure it is within the range listed in its documentation. The wireless access point might have been moved or might have fallen behind a user's desk. A wireless user will not be able to connect if the wireless access point is not within the required range.

> **NOTE** **Ethernet**   If you notice that a desk, chair, or other piece of furniture is positioned on top of an Ethernet cable, try replacing the cable with a new one. The cable could be damaged.

Installed Hardware

If, after checking physical network connections, you find no problem, you need to check the hardware used for the connections so that you can rule out malfunctioning hardware as the cause of the problem. Checking physical hardware connections includes verifying through Device Manager that the devices involved with connectivity are working properly and, if they aren't, troubleshooting those devices. If problems persist, you also need to verify that the hardware is installed properly both externally and on the motherboard.

Check Device Manager

Device Manager details the hardware components on the computer and denotes any malfunctioning hardware with either a red X or a yellow exclamation point. You should check Device Manager if physical connectivity is not the problem, and before other troubleshooting techniques are attempted. If you find a problem with a modem or NIC, the hardware can be repaired or replaced quickly, and the user can be connected to the network again promptly.

▶ **Locating problem hardware devices**

To use Device Manager to locate and troubleshoot hardware devices installed on the computer, follow these steps:

1. Open Control Panel, open System, and in the System Properties dialog box, select the Hardware tab.

2. Select Device Manager.

3. Check for red Xs or yellow exclamation points. Expand any tree to see the name of the device. Figure 8-1 shows Device Manager with the Modems and Network Adapters trees expanded. In this figure, each component is functioning correctly.

Figure 8-1   Device Manager shows installed hardware, including modems and NICs.

If there are problems denoted in Device Manager, the component most likely has a device driver issue, is disabled, or has malfunctioned. You can troubleshoot the device by using the device's Properties dialog box on the General tab. Figure 8-2 shows the General tab for a modem that appears to be working correctly. Notice that the device is enabled in Device Usage.

Figure 8-2   The General tab details the device status.

▶ **Troubleshooting hardware devices**

If you believe a device is the cause of the problem, if the device is disabled, or if it has a red X or a yellow exclamation point beside it, you can use Device Manager to troubleshoot it by following these steps:

1. Open Device Manager.

2. Expand the tree for the component to troubleshoot. Double-click the device name.

3. In the Properties dialog box, select the General tab.

4. Verify that the Device Usage list box is set to Use This Device (Enable). If it isn't, use the drop-down list to select it. (This might solve the problem.)

5. Select Troubleshoot.

6. Work through the Help and Support Center's Troubleshooting Wizard to resolve the problem.

The Help and Support troubleshooting wizards are a great way to troubleshoot a piece of hardware because they walk you though tried and true techniques for solving common problems with hardware. In addition, they offer exceptional learning tools for beginning technicians.

> **MORE INFO** *Device Manager*   *To learn more about Device Manager, read Knowledge Base article 314747.*

Check Physical Connections

If Device Manager finds a problem and you can't resolve it using the troubleshooting wizards, or if the device you are looking for is missing from the Device Manager list (no modem listed, no NIC listed), you need to check the physical connection of the hardware from inside the computer case.

Occasionally, especially after a computer has been moved or bumped, a component inside the computer slips out of place just enough to cause the component to fail. When a modem or NIC is not **seated** properly, it cannot work properly. If you have the proper credentials (A+ certification or approval from your superiors, for instance), you should open the case and check these connections.

▶ **Checking connections**

To check for the proper connections inside a computer case, follow these steps:

1. Turn off the computer and unplug it.

2. Remove the cover from the computer case.

3. Ground yourself to the computer using an antistatic wrist strap.

4. Locate the modem or NIC, and press lightly on the card to verify it is seated properly. If the card is not properly seated, unscrew the card from the computer chassis, remove and reseat the card, and replace the screw.

5. Replace the cover, plug in the computer, and turn it on.

If the connection still does not work or if there were no obvious problems with the hardware, continue working through the troubleshooting techniques listed in the following sections.

Using the Modem Troubleshooter

The Microsoft Windows Help and Support files offer a modem troubleshooter (among others). If you believe that the modem is the cause of the connectivity problem, it is configured correctly and enabled in Device Manager, and you know the modem is seated correctly or connected properly at the computer, you can try the Modem Troubleshooter in Help and Support.

This troubleshooter guides you through what to do if you have problems connecting to the Internet using the modem, if Windows does not detect the modem, or if the Network Setup and New Connection Wizards are not working properly. In this case, you'd choose to follow the wizard through the options for solving a problem using the modem to connect to the Internet.

▶ **Troubleshooting with the Modem Troubleshooter**

To use the Modem Troubleshooter, follow these steps:

1. From the Start menu, select Help And Support.

2. Under Pick A Help Topic, select Fixing A Problem.

3. Under Fixing A Problem, select Networking Problems, and from the right pane, select Modem Troubleshooter.

4. On the What Problem Are You Having page, select I Have Problems Using My Modem To Connect To The Internet. Click Next.

5. Work through the various troubleshooting pages to do the following:

   a. Verify that the **COM port** is turned on.

   b. Verify that the modem is functional.

   c. Verify that the physical connection is configured properly.

   d. Verify that the modem is turned on.

   e. Verify that the COM port settings are correct.

   f. Verify that the modem is on the Microsoft Hardware Compatibility List (HCL).

   g. Verify that the COM port, modem, or cable is not faulty.

   h. Upgrade the basic input/output system (BIOS) of the internal modem if necessary.

   i. Locate conflicting devices.

   j. Upgrade the modem's .inf (a file that lists commands the modem supports) file or driver.

   k. Verify that the modem is installed correctly.

   l. Re-create dial-up connections.

   m. Visit the Windows Update Web site or the manufacturer's Web site.

As you can see from this list, the Windows Help and Support troubleshooting wizards are quite thorough. Whenever possible, access these wizards to help you resolve end user problems. In your spare time, work through the wizards to learn new techniques for resolving problems.

> **NOTE** **NIC Troubleshooter** If you believe that the NIC is not functioning properly, work through Help and Support's Drives And Network Adapters Troubleshooter.

CONFIGURED NETWORK CONNECTIONS

If the physical connections aren't the cause of connectivity problems, the configuration of those connections might be. For instance, although the modem might be working properly, the user won't be able to connect to the Internet if the phone number used to dial the Internet service provider (ISP) is configured incorrectly. If a Digital Subscriber Line (DSL) line is used, but the connection is configured incorrectly or unavailable, the user won't be able to connect either. Configuration problems such as these are quite common. In this section you learn how to troubleshoot configuration settings for these types of Internet connections, plus two other types: workgroup connections and domain connections.

Modem Connections

Internet connectivity problems involving modems occur for a variety of reasons. The problem can be caused by something as simple as dialing an incorrect phone number or having the connection automatically disconnect after a period of time, to something as complicated as an improperly configured DNS server address. In this section, you learn about the most common problems with configured Internet connections; later you learn about more complicated name resolution problems and problems with DNS or WINS servers.

Users often report fairly common connectivity problems. These include statements such as these:

- My ISP isn't answering the phone.

- I get an error when the modem dials stating that the number isn't in service.

- I can't hear my modem when it dials.

- I hear my modem when it dials.

- I keep getting disconnected from the Internet after 20 minutes of inactivity.

- When I get disconnected from the Internet, the connection is not redialed automatically.

- When I disconnect from my ISP at night, the computer redials and connects even though I don't want it to.

- I keep getting prompted for my name and password, phone number, and other information.

- Sometimes my ISP's phone number is busy. I have a new number for a new server. How do I change it?

Each of these problems can be resolved in the same place: the Internet connection's Properties dialog box.

Resolving Tier 1 Internet Connectivity Calls

You can resolve the problems in the preceding list from the Internet connection's Properties dialog box, shown in Figure 8-3. To access this page, open Network Connections, right-click the Internet connection, and select Properties.

Figure 8-3   The Internet Properties dialog box offers a place to configure the modem.

Table 8-1 details how to resolve each of the calls in the preceding list using the Internet Properties dialog box.

Table 8-1   Resolving Common Internet Connectivity Calls

Complaint/Report	Possible Solution
My ISP isn't answering the phone.	Call the ISP and verify or obtain a phone number. On the General tab, retype the phone number.
I get an error when the modem dials stating that the number isn't in service.	Call the ISP and obtain a new phone number. On the General tab, insert the phone number.
I can't hear my modem when it dials.	On the General tab, click Configure. Select the Enable Modem Speaker check box. In Device Manager, double-click the modem and on the Modem tab, configure the speaker volume.
I hear my modem when it dials.	On the General tab, select Configure. Clear the Enable Modem Speaker check box.
I keep getting disconnected from the Internet after 20 minutes of inactivity.	On the Options tab, change the setting for Idle Time Before Hanging Up to Never, 24 Hours, 8 Hours, 4 Hours, or any other setting.

Table 8-1   Resolving Common Internet Connectivity Calls

Complaint/Report	Possible Solution
When I get disconnected from the Internet, the connection is not redialed automatically.	On the Options tab, select the Redial If Line Is Dropped check box.
When I disconnect from my ISP at night, the computer redials and connects even though I don't want it to.	On the Options tab, change the value for Redial Attempts to 0. Clear the Redial If Line Is Dropped check box.
I keep getting prompted for my name and password, phone number, and other information.	On the Options tab, clear the Prompt For Name And Password, Certificate, Etc., Include Windows Logon Domain, and Prompt For Phone Number check boxes as applicable to the network.
Sometimes my ISP's phone number is busy. I have a new number for a new server. How do I change it?	On the General tab, click Alternates. In the Alternate Phone Numbers dialog box, click Add. Add the new number, and click OK to exit the dialog boxes.

When you are finished making changes, click OK in the Internet Properties dialog box and disconnect and redial the number to activate the changes.

Cable and DSL Connections

Internet connectivity problems involving cable and DSL modems occur for a variety of reasons. The problem can be caused by something as simple as a disconnected cable or a dial-up modem that isn't disabled, to something as complicated as troubleshooting a slow connection or identifying the source of DSL interference. In this section, you learn about the most common problems with these types of configured Internet connections; later you learn about more complicated name resolution problems and problems with DNS or WINS servers.

Users often report fairly common connectivity problems. These include statements such as these:

- My dial-up modem keeps trying to dial out.
- My Internet connection is unavailable.
- I try to connect, but nothing happens at all.
- My Internet connection is slow.
- I think I'm getting interference. Could something be causing that?

Resolving Tier 1 Internet Connectivity Calls

You can resolve the problems in the preceding list using common sense and familiar troubleshooting techniques. Table 8-2 details how to resolve these calls.

Table 8-2   Resolving Common Internet Connectivity Calls

Complaint/Report	Possible Solution
My dial-up modem keeps trying to dial out.	Open Control Panel, and then Internet Options. Select the Connection tab, and select LAN Settings. Clear all check boxes. Click OK twice to close the two open dialog boxes. Open Internet Explorer, and from the Tools menu, select Internet Options. On the Connections tab, select Never Dial A Connection. Click OK.
My Internet connection is unavailable.	Check all physical connections to and from modems, routers, and the computer. Swap out questionable cables for new ones. If problems still exist, right-click the connection in Network Connections, select Properties, select the Networking tab, select Internet Protocol (TCP/IP), and click Properties. Verify that the settings are correct with the ISP. A common setting is Obtain An IP Address Automatically. Click OK to close all open dialog boxes.
I try to connect, but nothing happens at all.	Verify that all power supplies to modems or routers are plugged in and that all hardware is turned on. Verify that the NIC and all hardware is functional using Device Manager as detailed earlier.
My Internet connection is slow.	Contact the ISP first. The problem could lie in the ISP's capabilities. It could be "oversold," or servers could be overloaded. A newer modem might also be available.
I think I'm getting interference. Could something be causing that?	Yes. Lighting dimmer switches, AM radio stations, and other sources can cause interference. For more information, visit *http://cable-dsl.home.att.net.*

MORE INFO   Troubleshooting Cable Modems   For more information about troubleshooting cable modems, read Knowledge Base article 310089, "Troubleshooting Cable Modems."

Workgroup Connections

A workgroup is a common network configuration. Generally, a workgroup consists of a few computers, each of which is connected to a hub, router, or switch, through an Ethernet cable or wirelessly, for the purpose of sharing files in a small office or a home. Problems that occur in this type of network can occur for many reasons. When troubleshooting a user's access to another workgroup computer or resource on the network, you need to check the physical connections first, check the status of the hub and NIC, verify the workgroup name in My Computer, and try repairing or disabling and enabling the connection from Network Connections. If the problem cannot be resolved using any of these techniques, you might have to re-create the network connection.

> **NOTE** **Before Continuing** *Before performing any of the following troubleshooting techniques, verify that the user is logged on to the computer appropriately, that physical connections are solid, that the NIC has a green light indicating it is functional (if the NIC has diagnostic LEDs), and that the hub, switch, or other device is working properly.*

Resolving Tier 1 Workgroup Connectivity Calls

If the physical connections and hardware are all functional and connected properly, you can begin troubleshooting the connection's properties. These properties might have been changed because the user ran the Network Connections Wizard, the Network Setup Wizard, or the New Connection Wizard; changed the name of the workgroup or the name of the computer in the System Properties dialog box; or for a number of other reasons. You should first verify the workgroup name and computer name are correct in the System Properties dialog box by following these steps:

1. Open Control Panel and open System.

2. On the Computer Name tab, verify that the computer is a member of a workgroup, and that the workgroup name is correct. If these settings are correct, click OK.

3. If the workgroup name is incorrect, click Change, and in the Computer Name Changes dialog box shown in Figure 8-4, type the correct workgroup name and click OK.

Figure 8-4 Check the workgroup name from System in Control Panel.

4. If the computer name is incorrect, click Change, and in the Computer Name Changes dialog box shown in Figure 8-4, type in the correct computer name and click OK.

5. If the information on the Computer Name tab states that the computer is a member of a domain instead of a workgroup, click Change, and in the Computer Name Changes dialog box, select Workgroup, and type in the correct workgroup name. Click OK.

6. Click OK to close the System Properties dialog box, and reboot the computer if prompted.

You can also check the computer name, user name, workstation domain, and other information using the command-line utility net config workstation. The information provided can be quite useful when troubleshooting Tier 1 connectivity calls. To see what information can be obtained, follow these steps:

1. From the Start menu, select All Programs, Accessories, and then select Command Prompt.

2. At the prompt, type **net config workstation**, and press ENTER. Figure 8-5 shows a sample result.

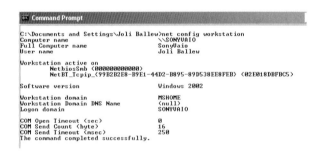

Figure 8-5   The command-line utility net config workstation offers plenty of information.

Notice in Figure 8-5 that the following pertinent information is offered (among other items):

- Computer name
- User name
- Workstation domain
- Logon domain

This command-line utility thus offers another way to locate and obtain information about the computer, and this information can prove quite helpful when troubleshooting connectivity problems. If the workgroup name and the computer name are correct, try repairing and then disabling and enabling the connection by following this procedure:

1. Open Control Panel and open Network Connections. Verify the local area connection is enabled. If it is not, right-click the connection and select Enable. Check to see if this resolves the problem.

2. Right-click Local Area Connection, and select Repair. Choosing this option forces a network adapter to acquire a new IP address, and thus "resets" the network connection for that computer. Wait to see the status of the attempted repair.

3. If the repair is successful, double-click the Local Area Connection icon. Verify that **packets** are being sent and received as shown in Figure 8-6. This denotes a healthy network connection. Click Close.

Figure 8-6   A working network connection shows packets being sent and received.

4. If the repair procedure fails, right-click Local Area Connection and select Disable. Right-click again and select Enable.

5. If enabling is successful, double-click the Local Area Connection icon. Verify that packets are being sent and received as shown in Figure 8-6. This denotes a healthy network connection. Click Close.

If the local area connection is still not working properly, clear all network connections by clicking an empty area of the Network Connections window. In the left pane, under See Also, click Network Troubleshooter. Next, follow these steps:

1. From the Help and Support Center Networking Problems page, select Home And Small Office Networking Troubleshooter.

2. On the first page, under What Problem Are You Having, select I'm Having Problems Sharing Files Or Printers. Click Next.

3. On the following wizard pages, make sure that I Want The Troubleshooter To Investigate Settings On This Computer is selected as you work through the options.

If the problem cannot be resolved using any of these techniques, you might have to re-create the network connection.

Re-Creating the Network Connection

As a last resort before tackling advanced command-line utility troubleshooting techniques, and prior to making complicated changes to DNS or WINS server addresses, re-create the network connection and reintroduce the computer to the network. This often works to bring the computer back online.

Because there are many ways a network can be configured, and because a computer in a network can be configured in multiple ways as well, the steps involved in re-creating a network connection can take on many different forms. For instance, a computer configured to provide (host) a shared dial-up Internet connection has a much different configuration than a computer that connects to the Internet through a router. Therefore, the following procedure walks through re-creating the connection for a computer that connects directly to the Internet and provides shared Internet access to the other computers on the network. Procedures for other configurations are performed similarly.

▶ **Re-creating a LAN connection**

To re-create a LAN connection and reintroduce the computer to the network, follow these steps:

1. From the Start menu, select All Programs, Accessories, Communications, and then select Network Setup Wizard. Click Next to start the wizard.

2. Read the information on the Before You Continue page, and click Next.

3. On the Select A Connection Method page shown in Figure 8-7, select the option that best describes the computer you are troubleshooting:

   ❑ This Computer Connects Directly To The Internet. The Other Computers On My Network Connect To The Internet Through This Computer. (The rest of the steps in this example show the procedure when this option is selected.)

   ❑ This Computer Connects To The Internet Through Another Computer On My Network Or Through A Residential Gateway.

   ❑ Other. (If you select this option, the Network Setup Wizard offers you additional choices, and you need to make the appropriate choice depending on the circumstances.)

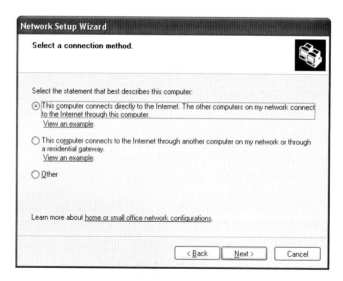

Figure 8-7   Select the option that best describes the computer.

4. When prompted to select an Internet connection, select the connection that the client uses to connect to the Internet from the list offered. Click Next.

5. If prompted that the computer has multiple connections, choose Let Me Choose The Connections To My Network. On the resulting wizard page, make the appropriate selections for your network. Click Next.

6. On the Give This Computer A Description And Name page, type a computer description (this is optional), and type the computer name. Click Next.

7. On the Name Your Network page, in the Workgroup Name box, type the name of the existing workgroup. Click Next.

8. On the Ready To Apply Network Settings page, verify that the settings are correct and click Next. (Click Back if they aren't and make any necessary changes.)

9. Wait while the Network Setup Wizard completes. When prompted to add other computers to the network, select Just Finish The Wizard; I Don't Need To Run The Wizard On Other Computers. Click Next, and then click Finish.

The user should now be able to access network resources on the Microsoft Windows XP computers on the network, and should have access to the Internet. Open My Network Places to verify this.

If problems still exist after you work through the troubleshooting techniques in this section, you need to apply some advanced techniques. These advanced procedures are detailed in the following sections of this chapter.

> **NOTE** **Automatic Private IP Addressing** Workgroups can use Automatic Private IP Addressing (APIPA) to connect workgroup resources, and this type of addressing can cause connectivity issues. APIPA can also be used in domains. For more information about APIPA, see the section "APIPA Connections" later in this chapter.

Domain Connections

A domain is another type of network configuration. Generally, a domain consists of many computers (10, 100, 1000, or more), each of which can be connected to a server (or servers) on the network through an Ethernet cable, wirelessly, through fiber optic cable, through a T1 line, over the Internet, or by using a combination of these or other connectivity options. A server authenticates the user onto the domain for the purpose of sharing files and folders, hardware, and other network resources. Those resources can be in the same office or anywhere in the world.

> **NOTE** **Windows XP Home Edition** Windows XP Home Edition cannot be used to join a domain.

Problems that occur in this type of network can occur for many reasons. When troubleshooting a user's access to a domain server or resource on the network, you need to verify that the user is logged on to the domain with the correct credentials and password, check the status of the servers and the physical connections, and check the status of the NIC. As with a workgroup connection, you can also try repairing and disabling and enabling the connection from Network Connections. If you cannot resolve the problem using any of these techniques, you will have to use more advanced troubleshooting techniques, including troubleshooting Transmission Control Protocol/Internet Protocol (TCP/IP) settings.

> **NOTE** **Before Continuing**   Before performing any of the following troubleshooting techniques, verify that physical connections are solid, that the NIC has a green light indicating it is functional (if the NIC has diagnostic LEDs), and that servers, hubs, switches, routers, and other devices are working properly and are available.

Resolving Tier 1 Domain Connectivity Calls

If the physical connections and hardware (including servers) are all in working order and connected properly, you can begin troubleshooting the connection's properties. You should first verify that the connection is functional, and that packets are being sent and received. As with a workgroup, try repairing and then disabling and enabling the connection by following these steps:

1. Open Control Panel and open Network Connections. Verify that the local area connection to the server is enabled if such a connection exists. If it is not enabled, right-click the connection and select Enable. Check to see if this resolves the problem.

2. Right-click the local area connection for the domain if it exists, and select Repair (see Figure 8-8). This connection might be a network bridge, a wireless connection, or another type of local area connection. Wait to see the status of the attempted repair.

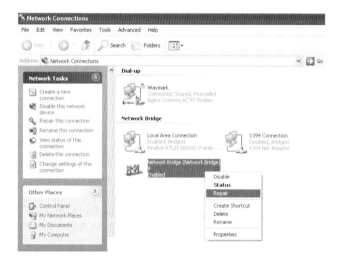

Figure 8-8   Repair network connections as a first step in troubleshooting.

3. If the repair is successful, double-click the connection's icon. Verify that packets are being sent and received. Click Close.

4. If the repair procedure fails, right-click the connection and select Disable. Right-click again and select Enable. Repeat this with the network bridge, if one exists.

5. If enabling is successful, double-click the Local Area Connection icon. Verify that packets are being sent and received. This denotes a healthy network connection. Click Close.

6. If the user connects to the domain over the Internet, verify that the user's Internet connection is active. If it is not, connect to the Internet before continuing. Double-click that connection to verify that data is being sent and received. Additionally, verify the speed, errors, and compression numbers. These might produce significant hints as to the source of the connectivity problem. For instance, if the user's Internet connection speed is 28.8 Kbps, the user's requests for data will probably **timeout** before they ever reach the server.

   NOTE **Internet Connections** If a user's Internet connection is the source of the problem, you might have to troubleshoot the modem or contact the ISP for information about the problem.

If the physical connection to the server or domain is functional and packets are being sent and received or an Internet connection is working properly, verify that the user is logging on to the domain and not the computer. When a Windows XP Professional computer is a member of a domain, users can log on to either the domain or the local computer. If a user has logged on to the computer instead of the domain, that user might not be able to access domain resources. To verify the user is logging on to the domain, follow these steps:

1. Open Control Panel, and open User Accounts.

2. From the User Accounts window, select User Accounts.

3. On the new User Accounts page, select Change The Way Users Log On Or Off.

4. On the Select Logon And Logoff Options page, clear Use The Welcome Screen if it is selected. Click Apply Options and close all windows.

5. Press CTRL + ALT + DEL on the keyboard, and select Log Off in the Windows Security dialog box. Select Log Off to verify when prompted.

6. On the Log On To Windows page, check to see how the user is logged on. If the user is logged on to the computer and not the domain, have the user log off and log on with a domain user account. If the user is logging on to an incorrect domain, continue your troubleshooting as detailed next.

If the user is logging on to an incorrect domain—for instance, if the user is trying to log on using a laptop normally used for accessing the corporate domain, and is now trying to use that same computer to log on to a different (perhaps) local domain—you have to change the computer's domain or workgroup membership on the Computer Name tab. To change the computer's domain membership, perform the following steps:

1. Right-click My Computer and select Properties, or, open System from Control Panel.

2. Select the Computer Name tab, and click Change.

3. In the Computer Name Changes dialog box, select Domain, and type the name of the new domain. Click OK. Figure 8-9 shows this dialog box.

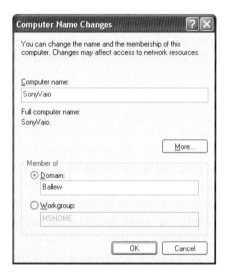

Figure 8-9   Make domain changes in the Computer Name Changes dialog box.

4. Reboot as prompted, and have the user log on to the new domain.

> **CAUTION**   **Use the Correct DNS Server Addres**   sIf the computer isn't configured with the correct DNS server addresses (or can't contact the DNS servers), you won't be able to change the computer's membership. There is more information on DNS servers later in this chapter.

If the user has logged on to the domain correctly and the connection is functioning properly, open Network Connections and clear all network connections by clicking an empty area of the Network Connections window. In the left pane, under See Also, click Network Troubleshooter, then follow these steps:

1. On the Help and Support Center Networking Problems page, select Diagnose Network Configuration And Run Automated Networking Tasks.

2. Select Set Scanning Options and select each item in the list. Click Save Options when you're done.

3. Click Scan Your System. The results will help you diagnose the problem, and this is a good first step. Figure 8-10 shows a sample report.

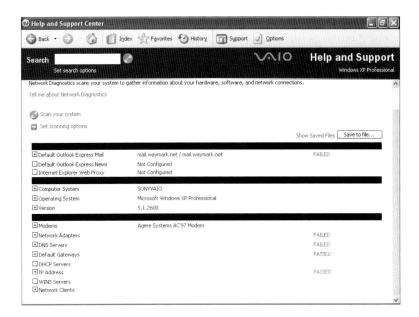

Figure 8-10   A system scan using the Network Troubleshooter can offer assistance.

Notice that this report produces a few failures, including contacting the mail server configured in Outlook Express, a problem with the wide area network (WAN) Miniport (IP) network adapter, and issues with the connection to a DNS server. Expanding each tree offers more information, including how the error was discovered (such as a ping failure or a server timeout).

In this case, each failure revolved around accessing the same IP address. All other network components, including modems, configured IP addresses on the local computer, default gateways, the ability to access other network resources, and configured network clients are functioning properly. The problem thus lies with that particular resource. Sometimes, the information here is just enough to get you started on the right track when troubleshooting domain access.

DHCP Connections

On a domain, most computers are configured to get their TCP/IP addresses automatically from a **Dynamic Host Configuration Protocol** (DHCP) server. These unique TCP/IP addresses allow computers to communicate with other computers and resources on the network and, in many cases, on the Internet. The DHCP server is responsible for automatically configuring IP addresses for computers and other resources on both local and remote networks. DHCP prevents an administrator from having to manually configure **static IP addresses** for individual resources.

When a problem occurs with users' TCP/IP configurations, the users will not be able to access the network's resources. For example, if the DHCP server is offline, users cannot obtain the necessary addresses from the DHCP server, and without a valid TCP/IP address from the DHCP server, users will not be able to communicate with anyone on the network or access network resources.

When a DHCP server is unavailable, APIPA takes over. APIPA offers a temporary TCP/IP addressing scheme so that computers on the local network can communicate with each other until a DHCP server becomes available again. However, because APIPA uses a different addressing scheme from all other networks (the addresses are reserved for this purpose), it also causes problems on networks that use DHCP because the two schemes aren't able to communicate. Even though APIPA causes some problems, it still allows communication between computers on the local network until the issue causing the problem is resolved. APIPA is detailed further next.

APIPA Connections

APIPA is a feature of Windows XP TCP/IP that automatically configures a unique IP address for each computer on a network when TCP/IP is configured for dynamic addressing and a DHCP server is not available. APIPA thus automates the IP configuration of all network resources and connections. These addresses are always in the range of 169.254.0.1 through 169.254.255.254 and use a **subnet mask** of 255.255.0.0. The purpose of APIPA is to allow a network to be easily and quickly configured for both workgroups and domains, and to allow resources to be available even if the DHCP server is offline.

When you configure a TCP/IP connection to obtain an IP address automatically, by default, the computer attempts to contact a DHCP server for that address. If the server is available, a user is given an address from the **scope of addresses** on the DHCP server. If a DHCP server is not configured or not available, the computer uses the alternate configuration to determine whether or not to use APIPA.

> **NOTE** **APIPA Addressing** APIPA addresses are never used on the Internet. In addition, because APIPA does not offer a **gateway address,** APIPA clients cannot access anything outside the LAN. APIPA is really only useful in emergencies in domain subnets and on small LANs that have only a single network segment and do not access outside resources.

▶ **Using automatic TCP/IP addressing and APIPA**

To configure a computer to use automatic TCP/IP addressing and APIPA when necessary, follow these steps:

1. Open Network Connections.

2. Right-click the configured network connection, and then select Properties.

3. On the General tab for a local area connection or on the Networking tab for all other connections, select Internet Protocol (TCP/IP), and then click Properties.

4. Verify that Obtain An IP Address Automatically is selected, and click OK. Click OK again to close the Local Area Connection Properties dialog box.

▶ **Determining if a computer is using APIPA**

You can easily find out if a computer is using an APIPA address and if APIPA is enabled by typing **ipconfig /all** at the command prompt and proceeding as follows:

1. From the Start menu, select All Programs, Accessories, Command Prompt.

2. Type **ipconfig /all** and press ENTER.

   TIP **Ipconfig** You can also type ipconfig without the /all switch if you need less information. Ipconfig with no switches offers the IP address, subnet mask, and default gateway of each connection, including any LANs and the Internet connections.

3. Under Windows IP Configuration, locate the Autoconfiguration IP Address. If the IP address is in the range of 169.254.0.1 through 169.254.255.254, the computer is configured with an APIPA address, and APIPA is active.

4. To see if APIPA is enabled, check the Autoconfiguration Enabled parameter. If the parameter is set to Yes, APIPA is enabled.

If APIPA is active, it automatically checks every five minutes for an available DHCP server, just in case one comes back online.

   TIP **Eureka** If a user is having problems connecting to a resource on the domain and APIPA addressing is active, you've found the problem. If the user is having problems connecting to resources on a workgroup that uses APIPA for its addressing scheme, you'll have to dig a little deeper.

Remote Access Connections

Corporate users can access a domain and network resources using routing and remote access servers and technology. Home users can access their workgroup's desktop computers using remote access technology, too. The Routing and Remote Access Service allows remote networking for telecommuters and mobile workers, and for system administrators who monitor network services. Users dial in to their networks to access file and printer sharing, e-mail, and other available resources.

Problems that occur when using remote access are similar to problems that occur when connecting to any other network or resource. In a domain, insufficient rights or privileges, an unavailable routing and remote access server, problematic physical connections, and dial-in properties can cause problems. In a workgroup, the problems are similar. When troubleshooting a remote access problem, follow the general troubleshooting principles outlined in this book and chapter, and search the Knowledge Base for solutions to specific problems and error messages.

RESOLVING COMPLEX NAME RESOLUTION PROBLEMS

If a domain or workgroup user is still unable to access a network resource on a domain or workgroup, and you've checked that the user has logged on correctly, that the physical connections are good, that the network connections are working properly, that an IP address problem (due to APIPA) isn't causing the problem, and the Network Troubleshooter did not help you solve the problem or only gave you a few hints, you have a more serious issue on your hands.

Complex problems generally require troubleshooting from the command line. In this section you learn some common commands, what type of information each of these commands offers, and how to work with the information you find. Commands detailed here include the following:

- Ping
- Ipconfig /All
- Net view
- Pathping
- Tracert

Using Ping

When the problem appears to have to do with TCP/IP, either because you have ruled out problems with NICs, physical connections, and the other causes detailed in the chapter, or because the Network Troubleshooter pointed out a TCP/IP address problem, you need to start the troubleshooting process with the Ping command. Ping allows you to check for connectivity between devices, including the local computer's NIC, the network's DNS server, DHCP server, gateway, and other resources.

When you use the Ping command, you'll ping from the inside out. You want to find out where the communication and connection fails. For example, you'll ping the **loopback address** first, then a local computer on the same **subnet** (basically, a subnet is the equivalent of a LAN), then a DNS or DHCP server on the local subnet if one exists, then the default gateway, then a remote computer on another subnet (a network outside of the LAN), and finally, a resource on the Internet. You should be able to find out where the breakdown occurs by compiling the results of these checks.

> **NOTE** **Ping by Name or IP Address** When using the Ping command, you can use either the computer name or the computer's IP address.

The Loopback Address
The loopback address (127.0.0.1) is the first thing you should check when a TCP/IP problem appears. If this check fails, the TCP/IP configuration for the local machine is not configured correctly.

▶ **Pinging the loopback address**

To ping the loopback address, follow these steps:

1. From the Start menu, select All Programs, Accessories, and select Command Prompt.

2. Type **ping 127.0.0.1**. A successful ping to a loopback address is shown in Figure 8-11.

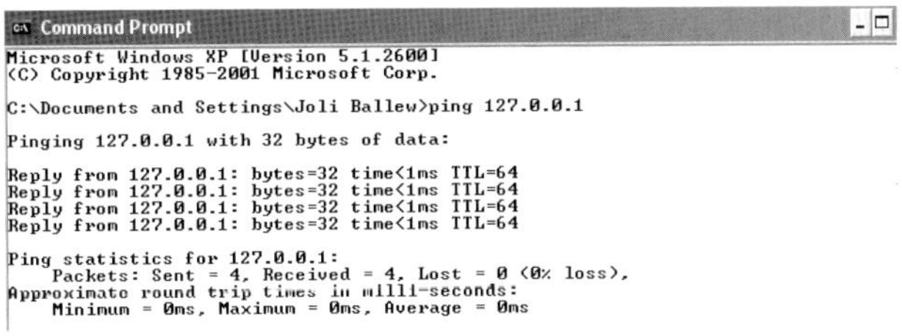

```
Command Prompt                                        _ □

Microsoft Windows XP [Version 5.1.2600]
(C) Copyright 1985-2001 Microsoft Corp.

C:\Documents and Settings\Joli Ballew>ping 127.0.0.1

Pinging 127.0.0.1 with 32 bytes of data:

Reply from 127.0.0.1: bytes=32 time<1ms TTL=64
Reply from 127.0.0.1: bytes=32 time<1ms TTL=64
Reply from 127.0.0.1: bytes=32 time<1ms TTL=64
Reply from 127.0.0.1: bytes=32 time<1ms TTL=64

Ping statistics for 127.0.0.1:
    Packets: Sent = 4, Received = 4, Lost = 0 (0% loss),
Approximate round trip times in milli-seconds:
    Minimum = 0ms, Maximum = 0ms, Average = 0ms
```

Figure 8-11 Ping the loopback address to verify that TCP/IP is configured correctly.

▶ **Checking the TCP/IP configuration**

If pinging the loopback address fails, check the configuration of TCP/IP by following this procedure:

1. Open Network Connections, right-click the configured connection, and select Properties.

2. Select Internet Protocol (TCP/IP) and click Properties to view the configuration. If a static address is configured and a DHCP server is available, select Obtain An IP Address Automatically. If Obtain An IP Address Automatically is selected, but a static IP address is necessary, select Use The Following IP Address, and then input the address, subnet mask, and gateway to use. If the configuration is correct, you might have to reset TCP/IP.

3. Click OK in the Properties dialog box, and click OK in the connection's Properties dialog box. Reboot the computer if prompted.

> **MORE INFO** **Reset TCP/IP in Windows XP** If reconfiguring the TCP/IP settings did not help solve the loopback problem, you can try resetting TCP/IP. Knowledge Base article 299357 details how.

Ping Other Resources

To ping any other computer on the network, simply replace the loopback address with the TCP/IP address of the resource on the network. Ping a local computer on the same subnet first, and then ping the gateway address. If you can ping the loopback address, a local computer on the same subnet, but the ping command to the gateway fails, you've probably found the problem. In this case, check the configuration on the local computer for the gateway address and verify that the gateway (or router) is operational. To check a computer's configured gateway address, follow these steps:

1. Open Network Connections, right-click the configured connection, and select Properties.

2. Select Internet Protocol (TCP/IP) and click Properties to view the configuration.

3. In the connection's Properties dialog box, click Advanced.

4. In the Advanced TCP/IP Settings dialog box, check the address for the default gateway. If the address is incorrect, click Edit. If no gateway is configured and one should be, click Add. To remove an address, click Remove.

5. If Edit or Add was selected in step 4, in the TCP/IP Gateway Address dialog box shown in Figure 8-12, type the correct address. Click OK.

Figure 8-12   Configure a gateway address.

6. Click OK twice to close the remaining dialog boxes, and click Close to apply the change.

If the ping to the gateway address is successful, however, continue to ping outward until you find the problem. For instance, ping a computer on a remote subnet next, and verify the DNS server is operational.

MORE INFO   **Troubleshooting TCP/IP Connectivity in Windows XP**   *For more information about troubleshooting using Ping and similar commands, read Knowledge Base article 314067.*

Using Ipconfig /All

The Ipconfig /All command displays statistics about the local computer's IP address, subnet mask, and default gateway, the physical address of the NIC(s), whether or not the computer is DHCP enabled, the addresses of the DNS servers, and more. This information can be quite useful in troubleshooting IP address problems, including improperly configured default gateways, subnet masks, and DNS server addresses.

Figure 8-13 shows an example of an Ipconfig /All report. There are three sections on this particular report (configurations and reports will vary):

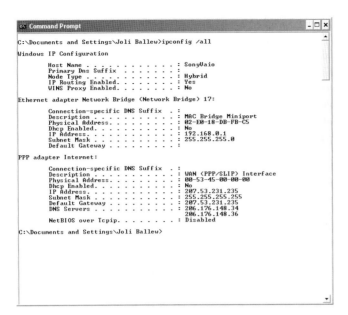

```
C:\Command Prompt                                          _ □ X

C:\Documents and Settings\Joli Ballew>ipconfig /all

Windows IP Configuration

        Host Name . . . . . . . . . . . . : SonyVaio
        Primary Dns Suffix  . . . . . . . :
        Node Type . . . . . . . . . . . . : Hybrid
        IP Routing Enabled. . . . . . . . : Yes
        WINS Proxy Enabled. . . . . . . . : No

Ethernet adapter Network Bridge (Network Bridge) 17:

        Connection-specific DNS Suffix  . :
        Description . . . . . . . . . . . : MAC Bridge Miniport
        Physical Address. . . . . . . . . : 02-E0-18-DB-FB-C5
        Dhcp Enabled. . . . . . . . . . . : No
        IP Address. . . . . . . . . . . . : 192.168.0.1
        Subnet Mask . . . . . . . . . . . : 255.255.255.0
        Default Gateway . . . . . . . . . :

PPP adapter Internet:

        Connection-specific DNS Suffix  . :
        Description . . . . . . . . . . . : WAN (PPP/SLIP) Interface
        Physical Address. . . . . . . . . : 00-53-45-00-00-00
        Dhcp Enabled. . . . . . . . . . . : No
        IP Address. . . . . . . . . . . . : 207.53.231.235
        Subnet Mask . . . . . . . . . . . : 255.255.255.255
        Default Gateway . . . . . . . . . : 207.53.231.235
        DNS Servers . . . . . . . . . . . : 206.176.148.34
                                            206.176.148.36
        NetBIOS over Tcpip. . . . . . . . : Disabled

C:\Documents and Settings\Joli Ballew>
```

Figure 8-13   The Ipconfig /All report offers a myriad of information.

- **Windows IP Configuration**   This section details the host name (computer name), the DNS suffix (the domain name), the node type (details how NetBIOS name queries are resolved), if IP routing is enabled or not, and if WINS Proxy is enabled or not.

- **Ethernet Adapter Network Bridge**   This section details the physical address of the network adapter, whether or not DHCP and autoconfiguration (APIPA) are enabled, the IP address, subnet mask, and default gateway.

- **PPP Adapter Internet**   This section details the physical address of the adapter, whether or not DHCP is enabled, the IP address, subnet mask, default gateway, and DNS server used in the connection, and whether or not NetBIOS over TCP/IP is enabled.

The information here can be especially useful when you need to verify that the IP address, subnet mask, and default gateway address are correct.

Rules About TCP/IP Addressing

When checking for problems using Ipconfig /All, you should verify that the IP address, subnet mask, and gateway address all jive. To do that, you need to know something about TCP/IP addressing.

There are five classes of IP addresses, but for the most part, you'll be concerned with only the first three. Table 8-3 details the various TCP/IP address classes you are likely to see on a home or corporate network and their start and end addresses.

An address in that range must have an associated subnet mask that agrees with the IP address. Subnet masks enable computers to determine when to send packets to the gateway to communicate with computers on remote subnets. When checking for TCP/IP configuration problems, verify that the IP address is using the correct subnet mask.

Table 8-3   **IP Addresses and Related Subnet Masks**

Class	Beginning IP Address	Ending IP Address	Default Subnet Mask
A	1.0.0.1	126.255.255.254	255.0.0.0
B	128.0.0.1	191.255.255.254	255.255.0.0
C	192.0.0.1	223.255.255.254	255.255.255.0

In addition to IP addresses and subnet masks, gateways and routers are used to connect users of the subnet to outside resources such as the Internet or other sub-nets on the network. The gateway or router must have an IP address also, and that IP address must be accessible from the user's local subnet. A router that connects a Class A network to a Class C network will need two IP addresses—one that is a Class A address and one that is a Class C address—so that the computers on each subnet can access it.

Finally, certain rules apply to all TCP/IP address schemes:

- IP addresses that start and end with 0 aren't allowed, so 0.208.254.121 is invalid, as is 10.1.10.0. However, addresses with 0 in the middle are allowed.

- The IP address 127.x.y.z is reserved as the loopback address and cannot be used.

- Each computer in each subnet must have a unique TCP/IP address. If two computers have the same IP address, problems will result.

- When you assign an IP address, you must also assign a subnet mask.

- Routers must be available from the subnet on which they reside. A Class C network with clients that use the IP addresses 192.168.1.2 through 192.168.1.14 might have a router configured at 192.168.1.1 or 192.168.1.15.

Net View

Net View is another command that can be used to test TCP/IP connections. To use the command, log on with the proper credentials required to view shares on a remote or local computer, open a command prompt, and type **net view *ComputerName*** or **net view *IP Address***. The resulting report lists the file and print shares on the computer. If there are no file or print shares on the computer, you see the message There Are No Entries In The List.

If the Net View command fails, check the following:

- The computer name in the System Properties dialog box

- The gateway or router address in the TCP/IP Properties dialog box

- The gateway or router's status
- The remote computer is running the File and Printer Sharing for Microsoft Networks Service (this service can be added in the TCP/IP Properties dialog box)

Tracert

When a route breaks down on the way from the destination computer to its target computer, communication fails. The Tracert command-line utility can help you figure out exactly where along the route this happened. Sometimes the connection breaks down at the gateway on the local network, and sometimes at a router on an external network.

To use Tracert, type **tracert** followed by the IP address of the remote computer. The resulting report shows where the packets were lost. You can use this information to uncover the source of the problem.

Pathping

Ping is used to test communication between one computer and another; Tracert is used to follow a particular route from one computer to another. Pathping is a combination of both Ping and Tracert, displaying information about packet loss at every router between the host computer and the remote one. Pathping provides information about data loss between the source and the destination, allowing you to determine which particular router or subnet might be having network problems. To use the Pathping command, type **pathping** followed by the target name or IP address.

> **NOTE** **More Commands** The Windows Help and Support files offer a list of all of the commands that can be performed at the command line. Search for Command-Line Reference A-Z. Each command reference includes a description of the command and how to use it.

ADVANCED NAME RESOLUTION COMPONENTS

Name resolution is the process that allows network and Internet users to access resources by their name instead of their IP address. The name used might be (among other things) a computer name, server name, a printer name, or a **fully qualified domain name** (FQDN). Without name resolution, users would be forced to remember the IP addresses of each resource on the network or on the Internet. Thus, name resolution makes accessing resources much simpler. Components of a network that assist in the name resolution process include the following:

- DNS servers
- WINS servers
- HOSTS files
- LMHOSTS files

When problems occur with accessing network resources, often the solution involves troubleshooting these components.

DNS

DNS servers resolve the names of network resources to their respective IP addresses. In a LAN, an administrator creates a DNS server and configures the information regarding the IP address of resources on the network. When something is wrong with the DNS configuration on a computer or the DNS server on a network, users will not be able to resolve computer names or FQDNs to their IP addresses and connectivity to those resources will fail.

If you believe (because of results of Ping, Ipconfig /All, Tracert, or other command-line tests) that an incorrect DNS configuration is preventing a user or users from resolving names to IP addresses, and you have verified the IP address of the DNS server and that it is online, you should check the DNS settings on the local computer. You can view and reconfigure the DNS configuration on a Windows XP computer quite easily by following these steps:

1. Open Network Connections, right-click the active local area connection, and choose Properties.

2. On the General tab of the Properties dialog box, select Internet Protocol (TCP/IP), and click Properties.

3. In the Internet Protocol (TCP/IP) Properties dialog box shown in Figure 8-14, select Obtain DNS Server Address Automatically, or select Use The Following DNS Server Addresses and type the IP address of the DNS server.

Figure 8-14   Set DNS properties.

4. If you need to configure an alternate DNS server address and you've configured the computer to obtain its IP and DNS server addresses automatically, on the Alternate Configuration tab, click User Configured, and type a preferred and alternate DNS server address. Click OK when you're done. (The Alternate Configuration tab only appears if you've

configured the computer to obtain its IP address and DNS server addresses automatically.)

5. To configure advanced DNS settings, on the General tab, click Advanced.

6. In the Advanced TCP/IP Settings dialog box, select the DNS tab.

7. In the DNS Server Addresses, In Order Of Use list, note the configured DNS server addresses. Use Add, Edit, or Remove to make configuration changes to the DNS servers listed. Use the arrows to move a DNS server up or down in the list. See Figure 8-15.

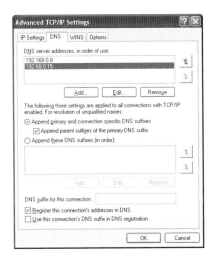

Figure 8-15   Configure advanced DNS settings.

8. Click OK three times to close the dialog boxes.

WINS

In addition to DNS, WINS is sometimes employed on a network. WINS servers resolve **NetBIOS names** to their associated IP addresses. NetBIOS names allow computers running older operating systems such as Microsoft Windows NT, Windows Me, and Windows 98 to participate in a network and to access resources. NetBIOS names are unique, and the name is generally a "friendly" name like Server01 or Computer 22.

> **NOTE** *No WINS Serve   rNot all networks use WINS servers. WINS integration is only necessary if the network includes computers running legacy operating systems.*

If the network includes a WINS server, and if you believe (because of results of Ping, Ipconfig /All, Tracert, or other command-line tests) that an incorrect WINS configuration is preventing a user or users from resolving NetBIOS names to IP addresses, and you have verified the IP address of the WINS server and that it is online, you should check the WINS settings on the local computer. You can view and reconfigure the WINS configuration on a Windows XP computer quite easily by following these steps:

1. Open Network Connections, right-click the active local area connection, and select Properties.

2. On the General tab of the Properties dialog box, select Internet Protocol (TCP/IP), and click Properties.

3. In the Internet Protocol (TCP/IP) Properties dialog box shown in Figure 8-14, click Advanced.

4. In the Advanced TCP/IP Settings dialog box, select the WINS tab. Use Add, Edit, or Remove to make configuration changes to the WINS servers listed. Use the arrows to move a WINS server up or down in the list. Leave the NetBIOS default settings, as shown in Figure 8-16. Click OK.

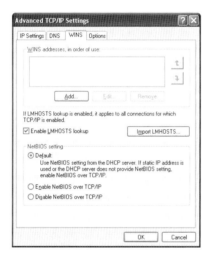

Figure 8-16   Configure advanced WINS settings using the Advanced TCP/IP Properties dialog box.

5. If you've configured the computer to obtain its IP address and DNS server address automatically and you need to configure an alternate WINS address, on the Alternate Configuration tab in the Internet Protocol (TCP/IP) Properties dialog box, click User Configured, and type a preferred and alternate WINS server. Click OK. Click Close.

LMHOSTS

An LMHOSTS file is a text file located on the local computer that maps NetBIOS names to their IP addresses for hosts that are not located on the local subnet. In Windows XP Professional, that file is located in the *%SystemRoot%*\System32\ Drivers\Etc folder.

LMHOSTS files can be manually updated and are useful in small networks where IP addresses change infrequently, or for networks with resources that have static IP addresses. When configuring WINS servers, make sure the Enable LMHOSTS Lookup check box is selected. LMHOSTS files serve as a backup for WINS servers.

HOSTS

HOSTS files are local text files that map host names and FQDNs to IP addresses. They are also located in the *%SystemRoot%*\System32\Drivers\Etc folder. Figure 8-17 shows a sample HOSTS file.

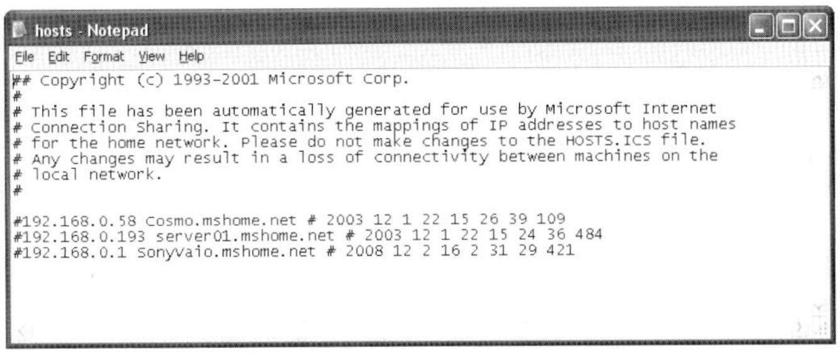


```
## Copyright (c) 1993-2001 Microsoft Corp.
#
# This file has been automatically generated for use by Microsoft Internet
# Connection Sharing. It contains the mappings of IP addresses to host names
# for the home network. Please do not make changes to the HOSTS.ICS file.
# Any changes may result in a loss of connectivity between machines on the
# local network.
#

#192.168.0.58 Cosmo.mshome.net # 2003 12 1 22 15 26 39 109
#192.168.0.193 server01.mshome.net # 2003 12 1 22 15 24 36 484
#192.168.0.1 SonyVaio.mshome.net # 2008 12 2 16 2 31 29 421
```

Figure 8-17 A HOSTS file maps host names and FQDNs to IP addresses.

Computers on the network are identified with their IP addresses. If a computer using a HOSTS file cannot connect to another using its host name, check this file for a bad entry.

TROUBLESHOOTING INTERNET CONNECTION SHARING

Internet Connection Sharing (ICS) offers a simple way to configure computers in a small home-office network to share a single Internet connection. One computer on the network acts as the host and connects to the Internet, and the other computers on the network connect through that computer's Internet connection when they need Internet access. In addition to providing Internet access, the ICS host computer also dynamically allocates IP addresses to the clients on the network, provides name resolution, and serves as the gateway for the other computers.

With that in mind, it makes sense that any other computer on the network that tries to pass out IP addresses, act as a gateway, or perform name resolution for clients will cause problems for the network. For these reasons, ICS is a good option only for the smallest of networks.

ICS Limitations

Because of what ICS does for a network (IP address allocation, name resolution, and acting as the network's gateway), and because the IP address the host computer uses is always 192.168.0.1 with a subnet mask of 255.255.255.0, there are several conditions that must be met while using ICS:

- The IP addresses of the computers on the network must also be in the 192.168.*x*.*y* range, and the subnet mask must always be 255.255.255.0. If network computers cannot use these addresses, ICS will not work properly.
- Microsoft Windows 2000 Server or Windows Server 2003 servers configured as domain controllers, DNS servers, gateways, and DHCP servers cannot be used on the network.

- Computers with static IP addresses will not work with ICS because IP addresses are automatically allocated.

- If more than one network adapter is available, and if two or more local area connections are configured and all of them connect to computers on the network, those connections will need to be bridged. Bridging a connection is as simple as right-clicking the connection and selecting Bridge Connections.

- ICS must be enabled from the dial-up, virtual private network (VPN), broadband, or other connection to the Internet.

Problems can also occur with ICS if the host computer originally had a static IP address on the network, or if the address 192.168.0.1 is being used by another computer on the network. (You can use Ipconfig to find out.)

NOTE **Troubleshooting** *If you are having problems with an ICS configuration, check the items in the preceding list. Make the appropriate changes to the network to resolve the problem.*

Enabling ICS

Although you can troubleshoot ICS in various ways, if the network is small with 10 or fewer computers, it's generally easiest to start over with ICS than to troubleshoot it. Once you know you've removed any offending DHCP or DNS servers, or any computers with static IP addresses, simply run the Network Setup Wizard on the host computer, create the network setup disk and run it on the other computers on the network, and then manually add any Windows servers that are not domain controllers.

HANDHELD AND MOBILE DEVICES

In this section you'll learn to resolve end user calls involving mobile devices and how to connect them to a user's desktop computer. These devices include personal organizers, PDAs, handheld computers, smart displays, and tablet PCs, among others. Making these connections requires an understanding of the devices themselves, available connection types, and the software required by the devices. Advanced skills include understanding BIOS requirements and port requirements and troubleshooting those aspects when the connection is not functioning properly.

Types of Devices

In this section you learn about the different types of devices you'll encounter as a Tier 1 desktop technician. You should make it a point to familiarize yourself with them, because you'll be called on to connect them for end users or troubleshoot existing connections.

Although there are different brands and types of peripherals, this section generically introduces the four main types of handheld devices you are likely to encounter:

- Simple pocket organizers that generally do not connect to the computer

- PDAs, handheld computers, and Pocket PCs that combine computing, Internet access, telephone, fax, and networking features

- Smart displays that act as mobile monitors for existing computers

- Tablet PCs that are an extension of the notebook computer

Simple Pocket Organizers

Sometimes referred to as personal organizers or electronic organizers, simple pocket organizers are the most basic of the handheld devices. They are similar in size to calculators, electronic dictionaries, or language translation devices (and they might include those things), but they have added functionality. Many simple pocket organizers also offer the following:

- A small memory for names and telephone numbers

- An alarm clock

- An area to write short notes using a notepad

- A dictionary, thesaurus, calculator, language translator, currency converter, or similar application

- Learning exercises such as spelling and vocabulary games

These devices generally do not connect to a computer, but earlier devices might connect through a serial port. Service calls regarding these devices generally involve explaining connection options. Some newer, high-end electronic organizers offer additional connectivity kits that allow for connections to PCs, but for the most part, they are not connection-enabled.

PDAs

PDAs are extensions of the earliest personal organizers. They are also referred to as digital organizers, digital assistants, handheld computers, and Pocket PCs, and offer features that were included with the earliest electronic handheld devices. Microsoft Pocket PC 2002 used a special operating system called Windows CE, which is a pared-down version of the full Windows operating system; Microsoft Pocket PC 2003 uses the Windows Mobile platform.

PDAs generally include a calculator, notepad, and address book, but now also include other features such as e-mail and Internet access, a way to organize contacts, a task list, a memo pad, and a calendar for keeping track of appointments. They usually consist of a touch screen with handwriting recognition capabilities, a processor and memory, as well as an operating system. PDAs can synchronize with desktop computers so that the information on both is always coordinated.

Users can add various applications to their PDAs, including the following:

- Streets and maps software

- Picture applications such as slide show software or photo editing software

- Database software

- Organizational software

- Language translation, currency converter, encyclopedia, dictionary, and thesaurus software

- Financial software

- Game software

For the most part, your job will consist of connecting these devices to a user's desktop computer, but that might extend to troubleshooting the device itself. Because this might be the case, you should familiarize yourself with the most popular PDAs, the software used on them, and how they are used in your workplace.

Smart Displays

A smart display is an additional monitor that connects wirelessly to a user's desktop PC, which allows a user to access his Windows XP Professional computer from anywhere in the home or office as long as he is within a specified distance (usually about 100 feet). The smart display remotely displays the computer desktop and the user can work while sitting on the couch, on the back porch, or from another office. This peripheral allows a user to do any task remotely that can be done at the computer.

Smart displays work by connecting to the computer using an **802.11b wireless connection**. The user uses a stylus to access the touch-sensitive screen, and also has available an on-screen keyboard. The smart display offers handwriting recognition and support for wireless mice and keyboards. Smart displays do not have an operating system installed; they simply provide remote access to a user's desktop computer.

Tablet PCs

Tablet PCs are powerful handheld computers that use a specialized version of the Windows XP operating system called Windows XP Tablet PC Edition. Tablet PCs support handwriting recognition, and can wirelessly share information with other computer users. With a tablet PC, a user writes directly on the screen and notes are saved in her own handwriting, which can then be converted easily to text. Tablet PCs also offer the following features:

- The ability to work from anywhere, as with a laptop, except the tablet PC is about the size of a legal pad

- Full computing capabilities, including available applications for word processing, database and spreadsheet work, graphic editing, and more

- Encryption, access control, and secure logon as with Windows XP Professional

- The ability to plug in keyboards and other peripherals

- Wireless connection to the Internet for e-mail, Web access, and more

Connection Types

Understanding the available types of mobile devices is an important part of being a knowledgeable desktop technician. Another important component is an understanding of how you connect these hardware devices to different types of computers. Most Tier 1 desktop support calls that involve mobile devices initiate at these connection points, so it's important to understand the different types.

Each computer has several ports, and they are generally accessed from the back of the computer. These ports offer a place to connect portable devices like printers, scanners, keyboards, and mice, or as you've seen in this chapter, PDAs, Pocket PCs, smart displays, and Tablet PCs. There are five types of ports you'll work with: serial ports, parallel ports, USB ports, FireWire ports, and Infrared Data Association (**IrDA**) ports. Smart displays and similar devices might also require a wireless access point, so this type of hardware is discussed as well.

Serial Port

Almost all computers come with a serial port. Serial ports were, at one time, the primary way that data was transferred between the computer and its peripheral devices. Today, serial ports are used to connect mice and keyboards, but can also be used to connect older modems, digital cameras, Global Positioning System (GPS) hardware, and musical synchronizers that offered only a serial connection when they were manufactured. A serial port transfers data between devices one **bit** at a time, which is quite slow; thus serial ports are unlikely candidates for peripherals needing fast transfer rates.

The cables that are used with serial ports vary. When connecting a mouse or keyboard, the cable is a thin one that is permanently connected to the device. When connecting a printer to a serial port, a special type of serial cable called a null modem cable is needed. Special conversion cables can be purchased, too, and these cables can connect a USB device (among other things) to an available serial port.

Many end users who have older computers have only serial ports and do not have other types of ports, and these users must have a way to connect their newer devices to their older computer's serial port. Because of this, manufacturers have created devices and converters that can connect to those ports for backward compatibility. These devices include (but are not limited to) the following:

- PDAs, Pocket PCs, and other personal organizers
- Synchronization cradles for PDAs and other personal organizers
- Card readers
- Digital converters
- Digitizer tablets
- Serial-to-USB adapters

When troubleshooting a device that connects using a serial port, always verify that there is not another, faster port available. If there isn't, verify that the port is functional by plugging in another device (like a mouse), that the connection to and from the peripheral and the computer is solid, and that the cable that connects the two is not worn or damaged.

Parallel Port

Almost all computers come with a parallel port. Parallel ports have 25 pins and are referred to as DB-25 ports; these use DB-25 cables. You most often use parallel ports to connect print devices, and they are common ports for connecting print servers. You can also use parallel ports to connect Zip drives, but you probably won't find many PDAs or similar devices connected there. Parallel ports send data one **byte** at a time.

USB Port

Almost all newer computers come with two or more USB ports. USB 1.1 supports 12 Mbps data transfer and is used to connect a myriad of devices. USB 2.0 supports transfer rates up to 480 Mbps and is quickly becoming standard equipment on all new computers. Connecting a USB 2.0 device to a USB 1.0 port generally produces problems and creates error messages, but it also slows the transfer rate down to USB 1.1 levels. Devices can include printers, scanners, flash drives, external drives, digital cameras, PDAs, and handheld devices.

You can also use USB ports to connect these PDA peripherals:

- Synchronization kits
- Charger kits
- Cradles
- Adapter cables

When troubleshooting a device that connects using a USB port, always verify that there is not another, faster port available, such as FireWire. If there isn't, verify that the port is functional by plugging in another device (like a printer, scanner, or flash drive), that the connection to and from the peripheral and the computer is solid, and that the cable that connects the two is not worn or damaged.

FireWire Port

Many newer media centers and high-end computers now come with FireWire (IEEE 1394) ports. FireWire can transfer data at a rate of 400 or 800 Mbps. It is used mainly for video transfer from digital movie cameras, but it will soon become a popular option for newer PDAs and handhelds, including cradles, chargers, and synchronizers.

When troubleshooting a device that connects using a FireWire port, always verify that the port is functional by plugging in another device (like a digital camera), that the connection to and from the peripheral and the computer is solid, and that the cable that connects the two is not worn or damaged.

IrDA Ports

Many newer media centers and high-end computers now come with IrDA ports. IrDA is another type of port used to transfer data between devices. IrDA data transfer requires a clear line of sight between devices and the devices should be in close proximity to each other. IrDA ports are found on many devices including the following:

- Media centers
- PDAs, handhelds, and portable computers
- Printers
- Digital cameras
- Other devices that connect and share information and data

When troubleshooting a device that connects using an IrDA port, always verify that the port is functional and that it is transmitting and receiving data, that the connection to and from the peripheral and the computer is within the required proximity, and that the two devices have a clear line of sight. You might also need to verify that the connection is enabled using the Network Connections window.

Wireless Access Points

Wireless local area networking is a technology that allows computers and other network devices like smart displays, PDAs, and handheld computers to transfer data without cables or wires. A wireless access point is a device that allows users to connect to a network using a wireless networking card installed in their computing device. The wireless access point functions as a bridge between the devices and allows them to communicate. Depending on the environment, one access point can offer up to 300 feet of wireless coverage.

Many devices have wireless networking cards and can communicate with a wireless access point, including the following:

- Media centers
- Smart displays
- Laptops
- Handheld computers, PDAs, and Tablet PCs
- Printers

When troubleshooting devices that use a wireless access point, verify that the connection is enabled and functioning using Network Connections, ping the access point's IP address, verify the signal strength by hovering over the network connection icon in the notification area, try changing channels if applicable, verify that the clients are in the required range, and verify that connectivity (if any exists to another network) is connected securely and properly.

Computer Requirements

PDAs, handhelds, and similar hardware require that the computer have the necessary ports as detailed in the previous section, but the computers must meet BIOS requirements for allowing port availability to the devices. Some IrDA adapter installations, for instance, require that the user enter the BIOS and make changes to it. In addition to BIOS compatibility, the user often must install software for synchronizing and working with the device after it has been connected.

BIOS Requirements

The BIOS is built-in software that contains the code required to boot the computer and control the keyboard, display, disk drives, and serial communications on a computer. The BIOS is stored on a chip that is connected to the computer motherboard, and is thus not affected by disk drive failures.

Some products—often printers or imaging devices—require that specific ports be configured in the BIOS before they can be used. Generally, configuring the BIOS involves booting the computer and pressing DEL or F1, F2, F3, or another function key before the operating system has started. The documentation that comes with the PDA, handheld, adapter, or other device will have specific directions if configuring these ports is required.

The BIOS also allows you to configure the hardware settings for both serial and parallel ports (the Base I/O address and interrupt) in the BIOS setup utility. You can enable or disable bidirectional printing with either the Extended Capabilities Port (ECP), or Enhanced Parallel Port (EPP) options for the parallel port, or enable or disable serial and parallel ports altogether. When troubleshooting devices that use these types of connections, make sure you verify that the ports are enabled in BIOS.

Software Installation

In addition to connecting the hardware to the required port and configuring the BIOS, a user might need help performing an initial setup when connecting the PDA to the computer for the first time. Generally, this consists of installing the client software, connecting the docking station, and doing an initial synchronization with the PDA. Because manufacturers differ, refer to the documentation that came with the hardware itself or visit the manufacturer's Web site.

> **NOTE**   **Compatibility**   Always verify that the software is compatible with Windows XP before installing. If the software doesn't list the operating system, visit the manufacturer's Web site.

General Troubleshooting

Because connectivity and synchronization generally occur between the PDA and the desktop PC using a synchronization cradle, when troubleshooting these types of calls, check this connection first. For the most part, you connect these devices using the serial and USB ports. The user should be able to place the PDA in the cradle and establish a connection either automatically or by pressing a button on the cradle, so if this doesn't happen, check the connections.

If hardware is not the issue, check the software. Make sure it was installed properly and, if necessary, reinstall it. Also, verify that the connection speeds on the PDA and the port used on the computer match. Although this differs for PDAs, for Windows XP you can check the port speed by following these steps:

1. Open Control Panel, and open System.

2. On the Hardware tab, select Device Manager.

3. Expand Ports, right-click the Communications Port and select Properties, and then select the Port Settings tab. See Figure 8-18.

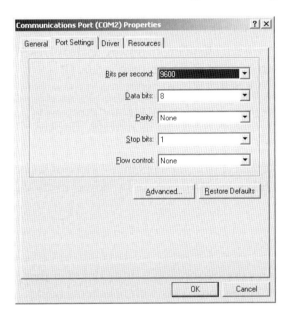

Figure 8-18   Check port settings on the Port Settings tab.

4. Click OK and close all of the open dialog boxes.

Finally, verify the port is functional by connecting a device that is known to be functional and Plug and Play–compatible, like a flash drive or mouse.

SUMMARY

- To resolve connectivity problems on a workgroup or a domain, check all physical connections, including cables, hubs, switches, routers, servers, and network computers first.

- To resolve connectivity problems that do not involve physical connectivity problems, troubleshoot the network connection in Network Connections.

- To resolve connectivity issues that have to do with TCP/IP, check for APIPA use, and use command-line utilities such as Ping, Ipconfig, Pathping, and others.

- To resolve name resolution problems, verify that DNS and WINS are properly configured and in working order, and that HOSTS and LMHOSTS files are correctly configured.

- To resolve problems with ICS, remove offending hardware such as DHCP and DNS servers, domain controllers, or computers with static IP addresses. Then, run the Network Setup Wizard again.

- Mobile and handheld devices vary in functionality and purpose. Some mobile devices act as remote terminals, some act as movable displays, and some simply hold data.

- Mobile and handheld devices connect to computers in a variety of ways including wirelessly, using a USB or FireWire port, or by slower methods such as a serial port.

REVIEW QUESTIONS

1. A user has set up Internet Connection Sharing on a host computer that runs Windows XP, but is experiencing problems with his clients being able to connect to both the Internet and other computers on the network. Which of the following items could be the cause of the problems? Select all that apply.

   a. There is a DHCP server on the network.

   b. There is a DNS server on the network.

   c. There are computers on the network with static IP addresses.

   d. There is a Windows 2000 server on the network.

2. You are troubleshooting a connectivity problem on a small home-office workgroup that includes four computers connected through an Ethernet hub. The user at Computer1 cannot access any workgroup resources but is able to access the shared printer connected directly to her computer; the other three computers can access all workgroup resources except for resources on Computer1, including the shared printer. What is most likely the problem?

   a. APIPA is in use.

   b. The network bridge is corrupt.

c. The configured DNS server is not available.

d. The Ethernet cable on Computer1 is disconnected from the NIC or the hub.

3. Match the troubleshooting scenarios on the left with the appropriate command on the right.

1. You need to check to see if TCP/IP is installed correctly on a user's computer.

a) Ipconfig

2. You need to find out the IP address, subnet mask, and default gateway of the user's computer.

b) Pathping *IPAddress*

3. You're unable to communicate with a remote computer. You suspect that that data loss is occurring at a remote router, but you aren't sure which one. You want to test the route that the packets take from your computer to the remote one and you want to view information about packet loss at every router along the way.

c) Ping 127.0.0.1.

4. You need to list the file shares on a remote computer running Windows XP.

d) Net View *ComputerName*

4. After using the command Ipconfig /All, the following results are given:

a. IP Address.........192.168.0.5

b. Subnet Mask.......255.255.255.255

c. Default Gateway............192.168.0.7

Which of these is most likely configured incorrectly?

5. You are troubleshooting a network connectivity problem for a workgroup containing 12 computers. One of the computers cannot access network resources. After verifying the physical connections are good, that the NIC light is on and the NIC produces no errors in Device Manager, and that the computer name and workgroup name are correct in System Properties, you still can't solve the problem. What should you try next?

a. Remove two of the computers from the workgroup; workgroups can only have 10 or fewer computers connected.

b. Open Network Connections and try to repair the connection.

c. Re-create the network connection.

d. Configure the workgroup to use APIPA.

6. For each of the devices listed, match its name on the left with its description on the right.

1. Pocket (personal) organizer	a) The operating system used on the Microsoft Pocket PC 2002 handheld computer.
2. PDA	b) Stores names and phone numbers; might also offer a calculator, dictionary, or thesaurus; and might not connect to a desktop computer.
3. Windows CE	c) A variation of the notebook computer where a stylus is used to write on an LCD screen, and where that handwriting is analyzed by the computer and stored as data. It has its own operating system and is a full-fledged computer.
4. Smart display	d) A handheld device that offers telephone and fax capabilities, Internet and e-mail access, and networking features. It can also have a Web browser, and offer handwriting recognition capabilities.
5. Tablet PC	e) A wireless handheld device that acts as an extension of the user's computer desktop, which allows the user to access the computer remotely when within a specified range.

7. A user has recently purchased a high-end PDA and wants to connect it to his Windows 98 computer. He has verified that the PDA software is compatible with Windows 98. He has several ports in the back of his computer and does not know to which port he should connect it. The PDA comes with a serial connection cable, a USB connection cable, and a FireWire connection cable. What connection will almost certainly work, what connection is more desirable, and what connection is unlikely to be an option (in that order)?

   a. USB, FireWire, serial

   b. FireWire, serial, USB

   c. Serial, USB, FireWire

   d. USB, serial, FireWire

   e. Serial, FireWire, USB

CASE SCENARIOS

Scenario 8-1: Resolving Issues Involving Joining Domains

An owner of a small business purchased Windows Server 2003, installed it on his best computer, and configured it to be the domain controller on his network. He has eight other computers in his office, and he was able to successfully connect all of them to the domain except for two. Of the following choices, which two computers will not be able to connect to the domain?

1. The two computers running Windows 98.
2. The two computers running Windows Me.
3. The two computers running Windows XP Home Edition.
4. The two computers running Windows 2000 Server.

Scenario 8-2: Troubleshooting Network Access to Resources

A user of a small office workgroup has returned from a weeklong vacation. She boots her computer and everything seems to be functional. As the day progresses, she accesses data from a workgroup file server and she prints to a network printer. Later, she tries to access another workgroup resource, a printer that is attached to a user's computer in the office upstairs, but she receives an error that the printer cannot be found. She reports that the Ethernet cable is connected and the NIC has a green light, and that she can access other resources on the network. What is the first thing you should do?

1. Check the status of the network router.
2. Check the status of the computer upstairs.
3. Ping the computer's loopback address.
4. Use the Tracert command at a command prompt to view the route and possible packet losses.

CHAPTER 9
SECURITY AND SECURITY PERMISSIONS

Upon completion of this chapter, you will be able to:

- Troubleshoot resource sharing in a small home-office workgroup

- Assign, configure, and troubleshoot share and NTFS permissions

- Understand how multiple permissions assignments affect resource access

- Understand privileges for built-in local groups, and troubleshoot access problems due to multiple group membership

- Determine what access problems are occurring due to local or group policies

- Understand the policies hierarchy

The purpose of this chapter is to teach you to troubleshoot end users' access to network or workgroup resources that are caused by permissions restrictions, multiple permissions, group membership, or local or group security policies. To troubleshoot these types of access problems, you need to be familiar with each, including how to create different types of shares, view and change settings for a local security policy, view and change settings for a group policy, and more. The topics in this chapter thus revolve around the following topics:

- Share permissions
- NTFS permissions
- Local security policies
- Group policies

UNDERSTANDING SECURITY PERMISSIONS

You assign permissions to files, folders, printers, and other network resources to protect them from unauthorized access. In a workgroup, the owner of the resource determines the level of access (if any) and assigns the permissions; in a domain, network administrators set permissions, and resources are accessed through the network servers.

As a Tier 1 technician, you'll be concerned with three types of permissions and file sharing:

- Simple file-sharing permissions on a Microsoft Windows XP workgroup
- Share folder permissions on workgroups and domains
- NTFS folder permissions on workgroups and domains

The Home Office: Windows XP and Simple File Sharing

When Windows XP is used to create a home office network, Simple File Sharing is enabled by default. This is exactly what it sounds like: a simple way for home users to share files on a network. When Simple File Sharing is configured, users share files by sharing the folders that hold them.

When using Simple File Sharing, users can do the following:

- Share folders with everyone on the network.
- Allow users who access the folder to view the files, edit the files, or both.
- Make folders in his user profile private.

Users cannot do the following:

- Prevent specific users and groups from accessing folders.
- Assign folder permissions for specific users and groups.
- View the Security tab of a shared folder's Properties dialog box.

▶ **Using Simple File Sharing**

To enable or disable Simple File Sharing or to see if Simple File Sharing is in use, follow these steps:

1. Open Control Panel and open Folder Options.
2. Select the View tab and, under Advanced Settings, scroll down the list of choices to the last option.
3. Simple File Sharing is enabled if the Use Simple File Sharing (Recommended) check box is selected. To disable it, clear the check box. For the purposes of this section, verify that it is selected. Click OK.

▶ **Sharing a file**

Once you've verified that Simple File Sharing is enabled, sharing a folder on the network is easy. Just follow these steps:

1. Right-click the Start menu, and choose Explore.
2. Locate the folder you want to share, right-click it, and select Sharing And Security.
3. In the Properties dialog box, select the Share This Folder On The Network check box. This is shown in Figure 9-1. Notice that a share name is automatically assigned. This is the name the users will see when they browse the network for this shared folder. Change the name if desired; the share

name must be 12 characters or less if you have clients that will be connecting to the share from computers running Windows Me, Windows 98, or earlier operating systems.

Figure 9-1   Sharing a folder with Simple File Sharing is easy.

4. To allow others to make changes to the files in the shared folder, also select the Allow Network Users To Change My Files check box. Click OK.

When sharing a folder on a network in this manner, you give permission for everyone on the network to access and read the files in the folder. With Simple File Sharing, you cannot choose who can and cannot access a folder. When you also choose to allow users to make changes to the files in the shared folder, you allow them to write to (or make changes to) those files as well.

There are two other options on the Sharing tab that were not discussed. Under Local Sharing And Security, you can share a folder with other users of the same computer by dragging it to the Shared Documents folder. The Shared Documents folder can be accessed by anyone logged on to the workgroup or the computer, and it is located in the C:\Documents And Settings\All Users folder, as shown in Figure 9-2. Sharing a folder in this manner only works for workgroups, however, not domains.

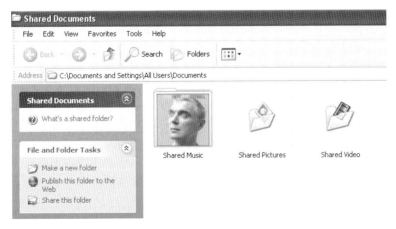

Figure 9-2   The Shared Documents folder can be used to share files on a computer or in a workgroup.

There's also the option to make a folder private. When you make a folder private, only the owner of the folder can access its contents. You can make folders private only if they are in the user's personal user profile (and only if the disk is formatted with NTFS). A personal user profile defines customized desktop environments, display settings, and network and printer connections, among other things. Personal user profile folders include My Documents and its subfolders, Desktop, Start Menu, Cookies, and Favorites.

To locate the list of local user profiles, right-click My Computer, select Properties and, on the Advanced tab, in the User Profiles section, select Settings. To view a personal user profile, browse to C:\Documents And Settings*User Name*, as shown in Figure 9-3.

> **MORE INFO**   **Learning More**   To learn more about user profiles, read Knowledge Base articles 314478 and 294887.

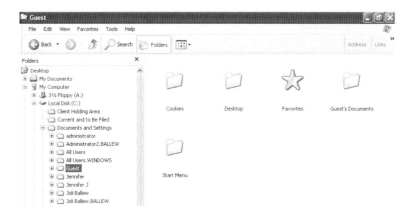

Figure 9-3   The Guest Account's personal profile folders are located under Documents and Settings.

> **NOTE**   **File Systems**   Simple File Sharing works for all Windows XP computers, whether they are formatted to use the **FAT** or **NTFS** file system.

Troubleshooting Simple File Sharing

There are only a few problems you'll run into when troubleshooting shares configured with Simple File Sharing, and they deal with user access to the shared resource. Assuming all network connections are functional, all computers and hubs are working properly, and Simple File Sharing is in use, Table 9-1 details some common problems and their solutions.

Table 9-1   **Troubleshooting Simple File Sharing**

Scenario/Report	Cause/Solution
A Microsoft Windows Me user reports he cannot access a shared folder named Working Files On Computer 01.	If the share name is longer than 12 characters, computers running Microsoft Windows 98 SE, Windows Me, or earlier operating systems cannot access the folder. Rename the share.
An owner of a file reports that users can access the file but cannot make changes. She wants users to be able to make changes.	On the Sharing tab of the shared folder, select the Allow Network Users To Change My Files check box.

Table 9-1   **Troubleshooting Simple File Sharing**

Scenario/Report	Cause/Solution
The owner of a file dragged the file to the Shared Documents folder and logged off the computer. When others log on, no one can access or even view the Shared Documents folders.	Users are logging on to a domain. Users will need to log on to the workgroup to access the file.
A user wants to share a file and assign specific permissions from the Security tab. However, the Security tab isn't available.	With Simple File Sharing, the Security tab is not available. This is by design.

Share Folder Permissions

You can use share permissions with both FAT and NTFS file systems, and they offer more configuration options than Simple File Sharing. Compare the Sharing tab in Figure 9-1, which uses Simple File Sharing, with the Sharing tab in Figure 9-4, which has Simple File Sharing disabled. On the Sharing tab in Figure 9-4, notice the Permissions button. This opens the Permissions dialog box, which allows the user to configure specific share permissions.

Figure 9-4   Share permissions can be configured by clicking Permissions.

There are three share permissions: Full Control, Read, and Change. You can configure these permissions only when Simple File Sharing is disabled, and you can use them to restrict who can access a particular resource and to what degree. You apply share permissions to folders, not files, and they're often adequate for securing a small home network. These three share permissions are detailed here:

■ **Read**   The Read permission is the most restrictive and allows the user to only view file names and subfolder names in the folder, view data in the folder, and run any program in the folder.

■ **Change**   This permission is less restrictive than the Read permission and allows a user to perform all Read tasks, add files or subfolders, change data in the files and save those changes, and delete any files or subfolders in the folder.

- **Full Control**   This permission is the least restrictive and allows a user to perform all Change tasks and change the permissions of the folder or take ownership of the share.

When applying permissions, you choose Allow or Deny for each available permission. Choosing Allow applies that permission to the group selected; Deny denies that permission. Deny always means deny, and this overrides any other permissions applied to the folder. To keep troubleshooting minimal, it is best to use the Deny option sparingly.

> **CAUTION   Be Careful**   Share permissions only apply if the user is accessing the resource over a network. The permissions do no good if the user is sitting at the computer that contains the shares. In addition, share permissions apply to all subfolders in the folder.

▶ **Sharing a folder**

To share a folder and apply share permissions, verify that Simple File Sharing is disabled on the View tab of the Folder Options dialog box, then follow these steps:

1. Use Windows Explorer to browse to the folder to share or locate it by other means.

2. Right-click the folder to share, and select Sharing And Security.

3. On the Sharing tab, select Share This Folder.

4. In the Share Name area, type a name for the share. Keep the name under 12 letters. (You'll be prompted if you use an invalid character.)

5. Type a comment if desired.

6. Next to User Limit, select Maximum Allowed or Allow This Number Of Users. If setting a user limit, enter the number of users to allow. By default, 10 is the maximum.

7. Click Permissions.

8. To add a group, click Add. To remove a group, select the group and click Remove. If applicable, in the Select Users Or Groups dialog box, add or remove any group. Separate multiple groups with semicolons. (You'll learn more about groups later in this chapter.) Click OK.

9. In the Group Or User Names list, select a group for which you want to configure permissions. In the Permissions For <*group name*> area, make changes to the permissions as desired. Figure 9-5 shows this dialog box. Click OK, and click OK to close the Properties dialog box.

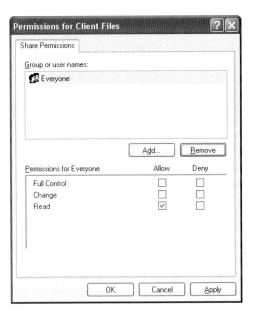

Figure 9-5   Set share permissions.

Troubleshooting Share Permissions

Problems can occur with share permissions just as they can with Simple File Sharing. Assuming all network connections are functional, all computers and hubs are working properly, and Simple File Sharing is not in use, Table 9-2 details some common problems with share permissions and their solutions.

Table 9-2   **Troubleshooting Share Permissions**

Scenario/Report	Cause/Solution
All network users report that when they access a particular shared folder on the network, they get a message that access is denied. This does not happen with any other share.	The share permissions for that resource might be set to Deny for the Everyone group. Also, the computer that is hosting the share might be turned off or not available, or the owner might have changed the share permissions recently.
An owner of a file reports that users can access the file but cannot make changes. He wants all users to be able to make changes.	On the Sharing tab of the shared folder, click Permissions. In the Share Permissions dialog box, select the Everyone group, and select the Read and Change check boxes.
The owner of a share reports that she opened her shared folder this morning to find that some of the items in the folder had been deleted. She states she did not assign the Full Control permission, but did assign the Read and Change permission to the Everyone group. She wants to know why users can delete her files.	By default, users with the Change permission for a folder can delete files in the folder. The user needs to reconfigure what files are in what shares, and who has access.
A user wants to share a file and assign specific permissions from the Security tab. However, the Security tab isn't available.	The file system used is FAT, not NTFS.

NTFS File and Folder Permissions

NTFS file and folder permissions are used with the NTFS file system and include Full Control, Modify, Read and Execute, List Folder Contents, Read, Write, and several special permissions. As with share permissions, they are assigned by selecting Allow or Deny. NTFS permissions are applied when a user is sitting at the machine or accessing the file or folder over the network, making it a better choice for offices and corporations. Unlike share permissions, NTFS permissions require the computer's partitions to be formatted using the NTFS file system.

Without including every aspect of each permission, the six basic NTFS folder permissions that you should be familiar with are introduced here:

- **Read**   This permission allows a user to view the files and subfolders.

- **Write**   This permission allows a user create files and folders and write data to files and subfolders.

- **List Folder Contents**   This permission allows a user to traverse the folder, execute files, and view files and subfolders.

- **Read and Execute**   This permission allows a user to view the files and subfolders, traverse folders, and execute files.

- **Modify**   This permission allows a user to view files and subfolders, traverse folders, execute files, create files, write data, create folders, and append data.

- **Full Control**   This permission allows a user to have complete control over the folder, including deleting files and subfolders, taking ownership, and all other tasks.

▶ Sharing a file or folder

To apply NTFS permissions, verify that Simple File Sharing is disabled on the View tab of the Folder Properties dialog box, that the file system is formatted using NTFS, then follow these steps:

1. Right-click the folder for which you want to assign NTFS permissions and select Sharing And Security.

2. On the Security tab, in the Group Or User Names list, select the group or user for which you want to set NTFS permissions. To add a user or group that isn't listed, click Add, and in the Select Users Or Groups dialog box, enter the object names to select. Click OK.

3. To change permissions for a group, select that group on the Security tab under Group Or User Names, and select or clear the permissions to apply or deny. Figure 9-6 shows the default NTFS permissions for the Power Users group.

Figure 9-6   Set NTFS permissions.

4. To access the advanced settings and to set special permissions, click Advanced.

5. In the Advanced Security Settings dialog box, notice the four tabs: Permissions, Auditing, Owner, and Effective Permissions. Select the Permissions tab.

6. On the Permissions tab, the default selection is Inherit From Parent The Permission Entries That Apply To Child Objects. Include These With Entries Explicitly Defined Here. When this check box is selected, the file, folder, or object will inherit the permission entries from the parent folder (or object). When this check box is cleared, the object will not inherit the permission entries. For more information on inheritance, see the Windows Help file Changing Inherited Permissions.

7. On the Permissions tab, the option to Replace Permission Entries On All Child Objects With Entries Shown Here That Apply To Child Objects is not selected. When selected, the permission entries on the child objects are reset so that they are identical to the current parent object. Click OK.

If you want to, you can also create share permissions at the same time you create NTFS permissions. Simply make the appropriate changes on the Sharing tab. Keep in mind, though, that share and NTFS permissions are independent of each other, and when you give a user NTFS permissions for a folder, that user cannot access the folder across the network unless you've also shared the folder and given the user share permissions.

Troubleshooting NTFS Permissions
Problems can occur with NTFS permissions just as they can with Simple File Sharing and share permissions. Assuming all network connections are functional, all computers and hubs are working properly, and that Simple File Sharing is not in use, Table 9-3 details some common problems and their solutions.

Table 9-3   **Troubleshooting NTFS Permissions**

Scenario/Report	Cause/Solution
A user reports he applied the NTFS permissions Read and Write for the group who will access a folder. However, when a member of the group opens the folder, she can't run the programs in it. He needs the users to be able to run the programs without giving them excess privileges.	The user can add the Read and Execute permission to the group. This gives users who access the folder the ability to execute files in the folder, without adding any other privileges.
A user wants to apply NTFS permissions but all of the options on the Security tab under Allow are unavailable and cannot be set.	The permissions for this subfolder have been inherited from the parent folder. To make the permissions accessible for this file, select the This Folder Only check box in Apply Onto when setting the permissions on the parent folder.
Although a network user is a member of the Power Users group, and this group has the Read NTFS permissions for a folder, the user cannot read the documents in the folder.	The user has been assigned a permission of Deny by another administrator or he is a member of another group that has been assigned the Deny permission to the folder. The user might also have the Deny share permission.
NTFS permissions can't be applied because the Security tab is missing.	The file system used is FAT, not NTFS.

When Both Share and NTFS Permissions Exist

When a user is assigned multiple share permissions, the user's effective permissions for the share are the combination of those permissions. For instance, if the share permissions applied to a folder are Change and Read, the user can change and read the folder's contents. When a user is assigned multiple NTFS permissions, the user's effective permissions for the folder are also the combination of those permissions. For instance, if the NTFS permissions Read, Write, and Modify exist, the user can read, write to, and modify the contents of the folder. However, if a user is assigned both share and NTFS permissions for a folder, the user's effective permissions for the folder are the more restrictive of the two cumulative permissions.

Here's an example: network user Brenda Diaz has access to a folder that has both share and NTFS permissions applied. The share permissions are Read and Change, and the NTFS permissions are Read and Read and Execute. Thus, Brenda's cumulative share permission is Change, and her cumulative NTFS permission is Read and Execute. To calculate Brenda's effective permissions, take the more restrictive of the two, which is Read and Execute. Brenda will not be able to change any data in the folder.

> **NOTE**   **Deny**   In all cases, if Deny is selected for a user, that user will not have access. Deny can be a share permission or an NTFS permission.

Built-In Local Groups and Their Privileges

As noted briefly in previous sections, there are a few built-in local groups: Administrators, Power Users, Users, and Backup Operators. Network administrators add end users to these groups manually. Each group (and each member of it) has specific user rights and privileges, and default permissions for file and folder access. Adding users to a group makes managing those users much easier, because instead of managing users separately, the administrator can manage the users as a single group.

To troubleshoot end-user access to shares in a workgroup or a domain, you'll need to understand what each group's default rights and permissions are. The four default user groups are detailed here.

Administrators

The Administrators group is the least restrictive group available. Administrators have full control of the computer, the files and folders on it, the local area network (if it exists), and the configured user accounts. Only a few users should be members of this group.

Besides being able to perform all of the tasks of any other group member, Administrators can also do the following:

- Take ownership of files and folders
- Back up and restore system data
- Set local policies
- Install service packs and Windows Updates
- Perform upgrades
- Perform system repairs such as installing device drivers and system services
- Audit the network and manage logs

Power Users

The Power Users group is the next least restrictive group. Power Users have more control over the computer than members of the Users group do, but less than administrators. Only users who are trusted employees and competent computer users should be members of this group.

Besides being able to perform all of the tasks a member of the Users group can, Power Users can also do the following:

- Modify computer-wide settings such as date, time, and power options
- Run legacy and noncertified Microsoft applications
- Install programs that do not modify operating system files or install system services

- Create local user accounts and local groups
- Manage local user accounts and local groups
- Stop and start system services that are not started by default
- Customize network printers
- Take ownership of files
- Back up and restore directories
- Install device drivers

Users

The Users group is the most secure group and is much more restrictive than the Administrators and the Power Users groups. The Users group is the most secure because members of this group cannot compromise the integrity of the operating system by modifying registry settings, operating system files, or application files. Most users should be members of this group.

Members of the Users group can do the following:

- Shut down their own workstations
- Lock the workstation
- Create local groups
- Manage the local groups they've created
- Run programs that are certified by Microsoft as compatible, and previously installed by administrators
- Retain ownership of files and folders they create

Members of the Users group cannot do the following:

- Modify system-wide registry settings, operating system files, or program files
- Shut down servers
- Manage local groups they did not create
- Run legacy applications or applications that are not certified by Microsoft
- Share directories
- Share printers

Backup Operators

The Backup Operators group can back up and restore files on the computer, regardless of the permissions on those files. Those files can include users' files and folders, system state files, and other critical operating system files. They can also log on to the computer and shut it down, but they cannot change security settings.

ADVANCED TROUBLESHOOTING

When resources are protected by both share and NTFS permissions, calculating effective permissions can be a little tricky. When a user can't access a particular resource, you have to take into account what share permissions are applied and what NTFS permissions are applied, and then take the more restrictive of the cumulative permissions for both. When a user is a member of more than one group, or if group membership has been recently changed, the problem in calculating effective permissions is exacerbated.

When Users Are Members of More Than One Group

When users are members of multiple groups, they'll have multiple permissions on the files and folders they have access to. When calculating effective permissions for a specific folder, do the following:

1. List the folder's assigned share permissions for each group the user is a member of, and calculate the effective share permissions. List the most lenient permission.

2. List the folder's assigned NTFS permissions for each group the user is a member of, and calculate the effective NTFS permissions. List the most lenient permission.

3. Compare the most lenient permissions in step 1 and step 2. Choose the more restrictive permission. This is the effective permission.

   NOTE **Deny** *Remember, if any group has the Deny permission configured for either type of permission, the user will not be able to access the resource.*

Changes in Group Membership

Other problems occur when a user's group membership changes. This is especially true if a user was a member of the Power Users group and has been downgraded to the Users group, or if a worker has been demoted and given more restrictive permissions to resources. When troubleshooting resource access, make sure to note any changes to the user's group status.

UNDERSTANDING LOCAL SECURITY SETTINGS

Local security settings are configured on the local computer and they affect everyone who logs on to it. The local security settings you'll be concerned with are account policies and local policies. There are two kinds of account policies—password policies and account lockout policies—and there are three kinds of local policies—audit policies, user rights assignments, and security options. These security policies define the rules for who can log on to the computer, what they can do once logged on, and more. These policies are configured for the purpose of protecting the computer and limiting a user's access. Local security policies are generally configured for computers in workgroups, especially in situations where multiple users access the same computer. They are also applied to computers accessed by people in kiosks or other public places.

Local policies can be applied to computers in domains, too, but the local security policy is overridden by any site policies, domain policies, and organizational unit policies (in that order) that are in place. If conflicts arise, the local security policy is ignored and the other policies in the hierarchy are applied. Therefore, local security policies in a domain are not very powerful. Local policies are set from the Local Security Policy administrative tool, available in Control Panel and shown in Figure 9-7.

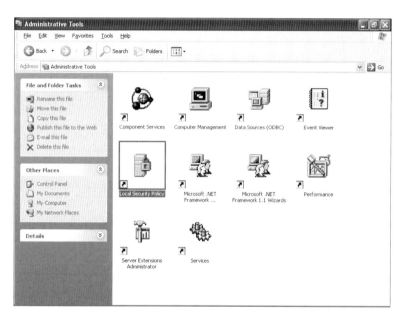

Figure 9-7   Local security policies protect the computer from harm.

Account Policies

There are two types of account policies, and in this section you'll learn about each of them. It is important to understand what policies can and might be set so that you can recognize and troubleshoot problems that occur because of policies put in place by administrators. For instance, one configurable account policy is to lock out a user when a specific number of failed logon attempts is met. This prevents someone from trying unlimited name and password combinations. Therefore, if a user reports he forgot his password, and he tried four different ones and is now locked out, you should be able to recognize this has to do with a local security policy put in place by administrators and have a fair understanding of how to resolve the problem. With that in mind, let's look at the available options for account policies.

Password Policies

To view the available password policies, open Control Panel, open Administrative Tools, open Local Security Policy, and expand Account Policies. Click Password Policy. Figure 9-8 shows the options that you can set.

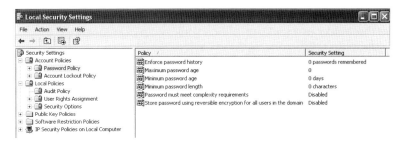

Figure 9-8 Password policies have several options that you can set.

If password policies have been set by local security policy or another policy on the network, an end user's password problem might be directly related to the policies configured. The six policies shown in Figure 9-8 allow an administrator to enable or enforce the following actions:

■ **Enforce Password History** Determines the number of unique new passwords that a user must create before she can reuse an old password. This prevents users from reusing the same two passwords over and over, forcing them to continually create new ones.

■ **Maximum Password Age** Determines the period of time (in days) that a user can use a password before the system requires the user to change it. This forces users to change their passwords every so often. If users do not change the password, they will not be able to log on and will need the assistance of a network administrator.

■ **Minimum Password Age** Determines the period of time (in days) that a user must use a password before he or she can change it. If a user reports he cannot change a password, this might be the issue.

■ **Minimum Password Length** Determines the least number of characters that a password must contain.

■ **Password Must Meet Complexity Requirements** Requires passwords to contain at least six characters, not contain a part of the user's name, and have three of the following four items: uppercase letters, lowercase letters, digits, and non-alphanumeric characters.

■ **Store Password Using Reversible Encryption For All Users In The Domain** Determines whether Microsoft Windows 2000 Server, Windows 2000 Professional, and Windows XP Professional store passwords using **reversible encryption**.

If a user has a problem with one of these items, logging on might require the assistance of a workgroup or network administrator. This is detailed shortly.

Account Lockout Policies

If account lockout policies have been set by local security policy or another policy on the network, an end user's logon problem might be directly related to the policies configured. The three account lockout policies allow an administrator to enable or force the following:

- **Account Lockout Duration**   Determines the number of minutes a locked out account remains locked before it automatically becomes unlocked. A user who has input too many incorrect passwords might become locked out, and either has to wait for the duration set here or ask an administrator for help.

- **Account Lockout Threshold**   Determines the number of failed logon attempts that causes an account to be locked out.

- **Reset Account Lockout Counter After**   Determines the number of minutes that must elapse before the failed logon attempt counter is reset to 0.

If a user is locked out and you have administrator privileges on the computer, you can unlock the user's account. This is detailed next.

Unlock a User Account, Reset a User's Password, or Force a Password Change

If you are the administrator of a workgroup and need to unlock an account, reset a user's password because he has forgotten it, force a user to change her password for security reasons, or perform similar tasks, you do that from the Administrative Tools option, Computer Management. As usual, you need to be logged on as an administrator.

▶ Unlocking an account

To unlock an account, follow these steps:

1. Log on to the computer using your Administrator account.

2. Open Control Panel, open Administrative Tools, and open Computer Management.

3. In the Computer Management console, expand System Tools and expand Local Users And Groups. Select Users.

4. In the right pane, locate the user whose account needs unlocking, right-click on that account, and select Properties.

5. To unlock the account, clear the Account Is Locked Out check box. (If the account is disabled, clear the Account Is Disabled check box.) Click OK.

▶ **Resetting a password**

To reset a user's password because he has forgotten it, follow these steps:

1. Log on to the computer using your Administrator account.

2. Open Control Panel, open Administrative Tools, and open Computer Management.

3. In the Computer Management console, expand System Tools and expand Local Users And Groups. Select Users.

4. In the right pane, locate the user whose account needs the password to be reset. Right-click and select Set Password.

5. Read the information in the Set Password dialog box. If a password reset disk is available, use it as suggested. If a password reset disk is not available, click Proceed.

6. In the Set Password dialog box, shown in Figure 9-9, type the new password and confirm it. Click OK.

Figure 9-9   The Set Password dialog box allows an administrator to reset a user's password if he has forgotten it.

7. Click OK to confirm the password has been set.

▶ **Forcing a password change**

To force a user to change her password at the next logon, follow these steps:

1. Log on to the computer using your Administrator account.

2. Open Control Panel, open Administrative Tools, and open Computer Management.

3. In the Computer Management console, expand System Tools and expand Local Users And Groups. Select Users.

4. In the right pane, locate the user whose password needs to be changed, right-click that account, and select Properties.

5. Select the User Must Change Password At Next Logon check box. Figure 9-10 shows an example. Click OK.

Figure 9-10   Require a user to change his password from the Computer Management console.

Local Security Policies

There are three types of local security policies that can be configured, and in this section you'll learn about each of them. It is important to understand what policies can and might be set so that you can recognize and troubleshoot problems that occur because of policies put in place by administrators. For instance, one configurable security policy prevents the installation of unsigned device drivers. Therefore, if a user reports that on his own computer he can install unsigned device drivers, but on the computer in the lobby he can't, you should be able to recognize that the computer in the lobby has a stricter local security policy than the one on the user's computer. With that in mind, let's look at the three available, configurable local security policy options.

Audit Policies

Audit policies can be set by administrators to log the success or failure of various events. This auditing can help an administrator determine if there are too many logon failures (implying someone might be trying to hack into the system), if someone has successfully changed a user rights assignment policy or audit policy, or a number of other events. As a Tier 1 technician, you won't be in charge of setting audit policies. However, because it is a configurable local security policy option, it bears a brief introduction.

▶ **Working with audit policies**

To view the available audit policies and learn the purpose of setting each, follow these steps:

1. Open Control Panel, open Administrative Tools, and open Local Security Policy.

2. Expand Local Policies if necessary, and select Audit Policies. Double-click any audit policy to change its properties, and to enable or disable auditing.

3. To learn more about audit policies, click Help, and click Help Topics. In the Microsoft Management Console help files, expand Local Security, expand concepts, expand Understanding Local Security Policy, and select Account And Local Policies. In the right pane, select Audit Policy.

User Rights Assignment

User rights assignment options are likely to be set on shared computers, computers in kiosks and public places, and workgroup computers. Setting a user rights assignment is the same as setting an audit policy: open Local Security Settings, expand Local Polices, select User Rights Assignment, and double-click the policy to change or set. Some user rights assignments policies that might be set on a computer include who or what might or might not be able to do the following:

- Access the computer from the network
- Add workstations to a domain
- Back up files and directories
- Change the system time
- Create permanent shared objects
- Load and unload device drivers
- Log on locally
- Manage auditing and the security log
- Remove a computer from a docking station
- Shut down the system
- Take ownership of objects

Therefore, if a user reports that she cannot perform a required function such as change the system time, shut down the system, or another task listed here, you might need to check the local security policy (and the user's group membership).

Security Options

Finally, security options are likely to be set, too. Setting a security option is the same as setting any policy: open Local Security Settings, expand Local Polices, select Security Options, and double-click the policy to change or set. Some security options policies that might be set on a computer include the following, and these can be enabled or disabled:

- Administrator account status
- Guest account status
- Renaming the Administrator or Guest account
- Shutting down the system if security audits cannot be logged
- Preventing users from installing printer drivers
- Unsigned device-driver installation behavior
- Displaying the last user name

- Requiring CTRL + ALT + DEL when logging on
- If message text is to appear when users log on
- If logoff is forced when users' logon hours expire
- If the virtual memory pagefile should be cleared when the computer is shut down

Because of the number of options available, it's important to view and understand what each option does or does not allow. This way, when a user reports an obscure problem, asks that you disable CTRL + ALT + DEL for logon, asks that you rename the Guest account, or wants you to configure message text that users must read when logging on, you know exactly where to look and how to configure the changes.

UNDERSTANDING GROUP POLICIES

Group policies can be set for a single computer with multiple users, for computers in workgroups, or for computers in domains. Group policies provide a way for administrators to customize or standardize how users' computers look and what can be accessed. In a workgroup or on a shared computer, a workgroup administrator uses the command-line utility Gpedit.msc to configure policies; in a domain, network administrators create domain group policies on network servers.

Administrators use group policies to customize and standardize many things, including but not limited to the following:

- What programs can be accessed by users
- What is shown on the desktop
- What the Start menu and taskbar look like
- What screen saver or wallpaper is used
- Where data is saved (which can be on a network server, not the local computer)
- What Control Panel tools can be accessed

To understand how group polices might be affecting an end user or causing an end user's problem, you need to understand what kinds of group policies can be set, how those polices will affect the end user, and how group policies are configured on the local computer.

> **NOTE** **Domain Group Policies** As with local security policies, group policies on a local computer, network, or workgroup are overridden by domain group policies.

Group Policies in a Workgroup

In a workgroup, administrators can configure group policies for computers, users, or both. The options for each are listed under the Computer Configuration option and the User Configuration option, respectively, in the Group Policy console. The

Computer Configuration options, shown in Figure 9-11, include several policies covered earlier (account policies and local policies). There is also a Software Settings option and an Administrative Templates option.

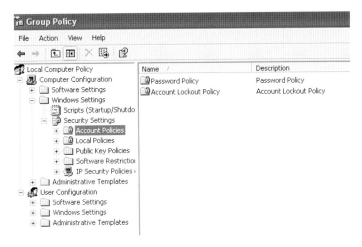

Figure 9-11   Computer Configuration options and group policies are shown in the Group Policy console.

To reinforce the power of configured group policy, consider this: A user reports he cannot add or delete sites from the Security Zones when using Microsoft Internet Explorer. The user would like to add a Web site to the Trusted Sites zone. The reason he can't is because a group policy has been set in the Computer Configuration option that disallows this. Policies for Internet Explorer and other components can be set under Computer Configuration, Administrative Templates. Some of these options are fairly complex, and you should work through each of them separately.

The User Configuration options are the ones we'll be most concerned with here, although you should familiarize yourself with all aspects of group policy. User configurations offer a myriad of customization or standardization options. To understand what group policies can be configured, open the Group Policy console on a local computer in a workgroup by following these steps:

1. From the Start menu, select Run, and type **gpedit.msc**. Click OK.

2. Expand User Configuration (if necessary).

3. Expand Administrative Templates.

4. Notice there are several options. Select Start Menu And Taskbar. Just within the Start Menu And Taskbar options alone, there are 32 configurable options.

5. To configure any option, double-click it. As an example, double-click Prevent Changes To Taskbar And Start Menu Settings. To enable this setting, in the Prevent Changes To Taskbar And Start Menu Settings dialog box, shown in Figure 9-12, select Enabled. Select the Explain tab to see an explanation of the setting.

6. Click OK when finished or click Previous Setting or Next Setting to make other changes.

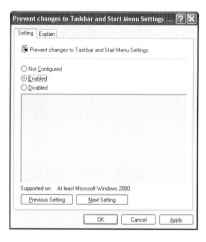

Figure 9-12   Enable a group policy setting.

Click and explore each item in the Administrative Templates options, including all of the items in Windows Components, Desktop, Control Panel, Shared Folders, Network, and System. You must become familiar with what can and might be set on an end user's computer so that you can successfully troubleshoot end-user issues.

NOTE Strong Restrictions *There are some extremely strong restrictions that can be placed on users of a computer using group policy. Access to the Control Panel can be disabled, Windows Messenger can be disabled, and items on the desktop or Start menu can be hidden.*

Group Policies in a Domain

If your end users are members of a domain, chances are good that domain group policies have been set. These domain group policies take precedence over any local group policies set on a local computer. Users might ask why specific group or local policies that they configured sometimes work and sometimes don't work; the answer to that is simple. If the user is logged on to the workgroup, the local group policies are applied; when the user logs on to the domain, those local policies are overridden.

Troubleshooting Group Policies

When problems arise that you suspect are related to group policies, either because both local group policies and domain policies exist, because local group policies are set and you aren't sure which ones, or because you can see that unusual restrictions are in place, you can view the policy information set for the computer from the Help and Support Center by following these steps:

1. From the Start menu, select Help And Support.

2. Below Pick A Task, select Use Tools To View Your Computer Information And Diagnose Problems.

3. In the Tools pane on the left, select Advanced System Information.

4. Click View Group Policy Settings Applied.

You can save, print, and e-mail the report for troubleshooting purposes. There are sections in the report for the last time a group policy was applied and, a listing of all of the configured group and local policies. This list can help you decide what, if any, group policies are causing the end user's problem. The Help and Support Center will most likely give you some insight into the problem at hand, and as you work with group policies, you'll begin to understand that they can have a huge impact on end users.

To help you get a feel for the types of calls you'll respond to that involve group policy settings, Table 9-4 lists some common reports from end users and the group policy associated with them.

Table 9-4   **Table 9-4 Common Group Policy Restrictions**

Report/Scenario	Associated Group Policy Folder
A user cannot enable AutoComplete for forms or passwords in Internet Explorer.	User Configuration, Administrative Templates, Windows Components, Internet Explorer, Disable AutoComplete For Forms.
The user cannot access My Documents from the Start menu.	User Configuration, Administrative Templates, Windows Components, Start Menu And Taskbar, Remove My Documents Icon From Start Menu.
A user cannot access the Control Panel.	User Configuration, Administrative Templates, Windows Components, Control Panel, Prohibit Access To The Control Panel.
When a user inserts a CD, AutoPlay never works and cannot be used.	Computer Configuration, Administrative Templates, System, Turn Off Autoplay.
A user does not want to be prompted to send a report each time an error occurs with a program.	Computer Configuration, Administrative Templates, System, Error Reporting, Report Errors.
A user does not have the option to Lock Computer when using CTRL + ALT + DEL.	User Configuration, Administrative Tools, Windows Components, System, CTRL + ALT + DEL Options, Remove Lock Computer.

Of course, there are hundreds of other configurations that can be made by administrators. Make sure you are at least familiar with all of them.

> **NOTE** **Application Deployment** Administrators who configure and use group policy to manage computers on a domain can also use the software installation and maintenance feature of IntelliMirror to install applications on computers. This is done in conjunction with **Active Directory directory service**, Group Policy, and **Windows Installer**. For more information on application deployment, visit TechNet.

SUMMARY

- There are several ways to configure sharing on a network, including using Simple File Sharing, setting share permissions, and setting NTFS permissions.

- Multiple permissions affect a user's access level. When share and NTFS permissions are applied, the cumulative permissions of both are determined, and the most restrictive of those create the user's effective permission.

- A user's group membership can determine the level of access to the computer and its files and folders.

- Local policies can restrict how users log on, what their passwords must consist of, and what they can access and change once logged on to the computer.

- Group policies can restrict the user's desktop, Start menu and taskbar, and what the user can access and change once logged on to the computer.

- When multiple policies exist, domain policies always override local policies.

REVIEW QUESTIONS

1. The company you work for hires quite a few temporary workers, and those workers need access to workgroup computers to perform their jobs. These employees are added to the default Users group when they are hired. Because they are members of the Users group, they have Read and Execute, List Folder Contents, and Read permissions by default. However, these users also need to be able to write data to the folders to which they have access. What's the best way to make this change without giving the users too much access?

    a. Add all new users to the Power Users group.

    b. Stop assigning NTFS permissions and assign the Read and Change share permissions.

    c. For the Users group on each share, assign the NTFS Write permission.

    d. Stop assigning NTFS permissions and assign the Full Control share permission.

2. A user's Windows 2000 Professional computer was recently upgraded to Windows XP Professional. A member of the Users group reports she can no longer run the legacy applications necessary to perform her job. You've looked for a newer version of the application, but cannot find one. The user is a Microsoft Certified Desktop Technician and a Microsoft Certified Professional, and has been with the company for many years, so you feel she's competent and will pose no threat if given extra leniency. You need to allow this user to run her legacy application. What's the best course of action?

    a. Move this end user from the Users group to the Power Users group.

    b. Decrease the default security settings for all members of the Users group.

    c. Purchase a new program that is Microsoft certified and train the users in the company to use it. Uninstall the legacy application.

    d. Move this end user from the Users group to the Administrators group.

3. A user named John is a member of several groups in a domain: the Research Group, the Marketing Group, and the Support Group. Each group he belongs to has access to a different set of folders and data. However, one folder named Help and Support is shared so that all users in the company can access it, although some users have more access than others. John's group membership and the permissions assigned to the Help and Support folder for each group are listed here. What is John's effective permission for the folder?

Group	Share Permissions	NTFS Permissions
Research	Read and Change	Read, Write, List Folder Contents, Read and Execute
Marketing	Read	Read, Read and Execute
Support	Full Control	Modify, Read and Execute, List Folder Contents, Read, Write

    a. Read

    b. Write

    c. Modify

    d. Full Control

4. A Windows XP Professional user reports she is unable to access the Add/ Remove Programs icon in Control Panel. What is most likely the problem?

    a. The Windows XP installation is corrupt.

    b. A group policy is in place that prevents access.

    c. The antivirus program is restricting access.

    d. There are no programs to add or remove.

    e. The user is not logged on as an administrator.

5. Select all of the ways the Group Policy console can be accessed.

    a. Type **gpedit.msc** at the Run line.

    b. Open the Group Policy console from Administrative Tools.

    c. Open Group Policy from Control Panel, using the Group Policy icon.

    d. Open Group Policy by choosing Start, pointing to All Programs, pointing to Accessories, pointing to System Tools, and selecting Group Policy.

6. In the following table, match the policy on the left with the appropriate security-setting policy folder on the right.

Policy	Local Security Setting Folder
1. Audit Logon Events	a) Local Policies, User Rights Assignment
2. Maximum Password Age	b) In Group Policy, User Configuration, Administrative Templates, Control Panel
3. Interactive Logon: Do Not Require CTRL + ALT + DEL	c) Local Policies, Security Options
4. Shut Down The System	d) Account Policies, Account Lockout Policy
5. Account Lockout Threshold	e) Local Policies, Audit Policy
6. Hide Specific Control Panel Tools	f) Account Policies, Password Policy

CASE SCENARIOS

Scenario 9-1: Understanding Windows XP File Sharing Options

A small-office user with three employees has just purchased a new Windows XP computer, and has set up a network using a four-port hub. She connected her three existing Windows 98 computers and her new Windows XP computer, and then used the Network Setup Wizard on the Windows XP machine to create the network. She reports she made no other changes. After sharing a few folders, the owner reports that everyone on the network can view and make changes to her shared files. She only wants the users on her network to be able to view the files, not edit or change them. What should you inform the owner to do? (Select all that apply.)

1. Disable Simple File Sharing.

2. Convert the file system of the Windows XP computer to NTFS.

3. Clear the Allow Users To Change My Files check box on the Sharing tab of each shared folder.

4. Drag the shared folders to the Shared Documents folder.

5. Upgrade all of the computers to Windows XP.

Scenario 9-2: Understanding Built-In Groups

The company you work for has its users separated into four user groups: the Administrators group, the Power Users group, the Users group, and the Temporary Workers group. The company's network is configured as a workgroup. The first three groups are built-in groups, and a network administrator created the last group. A user at your company who has previously been a member of the Administrators group has recently been demoted and placed in the Power Users group. He reports several problems:

- He cannot back up or restore files and folders on the network.
- He cannot manage auditing and security logs.
- He cannot take ownership of files and folders.
- He cannot force shutdown of a remote system.

What is the cause of this?

1. That's the nature of the default groups.
2. Local policies are preventing access.
3. Group policies are preventing access.
4. Public key policies are preventing access.

CHAPTER 10
PROTECT THE COMPUTER

Upon completion of this chapter, you will be able to:

- Apply critical updates, service packs, driver updates, and operating system updates

- Configure and use the Windows XP Internet Connection Firewall

- Enable and view the Internet Connection Firewall log files

- Modify the behavior of the Internet Connection Firewall by configuring advanced Internet Control Message Protocol settings

- Notice warning signs of viruses and apply, configure, and use virus scanning software

- Recover from a virus

- Use the Microsoft Baseline Security Analyzer to find out if a computer is secure

The goal of this chapter is to teach you to protect the computer using a variety of methods and techniques. Applying Windows updates, configuring the Internet Connection Firewall (ICF), and protecting the computer from viruses are all extremely important to the overall dependability and stability of a computer or network.

There are several objectives covered in this chapter, including these:

- Applying critical updates

- Identifying and troubleshooting problems caused by firewall configurations

- Identifying a virus attack

- Applying signature updates

- Identifying and responding to security incidents

WINDOWS UPDATE

Windows Update is an online update Web site provided by Microsoft to keep users' computers up to date and protected from the latest security threats. Windows Update provides and distributes security fixes, critical updates, updated Help files, newly released and signed drivers, and various other items. These updates can be downloaded and installed (for free) by anyone with valid administrator credentials on the computer and a licensed and valid copy of the operating system.

291

You can configure Windows Update to look for and obtain updates automatically. If a user reports problems acquiring updates on a regular basis, verify that Windows Update is enabled and configured appropriately by following these steps:

1. Open Control Panel and open System.

2. In the System Properties dialog box, on the Automatic Updates tab, select the Keep My Computer Up To Date check box.

3. Under Settings, verify that an appropriate option is selected. Options range from notifying a user before downloading updates to downloading and installing the updates automatically and on a specific schedule. Figure 10-1 shows an example.

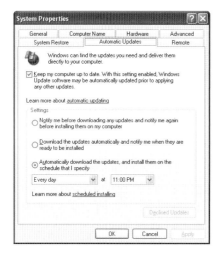

Figure 10-1 Automatic Update can be configured in a number of ways.

4. Click OK.

> **NOTE** **Manual Updates** End users can also obtain updates manually from the Windows Update Web site. To do so, from the Start menu, point to All Programs, and then select Windows Update. This process is discussed in depth later in this chapter.

There are three kinds of updates: critical updates and service packs, Windows updates, and driver updates. In the next three sections, these are discussed. However, downloading and installing updates is the same for each type, so the installation of updates is covered only in the first section.

Critical Updates and Service Packs

Critical updates and service packs are crucial to the operation of the computer and should always be installed. These updates provide solutions to known issues, include patches for security vulnerabilities, and might contain updates to the operating system or the applications installed on it, among other things.

If Windows Update is configured to download and install updates automatically, the end user only has to click Install when prompted by the operating system. If the user does not have this configured, or if the user is on a network that prevents it, the user might need help obtaining the updates manually. To obtain updates manually from the Windows Update Web site, follow these steps:

1. From the Start menu, point to All Programs, and then select Windows Update.

2. On the Microsoft Windows Update Web site, click Scan For Updates.

3. After the scan is complete, select a category under Pick Updates To Install, and then click Add for each update you want to install. Once the updates have been selected, click Review And Install Updates. (Critical updates and service packs will automatically be selected.)

4. When prompted, click Install Now.

5. Click Accept after reading the license agreement. Wait while the updates are installed and reboot if prompted.

It is imperative that you install all critical updates. Figure 10-2 shows a healthy system report from the Microsoft Windows Update Web site.

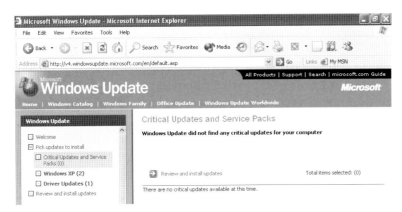

Figure 10-2 All critical updates and service packs are installed on this computer.

Windows Operating System Updates

Windows updates are less critical than the previously detailed updates, and these range from application updates for third-party software to updates for previously applied operating system service packs. Not everyone needs all updates, however, so a description of each is given with the update itself. You should read the descriptions prior to adding them to the installation list.

You download and install Windows updates in the same manner as critical updates and service packs; however, in most instances you can download and install multiple updates simultaneously. Figure 10-3 shows a download and installation in progress.

Figure 10-3   Windows Update shows its progress with a dialog box.

Driver Updates

Driver updates offer new and updated drivers for a user's particular computer system and setup. When Windows Update scans the computer, it acquires information about the modem, network card, printer, and similar hardware, and if an updated driver is available for any component, it is offered. End users find that driver updates enhance the performance of the computer because the newer drivers work better with Microsoft Windows XP than the older drivers do.

> **NOTE**   **Licensing**   End users will not be able to receive ongoing updates from Windows Update unless they have a valid and licensed copy of Windows XP.

Configuring automatic updates or obtaining the updates manually helps keep a computer running as smoothly as possible. When possible, encourage users, especially home users, to keep their computers as up to date as possible.

INTERNET CONNECTION FIREWALL

A firewall protects a computer from the outside world, specifically, the Internet. It acts as a security system that creates a border between the computer or network and the World Wide Web. This border determines what is allowed to come into or go out of the local intranet or standalone computer. This system assists in keeping hackers, viruses, and other evils from infiltrating the computer and network. Any computer connected directly to the Internet, whether it is a stand-alone computer or a computer that provides Internet Connection Sharing (ICS) services for other computers on a network should have the Internet Connection Firewall (ICF) enabled.

ICF has the following characteristics:

- ICF limits the data that comes into a computer or a network by scanning the data that tries to enter. Unwanted data is silently discarded.

- ICF does not limit what happens on a stand-alone computer or inside the network, or the data that passes between computers in an intranet.

- You can use ICF with dial-up connections, Digital Subscriber Line (DSL) modems, cable modems, and similar hardware.

- You can configure ICF to keep a security log of discarded packets so an administrator can view the types of packets that have been dropped, lost, opened, or closed.

- ICF does not protect against power surges, lightning, or natural disasters.

> **CAUTION**   **ICF and Virtual Private Networks**   You should not enable ICF on virtual private networks (VPNs). VPNs provide access to private networks through the Internet, and this access can incorporate the remote network's remote access rules, routed connections, and authentication procedures. When you enable ICF on a computer that uses a VPN, it can cause problems with file and printer sharing between that computer and resources on the network.

ICF and the Small Office

ICF is generally enabled on computers in small office networks and home networks because it is designed for use on computers that connect directly to the Internet, and in smaller networks there are usually one or more computers that do. (In larger companies, network computers connect to a network server that provides access, and the network servers have their own firewalls and security software and hardware.) You should not enable ICF on computers that do not access the Internet directly because ICF can interfere with communications between the computer and others on the network.

If a user wants to enable ICF or if you believe ICF has been enabled on a connection that does not access the Internet directly, you must access the Internet or Local Area Connection's Properties dialog box and make the appropriate changes, as follows:

1. Open Control Panel and open Network Connections.

2. Right-click the connection that connects to the Internet and select Properties.

3. In the Properties dialog box, select the Advanced tab.

4. To enable ICF, select the Protect My Computer And Network By Limiting Or Preventing Access To This Computer From The Internet check box. To disable ICF, clear this check box. Click OK. Figure 10-4 shows a sample connection with ICF and ICS enabled.

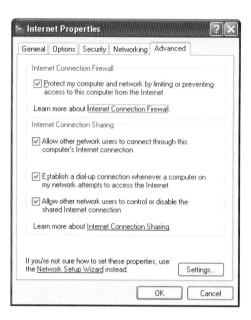

Figure 10-4   Enable Internet Connection Firewall through the local area connection's Properties dialog box.

Do not enable ICF on a local area network (LAN) connection that connects the user to the LAN. Do not enable ICF on a computer that accesses the Internet through a host computer's Internet connection either.

Configuring, Viewing, and Using Log Files

Security logging, the collecting of information that details dropped packets discarded by ICF, successful connections, and other firewall activity, is not enabled by default when you enable ICF. However, you can configure ICF to log activity, including logging what is permitted and what is rejected to and from the home or small office network and the Internet. Logging consists of three basic tasks: enabling logging, accessing the log, and reading log entries.

▶ **Enabling logging**

To view and use log file information, you need to enable logging by following these steps:

1. Open Control Panel and open Network Connections.

2. Right-click the connection that offers ICF and select Properties. Select the Advanced tab.

3. On the Advanced tab, click Settings.

4. In the Advanced Settings dialog box, select the Security Logging tab. Under Logging Options, select the Log Dropped Packets and/or Log Successful Connections check boxes.

❏ **Log Dropped Packets** Logs all dropped packets originating from the local network or the Internet.

❏ **Log Successful Connections** Logs all successful connections originating from the network or the Internet.

5. Note the location of the security log. By default it is in the \Windows\ Pfirewall.log file. Click OK. Click OK in the Properties dialog box to close it.

▶ **Accessing the log**

Once you have enabled logging, you can access the log by browsing to its location and opening the file. This file is most easily opened by browsing to it from Network Connections by following these steps:

1. Open Control Panel and open Network Connections.

2. Right-click the connection that offers ICF, and select Properties. Select the Advanced tab.

3. On the Advanced tab, click Settings.

4. In the Advanced Settings dialog box, select the Security Logging tab, and under Log File Options, click Browse.

5. Right-click the Pfirewall.txt file and select Open. Notice the text file has several headings including Date, Time, Action, Protocol, and more.

Reading Log Entries

Log entries give insight into what packets have been successful in getting into the network and which have been rejected. There are two sections, the header and the body. The header includes information about the version of ICF, the full name of ICF, where the time stamp on the log learned of the time, and the field names used by the body of the log entry to display data. The body details the log data.

There are 16 data entries per logged item. These include information about the date and time the log was written and information about the data that passed. Although this information is quite technical, briefly, it tells what types of packets were opened, closed, dropped, and lost; what **protocol** was used in the data transmission; the destination IP address of the data; the **port** used by the sending computer; the port of the destination computer; and the size of the packet logged.

> **NOTE** **Your Role as a Tier 1 Technician** As a Tier 1 desktop technician, your job is to understand where logs are stored, that logging is available, and that highly technical information can be obtained from the logs. As you gain experience, you'll learn more about these logs and the information that can be obtained from them.

ICMP and ICF

Internet Control Message Protocol (ICMP) allows routers and host computers to swap basic control information when data is sent from one computer to another. ICMP error and configuration information is attached to the data and includes whether or not the data sent reaches its final destination, if it can or cannot be forwarded by a specific router, and what the best route for the data is. ICMP tools such as Ping and Tracert are often used to troubleshoot network connectivity.

ICMP troubleshooting tools and their resulting messages can be helpful when used by a network administrator, but harmful when used by an attacker. For instance, a network administrator who sends a Ping request sends an ICMP packet that contains an Echo request message to the Internet Protocol (IP) address being tested. The reply allows the administrator to verify that the computer is reachable. An attacker, on the other hand, can send a **broadcast storm** of pings that can overpower a system so that it can't respond to legitimate traffic. By configuring ICMP, you can control how a system responds (or doesn't respond) to such requests. By default, no ICMP messages are enabled or allowed.

Configuring Advanced ICMP Settings

Desktop technicians and network administrators use ICMP requests to troubleshoot network connectivity. Generally, you enable the ICMP options when needed and then disable them once you've completed troubleshooting. You can set advanced ICMP options in the ICF host's Properties dialog box by following these steps:

1. Open Control Panel and open Network Connections.

2. Right-click the connection that has ICF configured and select Properties.

3. On the Advanced tab, click Settings.

4. In the Advanced Settings dialog box, select the ICMP tab. Figure 10-5 shows the default settings. Notice that no ICMP requests are enabled. To enable an option, select it.

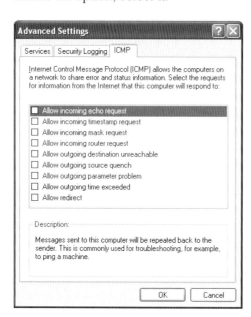

Figure 10-5   The default ICMP settings are shown here.

You can view what each option offers by selecting it on the ICMP tab. For instance, selecting the first option, Allow Incoming Echo Request, states that Echo messages sent to the computer will be repeated (echoed) back to the sender. This means that if a Ping message is sent to the computer, an ICMP message will be sent back noting that the ping was received. Although this can be an excellent tool for troubleshooting network connectivity, it isn't a good option to leave enabled all the time because it leaves the system vulnerable to Internet attacks.

ICMP Options

Table 10-1 details the available ICMP options shown in Figure 10-5. While on the job as a desktop technician, make sure that you do not allow or enable these options without a full understanding of them and the consequences and risks involved. Enable these options when troubleshooting connectivity, and then disable them when finished.

Table 10-1 **ICMP Options**

ICMP Option	Description
Allow Incoming Echo Request	Controls whether a remote computer can ask for and receive a response from the computer. Ping is a command that requires you to enable this option. When it is enabled (as with other options), attackers can see and contact the host computer.
Allow Incoming Timestamp Request	Sends a reply to another computer stating that an incoming message was received and includes time and date data.
Allow Incoming Mask Request	Provides the sender with the subnet mask for the network of which the computer is a member. The sender already has the IP address; giving the subnet mask is all an attacker or administrator needs to obtain the remaining network information about the computer's network.
Allow Incoming Router Request	Provides information about the routes the computer recognizes and will pass on information it has about any routers to which it is connected.
Allow Outgoing Destination Unreachable	The computer will send a "Destination Unreachable" message offering information about why discarded packets were not received. These messages refer to nonexistent and unreachable hosts on the network.
Allow Outgoing Source Quench	Offers information to routers about the rate at which data is received and tells routers to slow down if too much data is being sent and it cannot be received fast enough to keep up.
Allow Outgoing Parameter Problem	The computer sends a "Bad Header" error message when the computer discards data it has received that has a problematic header. This allows the sender to understand that the host exists, but that there were unknown problems with the message itself.

Table 10-1   **ICMP Options**

ICMP Option	Description
Allow Outgoing Time Exceeded	The computer sends the sender a "Time Expired" message when the computer must discard messages because the messages timed out.
Allow Redirect	Data sent from this computer will be rerouted if the path changes. This allows data to be pointed in the right direction so that data can flow more efficiently.

As you gain experience, you'll enable and disable these tools when troubleshooting the network and resource access.

Services

Generically, in computer terms, services are run either automatically or manually to support applications and programs available on the computer. You can view the services running on a Windows XP computer using Administrative Tools in Control Panel, under Services. Some services you might be familiar with include the Indexing service, the Messenger service, the Print Spooler service, the Smart Card service, and the Workstation service. ICF and ICS are also available services, as shown in Figure 10-6.

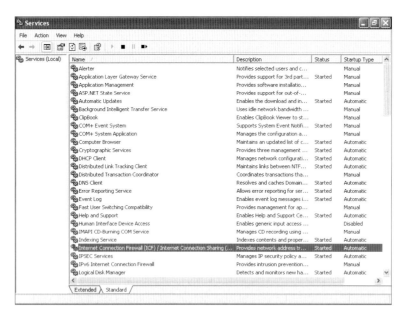

Figure 10-6   Services are accessed from Administrative Tools in Control Panel.

Some services offer their own services, and ICF is an example of this. Some ICF services run automatically, whereas you must configure others manually. Automatic services running with ICF allow someone from the Internet to contact a user or his computer on his private network in various secure ways. Other services that you must configure manually provide additional access to those users. For instance, if end users want to host Web pages from their home office and allow Internet users access to their personal Web server, they need to add the HTTP Web Server service. Adding this service tells ICF to allow the additional and required traffic.

In addition to Web servers, end users can create other types of servers or offer additional services. Each of the following servers or services requires you to manually configure the firewall to permit the service's traffic:

- File Transfer Protocol (FTP) server
- Incoming connection VPN (Layer 2 Tunneling Protocol or Point-to-Point Tunneling Protocol)
- Internet Message Access Protocol 3 (IMAP3), IMAP4, Post Office Protocol 3 (POP3), or Simple Mail Transfer Protocol (SMTP) mail servers
- IP Security (Internet Key Exchange)
- Remote Desktop
- Telnet server
- Secure Web server (HTTP Secure)

Once you know what a user wants to configure, adding the service is easy. This is detailed next.

Adding a Service Definition

To configure a firewall to permit service traffic that *you* define, you must have the following, which might need to be obtained from an administrator, from the service's documentation, or from the service's Web site:

- The name or IP address of the computer hosting the service
- ICF or ICS enabled on the connection
- The ability to log on as an administrator
- The necessary permissions on the network, if one exists
- The external port number for the service
- The internal port number for the service

To permit traffic for a *predefined* service, such as FTP, POP3, IMAP4, HTTP, and others, you need only the name or IP address of the computer hosting the service on the network.

▶ **Adding a predefined service definition**

To add a predefined service definition, follow these steps:

1. Open Control Panel and open Network Connections.

2. Right-click the shared connection or the Internet connection being protected by ICF, and select Properties.

3. In the Properties dialog box, on the Advanced tab, click Settings.

4. On the Services tab, select the check box for the service you want to add.

5. When prompted, type the name or IP address of the computer hosting the service on the network, as shown in Figure 10-7. Click OK.

Figure 10-7   Adding the Web Server (HTTP) service involves inputting the appropriate information.

6. After you've added the service or services, click OK in the Advanced Security dialog box to close it, and click OK in the Properties dialog box to apply the changes.

NOTE   Add a New Service Definition   *You can add new service definitions by clicking Add on the Services tab (see step 4 earlier). In the Service Settings dialog box, type the required information.*

Troubleshooting

There are a few fairly common problems that end users encounter when using ICF, including the inability to enable ICF on a connection, problems with file and print sharing, a network user's inability to access a server on the network (such as a Web server), problems with Remote Assistance, and problems running Internet programs. The solutions to all of these problems (and others) are well documented and easily available from the Microsoft Knowledge Base at *http://support.microsoft.com.*

When troubleshooting ICF, make sure you remember to check the obvious first. Listed next are some basic rules that must be followed, and any deviation from these can be the cause of many of the common problems encountered when using ICF:

- ICF can be enabled only by administrators, and can be enabled only on outgoing connections such as connections to the Internet. ICF can be disabled from a group or domain policy, preventing access even by a local administrator.

- ICF should be configured only on the computers on the network that connect directly to the Internet. If ICF is enabled on other computers on the network, problems with file and print sharing can ensue.

- Network users will not be able to access a Web server, FTP server, game server, or other network server unless the appropriate service definition has also been added.

- Remote Assistance can be affected if ICF has been enabled after a Remote Assistance invitation was created. This can be resolved by creating a new invitation while ICF is enabled or by disabling the firewall temporarily.

- Internet programs might not work as expected when ICF is enabled. To work around the problem, temporarily disable ICF.

As with other troubleshooting sections in previous chapters, you can find solutions to common problems in the Windows Help and Support files, the Knowledge Base, TechNet, third-party Web sites, and newsgroups.

TROUBLESHOOTING VIRUS ATTACKS

With Windows Update and ICF configured and enabled, it's time to turn your attention away from configuring operating system components and toward protecting the computer using third-party software. Protecting the computer from viruses and dealing with viruses that infiltrate the computer or the network can be a big part of a desktop technician's job. In this section you learn about installing, configuring, and using virus scanning software, and how and when you should apply **signature updates**. You also learn how to determine if a virus attack has occurred and where to go for help when a virus has been detected.

Virus Scanning Software

Virus scanning software, also called antivirus software, protects the computer or network from virus attacks. All of your end users should have antivirus software installed on their computers, but you'll learn that many (especially home users) do not. If, while on a service call, you discover that a user does not have virus scanning software, you should encourage her to get some type of protection immediately. Viruses can wreak havoc on unprotected computers, and those computers, once infected, are much more difficult to recover than those with antivirus software installed. In addition, users need to be told how and why to keep the software updated, because virus protection software is only as good as its last update.

Installing and Configuring

You install virus scanning software like any other software, generally by inserting a product CD and following the prompts provided, or by opening the executable file downloaded from a manufacturer's Web site. Configuring the software is an important part of the installation procedure, too, because improper configuration of the software can leave the computer vulnerable to attacks, even though you've installed the software.

> **NOTE   When Software Is Already in Place**   Larger companies and corporations will most likely have a combination of hardware and software already in place to protect the network, and if you are a Tier 1 network technician in a large company, you'll probably be involved only in applying updates or recovering from virus attacks.

After you've installed virus scanning software, browse through the software options and verify or enable the following settings:

- The software should start automatically when Windows is booted, and protection should be continuous. This prevents lapses in protection.

- Incoming and outgoing e-mail should be scanned for viruses every time. This prevents viruses from being propagated throughout the network through e-mail.

- Scripts should be blocked if possible. Scripts could contain viruses and cause harm to the computer or network.

- System scans should be configured to run daily or weekly to locate any previously undetected viruses.

- Virus definitions or signature updates should be configured to update themselves daily at a specified time. These definitions should be configured to install automatically when appropriate for the network. This confirms that the protection will always be current.

- The software should be renewed when the subscription on expires to prevent a lapse in protection.

- The software should be configured to protect instant messaging software and prevent **spyware** or **adware** from being installed on the computer.

- When viruses are detected, they should be quarantined or automatically repaired when possible.

With these configurations in place, the computer should be protected, and the user can feel confident that his data and network are safe. However, it is extremely important that signature updates be installed regularly; manually installing these updates is detailed next.

Applying Signature Updates

Signature updates are similar to the critical updates from the Windows Update Web site in that they contain the latest security patches and are created for the purpose of keeping the computer or network safe. They also contain the latest virus definitions and provide the best protection possible from the latest known security threats.

These updates can be configured as Windows Updates can, to download and install automatically, or they can be obtained manually. When possible, you should configure the updates to occur automatically. If this isn't possible due to network restrictions or group or domain policies, updates must be obtained manually. For most virus scanning software, obtaining updates manually is achieved as follows:

1. From the Start menu, point to All Programs, and then select the software scanning program name in the All Programs list.

2. From the options, locate the option to obtain updates. For example, Norton's is called LiveUpdate - Norton AntiVirus.

3. If the updates do not run automatically, work through the wizard that is offered, click Start, or otherwise follow the instructions on the screen.

Depending on the sensitivity of the system and of the data, automatic updates should be applied daily or weekly.

Taking Notice of Common Signs

No matter how secure a computer or network is, there is always a chance a virus can slip through and attack. Viruses can come through e-mail, floppy disk, or a downloaded application or network program, just to name a few ways. There are many kinds of viruses, too, including simple viruses that replicate themselves and are passed on without causing actual harm to the computer; Trojan Horse viruses that steal sensitive data; worms that infect computers even when the user has not opened any e-mail attachment, program, or other infected component; and combinations of these that cause an assortment of effects.

Even though there are numerous variations on what signs different viruses produce, the signs you should look for are quite similar:

- The computer system or network slows down.

- Network users all report similar problems almost simultaneously.

- Activity occurs on the computer, including messages, music, or pop-ups.

- A network e-mail server slows down or stops responding.

- Data files become corrupt or are missing.

- Files and folders are changed.

- Programs do not run or run chaotically.

- Computer partitions become unavailable.

- E-mail is sent from a computer automatically and to everyone in the user's address book.

Recovering from a Virus

Recovering from a virus might require a multifaceted approach. It likely will involve running the antivirus software installed on the computer first, or if that isn't possible, booting the computer using the virus scanning software recovery disk, if one exists. You can also access many third-party sites on the Internet for information, including the virus scanning software manufacturer's Web site. Many of these sites offer online tools to detect and remove a virus even if the end user doesn't own a copy of the software.

If the computer is so severely infected that you cannot access the online options and the computer won't boot to the recovery disk (or one is not available), you can use an uninfected computer to make a scan and install repair tools from most of the major antivirus manufacturer's Web sites. There are many options from these types of Web sites, and they can be extremely helpful in resolving problems.

Finally, if you know the name of the virus (perhaps you've seen it on the news, or it offers a name during infection) or if you've researched the symptoms and have narrowed down the virus to a single one, you can search the Internet for removal options. This information can be located in newsgroups or on third-party sites, but reliable information is also available from the Microsoft support pages. Figure 10-8 shows the Web page at *http://www.microsoft.com/security/antivirus*, which detailed the Swen worm, the Sobig virus and its variants, the Blaster worm, and other viruses.

Figure 10-8   Virus information is available from the Microsoft support pages.

Using the information here, network technicians and home users alike can locate information that details how to get rid of a virus once it's been detected, and stay up to date on other security issues.

MORE INFO *Get More Information* End users and desktop technicians can get more information about protecting a computer from *http://www.microsoft.com/ security/protect/windowsxp.*

USING MICROSOFT BASELINE SECURITY ANALYZER

The Microsoft Baseline Security Analyzer (MBSA) is one more way you can protect a computer system. MBSA scans computers for common security lapses and then generates individual security reports for each computer it scans. You can use these reports to determine what steps you should take to further secure the computer or computers on the network. MBSA runs on computers that are installed with Microsoft Windows 2000 and Windows XP, as well as Microsoft Windows Server 2003. You can use it to scan for security problems on computers that run Microsoft Windows NT 4.0, Windows 2000, Windows XP, and Windows Server 2003.

You must download the MBSA tool before you can use it; it is not an integral part of any computer operating system. You can download it from *http:// support.microsoft.com/default.aspx?kbid=320454.*

▶ **Installing and running the MBSA**

Once downloaded, you can install and run the MBSA to detect security vulnerabilities by following these steps:

1. Visit *http://support.microsoft.com/default.aspx?kbid=320454* and download the MBSA. When prompted, select Save.

2. Once the download is complete, in the Download Complete dialog box, click Open.

3. Install and start the application.

4. When prompted by MBSA, select Scan A Computer or Scan More Than One Computer.

5. Select the computer or computers to scan, and set the options for scanning. Options include the following:

   ❏ Windows Vulnerabilities

   ❏ Weak Passwords

   ❏ IIS Vulnerabilities

   ❏ SQL Vulnerabilities

   ❏ Security Updates

6. Click Start Scan.

7. Wait while the computer is scanned, then view the report. Part of a sample report is shown in Figure 10-9.

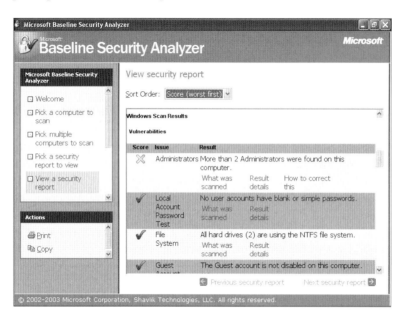

Figure 10-9   The MBSA report lists security lapses and vulnerabilities.

In this example, some of the Internet Explorer zones do not have secure settings, one Microsoft product has an issue with macro security, and multiple administrators exist. These are all security vulnerabilities that can be easily corrected. Notice that for each security lapse listed, options are given for resolution. To resolve any issue, click How To Correct This, also shown in Figure 10-9.

SUMMARY

- To install Windows updates as they become available, configure Automatic Updates to check for the updates regularly or set a schedule to obtain updates manually. Always install critical updates and service packs.

- To use ICF, verify that the computer connects directly to the Internet, then use the Internet connections Properties dialog box Advanced tab to enable it.

- To troubleshoot network and connectivity problems, enable ICMP options for the network connection configured to provide ICF.

- When adding servers and services to a LAN, add its respective service to ICF so that the required traffic for the service can pass.

- To get the best protection possible, install and properly configure virus scanning software to download signature updates automatically, automatically protect the computer, and scan incoming and outgoing e-mail.

- To use MBSA, download it from the Microsoft support pages, and then run it to obtain a detailed report listing the security vulnerabilities on the computer.

REVIEW QUESTIONS

1. An end user reports that although he was able to install Windows Update files when he first purchased his computer two years ago, he is now unable to install Service Pack 1 or 2. After a quick check, you discover that Windows Update is enabled in System Properties, and is configured to automatically download updates. You verify that the user can download Service Pack 1 but cannot install it. What is most likely the problem?

    a. The user has an unlicensed copy of Windows XP.

    b. The user is running Windows XP Home Edition and needs to upgrade to Windows XP Professional Edition.

    c. The user needs to register Windows XP with Microsoft.

    d. The user needs to activate Windows XP with Microsoft.

    e. Windows Update determined after scanning the computer that the user doesn't need to install the service packs.

2. A small office user has a network that consists of four computers. One Windows XP Professional Edition computer acts as the host and provides ICS services, and the other three computers access the Internet through this host computer's Internet connection. The administrator of the network wants to protect the network by using ICF. What must the administrator do?

    a. Purchase and install a router that is compatible with Windows XP and ICF.

    b. Upgrade to DSL or a cable modem; ICF doesn't work with a dial-up connection.

    c. Enable ICF on the host computer.

    d. Enable ICF on all four network computers.

3. You are troubleshooting a network connection and need to use the Ping command to see if a host is reachable. Which ICMP option should you enable on the host computer?

    a. Allow Incoming Router Request

    b. Allow Incoming Echo Request

    c. Allow Outgoing Source Quench

    d. Allow Redirect

4. An end user reports she has noticed some bizarre behavior on her computer all morning, and she believes it is getting worse. She reports the computer is displaying odd messages, that she cannot open her JPEG files, and that some programs won't run. She says she has not opened any e-mail attachments all morning, and that no one has accessed the computer but her. What is most likely the problem?

    a. The user has a virus on her computer and it is most likely a simple, replicating virus.

    b. The user has a virus on her computer and it is most likely a worm.

    c. The user has an internal problem that cannot be a virus, because the user states she did not open any e-mail attachments recently.

    d. The user's computer needs to be reinstalled; these are common signs of a corrupt installation.

5. You work for an Internet service provider (ISP). An end user calls and reports that he has a virus on his computer. He has discovered through his friends and from watching the national news that he has the Blaster worm. He does not have any antivirus software installed. Although it is not your job to assist the user in ridding the computer of the virus, you'd like to assist in some way in the time you are allotted. List four ways the user can get help in ridding the computer of the virus.

CASE SCENARIOS

Scenario 10-1: Allowing Specific Services on ICF

An end user is setting up a server that he will host himself using his small office network, and he wants Internet users to be able to connect to the Web pages stored on it. He is also setting up an additional server that will permit users to upload and download files using the Internet instead of the local network. What two services must he enable to permit the required traffic to flow through the ICF he currently has configured on this connection? Pick two.

1. Web Server (HTTP)

2. FTP Server

3. Telnet Server

4. POP3

5. Incoming Connection VPN (Point-to-Point Tunneling Protocol)

Scenario 10-2: Checking for Network Vulnerabilities

As a desktop technician for a small office network, it is your job to make sure all of the computers on the network are as secure and protected as possible. You've configured Windows Update to obtain and install updates automatically, you have ICF configured on all of the computers that need it, you have antivirus software installed on each computer, you incorporate a router for extra protection, and you enforce password policies that require users to create strong passwords on their computers. You now want to be able to test the computers on the network regularly from your desktop computer and check for additional vulnerabilities as they arise. The computers are all in the IP range of 192.168.0.1 to 192.168.0.12. You want to check the following:

- If the most recent security updates have been installed

- If password requirements are configured

- If the file systems are all configured as NTFS

- If the Guest account is enabled on any of the computers

- How many shares are present on each computer

- If Microsoft Outlook security zones have security issues

Is there a single, free program available to do this? Select the best answer.

1. There is no program like this available, but one is not needed; the computers are amply protected.

2. There is no program like this available, but the MBSA offers some of these options.

3. The MBSA offers all of these options, and can be used from the administrator's desktop.

4. There is no free program available, but several applications can be purchased that will perform these tasks.

CHAPTER 11

TROUBLESHOOTING APPLICATION ACCESS ON MULTIUSER, MULTIBOOT, AND NETWORKED COMPUTERS

Upon completion of this chapter, you will be able to:

- Configure application access for users of shared computers

- Configure and troubleshoot application access for users of multiboot computers

- Understand the three basic files system types—FAT, FAT32, and NTFS—and when and how they should be used

- Troubleshoot file system access on multiboot computers

- Use program compatibility mode

- Configure and troubleshoot application access for users of networked computers

The goal of this chapter is to teach you to work with various types of computer setups, specifically those with multiuser or multiboot configurations, as well as computers that participate on a network. For the most part, this chapter revolves around configuring applications and allowing access to them for each type of configuration. Other topics include understanding the three basic file system types—FAT, FAT32, and NTFS—and how applications should be configured when these file systems are used.

Briefly, the three computer configurations discussed in this chapter are as follows:

- **Multiuser** A multiuser computer can be a stand-alone computer, a computer in a workgroup, or a computer in a domain. Multiuser computers are accessed by two or more people, each of whom should have her own logon name and password. In a home environment, the users include family members and guests; in a work environment, the users might include network administrators, company employees, customers, and guests, among others. In all instances, the users who can log on to the computer each have various levels of access, which is determined by the type of user account they have been assigned, and any additional share or NTFS permissions, group policies, local policies, or domain policies that have been applied. Applications on multiuser computers are shared and only installed once.

- **Multiboot**   A multiboot computer can be a stand-alone computer, a computer in a workgroup, or a computer in a domain. Multiboot computers have more than one operating system installed (for instance, Microsoft Windows 98 and Microsoft Windows XP), and a user can boot to either. Applications used on multiboot computers must be installed on all **partitions** in which they'll be used. Multiboot computers can have more than two operating systems, but this is not common. Multiboot computers can also be multiuser computers.

- **Networked**   A networked computer can be a computer in a workgroup or a computer in a domain. Networked computers can also include stand-alone computers that are used as remote desktop servers for mobile hardware such as laptops and Pocket PCs. Networked computers can be multiuser and multiboot. Networked computers often have their installed applications stored directly on the machine in the Programs folder like most computers do, but some computers are configured to access the applications they need from a network server.

WORKING WITH MULTIUSER COMPUTERS

Multiuser computers support multiple users, and this means that several people log on to the computer at different times (one at a time) to work, play, e-mail, and perform other computing tasks. To resolve service calls involving multiuser computers, you need to have a basic understanding of the types of user accounts you'll encounter. You also need to have an understanding of how data and applications are shared among the users who log on to the computer. Once you have learned about user accounts and a little about how multiuser computers work, you'll learn how to configure application access on multiuser computers so that all users who access the computer can also access the applications installed on it.

Understanding User Accounts

Users who share a Microsoft Windows XP Home Edition or Windows XP Professional Edition computer are assigned a user account by the administrator of that computer. Each time the user logs on with this personal account, the computer retrieves the personalized settings, individual data, passwords, Internet and e-mail configurations, and other information for the user, so that the computer is always personalized for the user who accesses it. Configuring user accounts also serves as a way to keep the user's personal data safe from and inaccessible to other users who log on to the same computer.

The user account type also defines the level of access the user has while logged on to the computer, such as whether or not he can install software or hardware, create additional user accounts, make permanent changes to the computer, or change passwords. There are four types of user accounts you'll encounter:

- **Computer Administrator** This user account offers the user complete and unlimited authority to modify the computer in any way at all, including creating, changing, and deleting user accounts; making permanent changes to systemwide settings (such as setting local policies); and installing and uninstalling hardware and software. Local Administrator accounts are configured for stand-alone computers, as well as for computers in workgroups and domains.

- **Standard** This user account allows the user to install and uninstall software and hardware, and to make changes to the account password and picture. These accounts can be configured only for Windows XP Professional computers in domains.

- **Limited** This user account allows the user to make changes to her account password and picture, but does not allow the user to change computer settings, delete important files, install or uninstall hardware or software, or make changes to systemwide settings. These accounts are configured on stand-alone computers, as well as on computers in workgroups and domains.

- **Guest** This user account is a built-in account that can be enabled when needed, and allows a user to operate the computer in the same manner a user with a limited account can. Users can log on and check e-mail, browse the Internet, and use applications installed on the computer, but can cause no harm to the computer by installing programs or making permanent changes. The Guest account can be enabled on stand-alone computers, as well as on those in workgroups and domains.

Using a Shared Computer

Users who share a computer use their personal account to log on. That account can be configured on a single, stand-alone local computer, or the computer can be part of a workgroup or a domain. If a shared computer is a stand-alone computer or a member of a workgroup, users can share data on the computer by moving it to any of the Shared Documents folders. If the computer is a member of a domain, domain policies override any local settings, and the Shared Documents folders are not available. Figure 11-1 shows the Shared Documents folders on a Windows XP Professional computer that is not a member of a domain.

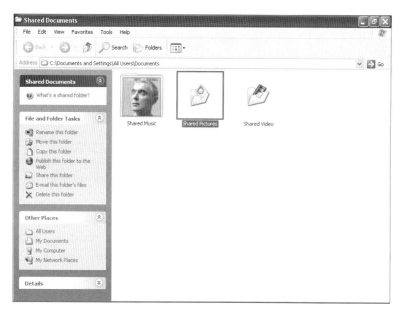

Figure 11-1   The Shared Documents folders offer an easy way to share files among multiple users.

Besides sharing data, applications can be shared among the users who log on to the computer. Applications do not need to be installed for each user who has access to the computer.

Configuring Access to Applications

When an administrator installs a program on the computer using the default settings, other administrators, limited or standard users, and guests who access the computer can use the installed programs. The user simply needs to select the program from the All Programs menu. The first time the user opens the application, it either configures itself automatically as shown in Figure 11-2, or prompts the user to input additional information (such as e-mail and Internet service provider [ISP] information). Virus scanning programs and other programs that are configured to protect the computer continue to work without additional configuration by users.

Figure 11-2   Application configuration in Microsoft Office can work automatically.

If the program is not compatible with Windows XP or was not installed using the installation defaults (for instance, if the program was installed to a private folder, recovered from the Recycle Bin, or otherwise modified so Windows does not recognize it as a shared application), you can place a shortcut to the application in the Shared Documents folder, and anyone who accesses the computer can then access the program.

If users cannot access an application installed on a Windows XP computer, follow these steps:

1. Log on as an administrator.

2. Right-click the Start button and select Explore All Users.

3. Using Windows Explorer, browse to the application that should be shared.

4. In the left pane of Windows Explorer, expand the drive on which Windows XP is installed (possibly C), expand Documents And Settings, expand All Users, and locate Shared Documents.

5. Right-click the application to share in the right pane, and drag its icon to the Shared Documents folder. Click Create Shortcut Here.

Any person who can log onto the computer can access items in the Shared Documents folder. In addition, you can add shortcuts to any user's desktop by copying a shortcut to the Desktop folder for each user who needs access.

WORKING WITH MULTIBOOT COMPUTERS

Multiboot computers run two or more operating systems and can have many combinations of them, including Windows XP, Microsoft Windows 2000, Windows NT, Windows 95, Windows 98, or Windows Me, and sometimes even Windows 3.1 or MS-DOS. As you gain experience working as a desktop technician, you'll see various configurations.

To troubleshoot these types of systems, you need to be familiar with the three basic file systems, how permissions play a role in users' access to them, and how installed programs should be configured.

> **NOTE**   *Order of Operating Systems*   *The order of the operating systems installed on a multiboot computer is generally from the earliest release to the latest. Windows XP should be installed last and on the last partition configured on the computer.*

File Systems and File System Access

Setting up or troubleshooting file system access on a multiboot computer requires that you understand why different file systems are required and some common issues that arise when different file systems are used in a multiboot environment. The three types of file systems discussed here are FAT and FAT32, which are earlier and simpler file systems, and NTFS, which is newer, more secure, and more complex.

On computers that contain multiple operating systems, compatibility and file access across operating systems becomes an issue because all operating systems do not provide support for all file systems. File compatibility problems result in files on a particular partition being unavailable when using another operating system on the computer. Having an understanding of the three file system types helps you troubleshoot these access problems.

FAT and FAT32

FAT is a file system used by MS-DOS and Windows-based operating systems to arrange and manage files stored on the computer. This type of file system organization allows information about the files to be accessed quickly and reliably. FAT is the only choice of file systems for MS-DOS, Windows 3.1, and Windows 95, because FAT is a 16-bit file system; FAT32 is a 32-bit file system, and is compatible with newer operating systems.

FAT32 is an offshoot of the FAT file system and supports larger **volumes** than FAT. It is thus a better choice when a larger hard disk is installed and when FAT must be used. FAT32 can be used with all of the latest operating systems, as detailed later in Table 11-1. You can convert a file system that is configured as FAT or FAT 32 to NTFS without loss of data, so if the operating system supports it, conversion is a good choice. However, converting back to FAT or FAT 32 from NTFS is not as forgiving; this type of conversion requires that you reformat the drive, which causes loss of data.

NTFS

NTFS is an advanced file system that provides organization, performance, security, reliability, and advanced features that the FAT and FAT32 file systems do not provide. NTFS offers encryption, file and folder permissions, **disk quotas**, and more. NTFS is supported only by the latest operating systems, as detailed in Table 11-1.

Supported File Systems

Table 11-1 shows the supported file systems for various Microsoft operating systems.

Table 11-1   **Supported File Systems**

Operating System	Supports FAT	Supports FAT32	Supports NTFS
MS-DOS	Yes	No	No
Windows 3.1	Yes	No	No
Windows NT	Yes	No	Yes
Windows 95	Yes	No	No
Windows 95 OSR2	Yes	Yes	No
Windows 98	Yes	Yes	No
Windows Me	Yes	Yes	No
Windows 2000	Yes	Yes	Yes
Windows XP	Yes	Yes	Yes

Thus, because of file system limitations, a multiboot computer offering Windows 98 and Windows XP will need to have one FAT or FAT 32 partition for Windows 98, and a FAT, FAT 32, or NTFS partition for Windows XP. However, although NTFS is the better choice for security, users will encounter file access problems when booted to the Windows 98 partition because Windows 98 does not support NTFS. These problems and others are detailed next.

Troubleshooting File System Access

Table 11-1 detailed which operating systems provide support for which file systems. It is important to understand the significance of this data. As just mentioned, file system access problems can occur when a user is logged on to one operating system and tries to access a file or folder on another partition using a file system that it does not support. An operating system that can access only a FAT partition will not recognize any files on a FAT32 or NTFS partition; an operating system that can access only FAT or FAT32 partitions will not recognize an NTFS partition.

When faced with problems caused by incompatible file systems, the only real solution is to **format** the partitions using the correct file system configuration. For instance, if users need to dual boot between Windows 95 and Windows XP, and need to be able to access files on each partition no matter to what operating system they've booted, the file systems for both partitions will need to be configured as FAT. This is because Windows 95 only recognizes FAT, so it would never be able to recognize the Windows XP partition unless it was formatted as FAT as well.

If file system configuration is not the problem, meaning the configured file systems and operating systems are compatible, consider these other items that can cause problems on multiboot computers:

■ Each operating system must be installed on a separate volume or partition. Microsoft does not support installing multiple operating systems on the same partition or volume, nor is this encouraged.

■ NTFS operating systems should not be installed on **compressed drives** that were not compressed using the NTFS compression utility.

■ You must install the operating systems in a specific order: MS-DOS, Windows 95, Windows 98, or Windows Me, Windows NT, Windows 2000, Windows XP.

■ If you're using Windows NT 4.0, apply Service Pack 4 or greater. Windows will automatically update all NTFS partitions to the version of NTFS used in Windows 2000 and Windows XP. This resolves most file access problems among NTFS partitions.

As with troubleshooting any problem you'll encounter, there are plenty of articles available from the Knowledge Base, TechNet, the Windows XP Expert Zone, and various newsgroups. When faced with a problem with file access and multiboot computers, access these sites and resources.

Troubleshooting Permissions Problems

Some end users might encounter file permission problems when working with multiboot computers, especially if those computers are also multiuser computers. As with a shared computer, a computer in a workgroup, or a computer in a domain, a user must have the correct permissions to access files and folders and to perform specific tasks on a multiboot computer. If those permissions aren't assigned to the user or the user's group, she receives a file permission error message, generally in the form of "Access Is Denied," as shown in Figure 11-3.

Figure 11-3   Access denied messages appear when permissions are not assigned or are not assigned correctly.

When users encounter access denied messages to a file or a folder, you'll be called on to resolve those errors. If the user needs access and the owner of the file wants to grant it, you can offer access by editing the share and NTFS permissions on the file or program in question to include that user by following these steps:

1. Use Windows Explorer to locate the problem folder.

2. Right-click the folder and select Properties.

3. On the Sharing tab, verify the folder is shared, and then click Permission.

4. In the Share Permissions dialog box, verify that the user has access to the folder. If the user does not have access, add the user or the user's group by clicking Add and selecting the user or group appropriately. If the user or group is already added, verify the permissions are configured correctly. Click OK.

5. If NTFS permissions have been applied, select the Security tab. Verify the user has access to the file or folder. If the user does not have access, add the user or the user's group by clicking Add and selecting the user or group appropriately. If the user or group is already added, verify the permissions are configured correctly. Click OK.

Users might also receive errors when installing programs. Remember, only users with Standard or Administrator accounts can install programs. To resolve this issue, the user will either have to be given additional, advanced permissions or assigned to a different group with the required permissions.

> **MORE INFO**   Troubleshooting Permissions   Chapter 9, "Security and Security Permissions," offers much more information on troubleshooting permissions. The topics covered there can be applied to multiboot computers. Make sure you review that chapter with multiboot computers in mind.

Difficult-to-Diagnose Errors

Access and permissions errors that are hard to diagnose can occur, especially when errors appear and everything seems to be in order, including the user name and password, permissions, and group membership. These errors are best resolved using the Knowledge Base or TechNet.

For instance, Knowledge Base article 810881 details how an Access Is Denied message can be issued to the owner of a folder if the original folder was created on an NTFS file system volume using a previous installation of Windows, and then Windows XP Professional was subsequently installed over it. It goes on to state that the error occurs because the **security ID** for the user has changed. Even if the user offers the same user name and password, the security ID no longer matches, and thus, the owner of the folder is unable to open his own folders. (The resolution of this requires logging on as an administrator and taking ownership of the folder.)

Additional problems can occur when folders have been moved and, of course, if a partition was formatted. When you encounter access problems after an upgrade or partition change, check the Knowledge Base first for answers.

Installing and Accessing Applications

When configuring a multiboot computer, many users incorrectly assume that they can install their programs once under a single partition and then browse to the program from any operating system to run it. They might get this idea because *multiuser* computers need only have their applications installed once, but that is an incorrect assumption about *multiboot* computers. When their applications don't work, you'll be called on to resolve the problem. For the most part, you'll only need to reinstall the required programs on each operating system for which the user requires access to them.

As you begin installing the applications for each operating system, you might run into compatibility problems. An application that runs well in Windows 98 might not run properly in Windows XP. When this happens, you'll need to install the program using program compatibility mode.

> **NOTE**   Application Installation   You do not need to install applications in each operating system on the computer for them to function properly. However, you do need to install the applications in each operating system from which they'll be used.

Multiple Installations
When a user complains that an application isn't working properly and won't run on a multiboot computer, verify that the application is installed on that operating system. If the user is simply browsing to the application's executable file and trying to run it, you've found the problem. To resolve the problem, reboot the computer and install the application on the operating system with which it is to be used.

Using Program Compatibility Mode
When troubleshooting applications on multiboot computers, you might find that the applications are installed correctly, but are still not functioning correctly. If the applications are installed correctly on the partition, the issue might lie with the program compatibility settings. Program compatibility settings allow older applications to work on newer operating systems, and newer applications to work on older ones.

In Chapter 6, "Install and Configure Office Applications," program compatibility mode was discussed in depth, but for the purpose of review you can configure program compatibility mode settings as follows:

1. Use Windows Explorer to locate the executable file for the application that is not running properly. It will most likely be in the Programs folder.

2. Right-click the executable file and select Properties.

3. In the file's Properties dialog box, select the Compatibility tab.

4. Select the Run This Program In Compatibility Mode For check box and from the available drop-down list, select the appropriate operating system. This is shown in Figure 11-4.

Figure 11-4 Configure Compatibility settings from the application's Properties dialog box.

5. If necessary, select any or all of the following check boxes:

❑ **Run In 256 Colors** This setting adjusts the color quality setting to 256 colors while the program is running. When the program is closed, the color quality settings return to the user's defaults.

❑ **Run In 640 x 480 Screen Resolution** This setting adjusts the screen resolution to 640 x 480 while the program is running. When the program is closed, the screen resolution settings return to the user's defaults.

❑ **Disable Visual Themes** This setting prevents visual themes from being applied to the program. This often works to resolve problems with menus or buttons in the program. When the program is closed, the theme setting returns to the user's default.

❑ **Turn Off Advanced Text Services For This Program** This setting turns off any advanced text services while the program is running. When the program is closed, the text settings return to the user's defaults and are available in other programs.

6. Click OK to apply.

WORKING WITH NETWORKED COMPUTERS

Clients who use networked computers, including desktop computers, multiuser computers, multiboot computers, handheld computers, laptop computers, and Pocket PCs, can access applications in one of two ways. They can have the applications they use installed directly on their computers' hard disks, or they can access the applications from a network server.

Configuring and troubleshooting access to applications installed on the computer's hard disk were detailed in the previous two sections. Configuring and troubleshooting access to applications when they are stored on and accessed from a network server is detailed here.

> **NOTE** **Network Administrator's Duties**   For users to access applications on a network, network administrators need to create and configure an application server. This network server can be a Windows XP Professional or Windows 2000 Professional desktop computer or a server running Microsoft Windows 2000 Server or Windows Server 2003.

Configuring Access to Applications

Users who access applications stored on application servers, network servers, or desktop computers can work with those applications from their own desktop, laptop, or handheld computer even if the application is not installed on it. The users accessing the applications can be members of a larger domain, members of a smaller workgroup, or single users with a mobile device who need access to their desktop computer's applications while away from their desktop computer.

The Larger Domain

When a user is a member of a corporate domain, he must install **Terminal Services client software** and use the Terminal Services Connection Manager to connect to the network through the Internet and a virtual private network (VPN), a wireless adapter, or a local area network (LAN); connect to the application server; log on; and then locate and run the application. When the session is complete, the user might log off of the application server and might even disconnect from the corporate network altogether. You are not likely to encounter problems involving this type of access as a Tier 1 desktop technician, because higher level network administrators usually configure and troubleshoot application servers and Terminal Services for network users.

The Smaller Workgroup

Windows XP Professional computers can serve as application servers, too, and can be used to provide both remote access to the computer from a laptop and application access for handheld PCs and Pocket PCs. You are more likely to see these configurations as a desktop technician, because these configurations use mobile devices that are becoming common among home and small office users, and are often resolved by Tier 1 technicians.

Although there are several configuration options you need to become familiar with, in this example, you learn the basic steps involved in turning a Windows XP computer into an application server, and then accessing the applications on that computer from a handheld PC. First, configure Windows XP Professional to serve as an application server (or in this case a remote terminal) by following these steps:

1. Open Control Panel, and then open System.

2. On the Remote Tab, select the Allow Users To Connect Remotely To This Computer check box.

3. Click Select Remote Users. Verify that the users who will access the computer remotely have access. Click OK.

4. Click OK to close the System dialog box.

5. Verify that remote users have passwords associated with their accounts.

6. Log off the computer, but leave it running.

This effectively turns the computer into a remote desktop server. A user can then connect her handheld PC to the computer using the Internet and a VPN, a local area connection, or a wireless connection, and use the applications on it. The Microsoft Handheld PC 2000 and the Microsoft Pocket PC 2002 and newer versions already have the Terminal Services client software installed, so there isn't a lot of other configuration to be done.

> **NOTE** **More Terminal Services Software** If the user needs Terminal Services software for other types of mobile hardware, visit the Microsoft Download Center at *http://www.microsoft.com/downloads*.

Troubleshooting Access to Applications

Some of the problems that occur with accessing applications on a network server, in a workgroup, or when using Remote Desktop are the same types of problems that occur when accessing any item on any network. The connection could have failed or the user might not have valid credentials on the network. Other problems can involve an incorrect version of Terminal Services client software, misspelled user names and passwords, and insufficient rights and privileges.

With that in mind, the following situations can cause application access problems (this is by no means a complete list):

- The client does not have sufficient permissions to access the network, the application folder, or the resources required of the application.
- The user is not logged on to the network segment appropriately.
- The user has mistyped a user name or password when prompted for credentials.
- The user is not a member of the appropriate group or has a Deny permission applied to the resource.
- The Remote Desktop port is not open on the Internet Connection Firewall.
- The user does not have the required software installed or the software is an earlier version.
- Remote access might be disabled by a group policy.
- The connection might have failed or requests could have timed out.

- The session might have been disconnected due to an Idle Session Limit setting under Group Policy.

- The user might not have the Log On Locally or the Allow Logon Through Terminal Services rights granted through local policies.

Large companies can lower support costs, increase the security of a network, and avoid potential downtime by installing applications on network servers instead of on each user's desktop computer. Home users can configure their computers to act as remote desktop servers for mobile hardware. These techniques simplify the burden of deploying applications to multiple desktops and purchasing expensive equipment, but can cause vulnerability to new problems, specifically difficult-to-diagnose application access problems.

SUMMARY

- When configuring a multiuser computer, configure a user account for each user who will log on to it, and verify that each user has access to the applications installed.

- When troubleshooting multiboot computers and file and folder access, verify the file systems used are compatible with the operating systems installed.

- When troubleshooting networked computers and application access, verify the user has the proper credentials, the appropriate permissions, is logged onto the network, and is a member of the appropriate groups. Also verify that a group policy is not preventing access.

REVIEW QUESTIONS

1. A multiuser computer running Windows XP has four user accounts configured for the four users who access the computer. Bob has an Administrator account and is in charge of the computer, John and Mary have Standard accounts and access the computer during the day, and Bill has a Limited User account and accesses the computer at night. Knowing this, which of the following must also be true? (Choose all that apply.)

   a. The computer is a member of a domain.

   b. The computer is running Windows XP Professional Edition.

   c. All users can change or delete their account password.

   d. The computer is running Windows XP Home Edition.

2. A user has a multiboot system that offers both Windows 98 and Windows XP. The Windows 98 partition is configured to use FAT32, and the Windows XP partition is configured to use NTFS. The client reports that when logged on to the Windows 98 partition, he cannot view files on the Windows XP partition. However, when he is logged on to the Windows XP partition, he can view files on the Windows 98 partition. How can he configure the computer so that he can view all of the files no matter what operating system he is running? Pick the best solution.

   a. Convert the Windows 98 partition to NTFS using the convert /fs:NTFS command at the command prompt.

   b. Convert the Windows XP partition to FAT32 using the convert /fs:FAT32 command at the command prompt.

   c. Reformat the Windows XP volume so that it uses FAT32.

   d. Reformat and repartition both partitions to use FAT.

3. A client calls to report she needs to share her single, stand-alone computer with a guest who will be visiting next month. She stresses that the computer contains highly personal documents, files, Internet history, personalization settings, e-mail configuration, and more. Her guest will stay

for two weeks and will need access to the computer for e-mailing, creating Microsoft Word documents, working on Microsoft Excel files, and creating Microsoft PowerPoint presentations. The client reports she has Microsoft Office 2003 Professional Edition installed on the computer. What should you advise the user to do to protect the computer from harmful downloads or program installations by her guest and keep her own documents safe, while still allowing the guest access to the applications on the computer?

   a. Create a Limited User account for the guest and reinstall Office 2003 under that account.

   b. Create a Standard user account for the user and drag Office 2003 to the Shared Documents folder.

   c. Enable the Guest account for the user.

   d. Create a Limited User account for the guest and create a local computer policy that does not allow access to the Add Or Remove Programs tool in Control Panel, and that disallows the downloading of programs.

4. Applying program compatibility settings to an executable file consists of several steps. Those steps are listed in the following table. Demonstrate your knowledge of this procedure by putting the steps in the correct order.

1.	a) Select the Run This Program In Compatibility Mode For check box and from the available drop-down list, select the appropriate operating system.
2.	b) Click OK.
3.	c) Right-click the executable file and choose Properties.
4.	d) Use Windows Explorer to locate the executable file for the application that is not running properly. It will most likely be in the Programs folder.
5.	e) In the file's Properties dialog box, select the Compatibility tab.

5. A user needs access to a new application recently installed on his corporation's application server. He has logged on to the network domain successfully and can access other, older applications, but he cannot access the new one. He reports he's getting an Access Is Denied error message. What is most likely the problem?

   a. The client does not have sufficient permissions to access the application folder, or the resources required of the application.

   b. The Remote Access port is not open on his Internet Connection Firewall.

   c. The user has an incorrect version of Terminal Services Client Services installed.

   d. Group policies are preventing access.

CASE SCENARIOS

Scenario 11-1: Troubleshooting Application Access on Multiboot Computers

A user has a multiboot computer that has Windows 2000 Professional with Service Pack 3 and Windows XP Professional Edition installed. Windows 2000 Professional is installed on the first partition, Windows XP Professional on the second, and both are configured with NTFS. Office 2003 is installed on the Windows XP partition. The user complains that she encounters problems when running Office 2003 from the Windows 2000 Professional partition. She needs to be able to access and run the program from both partitions. What can you do to solve this problem?

1. Install Office 2003 on the Windows 2000 Professional partition.

2. Purchase Microsoft Office 2000 and install it on the Windows 2000 Professional partition. Office 2003 works properly only on Windows XP computers and higher.

3. Reformat and reinstall the computer, and switch the order of the operating systems. Windows XP Professional should be on the first partition, Windows 2000 Professional on the second.

4. Run Office 2003 in program compatibility mode for Windows 2000.

Scenario 11-2: Troubleshooting Remote Desktop

A user has been trying to configure his Windows XP Home Edition computer to serve as an application server all morning. He needs to be able to access his computer from his laptop while he's away on business. Although he's been successful in initiating a Remote Assistance session with a friend, he has yet to be successful in initiating a Remote Desktop connection. What is most likely the problem?

1. He needs to install Terminal Services on his laptop computer.

2. The Remote Desktop port needs to opened on the Internet Connection Firewall.

3. Remote Desktop is not available on Windows XP Home Edition, only on Windows XP Professional Edition.

4. He needs to reinstall the TCP/IP services for his Internet connection.

APPENDIX A
MICROSOFT WINDOWS XP SERVICE PACK 2

As part of a major effort to increase the security of desktop computers, in summer 2004, Microsoft is releasing an update to Windows XP named Microsoft Windows XP Service Pack 2. As with all Windows service packs, Windows XP Service Pack 2 includes all of the critical updates released for Windows XP to date. In addition, Service Pack 2 includes a large number of new enhancements to Windows XP—enhancements aimed at increasing the default level of security for the operating system.

Although there is not room in a single appendix to detail all the enhancements provided in Windows XP Service Pack 2, there are many that will prove important to you as a desktop support technician. This chapter covers security enhancements in the following areas:

- **Automatic Updates** As you know, an important part of keeping Windows XP secure is keeping it up to date with the latest software updates released by Microsoft. You must also make sure that you understand what updates are available and how they affect a system. Windows XP Service Pack 2 provides a number of enhancements to the Automatic Updates feature in Windows XP, including the ability to download more categories of updates, better bandwidth management, and consolidation of updates so that less user input is required.

- **Windows Firewall** In the original release of Windows XP, the software-based firewall included with the operating system was named Internet Connection Firewall (ICF). With the release of Windows XP Service Pack 2, ICF has been renamed Windows Firewall and a number of features have been added. The updates include enabling Windows Firewall by default on all network connections, closing ports except when they are in use, improving the user interface, improving application compatibility when Windows Firewall is on, and providing a way to configure global settings for all network connections.

- **Internet Explorer** Security enhancements to Microsoft Internet Explorer provide improved protection against malicious content on the Web, and also provide interface enhancements that make configuring security easier. A new Information Bar consolidates many of the dialog boxes Internet Explorer uses to provide information to users. For the first time in its history, Internet Explorer now includes a built-in pop-up window blocker. Also, several new settings have been added to the security zones available in Internet Explorer.

- **Outlook Express** Service Pack 2 also provides security enhancements for Microsoft Outlook Express users. You can block external content from being automatically downloaded and displayed in HTML-formatted messages, and even configure Outlook Express to only display messages in plaintext format. As a result, potentially unsafe attachments that are sent through e-mail and instant messages are isolated so that they cannot affect other parts of the system.

- **Security Center** Security Center is an entirely new feature that provides a central interface for determining the status of security configurations of your computer. The Security Center window lets you view settings for Automatic Updates, Windows Firewall, and some third-party antivirus software. Security Center also runs as a background service and provides real-time alerts when certain security conditions are detected.

With the enhanced security technologies provided by Windows XP Service Pack 2, you and the users whom you support will experience a more secure desktop environment than ever before.

Also, when you study for the exam, make sure that you are familiar with the changes that are covered in this Appendix. Shortly after Windows XP Service Pack 2 is released, the exam will also be updated. Therefore, you might encounter questions that are based on the changes in Windows XP Service Pack 2.

> **MORE INFO** This chapter covers the aspects of Windows XP Service Pack 2 that are most important to you as a desktop support technician. This includes updates of many of the procedures found in this book, as well as new procedures for helping you support users. For detailed information on all features included with Service Pack 2, visit *http://www.microsoft.com/technet* and search using the keywords "changes to functionality in Microsoft Windows XP Service Pack 2."

AUTOMATIC UPDATES

Software updates help keep computers protected from new vulnerabilities that are discovered (and new threats that are created) after the initial shipping of an operating system. Updates are crucial to keeping computers secure and functioning properly. Updates provided by Microsoft include solutions to known issues, such as patches for security vulnerabilities and updates to the operating system and some applications.

Windows XP features an automatic updating service named Automatic Updates that can download and apply updates automatically in the background. Automatic Updates connects periodically to Windows Update on the Internet (or possibly to a Windows Update Services server on a corporate network). When Automatic Updates discovers new updates that apply to the computer, it can be configured to install all updates automatically (the preferred method) or to notify the computer's user that an update is available.

Windows XP Service Pack 2 provides several enhancements to the Automatic Updates feature, including the following:

- The latest version of Automatic Updates offers expanded support for Microsoft products, including Microsoft Office.

- Previous versions of Automatic Updates could only download critical updates. Now, Automatic Updates can download updates in the following categories: security updates, critical updates, update roll-ups, and service packs.

- Automatic Updates now prioritizes the download of available updates based on the importance and size of the updates. For example, if a large service pack is being downloaded and a smaller security update is released to address an exploit, that security update will be downloaded more quickly than the service pack.

- Automatic Updates is now more automated. The need for users to accept end user license agreements (EULAs) has been eliminated. Also, the user now has a choice of whether to restart the computer following the installation of updates that might require a restart. Updates that do require a restart can now be consolidated into a single installation so that only one restart is required.

- A forthcoming update to the online Windows Update Web site will provide users of Windows XP Service Pack 2 who choose not to use Automatic Updates with many of the same features as Automatic Updates provides. This includes the ability to download updates for Microsoft applications in addition to operating system updates, perform express installations that require minimal user input, and to research updates more easily.

When preparing for the exam, you should be familiar with the following updated (or new) procedures available after the installation of Windows XP Service Pack 2.

▶ Configuring Automatic Updates with Windows XP Service Pack 2

As a desktop support technician, you should make it a practice to recommend that users enable fully automatic updating in Windows. To configure Automatic Updates after Windows XP Service Pack 2 is installed, follow these steps:

1. Click Start, and then select Control Panel.

2. In the Control Panel window, select Performance And Maintenance.

3. In the Performance And Maintenance window, select System.

4. In the Automatic Updates tab, select the Automatic (Recommended) option, as shown in Figure A-1.

5. Select how often and at what time of day updates should be downloaded and installed. For users with high-bandwidth, dedicated connections (such as a cable modem), you should configure Windows to check for updates daily at a time when the user is not using the computer. Users with lower bandwidth connections might want to check less frequently, or even use one of the manual options.

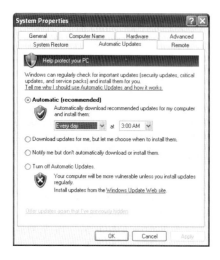

Figure A-1   The Automatic Updates interface changes slightly in Windows XP Service Pack 2.

6. Click OK.

▶ **Using the Windows Update Web site**

The Windows Update site offers a more hands-on approach to updating Windows than using Automatic Updates. If a user resists using the Automatic Updates feature, teach the user to frequently visit the Windows Update site and perform an Express Install that scans for, downloads, and then installs critical and security updates.

To perform an Express Install from the Windows Update site, follow these steps:

1. From the Start menu, select All Programs, and then select Windows Update.

2. On the Microsoft Windows Update Web site, shown in Figure A-2, click Express Install (Recommended).

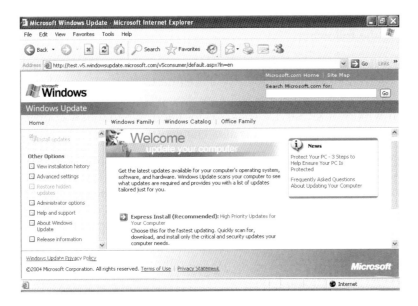

Figure A-2   Express Install scans a computer, downloads, and installs critical and security updates.

3. After the scan is complete (a process that is performed locally—no information is sent to Microsoft's servers), click Install.

4. If you are prompted with a EULA, read the agreement and click I Accept.

5. Wait while the updates are downloaded and installed. If you are prompted to restart your computer, click Restart Now. If you are not prompted to restart, click Close.

WINDOWS FIREWALL

A firewall protects a computer from malicious attacks originating outside the computer (specifically, the Internet) by blocking all incoming network traffic except that which you specifically configure the firewall to allow through. Any computer connected directly to the Internet, whether it is a stand-alone computer or a computer that provides Internet Connection Sharing (ICS) services for other computers on a network, should have a firewall enabled.

Previous versions of Windows XP include a software-based firewall, ICF. After installing Windows XP Service Pack 2, this firewall is renamed Windows Firewall. Windows Firewall is a stateful, host-based firewall that drops all incoming traffic that does not meet one of the following conditions:

- Solicited traffic (valid traffic that is sent in response to a request by the computer) is allowed through the firewall.

- Expected traffic (valid traffic that you have specifically configured the firewall to accept) is allowed through the firewall.

In addition to its new name, Windows Firewall also boasts a number of enhancements, including the following:

- **Enabled by default**   Windows Firewall is now enabled by default on all network connections. This includes local area network (LAN, wired and wireless), dial-up, and virtual private network (VPN) connections that exist when Windows XP Service Pack 2 is installed. When a new connection is created, Windows Firewall is also enabled by default.

- **Global settings**   In Windows XP (prior to installing Windows XP Service Pack 2), ICF settings must be configured individually for each connection. After installing Windows XP Service Pack 2, Windows Firewall provides an interface for configuring global settings that apply to all the connections of the computer. When you change a global Windows Firewall setting, the change is applied to all the connections on which Windows Firewall is enabled. Of course, you can still apply configurations to individual connections as well.

- **New interface**   In previous versions, ICF is enabled by selecting a single check box in the Advanced tab of the Properties dialog box for a connection. A Settings button opens a separate dialog box in which you can configure services, logging, and Internet Message Control Protocol (ICMP) allowances. In Windows XP Service Pack 2, the check box in the Advanced tab has been replaced with a Settings button that launches the new Windows Firewall Control Panel tool, which consolidates global and connection-specific settings, service and ICMP allowances, and log settings in a single, updated interface.

- **Prevent excepted traffic**   In previous versions, ICF is either enabled or disabled. When enabled, solicited traffic and excepted traffic are allowed. When disabled, all traffic is allowed. In Windows XP Service Pack 2, Windows Firewall supports a new feature that lets you keep Windows Firewall enabled and also not allow any exceptions; only solicited traffic is allowed. This new feature is intended to create an even more secure environment when connecting to the Internet in a public or other unsecured location.

- **Startup security**   In previous versions, ICF becomes active on connections only when the ICF/ICS service is started successfully. This means that when a computer is started, there is a delay between when the computer is active on the network and when the connections are protected with ICF. In Windows XP Service Pack 2, a startup Windows Firewall policy performs stateful packet filtering during startup so that the computer can perform basic network tasks (such as contacting DHCP and DNS servers) and still be protected.

- **Traffic source restrictions**   In previous versions, excepted traffic can originate from any Internet Protocol (IP) address. In Windows XP Service Pack 2, you can configure Windows Firewall so that excepted traffic is restricted by IP address (or IP address range), meaning that only traffic from computers with valid IP addresses is allowed through the firewall.

- **Create exceptions using application filenames** In previous versions, you configure excepted traffic by specifying the Transmission Control Protocol (TCP) and User Datagram Protocol (UDP) ports used by a service or application. In Windows XP Service Pack 2, you can also configure excepted traffic by specifying the filename of the application. When the application runs, Windows Firewall monitors the ports on which the application listens and automatically adds them to the list of allowed incoming traffic.

When preparing for the exam, you should be familiar with the following updated (or new) procedures available after the installation of Windows XP Service Pack 2.

▶ **Enabling or disabling Windows Firewall for all network connections**

The only users who can make changes to Windows Firewall settings are those who log on to the computer with a user account that is a member of the local Administrators group. To enable or disable Windows Firewall for a specific network connection, use these steps:

1. Click Start, and then select Control Panel.

2. In the Control Panel window, select Network And Internet Connections.

3. In the Network And Internet Connections window, select Windows Firewall.

4. In the General tab of the Windows Firewall dialog box, shown in Figure A-3, select the On (Recommended) option to enable the firewall for all connections. Select Off (Not Recommended) to disable the firewall for all connections.

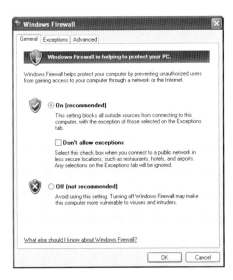

Figure A-3　You can enable and disable Windows Firewall for all network connections.

5. Click OK.

▶ **Enabling or disabling Windows Firewall for a specific network connection**

To enable or disable Windows Firewall for a specific network connection, follow these steps:

1. Click Start, and then select Control Panel.

2. In the Control Panel window, select Network And Internet Connections.

3. In the Network And Internet Connections window, select Network Connections.

4. In the Network Connections window, right-click the connection for which you want to enable or disable Windows Firewall and select Properties.

5. In the Properties dialog box of the network connection, select the Advanced tab.

6. In the Advanced tab, click Settings.

7. In the Windows Firewall dialog box, select the Advanced tab, shown in Figure A-4.

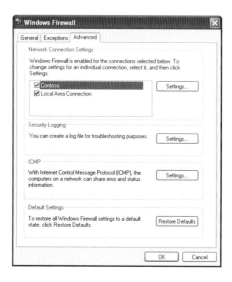

Figure A-4   You can enable and disable Windows Firewall for specific network connections.

8. To enable Windows Firewall for a connection, select the check box for that connection. To disable Windows Firewall for a connection, clear the check box for that connection.

9. Click OK to close the Windows Firewall dialog box.

10. Click OK to close the Properties dialog box for the network connection.

▶ **Enabling Windows Firewall logging**

You can configure Windows Firewall to log network activity, including any dropped packets or successful connections to the computer. Security logging is not enabled by default for Windows Firewall. To enable security logging for Windows Firewall, follow these steps:

1. Click Start, and then select Control Panel.

2. In the Control Panel window, select Network And Internet Connections.

3. In the Network And Internet Connections window, select Windows Firewall.

4. In the Windows Firewall dialog box, select the Advanced tab. In the Security Logging section, click Settings to open the Log Settings dialog box, shown in Figure A-5.

Figure A-5   You can enable security logging for Windows Firewall.

5. In the Logging Options section, select one or both of the following check boxes:

   ❑ **Log Dropped Packets**   Logs all dropped packets originating from the local network or the Internet.

   ❑ **Log Successful Connections**   Logs all successful connections originating from the network or the Internet.

6. Note the location of the security log. By default, it is in the \Windows\ Pfirewall.log file. Click OK to close the Log Settings dialog box. Click OK again to close the Windows Firewall dialog box.

▶ **Accessing the Windows Firewall log file**

After you enable logging, you can access the log file by browsing to its location and opening the file. To locate and open the Windows Firewall log file, follow these steps:

1. Click Start, and then select Control Panel.

2. In the Control Panel window, select Network And Internet Connections.

3. In the Network And Internet Connections window, select Windows Firewall.

4. In the Windows Firewall dialog box, select the Advanced tab.

5. In the Security Logging section, click Settings.

6. In the Log Settings dialog box, in the Log File Options section, click Save As.

7. In the Browse dialog box, right-click the Pfirewall.txt file and select Open. Notice that the text has several headings, including Date, Time, Action, Protocol, and more.

8. After reviewing the firewall log, close the Notepad window, click OK to exit the Log Settings dialog box, and then click OK again to close the Windows Firewall dialog box.

▶ **Creating an exception for a service or application**

By default, Windows Firewall blocks all unsolicited traffic. You can create exceptions so that particular types of unsolicited traffic are allowed through the firewall.

To create a global exception that applies to all network connections for which Windows Firewall is enabled, follow these steps:

1. Click Start, and then select Control Panel.

2. In the Control Panel window, select Network And Internet Connections.

3. In the Network And Internet Connections window, select Windows Firewall.

4. In the Windows Firewall dialog box, select the Exceptions tab, shown in Figure A-6.

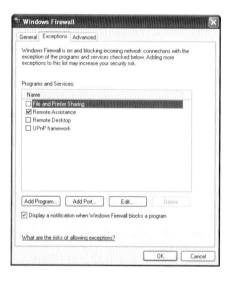

Figure A-6   You can create a global exception for all connections in Windows Firewall.

5. In the Programs And Services list, select the check box for the service you want to allow.

6. Click OK to close the Windows Firewall dialog box.

To create an exception for a particular network connection for which Windows Firewall is enabled, follow these steps:

1. Click Start, and then select Control Panel.

2. In the Control Panel window, select Network And Internet Connections.

3. In the Network And Internet Connections window, select Windows Firewall.

4. In the Windows Firewall dialog box, select the Advanced tab.

5. In the Network Connection Settings section, select the connection for which you want to configure an exception and click Settings.

6. In the Services tab of the Advanced Settings dialog box, shown in Figure A-7, select the check box for the service you want to allow.

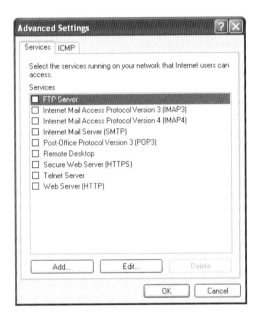

Figure A-7   You can create an exception for a particular network connection in Windows Firewall.

7. Click OK to close the Advanced Settings dialog box. Click OK again to close the Windows Firewall dialog box.

► Creating a custom service definition

In addition to the predefined services for which you can create an exception in Windows Firewall, you can also define a custom service and then configure it as an exception.

To create a global custom service exception that applies to all network connections for which Windows Firewall is enabled, follow these steps:

1. Click Start, and then select Control Panel.

2. In the Control Panel window, select Network And Internet Connections.

3. In the Network And Internet Connections window, select Windows Firewall.

4. In the Windows Firewall dialog box, select the Exceptions tab.

5. To create a global exception, do one of the following:

   ❑ Click Add Program to specify the executable file for a particular program installed on your computer. Windows Firewall will monitor the program and configure the proper TCP or UDP port information for you.

   ❑ Click Add Port to create an exception based on a TCP or UDP port number. You must know the proper port number used by an application or service to use this option.

6. Once you have added an exception, it shows up in the Programs And Services list in the Exceptions tab of the Windows Firewall dialog box. Select the check box for the exception to enable it.

7. Click OK to close the Windows Firewall dialog box.

To create a service exception for a particular network connection for which Windows Firewall is enabled, follow these steps:

1. Click Start, and then select Control Panel.

2. In the Control Panel window, select Network And Internet Connections.

3. In the Network And Internet Connections window, select Windows Firewall.

4. In the Windows Firewall dialog box, select the Advanced tab.

5. In the Network Connection Settings section, select the connection for which you want to configure an exception and click Settings.

6. In the Services tab of the Advanced Settings dialog box, click Add.

7. In the Service Settings dialog box, type a description of the service, type the IP address of the computer on the network that hosts the service, and configure the port information for the service.

8. Click OK to close the Service Settings dialog box. Click OK to close the Advanced Settings dialog box. Click OK again to close the Windows Firewall dialog box.

▶ **Configuring ICMP exceptions for a network connection**

Desktop technicians and network administrators use ICMP requests to troubleshoot network connectivity. Generally, you enable the ICMP options when you need them, and then disable them after you have completed troubleshooting. You cannot set global ICMP exceptions; you must create an exception for a particular network connection.

To create an ICMP exception for a network connection, follow these steps:

1. Click Start, and then select Control Panel.

2. In the Control Panel window, select Network And Internet Connections.

3. In the Network And Internet Connections window, select Windows Firewall.

4. In the Windows Firewall dialog box, select the Advanced tab.

5. In the Network Connection Settings section, select the connection for which you want to configure an exception and click Settings.

6. In the Advanced Settings dialog box, select the ICMP tab, shown in Figure A-8.

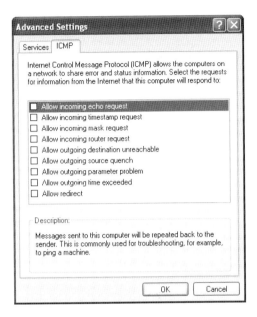

Figure A-8   You can configure an ICMP exception for a connection.

7. Select the check box for the exception you want to create.

8. Click OK to close the Advanced Settings dialog box. Click OK again to close the Windows Firewall dialog box.

INTERNET EXPLORER

Windows XP Service Pack 2 introduces a number of new security features to Internet Explorer 6. As with the rest of the enhancements introduced with Windows XP Service Pack 2, most of the updates to Internet Explorer are intended to provide better security. As a desktop support technician, you should understand how these enhancements affect the interface and the user experience.

Internet Explorer enhancements provided by Windows XP Service Pack 2 include the following:

- **Information Bar** The Internet Explorer Information Bar in Windows XP Service Pack 2 replaces many of the common dialog boxes that prompt users for information and provides a common area for displaying information. Notifications such as blocked ActiveX installs, blocked pop-up windows, and downloads all appear in the Information Bar, which appears below the toolbars and above the main browsing window, as shown in Figure A-9. Either clicking or right-clicking the Information Bar brings up a menu that relates to the notification that is presented. A new custom security zone setting lets users change the settings of the Information Bar for each security zone, including the ability to disable the Information Bar and return to using separate dialog boxes.

Figure A-9   The Internet Explorer Information Bar provides a common notification area.

NOTE   *Microsoft does not use pop-up ads or windows on the microsoft.com site. The Internet Explorer window in Figure A-9 was created to show the functionality of the new Information Bar and Pop-Up Blocker features in Windows XP Service Pack 2.*

- **Pop-Up Blocker**   When Windows XP Service Pack 2 is installed, Internet Explorer provides a Pop-Up Blocker feature for blocking pop-up windows (see Figure A-9) that displays a notification in the Information Bar when a pop-up is blocked. Clicking the Information Bar allows you to show the blocked pop-up, allow all pop-ups on the current site, and configure other settings.

- **File download prompt**   With Windows XP Service Pack 2 installed, Internet Explorer presents a new dialog box when a user downloads a file, as shown in Figure A-10. The new dialog box displays publisher information for the file (if available) and a section with information on the risks of downloading the file.

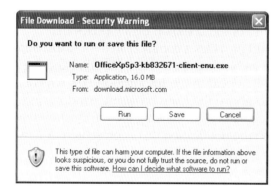

Figure A-10   The Internet Explorer File Download dialog box provides additional file information.

- **Add-on management** With Windows XP Service Pack 2 installed, Internet Explorer prompts users when add-on software tries to install itself into Internet Explorer. Users can also view and control the list of add-ons that can be loaded by Internet Explorer. Internet Explorer also attempts to detect crashes in Internet Explorer that are related to add-ons. If an add-on is identified, this information is presented to the user and the user can disable the add-ons to prevent future crashes.

When preparing for the exam, you should be familiar with the following updated (or new) procedures available after the installation of Windows XP Service Pack 2.

▶ Enabling the Pop-Up Blocker in Internet Explorer

Pop-up windows are not only annoying to users; they can also cause instability in Internet Explorer. Windows XP Service Pack 2 introduces the first Pop-Up Blocker built into Internet Explorer. To enable pop-up blocking in Internet Explorer, use these steps:

1. Click Start, and then select Control Panel.

2. In the Control Panel window, select Network And Internet Connections.

3. In the Network And Internet Connections window, select Internet Options.

4. In the Internet Properties dialog box, select the Privacy tab, shown in Figure A-11.

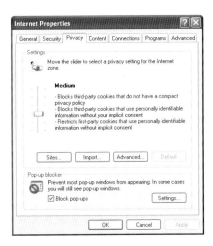

Figure A-11 Enabling the Pop-Up Blocker in Internet Explorer.

5. In the Pop-Up Blocker section, select the Block Pop-Ups check box.

6. Click OK to close the Internet Properties dialog box.

▶ Blocking or allowing a Web site regardless of Internet Explorer privacy settings

Although the ability to block or allow a Web site regardless of Internet Explorer privacy settings is present in previous versions of Windows XP, the interface changes slightly when you install Windows XP Service Pack 2.

To block or allow a Web site in Internet Explorer, use the following steps:

1. In Internet Explorer, from the Tools menu, select Internet Options.

2. In the Privacy tab of the Internet Options dialog box, click Sites.

3. In the Per Site Privacy Actions dialog box, in the Address Of Web Site text box, type the name of the site you want to block or allow.

4. Perform one of the following actions:

   ❑ Click Block to block access to the site you typed even if Internet Explorer's privacy settings would otherwise allow the site.

   ❑ Click Allow to allow access to the site you typed even if Internet Explorer's privacy settings would otherwise block the site.

5. Click OK to close the Per Site Privacy Actions dialog box.

6. Click OK to close the Internet Options dialog box.

▶ **Managing add-ons in Internet Explorer**

With Windows XP Service Pack 2, you can enable and disable each add-on individually and view information about how often the add-ons have been used by Internet Explorer. To manage add-ons in Internet Explorer, follow these steps:

1. Click Start, and then select Internet Explorer.

2. From the Tools menu, select Manage Add-Ons.

3. In the Manage Add-Ons dialog box (shown in Figure A-12), from the Show drop-down list, select one of the following options:

   ❑ **Add-Ons Currently Loaded In Internet Explorer**   This option lists the add-ons that have been loaded into memory within the current Internet Explorer process and those that have been blocked from loading. This includes ActiveX controls that were used by Web pages that were previously viewed within the current process.

   ❑ **Add-Ons That Have Been Used By Internet Explorer**   This option lists all add-ons that have been referenced by Internet Explorer and are still installed.

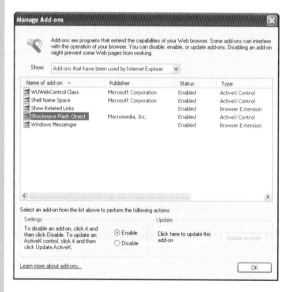

Figure A-12   You can manage add-ons in Internet Explorer.

4. Select any add-on from the list, and then perform one of the following actions:

   ❏ Select the Enable option to re-enable a previously disabled add-on. The add-on might have been disabled by the user or by Internet Explorer following a crash.

   ❏ Select the Disable option to disable an add-on.

   ❏ Click the Update ActiveX button to update ActiveX controls to their latest version. Windows searches for an update at the location where the original control was found. If a newer version is found at that location, Internet Explorer attempts to install the update.

5. Click OK to close the Manage Add-Ons dialog box.

OUTLOOK EXPRESS

Outlook Express is a basic e-mail and newsreader client application included with Internet Explorer and Windows XP. Windows XP Service Pack 2 includes a number of new security features, some of which made their debut in Microsoft Outlook 2003. As a desktop support technician, you'll find that a majority of home users and small business users use Outlook Express as their primary e-mail software. Enhancements to Outlook Express in Windows XP Service Pack 2 include the following:

- **Outlook Express e-mail attachment prompt**   When you open or save an attachment on a message, Outlook Express now uses the same technology used in Internet Explorer to control file downloads. Executable files are checked for a publisher and if the executable file does not include a publisher signature, has an invalid publisher, or has a publisher who has been previously blocked, the file is not allowed to run.

- **Plaintext mode**   With Windows XP Service Pack 2 installed, Outlook Express now gives you the option to display all incoming mail messages in plaintext instead of HTML, avoiding common security problems presented by HTML messages.

- **Block external HTML content**   HTML messages often include content that must be downloaded from an external server. Senders of spam frequently use this type of content to include references to images that reside on their Web servers (sometimes messages that are only a single pixel in size). When the user opens such a message, previous versions of Outlook Express automatically download and display the images, verifying to the sender that you have an active e-mail address. With Windows XP Service Pack 2 installed, the default setting in Outlook Express is to not automatically download external content.

When preparing for the exam, you should be familiar with the following updated (or new) procedures available after the installation of Windows XP Service Pack 2.

▶ Blocking images and external content in HTML e-mail

Blocking images and external content in HTML mail prevents senders of spam from including content in spam messages that is automatically downloaded from their servers when a user opens a message or views it in the Preview pane in

Outlook Express. Blocking external content also prevents Outlook Express from frequently needing to reconnect to the Internet when a user uses a dial-up Internet connection.

To block images and external content in HTML e-mail, follow these steps:

1. In Outlook Express, from the Tools menu, select Options.

2. In the Options dialog box, select the Security tab, shown in Figure A-13.

Figure A-13 Blocking external content in HTML e-mail in Outlook Express.

3. In the Security tab, select the Block Images And Other External Content In HTML E-Mail check box.

4. Click OK to close the Options dialog box.

▶ **Enabling plaintext mode in Outlook Express**

Users of Outlook Express frequently complain about delays when displaying HTML messages. In addition, HTML-formatted messages present security risks. Viewing messages in plaintext is safer, faster, and often easier for users.

To enable plaintext mode in Outlook Express, follow these steps:

1. In Outlook Express, from the Tools menu, select Options.

2. In the Options dialog box, select the Read tab, shown in Figure A-14.

Figure A-14 Enabling plaintext mode in Outlook Express.

3. In the Read tab, select the Read All Messages In Plain Text check box.

4. Click OK to close the Options dialog box.

SECURITY CENTER

Security Center is an entirely new feature provided by Windows XP Service Pack 2. The Security Center service runs as a background process in Windows XP and routinely checks the status of the following components.

■ **Windows Firewall**   Security Center detects whether Windows Firewall is enabled or disabled. Security Center can also detect the presence of some third-party software firewall products.

■ **Automatic Updates**   Security Center detects the current Automatic Updates setting in Windows XP. If Automatic Updates is turned off or is not set to the recommended settings, Security Center provides appropriate recommendations.

■ **Virus protection**   Security Center detects the presence of many third-party antivirus software programs. If the information is available, the Security Center service also determines whether the software is up to date and whether real-time scanning is turned on.

When Security Center is running, its presence is indicated by an icon in the notification area on the Windows taskbar, as shown in Figure A-15. When Security Center detects an important security condition (such as improper settings), it displays a pop-up notice in the notification area.

Figure A-15   The Security Center icon in the notification area provides access to the Security Center window and alerts the user to security conditions.

You can also double-click the Security Center icon in the notification area to open the main Security Center window, shown in Figure A-16. The Security Center window provides the following information:

■ Resources where you can learn more about security-related issues.

■ An indication of whether Windows Firewall is enabled or disabled, as well as a shortcut for opening the Windows Firewall dialog box.

■ The current configuration for Automatic Updates, as well as a link for changing Automatic Updates settings.

■ The current status of antivirus software installed on the computer. For some antivirus products, Security Center can also determine whether the antivirus software is up to date.

■ Additional shortcuts for opening the Internet Options and System dialog boxes.

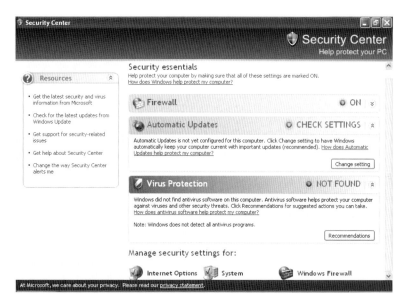

Figure A-16   The Security Center window provides a central interface for managing security on a computer running Windows XP.

> **NOTE**   In cases where you are running firewall or antivirus software that is not detected by Security Center, Security Center presents options for bypassing alerting for that component. If you see a Recommendations button, you can use it to open a window that lets you disable alerts or research appropriate third-party products.

GLOSSARY

.NET Programmability Support Support for developers of .NET Framework applications. Microsoft .NET Framework is a platform for building, deploying, and running Web services and applications.

802.11b wireless connection An industry standard for communicating through a wireless network. These network connections support a maximum bandwidth of 11 Mbps.

access point A device that provides wireless access to network resources. Users that have wireless networking cards in their computers can use this access point to wirelessly connect to the network.

access violation error Errors caused by corrupt files or low system resources. Access violation errors can occur due to inaccurate calculations, when launching programs, or when code is poorly written.

Active Directory A centralized database that contains information about a network's users, workstations, servers, printers, and other resources. Active Directory is essential to maintaining, organizing, and securing the resources on a larger network, because it allows network administrators to centrally manage resources. Active Directory is also extensible, meaning it can be configured to grow and to be personalized for any company.

ActiveX control Small programs and animations on Web pages. ActiveX controls are downloaded to and run on a computer to enhance the Web experience.

adware Software that shows ads that the program thinks the user would like to see. Adware is usually installed unknowingly and knows what a user likes because it watches what sites the user visits while online. Adware is a form of spyware.

AutoRecover files Files that are saved automatically when an application shuts down unexpectedly. AutoRecover files can help a user recover a document when the power goes out or when a computer shuts down unexpectedly.

basic input/output system (BIOS) A computer's BIOS program determines in what order the computer searches for system files on boot up, it manages communication between the operating system and the attached devices on boot up, and it is an integral part of the computer.

BIOS *See* basic input/output system (BIOS)

bit A binary digit, the smallest unit of information holding data on a computer. A single bit can only hold one of two values: 0 or 1.

broadcast storm When a single message is sent to all hosts on a network or network segment. Broadcast storms can be used by attackers to disable a network by sending too many messages for the network to handle.

byte A basic unit of computer storage. A byte contains 8 bits.

cache An area of the hard disk that holds temporary files. In the context of Internet Explorer, temporary Internet files are cached so a user can use the Back and Forward buttons, access History, and use offline files and folders. Retrieving information from the cache is much faster than retrieving information from the Internet.

COM port A computer's communication port. This port allows data to be sent one byte at a time, and is often referred to as a serial port.

compact privacy policy A Web site's privacy policy. The policy details what information is collected from visitors, who the information is given to, and how the owners of the Web site use the information, and it also conforms to the Platform for Privacy Preferences (P3P).

compressed drive A drive that has been condensed to take up less space on the hard disk by using a compression tool such as NTFS compression utilities.

Conflicts folder A folder in Outlook 2003 that holds multiple copies of conflicting items in the mailbox. If multiple changes have been made to an item, but the item is not updated correctly in the Navigation pane, check this folder.

cookie   A small text file that a Web site creates and stores on your computer. Cookies detail what users' preferences are, what they purchased, and any personal information offered by the user. Web sites place cookies on computers that visit them so that they can personalize the user's next visit. Generally, cookies are harmless.

device driver   Software that is used to allow a computer and a piece of hardware to communicate. Device drivers that are incompatible, corrupt, outdated, or of the wrong version for the hardware can cause errors that are difficult to diagnose.

digital signature   A digital identification tool that allows users to identify themselves in digital transactions. Digital signatures can also be used to encrypt messages, thus keeping them private.

disk quotas   A restriction that can be placed on users so that they can only use a predefined amount of a hard disk's available space.

DLL   *See* dynamic-link library (DLL)

DNS   *See* Domain Name System (DNS)

Domain Name System (DNS)   This technology maps user-friendly Internet addresses to the more complex numeric TCP/IP addresses. This enables users to type friendly Uniform Resource Locators (URLs), such as *www.microsoft.com*, in their Web browser instead of longer and more complicated numerical names.

Downloaded Program Files   A folder on a computer's hard disk that contains downloaded program files. These files can be ActiveX controls and Java applets, which are downloaded automatically from the Internet when you view certain pages.

Dynamic Host Configuration Protocol (DHCP)   A service that assigns TCP/IP addresses automatically to clients on a network. DHCP servers provide this service.

dynamic-link library (DLL)   DLL files are shared among multiple components of a computer and its applications and are used to run operating system components and applications. Missing DLL files cause multiple problems and usually generate an error message.

e-commerce   Conducting business on the Internet. E-commerce allows business-to-business transactions and business-to-consumer transactions. In general end user terms, it allows users to visit a Web site and purchase goods.

encryption   A process for converting plaintext to code for the purpose of security. Encrypted files use scrambled data that makes the file unreadable to everyone except the person who created it. Secure Web sites use encryption to secure transactions.

Ethernet   A type of cable that physically connects a computer to a network hub. This connection allows the computer and user to access network resources in a LAN.

Fast User Switching   A feature of Windows XP Home Edition and Windows XP Professional Edition, available for users who are not members of domains, which makes it possible for users to switch quickly between user accounts without having to actually log off and on, or reboot the computer. Running programs do not need to be closed before switching users.

FAT   *See* file allocation table (FAT)

file allocation table (FAT)   A type of file system used by older computers to organize the files and folders on the computer. FAT organizes the files on the computer so they can be accessed when they are needed.

format   The act of erasing all data on a computer drive, volume, or partition.

fully qualified domain name (FQDN)   A name used to identify an entity on the Internet and part of a Uniform Resource Locator (URL). For example, *www.microsoft.com* is a fully qualified domain name.

gateway address   A network point that allows access into and out of a network. Gateways can be routers, firewalls, or proxy servers. Gateways decide if a data packet belongs on the local network or on a remote one.

group policy   A policy created by an administrator that affects all users on a computer or all users in a domain, and are generally set by domain administrators on a domain level. Group policies are used to specify how a user's desktop looks, what wallpaper is used, and how the Internet Explorer Title bar looks, to name only a few options.

HTTP e-mail account An e-mail account that connects to an HTTP e-mail server, such as Hotmail. HTTP accounts can be added to Outlook 2003 or to Outlook Express and can download e-mail and synchronize mailbox folders.

IME *See* input method editor (IME)

input method editor (IME) A program that is used to enter different characters in Asian languages on a standard 101-key keyboard. As the user enters keystrokes, the program tries to identify the characters and convert them to phonetic and ideographic characters.

Internet cache files A temporary copy of a Web page's text and graphics. These temporary files are stored in random access memory (RAM) and on your hard disk and can be accessed more quickly than retrieving the files fresh from the Internet every time you visit the page. Internet cache files make browsing the Internet faster, because pages you visit often can be loaded more quickly than they can if no cache files exist.

IrDA Short for Infrared Data Association, a type of port installed on newer computers, printers, and other devices that allows them to communicate wirelessly. IrDA ports transmit data at about the same rate as a parallel port does, and the devices must be in close proximity and have a clear line of sight between them.

JavaScript A programming language. JavaScript is used on Web sites to open pop-up windows when a link is clicked, to change the color of text when a mouse is rolled over it, or to change formatted information such as the time or date.

kernel mode The computer mode that has direct access to hardware. Kernel mode maintains control over all resources and the system itself. Programs that run in kernel mode should not be run using program compatibility settings.

LAN *See* local area network (LAN)

local area network (LAN) A group of computers in a small geographic area such as a home, office, or floor of an office building. LANs can be workgroups or domains, can connect wirelessly or using Ethernet and a hub, or can connect by more complex connections such as fiber optic lines.

loopback address A TCP/IP address reserved for testing internal TCP/IP settings on any computer. The loopback address is any address in the range 127.x.y.z, and a successful ping to a computer's loopback address verifies that TCP/IP is installed correctly.

macro A set of actions used to automate tasks. Macros are recorded by the end user, and are then performed when a specific keystroke or menu selection is made.

Microsoft .NET Framework A platform for building, deploying, and running Web services and applications.

NetBIOS name A friendly name used by computers on a network to distinguish them from other resources. WINS servers resolve NetBIOS names to their associated IP addresses. NetBIOS names allow computers running older operating systems such as Windows NT, Windows Me, and Windows 98 to participate in a network and to access resources.

NetMeeting A real-time collaboration and conferencing application that combines application sharing, video and voice, and complete Internet conferencing.

NTFS A type of file system used by newer computers that is much more advanced than the FAT file system. NTFS provides advanced file and folder permissions, encryption, disk quotas, and compression. NTFS is supported by Windows NT, Windows 2000, and Windows XP.

packets Data sent over a network. Large messages and data are broken up into small pieces of data called packets. The individual packets might take different routes to the destination computer, but once there, they are reassembled to form the original data.

page fault An error that occurs when information cannot be found that the operating system needs to perform a task. This can occur due to lack of RAM or virtual memory, corrupt temporary files, a conflict between programs, missing or corrupt cookies, Favorites, History, or other Internet Explorer data.

partition   A smaller part of a larger hard disk. When a disk is partitioned, it is split into two or more smaller, virtual drives. Partitions can be created to hold data, hold applications, or create a multiboot computer.

personalized menu   Menu that shows most recently viewed or used commands. Hidden commands appear after a few seconds. Full menus can be configured if personalized menus are not desired.

port   An entry point or exit point for data on a computer. Printers use printer ports, universal serial bus (USB) devices use USB ports, and modems typically use serial ports. In addition, data that is sent or received from the Internet or a network also enters and exits using a port, defined by a number. For instance, HTTP traffic uses port 80, FTP traffic uses port 21, and Telnet traffic uses port 23.

post   A message sent to or read in a newsgroup.

protocol   A set of agreed-on rules for communicating among computers. Protocols are industry standards, and both the sending and receiving computer must agree on the protocols used for communication to take place.

retention policy   A company policy set by a network administrator. Retention policies are set to encourage users to keep e-mail and documents for a standard period of time and then delete or archive them. Retention policies override AutoArchive settings.

reversible encryption   A process used to camouflage a message or data. Encrypting data keeps data safe from access by intruders.

scope of addresses   The range of addresses a DHCP server can allocate to network clients.

ScreenTips   Reviewers' remarks. ScreenTips display comments in yellow pop-up boxes and the comments appear when the user holds the mouse over the comment.

search engine   An application that can search through every page on every Web site on the Internet for the purpose of offering those pages when a user searches for information. Major search engines include Google and Yahoo!.

seated   A hardware card's connection to the motherboard. A modem, network interface card, or sound card is considered seated if it is properly connected to the motherboard.

security ID   A unique identification number called a security identifier that identifies each user in a network.

security policy   Policies configured by domain, workgroup, or system administrators. The policies keep the computer and the computing environment secure by limiting what users can and cannot do while logged on to the computer or network.

service level agreement (SLA)   SLAs are agreements between parties (such as a call center and the company that hires it) that define how long a call should take, how much should be spent on each incident, and what reports and documents must be maintained. The SLA also defines penalties for not meeting those requirements.

shortcut key   A key combination associated with a macro for the purpose of running the macro. Common shortcut keys include CTRL+A, SHIFT+Z, and CTRL+V.

signature updates   Virus definition updates. Signature updates contain files that protect the computer from the latest security threats and are part of virus scanning software's options.

SLA   *See* service level agreement (SLA)

spyware   Software that monitors a user's Web surfing activities. Spyware is often installed unwittingly on a computer when free software is downloaded from the Internet.

static IP address   An address configured for a computer that is not allocated by a DHCP server. The address never changes, and must be manually input by a network administrator.

subnet   A separate and distinct part of a network, generally represented by one geographic location such as an office or building. Subnets use gateways to access the Internet, thus enabling all users to access the Internet through one shared network address.

subnetmask   Subnet masks enable computers to determine when to send packets to the gateway to communicate with computers on remote subnets.

system partition The physical area of the hard disk that holds the operating system files. The system partition is generally the C drive.

temporary files Files that are stored temporarily either in memory or on the computer's hard disk. These files are created to hold information such as computational output, copies of working documents (for recovery purposes), and for program execution.

temporary Internet files Cached files. Temporary Internet files allow a user to use the Back and Forward buttons, access History, and use offline files and folders. Retrieving information from the Temporary Internet Files folder is much faster than retrieving information from the Internet.

Terminal Services client software Software used for client computers that access applications remotely on a network.

timeout An error caused by an e-mail or news post that takes longer than the allotted time to download. Timeout errors can be eliminated by increasing how much

time Outlook is allotted to download messages from a mail server.

Uniform Resource Locator (URL) The URL of a Web site is its friendly name, for instance, *http://www.Microsoft.com*.

URL *See* Uniform Resource Locator (URL)

Visual Basic A programming language used for Web sites and applications. Macros created in Excel, Word, and other Office programs can be edited with the Visual Basic Editor, included with the applications.

volume An area of the hard disk used for storing data. See also partition.

Windows Installer A core component of IntelliMirror, which is used to deploy applications across a domain. Windows Installer is used to install applications and to manage user installation options.

wireless access point A part of a wireless network that acts as a transmitter for data on the network. Wireless access points can be bridges, routers, NICs, hubs, and switches.

XML tag A data marker used to retrieve data from a document.

BIBLIOGRAPHY

This is a list of all of the reference material mentioned in this book. Beside each is the chapter where the information was presented. Information that is listed here that does not have a chapter number by it is not specifically mentioned in the book. However, this additional material contains information worth noting.

URLS

http://www.Microsoft.com/technet (1, 2)
At TechNet, you'll find resources about Microsoft technologies, including solutions to documented problems, service packs, and security alerts. You can also access newsgroups, participate in chats, listen to Web casts, view events, and read columns.

http://www.Microsoft.com/windowsxp/expertzone/newsgroups/default.asp (1)
Join a myriad of newsgroups related to Windows XP here.

http://support.microsoft.com/default.aspx (2)
At the Microsoft Help and Support Web site you can access various support pages, including the Knowledge Base. Search the Knowledge Base to locate answers to known problems, access downloads and updates, contact Microsoft, get customer service, and access newsgroups. This is you one-stop shop for answers to documented problems.

http://www.microsoft.com/windowsxp/expertzone/default.asp (2)
At the Windows XP Expert Zone you can read articles, review frequently asked questions, locate newsgroups, participate in chats, join user groups, and much more.

http://www.verisign.com (5)
Verisign delivers critical infrastructure services that make the Internet safer and more reliable. Visit this site to learn more about digital signatures and Internet security.

http://www.thawte.com (5)
Visit this site to learn more about digital certificates, Internet security, and how to generate public and private keys.

http://www.win2000mag.com/Articles/Index.cfm?ArticleID=4773 (5)
This link offers the article Obtaining and Installing a Digital Certificate, written by Gary King, and published by Windows &.Net Magazine. It details how digital certificates verify a person's identity, and where and how to obtain a digital certificate.

http://www.microsoft.com/office/editions/prodinfo/sysreq.mspx (6)
Visit this site to view the minimum requirements for installing Office System 2003 editions.

http://office.microsoft.com/officeupdate/default.aspx (6)
Visit this site to check for and obtain updates to Microsoft Office products. You can also purchase Office products, order a trial CD, and search for solutions to problems.

http://www.shop.microsoft.com (6)
At this site, you'll find links to purchase almost any Microsoft product available, including operating systems, Office products, hardware, games, and developer tools.

http://www.oktec.com/help/file_types.htm (7)
This site contains information on the various file types you'll encounter as a technician. This comprehensive list offers information on what programs open a specific file type, what a file type is generally used for, and similar information.

http://cable-dsl.home.att.net (8)
This link takes you to the Navas Cable Modem/DSL Tuning Guide page, which contains information on increasing performance, sharing a connection, enhancing security, and resolving problems with modems and DSL connections.

http://www.microsoft.com/security/protect/windowsxp (10)
This Microsoft Web page details security for Windows XP, including setting up firewalls and similar security measures.

http://support.microsoft.com/default.aspx?kbid=320454 (10)
This Knowledge Base article, Microsoft Baseline Security Analyzer (MBSA) version 1.2 is available, contains information on how to use the MBSA.

http://www.microsoft.com/downloads (11)
Visit this site to access the latest downloads, including updates for Internet Explorer, security updates, worm removal tools, and virus deletion.

WHITE PAPERS

There are several places to get free white papers on Windows XP. A single Google search for *Windows XP White Papers* recently yielded 893,000 results. Here are some of my favorite white papers that relate to Windows XP, although doing a quick search will offer more than you can probably sift through in a lifetime.

http://techlibrary.banktech.com/data/detail?id=1078511663_21&type=RES&x= 1303610502 Microsoft Solutions for Management: Patch Management Using Microsoft Software Update Services Company: Microsoft Corporation.

> This solution accelerator provides guidance for deploying critical updates and security updates to Microsoft operating systems using Microsoft Software Update Services. It describes how Microsoft Software Update Services should be designed and configured to support patch management and provides details of the operational processes and procedures that need to be followed.

http://techlibrary.banktech.com/data/detail?id=1066238603_788&type=RES&x= 131330043 Guide to Securing Windows XP in Small and Medium Businesses Company: Microsoft Corporation.

> With the over-growing threat of malicious code -- such as worms, virus, and hacker threats -- it is critical that all customers take immediate action to help lock-down their desktop and laptop systems. This guide explains how to implement the security measures recommended in the Windows XP Security Guide in a small or medium business environment without an Active Directory deployment. In addition to the advanced step-by-step guidance in this document, you will also find information on the top security recommendations that Microsoft is making to all customers.

http://techlibrary.banktech.com/data/detail?id=1064427166_93&type=RES&x= 1644067792 Protect Your PC. Company: Microsoft Corporation.

> This article describes the three steps you can take to improve your computer's security. You can follow the three steps online, or print them for easy reference.

http://www.bitpipe.com/detail/RES/1048530283_979.html Eliminate XP Vulnerabilities. Company: Sygate Technologies.

> Implementing Sygate Secure Enterprise in combination with Windows XP will eliminate many of the vulnerabilities introduced into the enterprise network by Windows XP and provide a fundamental security platform that will enable enterprise to take advantage of new technology to increase productivity, while maintaining a secure and trustworthy environment.

http://itpapers.zdnet.com/abstract.aspx?scid=444&dtid=1&docid=59558 Reliability Improvements in Windows XP Professional: Microsoft.

> Learn how Windows XP Professional boosts user productivity with features that prevent many problems from occurring on users' systems and enable quick recovery from problems that do occur.

KNOWLEDGE BASE ARTICLES

Microsoft's Knowledge Base articles offer help on everything from Microsoft Access to Works for Windows. The articles offer solutions and workarounds to known issues, links to updates, extensive how-to articles, and tips for dealing with bugs and glitches. Information concerning compatibility with third-party hardware and software is also available. The Knowledge Base's data can be searched by article number, topic, keywords, date, and more, and offers a wealth of information. Listed next are the Knowledge Base articles introduced in this book.

KB 178342 (5)
"Profile Assistant Is Unavailable in Internet Explorer"
http://support.microsoft.com/default.aspx?scid=kb;en-us;178342

KB 290345 (5)
"Information About the Clear SSL State Option in Windows XP"
http://support.microsoft.com/default.aspx?scid=kb;en-us;290345

KB 291252 (2)
"How To Publish Pictures to the Internet in Windows XP"
http://support.microsoft.com/default.aspx?scid=kb;en-us;291252

KB 292106 (6)
"Changes to the Default Language Settings Are Not Retained"
http://support.microsoft.com/default.aspx?scid=kb;en-us;292106

KB 294519 (3)
"On-Screen Keyboard May Not Indicate External Keyboard Activity"
http://support.microsoft.com/default.aspx?scid=kb;en-us;294519

KB 294887 (9)
"How to Check User Profiles on a Windows XP-Based Computer"
http://support.microsoft.com/default.aspx?scid=kb;en-us;294887

KB 299357 (8)
"How to Reset Internet Protocol (TCP/IP) in Windows XP"
http://support.microsoft.com/default.aspx?scid=kb;en-us;299357

KB 302806 (6)
"Description of Microsoft Product Activation"
http://support.microsoft.com/default.aspx?scid=kb;en-us;302806

KB 302878 (6)
"Frequently Asked Questions About Microsoft Product Activation"
http://support.microsoft.com/default.aspx?scid=kb;en-us;302878

KB 303137 (3)
"Background Picture Is Not Displayed Correctly After You Move the Taskbar"
http://support.microsoft.com/default.aspx?scid=kb;en-us;303137

KB 307499 (3)
"ToolTips and Messages from the Status Area of the Taskbar May Remain"
http://support.microsoft.com/default.aspx?scid=kb;en-us;307499

KB 310089 (8)
"Troubleshooting Cable Modems"
http://support.microsoft.com/default.aspx?scid=kb;en-us;310089

KB 314067 (8)
"How to Troubleshoot TCP/IP Connectivity with Windows XP"
http://support.microsoft.com/default.aspx?scid=kb;en-us;314067

KB 314228 (3)
"The Windows XP Taskbar May Stop Responding for Some Time"
http://support.microsoft.com/default.aspx?scid=kb;en-us;314228

KB 314478 (9)
"How to Create and Copy Roaming User Profiles in Windows XP"
http://support.microsoft.com/default.aspx?scid=kb;en-us;314478

KB 314747 (8)
"Description of Device Manager in Windows 2000 and Windows XP"
http://support.microsoft.com/default.aspx?scid=kb;en-us;314747

KB 318027 (3)
"Taskbar Is Missing When You Log On to Windows"
http://support.microsoft.com/default.aspx?scid=kb;en-us;318027

KB 318388 (3)
"The Original Keyboard Layout Is Used After You Configure a New Default Input Method Editor"
http://support.microsoft.com/default.aspx?scid=kb;[LN];318388

KB 328010 (5)
"How to Configure Automatic Updates by Using Group Policy or Registry Settings"
http://support.microsoft.com/default.aspx?scid=kb;en-us;328010

KB 810881 (11)
"Access is Denied" Error Message When You Try to Open a Folder
http://support.microsoft.com/default.aspx?scid=kb;en-us;810881

KB 813938 (2)
"How to Set Up a Small Network with Windows Home Edition"
http://support.microsoft.com/default.aspx?scid=kb;en-us;813936 (an eight-part series of articles).

KB 826511 (6)
"HOW TO: Use an Office 2003 Setup Log File to Troubleshoot Setup Problems."
http://support.microsoft.com/default.aspx?scid=kb;en-us;826511

KB 831030 (6)
"Cannot Install German Language MUI Files"
http://support.microsoft.com/default.aspx?scid=kb;en-us;831030

KB 831591 (6)
"'The Dictionary For This Language Was Not Found' Error Message When You Try to Use Handwriting on the Language Bar"
http://support.microsoft.com/default.aspx?scid=kb;en-us;831591

THIRD-PARTY SITES OF NOTE

Although there is a wealth of information on the Internet and hundreds of thousands of sites you can visit, some sites stand above the others. I've listed several here that consistently offer valuable and reliable information on topics ranging from definitions, to drivers, to articles, and to quick fixes.

www.whatis.com (2)
Here you'll find definitions for technical words, as well as links to third party sites that offer more detailed information.

www.windrivers.com (2)
This site offers drivers for Windows-compatible products, including scanners, printers, cameras, and more.

www.kellys-korner-xp.com (2)
This site offers a myriad of troubleshooting tips, scripts, and frequently asked questions.

www.dougknox.com (2)
This site contains information about Windows XP and offers troubleshooting tips and solutions to recognized problems.

www.theeldergeek.com (2)
A Windows XP Home and Professional forum with information on file management, service packs, automatic updates, and more.

BOOKS

There are literally hundreds of books available to help you become more adept with Windows XP. Here are a few that I believe will help you in your quest to become a good desktop technician.

Ballew, Joli. 2003. *Microsoft Windows XP: Do Amazing Things. Seattle: Microsoft Press.*

Ballew, Joli. 2004. *Degunking Windows. Phoenix: Paraglyph Press.*

Bluttman, Ken. 2003. *Developing Microsoft Office Solutions: Answers for Office 2003, Office XP, Office 2000, and Office 97. Upper Saddle River, NJ: Pearson Higher Education.*

Bott, Ed, and Carl Siechert. 2001. *Microsoft Windows XP Inside Out. Seattle: Microsoft Press.*

Karp, David A. 2002. *Windows XP Annoyances. Sebastopol, CA: O'Reilly & Associates, Inc.*

Microsoft Corporation. 2001. *Microsoft Windows XP Professional: Exam 70 270 (With CD-ROM). Seattle: Microsoft Press.*

The Microsoft Office Team. 2003. *Microsoft Office 2003 Resource Kit. Seattle: Microsoft Press.*

The Microsoft Windows Team. 2003. *Microsoft Windows XP Professional Resource Kit. 2nd ed. Seattle: Microsoft Press.*

Simmons, Curt. 2003. A+ *Technician's On-the-Job Guide to Windows XP. Emeryville, CA: McGraw-Hill/Osborne Media.*

INDEX

SYSTEM REQUIREMENTS

STUDENT AND INSTRUCTOR WORKSTATIONS

To complete the exercises in this textbook, you need to meet the following minimum system requirements:

- Microsoft Windows XP Professional

- Microsoft Office Professional Edition 2003

- PC with 300 megahertz or higher processor clock speed recommended; 233 MHz minimum required (single or dual processor system)

- 128 MB RAM or higher recommended (64 MB minimum supported; may limit performance and some features)

- 4 GB or greater hard disk

- CD or DVD drive

- Keyboard and mouse

- Network adapter card

- VGA display adapter and monitor (Super VGA [800x600] display adapter and monitor capable of displaying 16-bit color recommended)

SERVER COMPUTER

The student and instructor computers will access a classroom server. To prepare this server, the instructor will need at least the Standard editions of both Microsoft Windows Server 2003 and Microsoft Exchange Server 2003.

All hardware must be in the Windows Server Catalog for the Windows Server 2003 family (*http://www.microsoft.com/windows/catalog/server/*).